Family Treatment

Evidence-Based Practice with Populations at Risk

FOURTH EDITION

Curtis Janzen
Oliver Harris
Catheleen Jordan
Cynthia Franklin

THOMSON

BROOKS/COLE

Australia • Brazil • Canada • Mexico • Singapore • Spain
United Kingdom • United States

THOMSON
™
BROOKS/COLE

Family Treatment: Evidence-Based Practice with Populations at Risk, *Fourth Edition*
Curtis Janzen, Oliver Harris, Catheleen Jordan, and Cynthia Franklin

Executive Editor: *Lisa Gebo*
Assistant Editor: *Alma Dea Michelena*
Editorial Assistant: *Sheila Walsh*
Technology Project Manager: *Barry Connolly*
Executive Marketing Manager: *Caroline Concilla*
Marketing Assistant: *Rebecca Weisman*
Senior Marketing Communications Manager: *Tami Strang*
Project Manager, Editorial Production: *Jennifer Klos*

Creative Director: *Rob Hugel*
Art Director: *Vernon Boes*
Print Buyer: *Lisa Claudeanos*
Permissions Editor: *Joohee Lee*
Production Service: *Sara Dovre Wudali, Buuji, Inc.*
Copy Editor: *Kristina Rose McComas*
Cover Designer: *Andrew Ogus*
Cover Image: *Vicki Wehrman/images.com*
Compositor: *Cadmus*
Printer: *Malloy Incorporated*

Thomson Higher Education
10 Davis Drive
Belmont, CA 94002-3098
USA

For more information about our products, contact us at:
Thomson Learning Academic Resource Center
1-800-423-0563

For permission to use material from this text or product, submit a request online at
http://www.thomsonrights.com.

Any additional questions about permissions can be submitted by e-mail to
thomsonrights@thomson.com.

Library of Congress Control Number:
2005921875

ISBN 0-534-64145-8

To Hobie, Netty, K-Bear, Chrissy, Shar, and Sweetie;
their capacity for love, growth, tolerance, and
fun never cease to amaze me. And in
memory of Shaye, my inspiration.

Catheleen Jordan

To my late mother, Gayle Southern, who always
encouraged creativity, persistence, and
excellence in all my pursuits.

Cynthia Franklin

Contents

Preface

We have restructured *Family Treatment* to focus on evidence-based approaches in family treatment in social work practice. In keeping with the evidence-based tradition, treatment manuals and case examples have been added.

Part I, Introduction to Evidence-Based Family Treatment, serves as the introduction to family treatment and presents our orientation and theoretical framework. The three chapters in Part I introduce the book's underlying philosophy and theoretical framework.

Chapter 1, Framework for Evidence-Based Family Treatment, provides an overview of the beginnings of treating families versus individuals, and then flows into cutting-edge trends and issues in family treatment, such as the influence of managed care, evidence-based practice, and measurement of practice.

Chapter 2, Theoretical and Treatment Approaches to Evidence-Based Family Treatment, is focused on presenting an overview of the models that will be the later focus of treatment manuals in the problem chapters to follow in Part II. These add more of the empirical basis or clinical wisdom that justifies the models' inclusion in the book. Family preservation and family psychoeducational approaches are newly added.

Chapter 3, Beginning Evidence-Based Treatment, is reorganized and refocused on using a systematic and planful evidence-based approach at all levels of intervention, from building rapport, to performing assessment, and to treatment planning.

Part II, Evidence-Based Intervention Strategies, consists of nine problem-focused chapters. Each chapter includes an assessment section with a table of several of the best, frequently used assessment measures for the population. The table will include basic information on validity, reliability, and contact information such as mailing address or Internet address. In the technique section, we include evidence-based treatment/best practices and give detail about evidenced-based treatments, give an example when citing information, and include a table with the major studies or a meta-analysis. Also, we include a detailed treatment manual that is summarized from one or more of the evidence-based practices available for that area. A case example is then provided.

Chapter 4, Evidence-Based Treatment of Families Headed by a Single Parent, focuses on important assessment criteria for single-parent headed households, including parental stress and child issues such as poor school performance, feelings of loss, conduct, and other adjustment disorders.

Chapter 5, Evidenced-Based Treatment of Families with Aging Members, spends more time on caregiving burden, caregiving roles, and elder abuse. This chapter includes a protocol on caregiving and resources for helping families.

Chapter 6, Evidence-Based Treatment of Families with Multiple Problems, includes issues such as income loss and poverty. This chapter focuses on families experiencing poverty and other issues. Treatments focus on multiple levels of social support, housing and other needed resources, children's school performance problems, and problems of parents.

Chapter 7, Evidenced-Based Treatment of Persistent Mental Disorders, includes a solid psychoeducational program and one of the multicomponent treatment programs that is well researched. We include a list of medications as well as a list of resources such as the Alliance for Mental Illness.

Chapter 8, Evidence-Based Treatment for Families with Chronically and Terminally Ill Members (Using HIV/AIDS as an example), is expanded to include more about other illnesses in addition to HIV/AIDS. These include pediatric illness as well as adult health problems. Evidence-based treatments tend toward the educational models; the new area of health promotions is introduced.

Chapter 9, Evidence-Based Treatment of Child Abuse and Other Family Violence, includes more emphasis on the use of risk factors to inform treatment options as well as on the role of explanations and hypothesis testing in treating traumatized and abused children. Promising though untested models also are presented.

Chapter 10, Evidence-Based Treatment of Substance Abuse, covers population and family dynamics and issues for adults and adolescents who abuse substances. Since substance abuse is a complex issue, a variety of individual and behavioral interventions are discussed.

Chapter 11, Evidence-Based Treatment during Separation and Divorce, presents information on how to help people who choose to divorce, and how to help people work through emotional divorce. Helping children to adjust is also addressed.

Chapter 12, Evidence-Based Treatment of the Reconstituted Family, includes new research that has been done, as well as resources from organizations such as the Stepfamily Association of America. These groups provide educational resources, support groups, and other programs and services.

Acknowledgements

We would like to gratefully acknowledge the staff at both Peacock Books and Brooks-Cole who provided professional support and guidance during the writing of the book. We especially thank Lisa Geebo, Alma Dea Michelena, Ted Peacock and Dick Welna. We also acknowledge the efforts of Marjorie Toensing with the index. Also gratefully acknowledged are our reviewers, including Marlene Belew Huff; Ellen Dunbar, California State University, Stanislaus; Miriam Freeman, University of South Carolina, Columbia; and Jackie A. Puckett, Limestone College.

About the Authors

Dr. Catheleen Jordan began her social work career as a Department of Public Welfare social worker in Bell County, Texas in 1974. She has an MSSW from the University of Texas at Arlington and a PhD in Social Welfare from the University of California-Berkeley. Catheleen currently is professor of social work at the University of Texas at Arlington, where she has taught since 1985. Her areas of expertise are family assessment/treatment and clinical research. She currently serves as a clinical supervisor in the UTA-SSW Community Service Clinic, is involved in clinical research with homeless dually diagnosed individuals, and serves as Chair of the UTA-SSW Direct Practice Sequence. Catheleen's involvement with the Texas Branch of the National Association of Social Workers includes Secretary of the Board of Directors, Unit Chair of the Tarrant County Unit, Chair of the NASW-State International Committee, and NASW State Conference Program Committee Member/fund raiser.

In addition to presentations internationally and locally, as well as numerous publications in the area of family practice, Catheleen has co-authored several books. These include *Evidence-Based Child Welfare Practice* (with Drs. Joan Rycraft and Debra Woody) and *Family Social Work*, 2nd edition (with Drs. Don Collins and Heather Coleman), both forthcoming from Brooks-Cole. Additionally, Catheleen serves on the editorial boards of the *Journal of Brief Therapy* and *Children and Schools*. More information can be found at http://www2.uta.edu/ssw/jordan/

Cynthia Franklin, Ph.D is Professor and holder of the Stiernberg/ Spencer Family Professorship in Mental Health at The University of Texas at Austin,

School of Social Work. She is also coordinator of the clinical concentration. Dr. Franklin teaches courses on practice theories, family therapy, and research methods at both the master's and doctoral levels. Dr. Franklin specializes in clinical practice with at-risk youth and families in school settings. She is an internationally known leader in school social work and school mental health practice. Dr. Franklin has over 100 publications in the professional literature on topics such as dropout prevention, clinical assessment, the effectiveness of solution-focused therapy in school settings, and adolescent pregnancy prevention. She served as the past editor-in-chief of The National Association of Social Worker's (NASW's) journal, *Children in Schools.* Dr. Franklin is author of several books, including *Family Practice; Brief Systems Methods for Social Work* (co-authored with Catheleen Jordan), published by Brooks/Cole Publications; and *Clinical Assessment for Social Workers,* now in its second edition (co-authored with Catheleen Jordan), published by Lyceum Press.

Dr. Franklin has won numerous awards, including a lifetime achievement award presented to her by the Solution-Focused Brief Therapy Association for her work with forgotten children in 2003, a statewide achievement award for her advocacy and work in school social work in Texas presented to her in 2003, and The Alumni of the Year Award from The University of Texas at Arlington in 2003. Dr. Franklin has also been active in the practice community. She is a clinical member of The American Association of Marriage and Family Therapy and holds practice licenses in clinical social work (LCSW), and marriage and family therapy (LMFT).

More information can be found at Cynthia Franklin, Professor, http://www.utexas.edu/ssw/faculty/franklin/

Theoretical Framework

The purpose of Part I is to introduce the field of family treatment and some of the most widely accepted support for the study and treatment of the family. No single theoretical structure for treating families has yet been developed, and we draw on several approaches to family treatment. All these approaches, however, use systems concepts to understand how the family operates to achieve growth and resolve problems. It is in this context that this part of the book has been written. Each of the chapters contributes to building an understanding of family functioning and suggests ways to plan appropriate strategies for changing interactional patterns when families become dysfunctional.

The first chapter gives a broad overview of family treatment in social work practice and of contributions by other professions. The underlying theoretical assumptions which provide the key concepts for understanding families and approaches to treatment are presented in greater depth. Chapter 2 overviews six models of family treatment, which will later be used in Part II to suggest treatment plans for specific family problems. Finally, Chapter 3 presents a systematic and planful evidence-based approach at all levels of intervention, from building rapport and performing assessment to treatment planning.

Framework for Evidence-Based Family Treatment

The idea of involving the entire family in resolving one member's problem originated in the 1950s; those at Mental Research Institute (MRI) in Palo Alto, California, were the pioneers in this approach. Virginia Satir, a social worker, was a prominent member of the group, which also included Paul Wazalwich, Greg Bateson, and others. Prior to the advent of treating the family as a client system, social workers and other therapists approached problem solving from the viewpoint of changing one individual's targeted behavior. It was believed that the cause of the maladaptive behavior was within the individual, so it was necessary to deal with the psychic aspects of the personality if problem-solving efforts were to be effective. This was supported by psychoanalytic theory and the prevailing emphasis on individual treatment.

These beliefs were largely discounted as therapists began to work with more than one member of the family. Social workers in public and private agencies were among those involved in this new movement that began in the early 1950s and was usually referred to in social work circles as multiple-client interviewing. At that time, only limited knowledge was available regarding the process and outcome of this mode of problem solving; yet, many practitioners were engaged in exploring this dimension of practice. Interviews usually involved two members of the nuclear family, most often the parents, seen together. New information not previously furnished by individuals when seen alone became available, revealing differences in the way family members perceived the same problem situation. This led social workers and other professionals working with more than one member of the family to seek better ways to understand these observations, and they began to pay more attention to the way family members experienced each other in their various encounters. This signaled the beginning of a new way of thinking about problem configuration and the ways of intervening with those involved in family conflict. The client was no longer identified as an individual with symptoms, but a family with a problem. We will discuss this movement from individual to family treatment in more detail, followed by a look at other professional contributions and a discussion of our theoretical assumptions, including the current focus on evidence-based practice.

FROM INDIVIDUAL TO FAMILY TREATMENT: THE HISTORY AND TODAY'S TREND TOWARD EVIDENCE-BASED PRACTICE

We will discuss in this section some of the historical underpinnings of the family approach from the social work literature and from literature in related fields. Family practice has been influenced by a diverse group of practitioners and researchers. The movement away from the traditional approach of treating an individual with a problem to treatment of the family as a unit has been a gradual process. Though family treatment as a mode of practice was formally introduced in the 1950s, some of the underlying ideas and observations that support this process appeared in the social work literature as early as the first quarter of the century. Mary Richmond addressed the components of problem assessment in her book *Social Diagnosis* (1917); this writing reflected the beginning of a family orientation in casework practice. In discussing the caseworker's activity in diagnosing problem situations, Richmond noted the importance of knowing the main "drift" of the family's life as a key to understanding what might be troubling the individual family member. In other words, she was emphasizing the importance of family history in delivering casework services to individuals. Richmond also recognized the importance of family unity and suggested that it would be useful to learn of the difference between the power of cohesion in stable and unstable families. She believed that the caseworker should inquire about the family's interest, its hope and ambition, and the activities its members engaged in together.

While Richmond stopped short of suggesting family interviews, she moved closer to this a few years later. In commenting on the development of casework, she suggested, "The next stage in development is to bring the client and those to whom he is socially related together and then to observe the relationship in being, instead of merely gathering a report of it second hand" (Richmond, 1922, p. 138). This also hints at the importance of family interaction, which is accepted as the "centerpiece" of contemporary work with families.

It is fair to say that Richmond's perception of the caseworker's activity in providing services to clients is reflected in contemporary family treatment. Her vision of involving family members in change efforts takes on additional significance when we consider the fact that it occurred at a time when psycho-analytic theory and individual treatment formed the prevailing base of social work practice.

Further development of the observations set forth by Richmond and others continued over the years and culminated in a thrust toward working with families. This movement to family treatment was widely reflected in the literature through the writings of a number of social workers who viewed the interactions of family members as an appropriate area of attention. Scherz (1953), in writing about family-centered casework, saw the individual as a part of the family constellation and suggested this individual "could not be adequately understood or helped in isolation from persons with whom he had close emotional ties" (p. 343). She also emphasized the value of seeing more than one family member when exploring family difficulties. By seeing more than one member, knowledge of family interaction and the role of each participant in this process could be obtained. The move toward treating the family was also supported by Siporin (1956), who recognized the importance of the role theory and small group theory in the conceptualization of theory and practice relative to changing the behavior of the family group. He was among those who initially visualized the necessity of understanding family structure and viewing the family as a social system.

Gomberg (1958) pointed up the limitations implicit in relying solely on individual psychology for an understanding of human problems and stressed the need to include social factors and the family in order to encompass the larger whole. He cautioned that we should not choose between a concept of the family and a psychology of the individual, but should seek a balanced understanding of the interrelatedness between the two. Gomberg was aware of the growing importance of such phenomena as complementarity, role reciprocity, and the congruence of relationships in understanding the family. He further recognized the need to understand "the nature of family equilibrium, social roles, and role expectations characteristic between husband and wife, parent and child, siblings, and within the family group as a whole" (p. 75).

About the same time that Gomberg was reporting on the limitations of individual psychology as the single theoretical base for intervention, Sherman (1959) was writing about the growing trend of seeing two or more family members in an interview, which he defined as joint interviewing. This reflected a shift from viewing the distress of the individual as the problem to recognizing this distress as symptomatic of a family problem or as pathology in the whole family. Sherman also saw a connection between individual treatment and family treatment and suggested that "sometimes the best treatment for the individual is treatment of his family" (p. 22).

Coyle (1962), like Siporin, advanced the idea of the applicability of small group theory in helping the family. She emphasized group structure and dynamics as relevant to family organization and the distribution of power and authority. Coyle also likened the emergence of subgroups within the group process to subsystems in the family, each with specific roles and responsibilities for achieving the goals of their respective organizations.

Pollak and Brieland (1961), reporting on the Midwest Seminars on Family Diagnosis and Treatment, recognized the importance of understanding breakdown in interpersonal relationships within the family. They found that relationships became more complicated as family size increased and additional subsystems came into being. The interrelatedness of the subsystems was such that deterioration in one was likely to cause deterioration in others. Focusing on the whole family was strongly supported, including concern for the development stage of the problem family and viewing the family group in its natural habitat through home visits and partaking of a meal or other hospitality in the home as a way of better understanding family interactions. This was quite a departure from the traditional hour with an individual in the caseworker's office.

Scherz (1962), continuing the move from individual to family treatment, stressed the necessity of focusing on the whole family in order to gain sufficient understanding to diagnose and treat the problems expressed by individual family members. She recognized that this way of dealing with family interactional processes introduced more complications and placed more demands on the caseworker than would be experienced in working with an individual client. In spite of her acceptance of the contributions of multiple-client interviewing, she did not see this as something to be used exclusively, suggesting that both multiple-client and individual interviews should be used in some cases. She wrote, for example, "The emergence of strong dependency needs that cannot be sufficiently gratified in a group treatment process is an indication that individual treatment should supplement family group treatment" (p. 123).

Klein (1963), writing about the systemic aspects of the family, recognized the difference in treating the family as a system instead of treating the individual. He viewed the family group as a medium through which individual change is realized. In other words, he proposed that a change in family interactional patterns would produce change in the way the individual interacted with others within and outside of the family.

Hollis (1981), a much-read authority on a psychodynamic approach to social work treatment with individuals, expanded the attention she gave to family work in the 1981 edition of her book. A fifth edition (Woods & Hollis, 1999) expanded the emphasis on family work even more. The view of the family as a system, on which we elaborate in Chapter 2, is increasingly adopted by social work authors. The eco-systems perspective (Meyer, 1988) utilizes systems concepts that locate the family as a subsystem in the context of the multiplicity of systems with which family members have to deal. These developments can be seen as bringing a shift in emphasis from individual to family functioning and a shift from individual treatment to family group methods of treatment. We fully agree with Sherman that this is not just a shift in intensity but represents a basic shift in the way problems of individual and family functioning are conceptualized. While the field at the time was clearly trying to find a new way and many of the concepts were in early stages of definition, it is clear that core concepts were identified.

Over the last decade, with the advent of managed care and clients' rights groups, a focus has been on the development of brief family interventions (Franklin & Jordan, 1999). These interventions are amenable to a measurement approach so that evidence of their efficacy may be provided to clients and to third-party payers. Social workers such as Steve de Shazer and InSoo Kim Berg were in the forefront of developing solution-focused brief therapies. Brief cognitive behavioral approaches were developed for children and families by Eileen Gambrill, Richard Barth, and others. In the mental health area, social workers such as Gerald Hogarty developed brief psychosocial interventions for families with a member suffering from mental illness. These individuals have developed techniques for working with families systemically from a brief therapeutic framework; these techniques will be reviewed in subsequent chapters. The brief therapy techniques focus on the family as a system and assume that information coming from an outside source (for example, the social worker) can expedite family change. Gambrill (2003) is responsible for introducing evidence-based practice into social work. This approach calls for using empirically validated or supported treatment approaches versus those with no known efficacy or shown to be harmful.

To summarize the current status of family treatment in social work, the social worker helping families cannot be solely concerned about what one person is doing but must think in terms of two or more people interacting and influencing each other. For example, if a child is experiencing problems at school or is involved in negative peer group behavior outside the home, the problem should not be viewed solely as the child's. It must be remembered that the child is a member of a family system that includes others, such as parents and siblings, and experiences a relationship that is influenced by the behavior of those with whom she is interacting. Therefore, it becomes necessary to acquire a different perspective of problem formation and problem solution when treating the family as a unit than when working with an individual.

It might be helpful to remind social workers making the transition from work with individual clients to work with families that breaking old patterns of behavior is not always easy. It is not uncommon for the new family therapist to approach the task by interviewing individuals in the presence of other family members. This is to say that the social worker may carry on a dialogue with one family member at a time, which can result in an overemphasis on changing individual behavior rather than focusing on changing the way family members relate to each other. In this case, the family's participation as a unit is limited, and the opportunity to assess family interactional patterns will be impaired. This is not to suggest that attention should never be focused on the individual in family treatment. It may indeed be necessary at times to focus on an individual in certain situations, such as when the family should listen to a member who is seldom heard or to give support to a family member who needs help in gaining or maintaining a sense of individuation.

To illustrate the change in therapeutic considerations between the traditional one-to-one approach and the family treatment perspective, consider an adolescent client who is truant and has difficulty in school. In the traditional approach, therapeutic efforts would likely focus on the client's fears, feelings of inadequacy, and so on. The objective would be to help the client develop insight into the cause of the problem, which would pave the way for a change in behavior. The involvement of parents and siblings would most likely be peripheral. The parents might be asked to provide some information about the problem; contacts with them would likely be separate from those with the child; and neither they nor other children would be given more than minimum responsibility for the problem.

Conceptualization of the problem is quite different in the family treatment method. The family member whose behavior is in question is thought of as the symptom bearer of a family problem. Among the objectives of the social worker is the shifting of attention from the symptom bearer to the family and involving other members in working toward necessary changes. Seeing family members together is useful because it provides an opportunity to observe various family patterns as members interact around the problem, and this reveals a more complete picture of the issue to be addressed. The therapist who sees only one family member gets only that person's view of the problem, which represents the way it is experienced from the unique position held in the family by that individual.

Take the case of a child in treatment who reveals a reluctance to play with other children in the neighborhood. The mother responds to the child's remarks by saying she realizes this isn't good, but the playgrounds are unsafe and she is fearful that the child might get hurt if allowed outside to play. The mother's comment gives the social worker and the child a different idea about the problem. The child experiences a conflicting message with regard to the inappropriateness of staying in the house and the danger of going outside to play. And the worker now has a notion about the mother's role in the child's behavior. If they had not been seen together, the manner in which the mother impacts on the child's behavior might never have been connected in this way.

To understand the way people interact and perform as members of a family, it is necessary to be aware of conceptualizations about the family as a functioning unit. For example, some notion of family structure and the processes in which the family engages as it maintains its existence is necessary. In the remainder of this chapter, we will present some of the essential concepts used in family treatment. We also broaden the definition of family beyond the usual conception of the isolated nuclear family, doing so to underscore our position that the framework we present is applicable to a variety of family types. Presentation of these concepts will lay the groundwork for a theoretical framework for understanding the dynamics of the family as a complex interactive system, and this will be developed further later in this chapter.

Other Professional Contributions

Men and women from different professions have contributed a great deal to the development of family treatment. Included among the earlier originators were Gregory Bateson, Don Jackson, Jay Haley, John Weakland (Bateson, Jackson, Haley, & Weakland, 1963), and Virginia Satir (1964), the lone social worker, sometimes known as the Palo Alto group and known for their development of communications theory. Coming from a base in psychoanalysis in his work with schizophrenic patients was Murray Bowen (1978). Nathan Ackerman (1958) and Carl Whitaker, as well, moved from individual to family treatment with psychiatric patients. Also among the early developers were Ivan Boszormeny-Nagy (1965), James Framo (1970), and Gerald Zuk (1971) in the Philadelphia area, as well as Salvador Minuchin (1974) and the Child Guidance Center. These pioneering family therapy authors have influenced social work family practitioners, as we have borrowed methodologies from these approaches as they fit with our ecological systems perspective. Specific theories will be discussed in the next chapter; here we will next discuss our theoretical assumptions as themes underlying our systems approach.

THEORETICAL ASSUMPTIONS

Developments within social work as well as in the broader mental health field have led to a proliferation of theories of family treatment. The various theories set forth a variety of concepts in promoting the understanding of individual and family functioning, and of what goes wrong and needs to be righted. Upon closer examination, some similarities are obscured by differences in emphasis on one or another aspect of family structure or process, or in the language used to describe them. Theorists also differ in their thinking about the goals and means of treatment. We note that while the frameworks differ in these ways, they turn out to be neither mutually exclusive nor limited to a theoretical approach. Space allows us neither to introduce nor provide a detailed understanding of all of them. The following discussion will introduce core ideas, principles, and richness of thinking available, drawing attention to similarities and differences among some of them, specifying the concepts we have drawn upon in developing the framework we wish to present to you.

As many as 17 different approaches to family treatment have been identified, described, and compared (Horne & Passmore, 1999). These include approaches that are derivatives of other therapies and attempts to integrate several approaches. Other writers have seen fewer types (Nichols, 1984). Still other authors have made efforts to classify approaches according to the followers of a particular theorist (Hoffman, 1981), basic belief systems, or similarities of thinking about the goals and methods of change. Efforts to identify areas of overlap and similarity, as well as areas of difference and uniqueness, have resulted in a variety of classifications of treatment approaches. In Chapter 2, we present specific helping models; but first we present our underlying theoretical assumptions about working with families, including an investigative stance, evidence-based practice, a systems and communication orientation, a feminist orientation, strengthening of family structures, and a past versus present orientation.

Investigative Stance

Our emphasis on an investigative stance in treatment is in harmony with the social work principle of starting where the client is and with the need to involve the client family in the problem-solving process. Our clear preference for focus in treatment is on here-and-now behavior and feelings determined by a selective investigation of history, including both events and relationships often serving a useful purpose in the production of change. Since families live in a social context, we see that it is important to build effective linkages between family and other systems when other systems undermine or fail to support the family or when families fail to use the support and guidance of those systems.

Areas of focal attention in the treatment process are the family's communication patterns, its structure, and its regulation of interpersonal distance. Families and family subsystems need boundaries and a balance of leadership, direction, rules, hierarchy, separateness, and belonging for effective functioning, and constructive communication processes that clarify all of these for family members. In some cases, all these aspects of functioning may need work; in other cases, only some aspects will need improvement.

Evidence-Based Practice

Along with the trend toward greater accountability is the trend toward evidence-based approaches. Roberts and Yeager (2004) define evidence-based practice as the use of the best scientific evidence when making a clinical decision, that is, use of techniques proven to work. Further, the authors discuss evidence-based social work, which not only encompasses the principles of evidence-based practice but additionally calls for evaluation of one's own practice activities (Cournoyer & Powers, 2004). Systems for monitoring practice will be discussed in Chapter 3.

Of importance in today's behavioral managed care environment is use of accountable methods, selected from knowledge of the evidence-based literature. This trend has encouraged the use of brief therapies that are proven to be effective with client problems. Also important is the use of measurement to assess client problems and to monitor treatment (Jordan & Franklin, 2003).

Systems and Communication Orientation

Aspects of systems theory are inherent in all of the approaches to family treatment in the social work profession. Family therapy approaches, whether psychodynamic, behavioral, client centered, or gestalt, among others, address the family as social system. Individuals in the family, over time, come to have a particular role within the system. Change for better or worse in individual functioning and performance requires change in the functioning and role performance of other members of the system. Likewise, changes in membership, role demands, communicative processes, or other events in the family necessitate change in individual functioning. The functioning of any individual may thus be seen as both an effect and cause of the functioning of other parts or the whole of the family system. The various approaches differ in the degree to which they are explicit in developing such ideas and in the extent of family membership included.

Inherent also in family treatment theories is a more or less explicit emphasis on the need for, and modes of communication between, family members in the promotion and maintenance of family health and in family problem solving. Persons cannot "not" communicate because nonverbal behavior communicates just as do words. Communication modes and problems can be separately assessed, but they are in fact inherent in family structure and role divisions. Family rules and structure are evident in the freedom or lack of it in expressing doubt or difference, and in who can say what to whom and when. Communication conveys how much each family member is valued and who has power in the system.

Systemic Concepts

The systemic concepts we will discuss include social roles and the function of homeostasis, triangulation, family rules, and family myths, and separateness versus connectedness, all of which are important considerations for social workers and other professionals engaged in treating families.

Social Role   The concept of role within the context of family functioning may be viewed as a prescription for interpersonal behavior, associated with individuals as actors and the status of positions. Role requirements are learned in the process of social interaction, and the occupants of a role see it as carrying a specific status for the occupant and for others with whom the occupant interacts. Learning the behaviors expected in various roles involves both observation and teaching.

Learning role expectations by observation may be realized through role taking, imagining oneself to be in the position of another person. This occurs through the process of observing and initiating the behavior of someone whose behavior is accepted by the role taker. In the best of all worlds, this would reflect that which is good and supportive of positive interaction. However, role taking may not always involve behavior that society defines as positive. This is because admired and accepted behavior is often brought on by negative experiences of a hostile environment, including discrimination, poverty, and crime. As a result, social roles do not always make positive impressions or support that which is considered ideal in contemporary society. For example, a young teen imitates his older brother's gang behavior.

In the case of role teaching, information about the role is conveyed when one directly communicates a set of expectations to the role occupant. Through the process of interaction, people learn what is expected in their respective roles. For example, the wife does not make decisions and repeatedly refers all family matters to the husband; this behavior communicates the expectation that he is to be the decision maker. As the husband continues to make decisions, it reinforces the behavior and defines the dependency of the wife with regard to decision making. In the meantime, the role of decision maker is established, and it is expected that this person will behave in this way.

If both partners are satisfied with their respective role behaviors, this indicates that they have harmonized their interpersonal roles around this independent-dependent relationship and that role complementarity exists between them. In this case, the complementary needs of both are fulfilled by this independent-dependent interaction. And in spite of the appearance of an unequal relationship, this couple may function satisfactorily due to a congruence of roles.

Their relationship would be quite different if an incongruity of roles existed, that is, if the couple did not agree on the appropriate behavior to be associated with the roles they are expected to fill. For example, if the wife expects to make all decisions about family matters but is denied this opportunity by her husband who expects shared decision making, this will result in role conflict and an incongruity of roles will exist.

It should not be assumed that a lack of congruence in the relationship means there is also disagreement. Since an individual takes on a series of roles in the process of identifying and developing a self, a lack of congruence might arise as a result of inconsistencies between identities that surface in response to situations experienced by the role occupant. This can be seen when the occupant interacts with various others where existing relationships call forth incompatible identities, as in the case of a teacher interacting with a student who is also a friend. The identity compatible with exchanges between friends is usually characterized by a symmetrical relationship, where both communicators behave equally. However, when a superior and a subordinate attempt a friendship relationship, incongruence develops. In other words, congruence cannot occur when both equal and unequal behaviors are required simultaneously.

To this point we have been concerned primarily with role as related to various role images. Finally, we will focus on roles from an intrafamilial perspective. Since the parent role is invested with the responsibility for the family system, it represents a logical point at which to begin the intrafamilial focus. Then we follow with a discussion of the role of children in the family.

Assimilation into the role of parent, as well as the role of child, occurs through the same learning process described earlier. The role prescription for parent requires the exercise of authority in the interest of the development of children, while at the same time providing the opportunity for growth as reflected in separation and individuation. Preferred behaviors for the parent role can be learned through teaching as exemplified in parent effectiveness training. Nevertheless, the first and perhaps most important learning of role behavior occurs through observation and role taking. This is to say that children learn parenting behavior from their relationship with parents as they move through the life cycle. Thus, much of the behavior demonstrated by parents in association with their children becomes the behavior that the children will demonstrate in the future when they become parents. For example, several studies have found that children who are abused by their parents also abuse their children when they become parents. Positive qualities will likewise be transferred to the future parent role.

The role of the child comes with the birth of the infant, and much of the early role behavior is characterized as instinctive and dependent. However, the infant's behavior is also influenced by the responses of the parents in their effort to meet the child's needs. If the children are provided appropriate physical and emotional comfort by the parents and given food when hungry, they are likely to respond in ways that reflect contentment. Children's contented behavior pleases the parents and elicits more of the parental responses that produced this behavior, thus defining expected role behavior for both parents and children. The parent role is to provide appropriate nourishment for the child, while the child is to behave in ways that reflect happiness and contentment. Even at this early stage of life, role behavior is learned through the process of interacting with others.

As children grow, they learn expected role behavior from a number of associations and experiences, including siblings, peers, and various adults. One of the most influential sources of learning from adults other than parents is experienced when children enter school and take on the role of student. This is a new role, and children must learn how to behave as students whose primary objective is to gain specific knowledge designed to facilitate movement through various stages of life. Teaching and observation are again the primary vehicles for communicating what is required of children in the student role. The teacher communicates specific information and requires children to demonstrate the extent to which this information is understood and integrated into an orderly body of knowledge commensurate with the children's level of development. In addition to providing information and guiding the children's quest for knowledge, the teacher almost always becomes a role model for the children and thereby enhances the role-taking process through which role expectations are learned. This interaction defines how the children should behave as students: That is, that they should acquire knowledge under the guidance of the teacher and be able to demonstrate this achievement in communication with others. Understanding various role sets as experienced by family members and the way in which these roles are defined will greatly assist social workers and other professionals in determining appropriate strategies for intervening in family conflict.

Family Homeostasis   All systems have a self-regulatory mechanism through which a state of equilibrium is maintained. They seek to maintain a steady state, or a desired balance in their existence, through an error-activated feedback process. In regard to maintaining balance in relationships, if one person shows a change in relationship to another person, that person will react in a manner designed to modify and decrease the impact of that change. In the case of the family, homeostasis implies that the family acts so as to achieve a balance in relationships. This means that all parts of the system function in such a way that change is unnecessary for realization of family goals.

Most, but not all, families maintain a balance in relationships through wholesome growth-producing transactions. This implies that permeable boundaries facilitate feedback, and the feedback process promotes adjustments to life cycle developments, which maintain the desired balance. However, family homeostasis may be achieved in a variety of ways. For example, as early as the 1950s, study of schizophrenic patients and their families revealed that in some of these families there was a vested interest in the patient's illness. In this case, when the patient began to improve, family members exerted pressure to maintain the illness. In other situations when the patient got well, someone else in the family became symptomatic. This behavior suggests the need for a symptom bearer in the family in order to maintain the established pattern of relationships.

In such cases, the family, in its efforts to maintain a homeostatic state, may not always serve the best interests of all its members. Therefore, the worker should keep in mind that in maintaining its emotional balance, the family may try to prevent unwanted change in the system by encouraging role performance that is destructive for the role occupant. Yet, much of the behavior that maintains the status quo within the family is accepted by its members as a legitimate part of the family's operation. This supports the suggestion that someone outside of the family is most often the first to identify such behavior as deviant and to send out the call for help. For example, the school is often the first to call attention to the deviant behavior exhibited by the child. The family fails to recognize this behavior as deviant because it serves the function of maintaining equilibrium within the family.

To further illustrate the homeostatic process, consider the case of parents who fight in the presence of a child and frequently threaten to separate. The child fears loss of the parents and reacts to prevent this loss by displaying behavior that claims the parents' attention. When the parents focus their attention on the child, they must discontinue their fighting. The threat of loss for the child subsides, and the family remains intact. As this transaction is repeated, it becomes a pattern of behavior in the family; the parents fight and the child acts out to keep them together.

Family Triangulation   A number of theorists have contributed to the development of the concept of triangulation in family relations. In keeping with this concept, it is accepted that the formation of a unit of three as a way of relating is a process common to all emotional systems. Knowledge of this process is essential to understanding the family as it struggles to maintain itself as a viable system. The triangle, as most commonly perceived, involves three persons (for example, parents and a child) or two persons and an issue (for example, a couple and alcohol). The two-person system has difficulty maintaining its stability under the pressure of anxiety and tension. When this system experiences intolerable frustration, it triangulates a third person or an issue in the hope of reducing the level of tension. The social worker engaged in family treatment is also a likely object of triangulation, especially when dealing with a two-person system. In a triangle situation, the third operative person or issue becomes the object of attention for at least one of the original two, and sometimes both engage in a struggle for the advantages offered by the third component of the triangle.

The concept of triangles in human relationships is most often applied as a way of describing the relations of a unit of three. However, more than three persons, or a combination of persons and issues, may be involved, as demonstrated in the family where two or more children alternate as the triangulated family member. In other families, more than one child may be brought into the relationship struggle between parents at the same time. As an example, consider the parent whose actions convey to the children that the other parent is not interested in the welfare of the family. This encourages the children to join with the first parent to ensure survival. It creates a situation in which at least three have come together against one, and at least four people are actively involved in the triangulation process.

It is important to recognize the existence of a perverse triangle within the process of family relating. This triangle is potentially pathological and can lead to conflict and possible dissolution of the system. In describing the perverse triangle, Haley (1987) suggests that one member is of a different generation (such as parent and child). These two people of different generations form a coalition against the peer of one of the members (for example, one parent and child against the other parent) but deny the presence of the coalition, in spite of behavior that confirms its existence. If the coalition continues and the denial of its existence is repeatedly offered, this pattern of relating is established and a pathological situation exists.

The concept of the triangle in human relationships provides the social worker with a way of viewing the patterns of relating within the family. To illustrate the working of this concept as it is frequently observed in family treatment, a case example from our experience is the H family:

Mr. and Mrs. H were both 31 years of age. He was a successful executive and she was a housewife and mother. They were married at 21, when both were in their last year of college. Their first and only child was a son, D, who was born one year after the marriage. D had just celebrated his ninth birthday when the family came for treatment.

The parents were very articulate, and Mr. H's skills in public relations and sales, areas in which he had been quite successful, were readily observed in the early sessions. He explained the family's route to therapy as a mutual decision, coming after D's increasing show of dependent behavior. In school he was demanding more attention, and the teachers thought he was showing signs of insecurity. At home his behavior was somewhat confusing to the parents, as he demanded more attention, yet at times he withdrew from their efforts to engage with him.

It was learned during the course of treatment that the beginning of this behavior followed closely what Mrs. H described as rather serious misunderstandings between her and Mr. H. For the past five years, Mr. H had advanced steadily with his company and, about one year ago, had been promoted to a position of increased responsibility. This position required travel and a good deal of entertaining, which forced curtailment of many activities the family had previously enjoyed. Mrs. H was feeling left out of her husband's life, and as both she and the job demanded more and more of Mr. H's time, anxiety and tension developed. In commenting on this Mrs. H stated that the job seemed to be winning and that they had more than once discussed divorce.

As a result of the increasing anxiety Mrs. H experienced, she began to do more things with her son, shared her loneliness with him, and in various ways conveyed abandonment by Mr. H and their need to be together. This led to a coalition between mother and son, as the son was triangulated by the mother to help in dealing with her relationship with her husband. Nevertheless, this was an uneasy coalition, as D was very fond of his father. When the father also bid for D's attention, D withdrew out of fear of hurting one of his parents. The burden this placed on D was too great to be contained within the family relationship and spilled over into his relationship within the school system.

The family triangle does not necessarily involve the same third person or object throughout the triangulation process, and usually a number of alternatives are available to complete it. In the H case, for example, Mrs. H might also have chosen to attach herself to her parents to help in dealing with her husband or attempted a coalition with the therapist for the same purpose.

It should also be noted that triangulation is not always an indication of pathology in the family. For example, either parent may develop an interest in an outside activity such as volunteer work as a way of spreading out the tension that usually develops in intense intimate relating. It is not likely that bringing this third component into the relationship will become problematic, as long as it does not replace the other principal participant in the relationship. By redirecting some of the energy that otherwise goes into the buildup of tension, both partners are better able to carry out normal functions. In summary, triangulation is a predictable way in which human systems handle problems in relating as they seek to relieve the buildup of tension. While it can, under certain circumstances, contribute to family dysfunction, it can also be an alternative that leaves the participants in an intimate relationship somewhat more free to function effectively.

Family Rules   Family rules are essentially relationship agreements that influence family behavior. Some rules are explicit and established along the lines of specific roles and expectations of family members. With these rules, what is desired is likely to be discussed, which opens the rules to the possibility of negotiation and change. The most powerful family rules, however, are those that are implicit, having been established over time by repeated family transaction. For example, consider the case of a family in which one parent is involved in an extramarital love affair. This affair has generated repeated experiences through which family members have come to realize that the extramarital relationship exists. The parents never openly talk about the relationship themselves or entertain discussion of it by the children. As this scenario is repeated, it becomes an established rule that the family will not talk about the parent's affair. The strength of this rule lies in the fact that, without discussion, relevant information about the experience is not processed. When discussion does not occur, the family is less likely to take actions to alter the status quo. The self-perpetuating mechanisms within the family system take over and reinforce the implicit rule, which continues unchanged among family members.

Families also have different ways of enforcing rules in treatment. For example, if the social worker seems to be getting too close to a family secret in an interchange with one family member, someone else may enter the discussion with a different idea that changes the flow of information. In another situation, especially where children are involved, a child may suddenly display some form of disruptive behavior. This claims the attention of the group, taking the focus away from the possible revelation of the secret as awareness turns to this new and unexpected activity. Some families also have rules governing communication around valued areas of family life, such as sexual behavior and family illness. Whatever the governing mechanism, when it interferes with the effective course of treatment, preventive measures should be taken.

The Family Myth   The family myth essentially consists of family members' shared beliefs and expectations of each other and their relationships. It is characterized by unquestioned sharing of beliefs and expectations by all family members, which results in automatic agreement on the myth without further thought by any member. Ferreira (1977) gives this example:

> The wife in a family of 16 years' duration did not drive an automobile, nor did she care to learn. It was necessary for the husband to drive her everywhere she wished to go, which he did at whatever personal sacrifice it required. The wife explained her position by saying she was not mechanically inclined. The husband immediately agreed with his wife and corroborated her statement by adding that she often let things fall from her hands around the house, and had always been that way. He further reported that she also did not trust cab drivers, while the wife nodded her approval. (p. 51)

The husband so completely shared the belief that his wife was not mechanically inclined and needed his assistance that he not only agreed with her statement but supported the belief by offering an example of her awkwardness. He obviously had no thought of questioning her position.

It is also important to keep in mind that, in spite of the irrationality often apparent in the existence of a family myth, family members perceive it as an emotionally indispensable and necessary part of their reality. As such, it not only determines the behavior of all family members but also reveals something about family relationships. It implies the existence of reciprocal roles in the family, which is to say, if the myth is around something someone in the family cannot do, it implies that it can be done by someone else in the family. As further emphasis on the myth in family relating, consider the central characters, George and Martha, in the drama *Who's Afraid of Virginia Woolf?* Much of the discussion between the characters in this drama centers on the existence of an imaginary son. Although the son does not exist, both Martha and George believe him to be real and repeatedly express agreement on matters pertaining to him. Myths may also serve a homeostatic function within the family and are likely to surface at times of extreme tension that threaten to disrupt family relationships. The myth prevents change in relationships, as do all balancing mechanisms, enabling the family to continue functioning in its customary manner.

Separateness and Connectedness   It is important that family members act both in concert with others and individually. A process of being together and being apart from one another characterizes human relationships. Two strong emotional forces are at work in this process: the need for emotional closeness, which brings people together; and the desire for individuality and autonomy, which moves the individual away from the control of others.

The family is characterized by a connectedness between members and also separateness of members from one another. This duality is reflected in the situation surrounding the newborn infant. Although coming from the parents, the infant is physically a separate individual and must remain so. Returning to the womb is impossible, and the child's psychobiological individuality will exist despite experience with the socialization process. The parents must maintain their psychobiological individuality regardless of their emotional closeness. The infant also exemplifies connectedness among family members. The newborn must depend on parents for nurturance in order to survive and therefore cannot sever this connection. And if the parents are to fulfill the infant's needs, they must come together and accommodate each other in the parenting role.

The other side of being separate and connected involves emotional issues. Fusion and differentiation behavior among family members are essential elements in their coming together and being able to separate. Fusion behavior is an adaptation of speech and actions designed to establish a system of feeling and responses that is in keeping with the family's preferred pattern of behavior. Differentiation behavior is the opposite of fusion behavior in that the individual develops speech and actions that will disengage her own feelings and responses from a pattern of automatic compliance with what is preferred by others. This means that the individual seeks freedom from control by others, freedom to be different from others, and freedom to be apart from others.

Maintaining connectedness to others creates a sense of belonging, which satisfies the basic human need for closeness and identification. Yet, we must keep in mind that excessive closeness minimizes the opportunity for separateness; and if this condition exists, enmeshment and loss of identity may result. Separateness has a similar quality in that it contributes to individuality and autonomy, but when carried to the extreme, it can produce loneliness and isolation. Therefore, a balance must be sought that will allow family members to come together to share and support, but also to separate and follow individual pathways to fulfillment and satisfaction.

The ways in which family members want to be together and the ways they want to be apart are reflected in the family's patterns of behavior. Some families develop around an excessive need for emotional closeness, while other families place great emphasis on separateness as shown in autonomy of behavior. If the need for closeness is too great, fusion within family relationships is likely to result. And when fusion occurs, family members will not be able to express themselves in a manner other than what is preferred by the family. If the drive for individuality and self-determination exceeds all other interests, the ability of family members to be close and supportive in relationships with one another is lessened. Extremes in either case contribute to family dysfunction.

The pattern of relating within a family is not the result of an accidental process. It is influenced by the patterns established in the parents' families of origin. If the parents were never given permission to separate from their own families of origin, they will experience difficulty in establishing separate ego boundaries between themselves. The new parents will then transmit this need for togetherness to their children, who will also have difficulty separating from them. The implicit obligation in this type of family is to remain devoted to the families of origin. Individuation is not encouraged among family members, and the avenues through which this might take place are frequently blocked. This blocking behavior is often subtle. It can be seen in the family that permits members to transcend its boundaries but systematically rejects all feedback from such encounters. A typical example is the adolescent who is allowed to interact with systems outside the family but is denied the opportunity to use this experience for personal growth. Families accomplish this denial in various ways. Sometimes they discourage differentiation indirectly by disqualifying the child's attempts at new behavior or expressing fear that great danger is associated with her wish to be different at such a tender age. In this way the avenue to differentiation is blocked, and the family goal of maintaining the devotion of its members is supported.

The experience of separateness in relationship is not entirely a physical phenomenon but may be a psychic boundary. For example, parents may help their child to dress herself at an early age, thus creating a psychic sense of separateness and empowerment in the child. We believe that one of the most important developments within the family as it passes through its life cycle is the determination of what it will do about closeness and separation in family relations. Most families are able to establish a workable balance in how its members will come together and support each other, and how they will be different and able to be apart from each other. The extent to which this balance is achieved is crucial, and social workers may often find this a necessary target area for their change efforts.

Feminist Orientation

The feminist perspective in family treatment provides the therapist with a necessary reminder of the impact of gender difference in the helping process. We believe it is important to present this view in connection with theoretical and systems thinking as applied to family treatment. Both male and female therapists should be mindful of the feminist perspective as they engage with families in a mutual effort to improve family functioning.

Feminist therapists have drawn attention to several aspects of systems thinking that do not adequately represent the real position of women. The systems concepts that a change in one part of the system affects other parts of the system and that a change in the definition of the male role and the functioning of male members affects the role definition and functioning of the female member of the system are not doubted. What feminists question is the view that the power to influence is as great from female to male as it is in the reverse direction. Therapists need to take into account society's patriarchal definitions of the male role as breadwinner and head of the family, and how this has given males authority and power of decision over wife and children. Definition of the woman's role as confined to the family with responsibility as the nurturing and caretaking member leaves women relatively powerless. Structural therapists who assume equality in reciprocity only reinforce the limited role for wives and mothers.

In observation of family situations, therapists have sometimes noted that the male is peripherally involved in household and family operations, and that his marginal involvement is seen as contributory to family malfunction. Interventions designed to move him back into a more central role are seen as degrading to the wife, reinforcing the traditional patriarchal view of her position and power in the family. A therapist who is aware of the traditional orientation may, even so, assess the family as needing more investment from the peripheral male but will intervene in a way that sees the wife as, and enables her to function as, an equally powerful partner. Interventions designed to expand the male role definition from its directive and authoritative aspects to include connecting and nurturing functions serve to improve family functioning without depreciating the woman's role, while also increasing male satisfaction.

The traditional view of the male role can be seen as limiting the male experience (Dienhart & Avis, 1991) by keeping him in the instrumental role. Feminist therapists would help males to move from their individualistic and competitive positions and encourage more mutuality and sharing from which they can profit and grow.

The achievement of separateness, individuality, and autonomy or differentiation of self, as it is called in Bowen's systems theory, is seen in all therapeutic approaches as important to individual and family functioning. It results in giving members a feeling of competence and a sense of empowerment. It enables family members to see and relate to other members as individuals and not solely as someone to meet the self's needs. From this emphasis on separateness, the nurturing activity of wives/mothers in fostering and regulating relatedness between family members has sometimes been seen as overinvolvement and denying of their separateness. On this point, feminists assert that women develop a connected sense of self and define themselves through attachments to others (Knudson-Martin, 1994, p. 36). Further, it is important to recognize that nurturance, connectedness, and involvement have been society's expectation for women; they have been socialized into a gender identity that expects them to do just that (Longres, 2000). Their separateness and definition of self have come through engagement in relationships. The goal for themselves and their family is to develop their separateness while maintaining connectedness. By contrast, males' achievement of a sense of separateness is a process of separating from the primary caregiver, who is almost always female. This separation process stresses differences rather than similarities. The process of separating from the primary caregiver typically leaves men with a deficit in the relational capacities and skills that their female counterparts have developed (Dienhart & Avis, 1991, p. 27).

Feminist family therapists view attempts to help men and women fit into traditional role definitions as unhelpful and destructive. Therapists should take a political position as well as a therapeutic one that challenges stereotyped sex roles, as well as sexist assumptions about family structure, society, and culture. Neutrality in the conventional therapeutic sense is believed to reinforce the status quo (i.e., the socioeconomic oppression of women). The client is encouraged not only to develop insights about her role in maintaining the familial and societal contexts of which she is a part but also to take responsibility for changing them (Ault-Riche, 1986). Leeder (1994, p. 2) similarly advocates a feminist view of treatment that is dedicated to overcoming and working with gender discrimination as a political and therapeutic goal.

Strengthening Family Structure

Elements of family structure are observable in the communication processes of the family. Who speaks to whom; who listens to whom; whose ideas are adopted; who gets put down, shut out, or ignored; and who seldom or never speaks are aspects of communications that tell of role, status, power, control, affection, and distance regulation in relationships. Communications contribute to the shaping of family structure, and family structure in turn serves to shape the pattern of communications. Other aspects of structure that need worker attention in the helping process are factors of stability and changeability, family hierarchy, family subsystems, and distance regulation.

Changeability   One concern about structure is that it should not be so rigid as to prohibit variability and change. At the same time, it should be sufficiently stable so that members can experience the family as dependable and predictable enough to provide some guidelines by which the individual members can be clear about what roles and behaviors are expected. On the other hand, structure should also not be so changeable as to be chaotic, with no clearly defined roles or rules for behavior, with only vaguely defined subsystems within the family and no sense of leadership and control. For individuals, subsystems, and the family as a whole to function properly, subsystem boundaries, roles for individuals, and rules of the system need to be clearly defined without being permanently fixed, subject to change as the needs of and demands on individual members and the system as a whole change. Achieving clarity about boundaries, roles, and rules in the interest of stability, and at the same time enabling the family to allow for needed change, is a central task in the treatment process.

Past versus Present Orientation

Simply stated, family treatment approaches may be classified as psychoanalytic (insight-oriented), experiential, or cognitive-behavioral (action-oriented).
These approaches are similar in their systemic view of the family but differ on
some other key characteristics that are reviewed here.

Some approaches to family treatment are based on the idea that past experiences determine present individual and family behavior, and that becoming
aware of and understanding them is important in changing behavior.
Approaches classified as historical and psychoanalytic are congruent with
such an emphasis. There is little disagreement among all treatment approaches
that the past experience in the family of origin has been influential in the problems and behavior of the individual and the family. But the way in which the
past is dealt with differs greatly among approaches. Those based on psychoanalytic therapy elicit the individual's past negative experience with parents or
siblings or family events. Scharff and Scharff (1991) note that psychoanalytic
and object relations theories allow a focus on recognizing and surfacing feelings about the past that adds depth to the understanding of each individual
family member. This understanding may be integrated with techniques that
attend primarily to here-and-now interactions between family members to
promote changed behavior and that minimize the necessity of awareness and
understanding. For example, couples therapy may include a component aimed
at resolving or renewing ties by bringing in family-of-origin members primarily at a later phase of treatment.

Systems approaches view problematic individuals and families as overinvolved and emotional about their families of origin. Two or three generations
of family history play into present difficulties. The goal of treatment is
for individuals to be less tied to, but not cut off from, family of origin. One of
the means is through cognitive understanding, acquired through a dispassion-
ate search for information from members of the extended family. This
(systems) approach directs attention to achieving a more objective (rational)
view of relationships among all family members over several generations.
Relationships within a generation affect and are affected by those across generational lines, and understanding and interpretation of these relationships is
a major focus of treatment. On the other hand, treatment does not necessarily
draw in all family members. One person's change as a result of family-focused
treatment can effect changes in the entire system. Rationality is valued over
emotionality in relating to family and achieving change.

At the other end of this past/present continuum are approaches that
inquire little or not at all about the past, forgoing interpretation and insight
and focusing on present interactions between family members and the structure or organization of the current family. Some treatment approaches make
no effort to learn specifics of the past, looking only at the present problem
and what keeps the family functioning in a problem-perpetuating manner.
The strategic approach developed by Madanes (1981) would be an example.
This focus is on the here-and-now.

Interpretation versus Behavior Change   Here the distinction between approaches is on the means of bringing about change in the family. As indicated in the previous section, psychodynamic approaches assume that talking and developing awareness of the origin of the problem provide the basis for change.

Action-oriented techniques, on the other hand, focus primarily on the here-and-now of family relationships, on promoting changed behavior more than on understanding, and on restructuring the role network. Structural practitioners (Minuchin, 1974) hold images of how families need to be organized in order to solve the problems of the family and its individual members. Role definitions for husbands and wives, mothers and fathers, and parents and children, as well as clarity about who is in charge, the importance of generational distinctions and boundaries, and clarity about rules for behavior, all need to be understood and corrected. Parents are helped to be parental and children to be children; males and females have specific roles to perform. In developing their image of the properly structured family, therapists need to be aware of the ways in which their image of the well-functioning family is shaped by their experience in their family of origin and its religious and ethnic environment. A sexist bias is seen by some therapists to be inherent in the structural approach.

Seeing family members together to observe how they deal with each other, the reenactment of family events, giving direction to change unhelpful responses, suggesting new responses in the interview, and assigning tasks to be carried out between interviews are also among the primary methods of promoting change. Recurring sequences of interaction consist of helpful or unhelpful actions in solving the family's problems; responses reward or discourage desirable behavior or problem solution.

Differences between the approaches to behavior change also lie in the degree to which the family is involved in producing a problem solution and the level of responsibility taken by the therapist. In strategic approaches, for example, the therapist might unilaterally determine which family members would be seen, how to frame the problem, and the number of steps needed to solve it. This might occur without any effort to develop the family's understanding of causation or reasons for perpetuation of the problem. Directions are given for things to do between sessions. The emphasis is clearly on problem solution and not on giving family members the opportunity for personal growth or an emotional experience with each other.

Social learning approaches promote behavior change by developing a detailed understanding of which actions by family members reward or discourage desirable behavior and what new behaviors need to be acquired in order to promote the desired behavior. Family members are instructed to instrument new behaviors that will encourage desired responses from others and to eliminate behaviors that encourage undesired responses. Family preservation and family psychoeducation approaches are integrative and utilize many action-oriented techniques.

Growth versus Problem Solution   The main distinction in this dichotomy is whether the primary goal of treatment is individual growth and change or solution of the presenting problem. In one sense, solution of the presenting problem may result from growth of family members as autonomous persons. Helping them to experience themselves as separate and whole persons helps them and the family to function better. Alternately, solution of the problem may occur through change in family roles, alliances, or other aspects of structure. Such changes allow as well for generally better relationships and ongoing problem solution.

Several aspects of treatment are included in the label of "experiential." As implied, the intent is to allow during the sessions for clarification of relationships and expression of feelings between family members, to enable them to experience and understand each other in new ways, as separate and unique, different but valued. The means for achieving this may be through verbal exchange or through physical means such as decreasing or increasing distance, or having family members face each other or change the seating arrangement during a treatment session.

A second aspect of the experiential approach is the use of the therapist's own emotional response to the family to enable family members to become "real people" in their own right. In context of supportive actions that are clearly directed to such a goal, the therapist fosters emotional intensity, spontaneity, and genuineness by direct, sometimes provocative, response to the family or individual behavior. Such therapist behavior serves as a model for the family but requires therapists who are themselves mature, open, spontaneous, self-aware, and aware of how far the family can be "pushed" on this experiential level.

Emotionality–Rationality–Activity   Emotional overinvolvement is the key here. The term "rationality" emphasizes achieving rational understanding of the problems, then dealing with them in a rational rather than emotionally based manner. Viewing the family as a system could result in neglect of the affective component and the experience of the individual in the family. Experiential and individual-growth oriented approaches deal with emotional issues.

It should be clear from this brief overview of different approaches to treatment of the family that there are many variations in ways of conceptualizing the problems of the family or the individual in it, in the methods of treatment, and in the goals to be achieved. Similar ways of defining the problem may lead to different methods of treatment, and different problem definitions may use similar methods of treatment. Goals may be achieved by more than one method and, conversely, similar methods may achieve different or several ends. While identifying them, we have given only a sketchy picture of the different approaches. In the following chapters we define our own understandings of the family and the means and goals of treatment, and we will demonstrate where our approach draws from the ones we have already mentioned. Our elaboration will convey that we are clearly in favor of individual growth and overall family well-being but that solution of the presenting problem is our priority. Our method is more focused on changing behavior and relationships than on interpretation and acquisition of understanding by family members. At the same time, we actively involve family members in developing problem solutions. And while we see history and past relationships with extended family as significant and useful in developing our understanding, our approach focuses more on the set of present relationships.

Not accounted for in the preceding classification of approaches is the great emphasis on a different understanding of sex roles brought by feminist thinkers and therapists. Their look at aspects of the different approaches leads to a different understanding of the male and female roles in and accountability for events and transactions in the family. Two separate critiques (Dienhart & Avis, 1991; Ault-Riche, 1986) from a feminist point of view of five of the major approaches to family treatment introduce feminist concerns and suggest modifications to accommodate those concerns. Further reference to feminist thinking will be made in subsequent chapters.

Before embarking on the more detailed exposition of our theoretical understanding of families and approach to treatment, it is important to draw attention to several broad themes that are significant in our overall exposition.

We want to be clear about our conception of what is and who is in a family. The theory to be set forth is relevant to the structure, process, and situation of all kinds of families. The image of family that first comes to mind may not be the same for all readers and is likely formed out of one's own experience as much as out of a scientific definition. Different images will reflect the fact that not all families are the same—not all fit into the category of "typical nuclear family," with two parents and two children. In fact, other family types are more likely to be encountered in social work practice, including unmarried partners, remarried couples and their children, single-parent households, gay or lesbian partners—any of whom may include significant other extended family members or nonrelative others. Beyond the differences in family membership, it is obvious that families differ according to the culture, class, or ethnic group of which they are a part and the life circumstances with which they have had to cope.

While we devote separate chapters to some of these different types of families, our theory in the sections that follow attempts to outline a framework for looking at the structure and process of families that allows for understanding the sameness among them as well as the obvious differences. To that end, we will approach each of these chapters with a framework of population definition, assessment issues, and evidence-based treatment recommendations. In Part II, the problem-focused chapters, we will conclude the assessment section of each chapter with a table of several of the best assessment measures that are frequently used for the populations. The tables will include basic information on validity, reliability, and contact information.

In the technique section, we will include evidence-based treatment/best practices and give detail about evidenced-based treatments, give an example when citing information, and include a table with the major studies or a meta-analysis.

We will also include a treatment manual, which will be summarized from one or more of the evidence-based practices available for that area. A case example will be provided.

Our approach thus far has examined mainly the internal operations of families and has not put the family system into the larger social context—the community or communities in which the family resides or of which it is a part. Families acquire values, standards, and modes of operation not only from their families or origin but also from the ethnic and religious communities to which they are attached. Therapeutic involvement requires attention to the physical environment in which the family resides as well as to the institutional communities—the work and school environments—that ordinarily impinge on family functioning and to the systems offering services to the family in need of help.

SUMMARY

We have tracked a transition in social work practice from a primary focus on work with individuals to work with the family as a group. A key trend is evidence-based practice, and our treatment recommendations will reflect this approach. A similar course has been identified in psychiatry and the mental health professions, generally. We have identified and discussed the underlying theoretical assumptions of our approach. These are an investigative stance, evidence-based practice, a systems and communication orientation, a feminist orientation, a strengthening of family structure, and a past versus present focus. The next chapter continues this discussion by describing several treatment approaches to family therapy based on the theoretical assumptions presented here.

References

Ackerman, N. W. 1958. *The Psychodynamics of Family Life*. New York: Basic Books.

Ault-Riche, Marianne. 1986. "A Feminist Critique of Five Schools of Family Therapy." In *Women and Family Therapy*, ed. Marianne Ault-Riche. Rockville, MD: Aspen Systems Corporation.

Bateson, G., Jackson, D. D., Haley, J., and Weakland, J. H. 1963. "Toward a Theory of Schizophrenia." *Behavioral Science* 1:251–54.

Benson, Mark, Schindler-Zimmerman, Toni, and Martin, Doris. 1991. "Assessing Children's Perceptions of Their Family: Circular Questioning Revisited." *Journal of Marital and Family Therapy* 17(4): 363–72.

Boszormeny-Nagy, I., and Framo, J. L. (eds.). 1965. *Intensive Family Therapy*. New York: Harper & Row.

Bowen, M. 1978. *Family Therapy in Clinical Practice*. New York: Jason Aronson.

Corcoran, K., and Fischer, J. 2000. *Measures for Clinical Practice*. New York: Free Press.

Cournoyer, and Powers. 2004. "Chapter 1 Systematic Reviews of Evidence-Based

Studies and Practice-Based Research: How to Search for, Develop, and Use Them. In *Evidence-Based Practice Manual: Research and Outcome Measures in Health and Human Services*. eds. A. R. Roberts and K. R. Yeager. New York: Oxford University Press, p. 7.

Coyle, Grace L. 1962. Concepts Relevant to Helping the Family as a Group. *Social Casework* 43:347–54.

Dienhart, Anna, and Avis, Judith. 1991. "Men in Therapy: Exploring Feminist Informed Alternatives." In *Feminist Approaches for Men in Family Therapy*, ed. Michelle Bograd. Binghamton, NY: Harrington Park Press.

Framo, J. L. 1970. "Symptoms from a Family Transactional Viewpoint. In *Family Therapy in Transition*, ed. N. W. Ackerman. Boston: Little, Brown.

Franklin, C., and Jordan, C. 1999. *Family Practice: Brief Systems Interventions for Social Work*. Pacific Grove, CA: Brooks/Cole.

Friedman, Gary. 1994. *Primer of Epidemiology*. New York: McGraw-Hill.

Friedman, L. J. 1980. "Integrating Psychoanalytic Object-Relations Understanding with Family and Systems Intervention in Couples Therapy. In *Family Therapy*, eds. J. Pierce and L.J. Friedman. New York: Grune and Stratton.

Gambrill, E. 2003. "Editorial: Evidence-Based Practice: Sea Change or the Emperor's New Clothes? *Journal of Social Work Education* 39(1):1–18.

Gomberg, Robert M. 1958. "Trends in Theory and Practice." *Social Casework* 39:73–83.

Haley, J. 1987. *Problem-Solving Therapy*. 2nd Edition. San Francisco: Jossey-Bass.

Hansen, J. C., and L'Abate, L. 1982. *Approaches to Family Therapy*. New York: Macmillan.

Hess, R., and Handel, G. 1985. *The Psychosocial Interior of the Family*. New York: Aldine Publishing Co.

Hoffman, L. 1981. *Foundations of Family Therapy*. New York: Basic Books.

Hollis, F. 1981. *Casework: A Psychosocial Therapy*. New York: Random House.

Horne, Arthur, and Passmore, J. Laurence. 1999. *Family Counseling and Therapy*. Itasca, IL: F. E. Peacock Publishers.

Jordan, C., and Franklin, C. 2003. *Clinical Assessment for Social Workers: Quantitative and Qualitative Measures*. 2nd edition. Chicago: Lyceum.

Klein, Alan. 1963. "Exploring Family Group Counseling." *Social Work* 8:23–29.

Knudson-Martin, C. 1994. The Female Voice: Applications to Bowen's Family Systems Theory. *Journal of Marital and Family Therapy* 20(1):35–46.

Kolevson, Michael, and Green, Robert. 1985. *Family Therapy Models*. New York: Springer Publishing Co.

L'Abate, L., and Frey, J. 1981. "The E-R-A Model: The Role of Feelings in Family Therapy Reconsidered: Implications for a Classification of Theories of Family Therapy. *Journal of Marital and Family Therapy* 7(2):143–150.

Leeder, E. 1994. *Treating Abuse in Familes: A Feminist and Community Approach*. New York: Springer Publishing Company.

Levant, R. F. 1980. A Classification of Family Therapy: A Review of Prior Attempts and a New Paradigmatic Model. *American Journal of Family Therapy* 8:3–16.

Longres, J. F. 2000. *Human Behavior and the Social Environment*, 3rd edition. Itasca, IL: Peacock.

Madanes, C. 1981. *Strategic Family Therapy*. San Francisco: Jossey-Bass.

Madanes, C., and Haley, J. 1977. "Dimensions of Family Therapy." *Journal of Nervous and Mental Disease* 165:88–97.

McGill, David. 1992. "The Cultural Story in Multicultural Family Therapy." *Families in Society* 73:339–49.

Meyer, C. 1988. "The Eco-Systems Perspective." In *Paradigms of Clinical*

Social Work, ed. R. Dorfman. New York: Brunner/Mazel Publishers.

Minuchin, S. 1974. *Families and Family Therapy.* Cambridge, MA: Harvard University Press.

Nichols, Michael. 1984. *Family Therapy: Concepts and Methods.* New York: Gardner Press.

Nichols, Michael, Schwartz, Richard Z., and Minuchin, Salvador. 2003. *Family Therapy: Concepts and Methods.* 5th edition. New York: Gardner Press.

Olson, D., Russell, C. S., and Sprenkle, D. H. 1980. "Marital and Family Therapy." *Journal of Marriage and the Family* 42:973–94.

Penn, Peggy. 1985. "Feed Forward: Future Questions, Future Maps." *Family Process* 24(3):299–310.

Pollak, Otto, and Brieland, Donald. 1961. "The Midwest Seminar on Family Diagnosis and Treatment." *Social Casework* 42:319–24.

Richmond, Mary E. 1917. *Social Diagnosis.* New York: Russell Sage Foundation.

Richmond, Mary E. 1922. *What Is Social Casework?* New York: Russell Sage Foundation.

Roberts, A. R., and Yeager, K. R. 2004. "Chapter 1 Systematic Reviews of Evidence-Based Studies and Practice-Based Research: How to Search for, Develop, and Use Them." In *Evidence-Based Practice Manual: Research and Outcome Measures in Health and Human Services.* eds. A. R. Roberts and K. R.Yeager. New York Oxford University Press, p. 5.

Satir, V. 1964. *Conjoint Family Therapy.* Palo Alto, CA: Science and Behavior Books.

———. 1983. *Conjoint Family Therapy,* rev. ed. Palo Alto, CA: Science and Behavior Books.

Sattler, Jerome. 1997. *Clinical and Forensic Interviewing of Children and Families: Guidelines for the Mental Health, Education, Pediatric, and Child Maltreatment Fields.* San Diego, CA: Jerome Sattler Publisher.

Scharff, David, and Scharff, Jill. 1991. *Object Relations Family Therapy.* New York: Jason Aronson.

Scherz, Frances H. 1953. "What Is Family-Centered Casework? *Social Casework* 34:343–49.

Scherz, Frances H. 1962. "Multiple-Client Interviewing: Treatment Implications." *Social Casework* 43:120–24.

Selvini-Palazolli, M., Boscolo, L., Cecchin, G., and Prata, G. 1980. "Hypothesizing, Circularity, Neutrality: Three Guidelines for the Conductor of the Session." *Family Process* 19:3–12.

Sherman, Sanford N. 1959. "Joint Interviews in Casework Practice." *Social Work* 4:20–28.

Siporin, Max. 1956. "Family-Centered Casework in a Psychiatric Setting." *Social Casework* 37:167–74.

Sturkie, Kinly. 1986. "Framework for Comparing Approaches to Family Therapy." *Social Casework* 67:613–21.

Tomm, K. 1987. "Interventive Interviewing: Part II. Reflexive Questioning as a Means to Enable Self-Healing." *Family Process* 26:167–83.

———. 1988. "Interventive Interviewing: Part III. Intending to Ask Lineal, Circular, Strategic or Reflective Questions?" *Family Process* 27(1):1–15.

Whitehead, Barbara. 1993. "The New Family Values." *UTNE Reader* No. 57, May–June, 61–65.

Willbach, Daniel. 1989. "Ethics and Family Therapy: The Case Management of Family Violence." *Journal of Marital and Family Therapy* 15(1):43–52.

Woods, M., and Hollis, F. 1999. *Casework: A Psychosocial Therapy.* 5th edition. New York: McGraw-Hill.

Zuk, G. H. 1971. "Family Therapy: 1964–1970." *Psychotherapy: Theory, Research and Practice* 8:90–97.

Theoretical and Treatment Approaches to Evidence-Based Family Treatment

Understanding the family as a system and planning intervention require the family practitioner to be knowledgeable about family interactions, as presented in Chapter 1, as well as family therapy interventions. In Chapter 2, we describe selected therapeutic approaches. New to this edition are two models developed by social workers, psychoeducational family therapy and family preservation. Also new is the addition of a discussion of the evidence base for each of the theoretical models.

We will concentrate on only six specific models even though many approaches to family treatment exist. Many of the concepts and techniques we will discuss are applicable to other theoretical approaches, however. We believe the presentation of these approaches, together with the concepts and techniques they embrace, will help professionals working with families to better understand the dynamics of the family as a complex interactive system amenable to intervention and change. The following are the approaches we will discuss: (1) the structural approach, (2) the communications approach, (3) the strategic approach, (4) the social learning approach, (5) the family preservation approach, and (6) the family psychoeducational approach.

THE STRUCTURAL APPROACH

The structural approach to therapeutic intervention with families emphasizes the importance of family structure, family subsystems, and boundaries around the family, its individual members, and its subsystems. Although reference to these concepts will appear at other points in this book, these components are integral to other models as well as to structural family therapy, and it is here that we hope to provide a definition and fully describe the functions of each. Our discussion will reflect our experiences and writings (Franklin & Jordan, 1999) as well as the thinking of others, including Nichols, Schwartz, and Minuchin (2003). Salvatore Minuchin is attributed with development of the model.

Family Structure

Minuchin (1974) defines *family structure* as "The invisible set of functional demands that organizes the ways in which family members interact. Repeated transactions establish patterns of how, when, and to whom to relate and these patterns underpin the system" (p. 51). For example, one parent tells a child to stop playing and go to bed. When the child refuses, the other parent becomes infuriated by this display of disobedience and yells at the child, after which the child complies with the wish of the other parent and goes to bed. Repetition of this way of dealing with the child establishes a transactional pattern and creates a structure in which the parent who first gave the child the order to go to bed is viewed as an incompetent disciplinarian and the parent who enforced the order is considered competent.

Another aspect of family structure is the rules that govern family organization and transactions within the family. Such rules are often recognized in the way various family members protect each other. If the parents cannot handle intimacy and closeness in their relationship, the child behaves in such a way as to demand their attention and thereby prevent the necessity of the parents having to relate to each other on an intimate level. Nichols (2003) suggests that family structure is also shaped by universal and idiosyncratic constraints. This involves a power hierarchy in which parents and children have different levels of authority. A complementarity of functions is also necessary, with both parents accepting an interdependency of functioning and supporting each other as a team.

Family Subsystems

The second component of structural family therapy is *family subsystems*. Family members joining together to carry out various functions create subsystems. Coming together in this way may be centered around age (generation), gender function, or common interest. Among the natural groupings that form subsystems are adult couples, siblings, and parent and child. There are many roles to be filled in the family, and each member may play several roles in a number of subgroups. One parent may be at different times a father, son, or nephew, while the other may be a mother, daughter, or niece depending on time, place, and circumstances. Among the basic underpinnings of the structural approach to family treatment is the belief that the family is a system that functions through the support of subsystems. The major subsystems that develop over time within the nuclear family structure are the *couple subsystem,* the *parental subsystem,* the *sibling subsystem,* and the *parent–child subsystem.* It should be noted that the adults involved in the couple subsystem, the parental subsystem, and the parent–child subsystem are not always a married couple. These parent roles are sometimes filled by extended family members, including grandparents, uncles, aunts, or other relatives who assume responsibility for the child. The significant other of the child's responsible relative may also fill the role of parent.

Couple Subsystem

The *couple subsystem* is the first to emerge and comes into being when two adults come together with the desire to exist as a unit, sharing and accommodating each other. Complementarity and accommodation are the primary components of a successful couple subsystem. This means that each partner should develop patterns of behavior that lend support to effective functioning of the other. In carrying this out, a kind of joining and cooperating takes place. Yet, the ability to be and act separately is also essential to effective functioning of the couple subsystem. Therefore, the two people involved must seek a balance between being close and supportive, and maintaining the individuality necessary for independent action.

Thus the couple subsystem, like all subsystems, is characterized by a boundary within a boundary structure. The inner boundary maintains the individuality of the participants, while the outer boundary defines the subsystem and protects it from the intrusion of outside forces. The outer boundary that surrounds the couple subsystem also differentiates it from other family systems and provides a turf over which these two participants are the rulers. When the boundary is appropriately in place, the couple subsystem is clearly separated from families of origin, and extended family interference is controlled. At the same time, the individual boundaries provide the partners turf over which each can rule within the subsystem boundary, as exemplified by the ability of each to act without complete support and validation from the other. This also allows a self to be identified and responsibility to be taken for individual action. When children come into the family, the couple subsystem boundary also protects against the children's intrusion into the couple's domain. This does not mean the couple subsystem is isolated from other systems. However, it symbolizes the right of the couple subsystem to engage in its own internal processes without interference from outside its boundary.

In spite of the boundary's objective of safeguarding the integrity of the system, boundary violations do occur. Take the case of a newly formed couple whose parents are consistently interfering with the new relationship by invading its psychosocial space, which is a serious threat to the boundary around this subsystem. If the new couple accepts the efforts of these relatives to control their lives, these two subsystems become diffuse, and the identity of two separate systems does not exist. In the case of such encroachment, it is not uncommon to find a coalition existing between two principals of different generations. For example, one partner may join with a parent in a coalition against the other partner of the newly formed couple. This is a generational boundary violation that reflects the lack of a clear boundary between the partner and the parent, and this contributes to dysfunction in both couple and parent systems. While the parent is involved with the kinship partner against the other partner of the couple, it is likely that the parent's relationship will be neglected, giving rise to yet another relationship problem.

Parental Subsystem

Until the arrival of the first child by birth, adoption, or custody proceedings, the partners are viewed as a couple subsystem reflecting primary concern for their roles as partners. With the arrival of the first child (or children), three new subsystems come into being that must be recognized in considering family functioning. The new family units are the parental subsystem, composed of two adults; the sibling subsystem, which may be one child or two or more children; and the parent–child subsystem, which comes into existence as a functional unit when the parents individually or collectively interact with a child.

The parental subsystem is largely child-focused and has executive responsibility for the entire family system. This responsibility is rooted in the hierarchical position accorded the parents, who provide the leadership and authority necessary for family growth and development. If parents do not demonstrate leadership and authority, the family system, including wholesome development of their children, is placed at risk. Parents who do not direct and lead children leave them on their own to find appropriate role models and authority figures by trial and error, which can be devastating for a child. A problem is also presented in cases where one part of the hierarchical system is absent. This creates a void into which a child may be elevated for a number of reasons. For example, a lonely and distraught parent may turn to a child to replace the affections of the absent parent and thereby create closeness in the parent–child relationship that denies the child the opportunity to develop autonomy. At the same time, this closeness may tie the two participants together so closely that one cannot function without the other. If this occurs, a symbiotic relationship can develop that seriously impairs the adjustment of parent and child.

In order to perform effectively as a parental subsystem, parents must be flexible and maintain a delicate balance between exercising control over their children and promoting their independence. Unlike the couple subsystem, which is protected from the intrusion of children, the parental subsystem operates differently where children are concerned. The boundary of the parental subsystem permits free movement of children back and forth across the perimeters of the system. This new role of parent carries with it responsibility for the rearing of children. One of the first things parents must do is give up some of what they previously shared exclusively when occupying only the role of partner in the couple relationship.

In systems theory, a change in one part of the system requires change in other parts. With the introduction of a child (or children) into the couple system, the partners in this system become parents. The additional member(s) impacts the relationship and sets a change process in motion. The previous balance in relationship enjoyed by the parents is disrupted, and a new boundary must be established around themselves and the child (or children). This boundary expansion presents the parents with new responsibilities as children must be nurtured. This nurturing requires parents to restructure their own need-meeting activities in order to meet the physical and emotional needs of their children.

Sometimes changing to include a child is difficult for new parents. Before the introduction of children into the system, parents are primarily concerned with their own and each other's needs and expectations, in an intimate and personal relationship. When they become parents, there is likely to be less time for enjoying each other. Leisure time may have to be spent differently, or recreational activities may be sharply curtailed in the interest of childcare. If parents are unable to make these adjustments by redefining the manner in which they interact within their own life space, functioning as a family is likely to be problematic.

These role adjustments must be repeated with each addition of another child to the family. The older children also become involved in the sharing and need-meeting process as it relates to each new member. For example, when a younger child joins the family by birth, adoption, or through the exercise of parental custody, it affects the next oldest child, who must give up the role of baby in the family and relinquish some of the closeness previously shared with parents. The parents must extend the nurturing role to include the new member, and by so doing alter their relationship with the other children. Physical accommodations must also be made for the new child that may affect the other children's play activities, sleeping arrangements, and so on. Sometimes these changes will impact negatively on the older children, who may react with such behavior as withdrawing, thumb sucking, or bed-wetting. Such behavior is usually temporary if parents are able to demonstrate caring for the older children. However, the role of parents can become more difficult as the children grow and seek increased individuality. This places great demands on the control and permission functions of the parental subsystem. Maintaining a balance between these functions in a manner that supports autonomy, while exercising the necessary control at appropriate points in the developmental process, can be a difficult task for parents. The difficulty is enhanced by our changing society, in which values are continuously tested and disagreements are evidenced in many areas.

We believe conflict is inherent in the parenting role, and this should be kept in mind when working with families, especially around problems involving adolescents. This is the time when parents attempt to guide and protect children, and it may include measures that are controlling and restricting. And children who are striving to grow and become individuated may reject their parents' efforts to guide them in this direction. This presents a difficult problem for parents and children, and a challenging situation for social workers intervening with families unable to cope with these interlocking conflicts.

Sibling Subsystem

In order to grow and develop individuality, children need their own turf where experimentation and learning can take place without interference from adults. This makes the sibling subsystem a very important part of the family organization. It is in this subgroup that children learn how to relate to each other, including how to share, disagree, make friends, bargain, and protect themselves from the down position of a complementary relationship. Also, this experience serves as a shield of protection for the child in encounters with other systems. The first use of this experience may be seen as the child interacts with the parents and learns to adjust to a relationship of unequal power. Although the young child does not master the skill of negotiation and compromise from the sibling subgroup experience, alternative behaviors in personal encounters are likely to be learned and will be further tested with elders in the future. In this way, the child establishes and broadens patterns of relating. This is not to imply that the child learns only within the conflicts of the sibling subsystem experience. Much is also learned from interacting with parents and later with extrafamilial systems. However, experiences in this subsystem remain among the most important for the child, as they provide one of the earliest opportunities to test behavior and to learn from trial and error. And this type of learning is essential for the child's growth and development.

Like other subsystems, the sibling subsystem has a boundary that protects the system from intrusion by adults. Nevertheless, the boundary is permeable. This allows parents to move back and forth across it but gives children the right to privacy without parental interference when the need arises. For example, children need the opportunity to have their own special interests, try out their own thinking in specific areas, and offer their own kind of support to each other in times of stress, without direct guidance from parents. Some adjustment becomes necessary in this system as a result of the growth and development of children. With this growth and age differential come different interests, privileges, and responsibilities. At this point the subsystem is usually divided into two groups, along the lines of teenagers and preteenagers. Such a division ensures more effective functioning of the system, while at the same time it protects the integrity of the system as it relates to the life cycle of participants.

If a permeable boundary exists around the family, children should be able to interact freely with extrafamilial systems involving age-appropriate activities. The children will make inputs into the family system from these experiences, and if the substance of these inputs seriously threatens the way the family wishes to operate, the boundary around the family may become inappropriately rigid.

For example, consider the teenage daughter who shares with her parents the desire to spend a weekend camping with her boyfriend, as others among her peer group are doing. The parents are very much opposed to such association between boys and girls and disapprove not only of the weekend camping but also of the daughter's association with the peer group. This reflects increasing rigidity in the family boundary and may well interfere with the daughter's separation from the family.

Parent–Child Subsystem

In the parent–child subsystem, parent(s) and child or parent(s) and children interact as a functional unit within a boundary. It is different from the three subsystems previously discussed in that at least one of the persons composing it is of a different generation. While a subsystem composed of different generations can become dysfunctional, this is not an automatic outcome. For example, a parent and young child may be closely involved in an interactional process that forms a subsystem of two different generations, but as long as the boundary around this system is not inappropriately rigid and permits crossing by other family members, it is not likely to become pathological. If, on the other hand, one parent and a child should become aligned in such a way as to exclude the other parent from entering the system, it would then be dysfunctional. Minuchin (1974) suggests that the clarity of boundaries surrounding a subsystem is more important than who makes up the subsystem. Take the case of a single-parent family, in which the parent is employed and depends on the oldest child to help with the care of younger children. This places them in a boundary together with shared responsibility. However, this boundary will remain functional as long as the limits of authority and responsibility placed with the child are clearly defined and the hierarchy is maintained. In other words, if the parent tells the child that overseeing the behavior of younger children is to be done only in the parent's absence and that when at home the parent will be in charge of the family, the system can function smoothly.

Difficulty will develop when the lines of authority are not clear and the child becomes locked in a rigid boundary with the parent. In this case, the individual boundaries around parent and child become diffused, and the child's authority will not be limited by the parent's presence. The child then becomes a parental-child and may act indiscriminately as an extension of the parent where younger children are concerned. This denies the other children free access to the parent and may result in problem behavior for these children.

Boundaries

The third component of structural family therapy is boundaries. Boundaries are "invisible barriers which surround individuals and subsystems, regulating the amount of contact with others" (Nichols, 2003, p. 474). The function of boundaries is to safeguard the differentiation and autonomy of the family and its subsystems. For example, if a parent restricts a child's play to the immediate neighborhood and this is accepted, a boundary is established that protects the child from wandering far from home and perhaps becoming lost. Boundaries may vary from being rigid to being diffuse. Rigid boundaries allow little contact with outside systems, which promotes disengagement and isolates the individuals and subsystems involved. While this permits growth and independence, it also limits warmth, affection, and mutual support. Diffuse boundaries produce enmeshment, which is characterized by extreme closeness. Enmeshed subsystems promote a heightened sense of mutual support, but lack independence and autonomy. Children who are enmeshed with their parents are likely to be uncomfortable when left by them and may have difficulty relating to people outside the family (Nichols et al., 2003). Other boundary characteristics have been presented in our discussion of the couple and sibling subsystems and will not be repeated here. (For details, see those sections.)

In structural family therapy, the family is conceptualized as an open system and as such is influenced by and impacts the surrounding environment. The family is also perceived as being in constant transformation, and over time transactional rules evolve as each family group negotiates arrangements that are syntonic and effective for a given period. This evolution is influenced by the interplay of homeostasis and change (Colapinto, 1999). Homeostasis serves as a balancing mechanism whenever the family system is threatened. And change is seen as the family system's adjustment to a different set of environmental circumstances or to essential developmental needs. In moments of crisis, homeostasis plays a role in maintaining equilibrium.

Structural family therapy focuses on the current relationship between system and problem behavior and accepts that the knowledge of the origin of a problem is largely irrelevant to the process of therapeutic change (Minuchin & Fishman, 1981). This approach also holds that problems brought to therapy are essentially dysfunctions of the family's structure, and efforts are focused on changing the structure, which means change in the relative positions of family members. For example, the therapist may need to bring the executive branch of the family closer together or provide for more distance between a parent and child. Structural therapy perceives change as the process of helping families outgrow their stereotyped pattern of behavior. Releasing underutilized resources that keep the family functioning at an adequate level does this, and this release will create a climate for system change.

Role of the Therapist

The structural family therapist must enter the system that needs to be changed by accommodating to the rules of the system and joining with the family. The therapist brings to the family encounter a series of hypotheses that are tested, expanded, and corrected when necessary (Colapinto, 1999). Mobility on the part of the therapist is required as she moves from one role to another and forms alliances with different family members while maintaining a focus that connects all of this activity to the presenting problem.

This approach prescribes activity, initiative, and directiveness for the therapist who organizes and starts family interaction but refrains from becoming too central in order to allow the family to display its limitations and potentialities. In summary, "the role of the therapist is to move around within the system, blocking existing stereotyped patterns of transactions and fostering the development of more flexible ones" (Colapinto, 1999, p. 91).

Techniques

Structural family therapists have developed a number of techniques, some of which are applicable to other approaches and demonstrated in other chapters in this book. The following are some of the techniques frequently used in restructuring families.

Confirmation   The therapist who is giving a sympathetic response to a family member's affective presentation of herself, for example, may employ this technique: "You seem to be worried." Confirmation can also be executed by describing an obviously negative characteristic of the client, followed immediately by a statement that removes blame for the behavior; for example, the therapist may say to the wife, "You are very critical of your husband. What does he do to make you unhappy?"

Reversal   The therapist directing a family member to reverse her attitude or behavior regarding a crucial issue that elicits a paradoxical response from another member operationalizes this technique. For example, Minuchin and Fishman (1981) report a situation in which the wife resented her husband's overly close relationship with his mother. The therapist instructed the wife (in private) to reverse her attitude regarding the relationship. Instead of opposing it, she should praise the beauty of the devotion between mother and son and encourage her husband to spend more time with his mother. The husband did not appreciate his wife telling him what he should do and defied her instructions by becoming less involved with his mother (p. 248). This technique is used when one family member is cooperative and will follow advice while another member will resist it. The person on the receiving end should not be present when the reversal is given, as success depends on that individual's being surprised by the change in attitude of the other person and, therefore, reacting spontaneously to the unexpected change. Reversals have also been used in helping parents manage rebellious children.

Boundary Making   Boundary making occurs when the therapist defines an area of interaction as being open to some family members but closed to others (Colapinto, 1999). When the mother who is overinvolved with the children is asked to leave her seat between the children and take a seat next to her husband, this is a beginning effort on the part of the therapist to establish appropriate boundaries around both the parental and sibling subsystems.

Joining   The technique of joining is letting the family know that the therapist understands them and is working with and for them (Minuchin & Fishman, 1981). Joining is realized when the therapist becomes accepted as such by the family and the therapist understands the family's organization and style and blends with them. Joining is facilitated as the therapist listens to and speaks the family's language and views the problem through the family's eyes, making comments and asking questions where necessary, but always with sufficient distance to claim and maintain leadership throughout the course of therapy. Joining between the therapist and one family member may also occur during the treatment process. For example, the therapist may support the father in revealing his experiences in the family; may follow this with support of the mother in explaining her frustration in trying to cope with family disorganization; and later join with the children as they describe how difficult it is for them to know what to expect and how to behave. By joining with the family in this way, the therapist is positioning himself to be able to move the family toward positive change, which is the goal of therapy.

Evidence Base

Salvatore Minuchin, the originator of structural family therapy, and his colleagues conducted the early studies in the key concepts of structural family therapy (1967, 1978). He studied the concepts of enmeshment and engagement and found that patient families were at extremes on these concepts compared with nonpatient control families. Other research supported this finding and also showed support for the concept of subsystems (Davis, Stern, & Van Deusen, 1977). A later study by Minuchin and colleagues (1978) showed that normal families were less enmeshed and had clearer subsystem boundaries than did patient families. More recent research treatment development (Szapocznik & Kurtines, 1989) and research (Santisteban et al., 1997) focused on treatment of adolescents at risk of drug abuse and conduct or antisocial personality. Findings were both clinically and statistically significant. Other groups shown to be helped by structural family therapy include families with low socioeconomic status (Minuchin, 1967), families with psychosomatic members (Harkaway, 1987; Rosman, Minuchin, Liebman, & Baker, 1978; Rosman, Minuchin, & Liebman, 1977), and families with addictions (Zeigler-Driscoll, 1979).

THE COMMUNICATIONS APPROACH

The communications approach to the study and treatment of the family developed largely from the work of the Palo Alto Medical Research Foundation Project. The focus of this project was on treating families of schizophrenic patients. Among those who were connected with it and contributed to the basic concepts of the communication approach were Gregory Bateson, Jay Haley, Don Jackson, and Virginia Satir. It is accepted in this approach to family treatment that all behavior has communication value and conveys several messages on different levels. The family is seen as a living system that maintains a relationship with the environment through communication, which involves the sending and receiving of messages and a feedback process. As a result, family relationships are products of communication. Family members establish rules that regulate the ways they relate to each other and to the outside world. Once these rules are established, the family seeks to maintain the status quo. In other words, the family is viewed as a rule-governed, complex, interactive system, with communication patterns playing a primary role in family functioning. Communication is defined as all verbal and nonverbal behavior within a social context. This speaks to the complexity of the process of communication. We can readily imagine a simultaneous sending and receiving of messages by gesture, manner of dress, tone of voice, facial expression, body posture, and so on.

In order to understand dysfunction in the family, the communication process operating within family relationships must also be understood. It is important to realize that the way a family communicates, member to member, and member to the outside world, reflects the way the family perceives itself and how it will function. The way members of a family communicate with each other shapes the view they have of themselves and others. This in turn influences the way members report themselves to others, including those outside the family. For example, if the family perceives a member's behavior as good and in keeping with the way it views itself and it repeatedly communicates satisfaction with this behavior, the response will impact on the individual. This member's perception of self will likely be one of value, and this perception will manifest in transactions with others. If, however, family feedback to a member is constantly negative, the reverse will most likely happen.

If the family decides it is best to rely on its own internal processes for validation of its functioning and it intensifies interaction between members, the freedom to communicate across family boundaries will be restricted. This encourages more communication within the family and more dependence upon one another. If the family is successful in establishing this pattern of behavior, communications from family members will reflect sameness, and family functioning will likely be characterized by enmeshment.

The existence of one person in the presence of another sets the stage for communication and, at the same time, assures that the process will take place. This obviously makes possible the act of verbal exchange, which is the most widely understood form of communication. However, both persons may choose to remain silent, and communication will still take place. Messages are conveyed by silence and inactivity as well as by language and activity. The silence of a person who refrains from talking in the presence of another conveys a message to the other, who in turn responds to this silence. Communication has taken place. For example, if the message sent by silence is interpreted as a desire not to engage with the receiver, who respects the wish by also remaining silent, the communication cycle has been completed. The message has been sent, received, and interpreted, and the receiver has responded by the conscious decision to remain silent. And if these two people remain in an interactional situation, despite their silence, they will continue the communication process, with each being aware of the other and conveying messages one to the other through body language, if nothing more. In other words, one cannot refrain from communicating when in the presence of another.

The content and relationship of messages provide additional material for social workers in understanding human communication. Bateson, Haley, Jackson, and Satir, of the Palo Alto project, suggest that every communication carries many levels of information. One of these levels is concerned with the relationship in which the communication occurs; people in communication with each other are constantly attempting to define their positions in this relationship. There are two types of relationships, complementary and symmetrical. In the complementary relationship, the communication involves two people of unequal status. The behavior of each participant identifies her status in the relationship. For example, in a complementary relationship, one person initiates action and the other person follows that action, which indicates that these individuals complement each other. The opposite exists in the case of a symmetrical relationship, where two individuals react to each other from positions of equal status. This means that each person exercises the right to initiate action, offer advice, and criticize the other.

Double-Binding Communication

The existence of a paradox in human communication, represented by the double-bind phenomenon, may be observed in some families. The exchange of communication in these families is characterized by the sending of incongruent messages, usually within the boundary of a complementary relationship. The incongruence of the double message is reflected in its request that the receiver obey and disobey the message simultaneously. This, of course, cannot be done, and if this type of communication is used repeatedly, paradoxical behavior will result. To further illustrate double-binding communication, take the case of an adolescent who wishes to spend the night with a friend. As he and his mother talk this over, she remarks after much discussion, "You know I want you to go and be with your friend; don't worry that I'll be here alone in this big house." This message tells the youngster to go, but at the same time it calls his loyalty to his mother into question and speaks to her fear of being alone, which also says "Don't go."

Incongruent messages may become a double bind in certain relationships when a necessary set of conditions is present. The following conditions are set forth as the essential ingredients of double-bind communication by Watzlawick and Jackson (1967, p. 212):

1. There are two or more persons involved in an intense relationship that has a high degree of survival value for one or more of the participants.
2. In this context, messages are given that assert opposing commands, i.e., the assertions are always mutually exclusive, which means neither assertion can be obeyed without disobeying the other.
3. The recipient of the message is prevented from commenting on it or walking away from it.

Consider the case of the parent–child relationship. Here the relationship is likely to be intense and to have survival value for the child, who needs nourishment from the parent. This places the child in the position of being unable to comment on the opposing commands of the parent successfully or to walk away from them. As a result, the child is often exposed to the double-bind effect.

Double-bind communication is not peculiar to pathologic families. It may be observed to a greater or lesser extent in a wide variety of families, most of whom do not require professional intervention. The issue of family pathology may be determined by whether or not the double-binding transaction is repeated sufficiently to become an established pattern in family communication. When this has occurred and the self-perpetuating force of the pathological system takes over, family dysfunctioning results. It should also be kept in mind that the double-bind process is not a unidirectional phenomenon. The paradoxical behavior that results from the double-binding message in turn creates a double bind for the sender of the message, thus creating and perpetuating pathologic communication.

Metacommunication

Metacommunication is an important part of the communication pattern observed in human interaction. Metacommunication may be defined as the sending of a message about a message, both of which are sent at the same time. The message conveys to the receiver how the sender wishes it to be received and how the receiver should react to it. Metacommunication also comments on the nature of the relationship between the persons involved, indicating the way the sender perceives the receiver and the attitude the sender has toward the message and the self. The content of the message, tone of voice, facial expression, body posture, and so on serve to shape and define further what is verbalized by the sender. This adds to the complexity of the communication process and forces the receiver of metacommunicative messages to assess not only the content but also the content within the context of the message.

For example, consider an interchange between husband and wife in which the husband comments, "The children really keep you busy." The literal content of the message is that the children are claiming the wife's attention in such a way that she spends a good ideal of time responding. However, this seemingly simple statement may carry a number of messages on a metacommunicative level. First, the context within which the message is sent will help the receiver define it. If it occurs in a relaxed conversation after dinner and in a tone of voice that recognizes the wife's many responsibilities, it may convey the message, "I value you and I appreciate your accomplishments as a wife and mother." Here the sender's attitude toward the message, the receiver, and himself is one of friendliness. On the other hand, if the same comment is made in a sarcastic manner as the husband restlessly awaits his wife's preparation of dinner, it may well carry the message, "I want you to give greater priority to preparing meals on time." The sender's attitude in this case would likely be, "I am not friendly, you are not treating me in a friendly manner, and the message is a warning to be heeded."

Metacommunication can also be sent on a verbal level when the sender verbally explains the message being sent. This, too, can occur at various levels of abstraction. For example:

1. It may involve labeling the kind of message sent and telling the receiver how the sender wishes it to be received: "It was a joke (laugh at it)."
2. The sender can verbalize the reason for sending the message by referring to a previous perception from the other: "You hit me. So I hit you back. I thought you were tired and wanted my help."

The combination of verbal and nonverbal metacommunication creates for the receiver a complex situation from which to determine the meaning of messages received. Making this determination usually requires more attention to the context of the message and the nonverbal metacommunication than to the verbal aspects, as the latter is more explicit. When a person communicates, he is often asking something of the receiver and trying to influence the receiver to give him what he wants. Since such requests are not always expressed verbally, those on the receiving end of messages must rely on metacommunication to understand what is asked of them and to determine how they will respond.

Accepted Principles

The communications approach to family therapy does not emphasize the internal structure of family members but concentrates on their communication in order to determine what is cause and what is effect. This model accepts communication as having both a report and a command function. Information is conveyed through the report function while the command function defines relationships. This is demonstrated when one family member speaks to another member and by so doing delivers a message. At the same time, a statement is also made about how the deliverer of the message views both herself and the receiver of the message. For example, when a child in tears reports to a parent that a sibling has mistreated her, the message carries information but also delivers a command to the parent who is viewed as an authority figure to do something about it.

This model of family therapy assumes that functional families are characterized by a set of properties that includes equality in relationships, an appreciation for similarities and differences, an openness to change, and maintenance of congruent communication. In the functional family, only a few rules are observed, but these rules are consistently applied. The dysfunctional family has rigid rules that are inconsistently applied. Family communication is also used to gain access to family rules and clarify coping styles within the family.

Role of the Therapist

In the communications model of family therapy, the therapist identifies the symptom to be changed as a communicative message (Nichols et al., 2003). In the first contact with the family, the therapist focuses attention on each family member and demonstrates a readiness to listen and to touch and be touched. It is not unusual for the therapist to hold the hand of a family member during the therapeutic encounter. This reflects the therapist's humanness and establishes the foundation for trust in his leadership to guide the family through the process of change. In the role of leadership, the personhood and humanness of the therapist is more important than any set of skills he might possess (Satir & Bitter, 1991). The therapist must also model congruence and respond in a completely nonjudgmental manner to the communication and metacommunication of the family.

It is essential for the therapist to have faith in the ability of the family to grow and change. In addition, a therapeutic posture that includes humanness, a readiness to listen and respond appropriately to different modes of family communication, and the ability to assume leadership of the therapeutic process must be maintained at every stage of treatment.

Techniques

The communications approach to treating families has developed a number of techniques that have been used successfully in changing undesirable behaviors. Most of these techniques involve teaching rules of clear communication and manipulating family interactions (Nichols et al., 2003). We will not attempt to discuss all of these techniques, but following are two that are frequently used by communication therapists.

Sculpting   Arranging family members or objects in such a way as to symbolize the family's emotional relationships creates a family sculpture. Each member's perceived position in the family system is identified. As sculpting takes place, each family member may be asked to create a live family portrait by placing members together with reference to their posture and spatial relationships, depicting both action and feelings. In this way a visual picture of each member's experience in the family is placed in evidence (Sherman & Fredman, 1986). Sculpting helps the therapist handle excessive verbalization, defensiveness, projection of blame, and so forth by removing the family's familiar ways of communicating and forcing them to communicate with each other in a new and different way.

Family sculpting may be operationalized at any time during the therapeutic process by explaining it as a useful way to see how it feels to be each member of the family. Each family member is asked to arrange the family in a way that defines his or her position in the family. After each member has shown, through sculpting, how he or she currently experiences the family, they may be asked to rearrange the positions of members to reflect the family as they would like it to be.

Sculpting can be used in different ways. Some therapists may ask the sculptor to assign a word or phrase to each member that describes that member's behavior, for example, "supportive" or "controlling." The therapist may also intervene during the sculpting process by suggesting possibilities or coaching the sculptor in order to enhance or clarify the family portraits. Questions may be asked of family members regarding their feelings about occupying the position given to them by the sculptor: For example, do they agree with this portrait of the family? Some therapists may choose not to engage in a discussion of the family sculpting, and may allow them to integrate the experience on their own (Sherman & Fredman, 1986).

Metaphor   A metaphor is a statement about one thing that resembles something else. The therapist uses a metaphor that is familiar to the family to talk about issues. For example, a family who is very involved in team sports may be helped by the therapist using the metaphor of a team to refer to the family. In other words, it is a symbolic and nonthreatening way of communicating with the family. A metaphor may be used to convey an idea or feeling or to suggest options that are not readily apparent. To demonstrate the use of this technique, we borrow an example from Erickson's work with a couple experiencing difficulty in sexual relations. The experience of eating together is introduced and discussion developed concerning the conditions surrounding the meal. The therapist may ask if there are times when the couple has dinner without the children present, then move to talk about some aspect of eating that resembles sexual relations. For example, the therapist may say that sometimes a wife may want to begin the meal slowly by having an appetizer before the main course is served, while her husband likes to receive the main course without delay. If the couple appears to understand the analogy, the therapist may return to some aspect of the dinner that does not relate so closely to sexual activity, such as commenting that some people like dinner by candlelight, while others like to eat with bright lights. At the end of the discussion, the therapist may move toward assigning a task around dinner to be carried out as homework before the next appointment, with the hope that if the dinner is successful the mood will carry over to improved sexual relations.

Evidence Base   While this approach has not been extensively studied on its own, it is a part of the theoretical base of strategic therapies to be discussed next. The systemic approaches, including strategic family therapy, have an evidence base for helping some families with some types of problems. We include the techniques of communication theory here due to their clinical usefulness in establishing rapport and establishing a therapeutic alliance between family and therapist/social worker. Therapeutic alliance has demonstrated importance as a factor in clients staying in treatment, thus facilitating positive changes (Lambert, 2004).

THE STRATEGIC APPROACH

Strategic family therapy is a problem-focused strategy concerned with repeated sequences of behavior and dysfunctional hierarchies within the family. Jay Haley is perhaps the most well-known figure associated with the strategic approach to family treatment. While there are distinct differences between the various approaches to family therapy, there are also a number of similarities. This is especially so in the case of the structural, communications, and strategic approaches. This may be due in part to Haley's close association with the Palo Alto group of Bateson and others, who developed the communications approach, and also with Minuchin at the Philadelphia Child Guidance Clinic, where structural family therapy began. Among other things, all three approaches give some attention to family homeostasis, communication, boundaries, and triangles involved in family relationships.

These common characteristics have already been discussed as they relate to the structural and communication approaches and will not be repeated in our discussion of strategic family therapy. We will include the role of the therapist, the accepted principles of the approach, and the techniques used to solve family problems.

The theoretical support for strategic therapy is based on general systems theory and cybernetics (Nichols et al., 2003). The therapist is at the center of all activity, and each family is seen as unique. Therefore, emphasis is placed on designed strategies to solve each family's specific problems rather than developing strategies for use with all families. Since the primary focus is problem solving and not the development of insight, restructuring the family system is not always required. Therapy is typically accomplished by the therapist's assessing and understanding the family's life cycle stage of development, the hierarchical dysfunction, and the repetitive sequence or cycle of family interactions, then correcting the hierarchy and breaking the cycle through straightforward or paradoxical directives (Schilson, 1991, p. 142).

Accepted Principles

Schilson (1991) suggests several tenets upon which strategic therapy is based. These tenets will serve as the basis for the principles we will develop as the cornerstone of the strategic therapist's work with families. As previously mentioned, strategic therapy and structural therapy embrace many common principles, some of which will be reflected in those we develop and list here.

1. Each family is seen as a unique entity with its own rules and its own set of identifying factors.
2. A functional family is seen as reflecting appropriate distribution of power within the family, with parents having more power than children.
3. Family problems are viewed not in terms of an identified patient but as interactions between family members.

4. Strategic therapists are active in directing the therapy process, with much emphasis placed on giving directives to be carried out at home, sometimes referred to as "homework."

5. In diagnosing dysfunctional families, the strategic therapist emphasizes the present rather than the past; the family life cycle; and the concepts of systems theory (i.e., coalitions, circularity, boundaries, etc).

6. The development of insight is not required for change in daily functioning. Emphasis is placed on relabeling or reframing, which is designed to give the family a different perception of the difficulty it is experiencing, and this will increase the family's effectiveness in solving its problem.

7. Primary attention is given to the problem brought to the therapist's attention in the first interview. This reflects the symptom-focused, problem-solving emphasis of the strategic approach to family therapy.

8. The expression of feelings or emotions per se is not encouraged by strategic therapists, who see such expression as diverting attention from the interactional process within the family that needs to be changed.

9. The family system is seen as operating by repeated interactional patterns, and in dysfunctional families, problems are maintained by these ongoing interactional patterns.

10. The therapist is responsible for success in therapy, and if it fails, the therapist is blamed for the failure. If it is successful, the therapist does not take credit for it but gives the credit to the family. In order to be considered successful, the therapeutic experience must produce beneficial change in the presenting problem.

11. The strategic approach supports the belief that triangulation is a part of family interaction. When the problem involving two family members becomes too stressful for these members to resolve, a third person is brought into the conflict.

12. When the presenting problem has been eliminated, the strategic therapist will likely discontinue therapy.

Haley and Richeport-Haley (2003) suggest intense involvement and rapid disengagement following positive change. During the course of therapy, the strategic therapist often works with individuals and subsystems of the family. Attention is given to four interrelated elements: symptoms, metaphors, hierarchy and power, and the life cycle development of the family (Schilson, 1991, p. 153).

Role of Therapist

The therapist must be in control of what happens in the therapy session. This includes being directive and persuasive, yet remaining sensitive to client concerns. The presenting problem is important to the strategic therapist and should be given a great deal of consideration in the initial interview and throughout treatment. The therapist's activity is pivotal in the initial interview, which is conducted in stages that each have a specific purpose. The therapist is considered the expert in her interaction with the family and should be comfortable with this role (Schilson, 1991). In keeping with the emphasis placed on the hierarchy of the family in strategic therapy, the therapist must help the parents feel sufficiently empowered to appropriately carry out their executive function. The elimination of the presenting problem is of primary concern to the strategic therapist, who reframes this problem in such a way that it is seen as manageable by the parents.

Techniques

Most strategic therapists believe common-sense solutions to problems experienced by dysfunctional families are usually ineffective because these families are unable to move far enough outside of their environment to see what maintains the problem (Nichols et al., 2003). As a result, "uncommon techniques" are usually used. These techniques include directives and homework tasks, relabeling or reframing, empowerment, straightforward directives, and paradoxical directives (Schilson, 1991, pp. 168–73).

Directives and Homework Tasks   A directive may be defined simply as the therapist telling someone what to do. For example, Haley and Richeport-Haley (2003) suggest that when the therapist addresses a specific question to the client to "tell me more about that," he is giving a directive. When dealing with inappropriate sequences of behavior, the therapist may use directives or tasks to break through this behavior if other efforts are ineffective (Schilson, 1991). When a family is given directives or homework, it accomplishes three things. First, it provides new subjective experiences that change the family's pattern of behavior. Second, it keeps the family connected to the therapist and intensifies their relationship. Third, the way the family responds to the directive will provide the therapist with information about the family.

When selecting a task for the family, the therapist should choose one that changes the dysfunctional hierarchy and the behavioral sequence in the family. At the same time, a directive should be in keeping with what the family can afford in terms of time and resources. It should also be formulated on a level commensurate with the family's ability to accomplish and be stated clearly in language that the family can understand. They should be made to understand that the directive is important, and congratulations should be offered by the therapist if it is successfully completed. If, however, the assigned tasks are not carried out, the reasons for this must be explored, and the family should not be excused without a valid reason.

Relabeling   Relabeling, sometimes referred to as reframing, is the therapist's way of giving a positive view to a family member's behavior, the objective of which is to alter the way the family views the presenting problem. This technique is demonstrated in the family where criticism, fighting, and bickering are always present. The therapist may relabel this behavior by telling the family that this is their way of expressing affection for each other: There is lots of love and caring in the family, but this is the only way they know to show it. This gives the family a new way of looking at the problem and a new approach to changing their patterns of behavior.

Empowerment   This technique is used to help the family realize that their efforts to deal with the presenting problem have not been ineffective. They may be told they have done some things right; that if not, the problem would be worse. Also, they have within themselves the ability to improve their coping skills and redirect their efforts toward different objectives. It is believed that this gives the family confidence and new energy with which to carry out directives from the therapist.

Straightforward Directives   These directives are given in a straightforward manner and are usually used with families that are cooperative and can use cognitive information. The straightforward directive or task is given with the expectation that family members will comply. These directives may consist of a straightforward task designed to change family interactional patterns. For example, in an interview, the therapist may tell the mother who continues to interrupt a discussion between the father and son that this is the father and son's time and she must not interrupt. She will have the opportunity to share her views later. The message here is clear and straightforward, and the therapist has no reason to think the mother will not follow the directive.

Paradoxical Directives   Paradoxical directives may be used when the family is uncooperative and resistive to the help being offered, when they are fighting among themselves with a lack of support for their members, and when parental guidance for children is lacking (Weeks & L'Abate, 1982). In these situations, the therapist, in giving the directive, actually instructs the family to do the exact opposite of what she would like them to do. In other words, the directive asks the family not to change but to continue the dysfunctional behavior for which they are seeking help. Paradoxical directives are based on the assumption that the resistive family will defy the therapist and discontinue their dysfunctional behavior, which produces the desired change. As an example of a paradoxical directive, consider parents who have failed to provide guidance for their 14-year-old son and have resisted all efforts to change their behavior. The therapist tells the parents she has given their situation a good deal of thought and has decided they need to give the boy more freedom to do the things he likes to do because he is at a point where he needs to grow up and become more independent. And they should start by increasing his allowance to show their support for this growth and development. The therapist then tells the boy he should help his parents understand the progress he is making in becoming more mature by taking more responsibility for doing some of the things he likes, such as shopping at the mall. In order to do this, he should ask his parents for a specific increase in his allowance sufficient to go shopping at least once each week to buy the clothes he likes. If he runs short of money, he should ask for more because he has reached the age where he needs to be concerned about the clothes he wears. If he and his parents cooperate in carrying out this task, it should bring them much satisfaction. The parents will most likely resent the boy's increasing demands and show their resistance to the therapist by failing to follow the directive and beginning to set limits on what the boy is allowed to do.

Sometimes when the family realizes positive behavior changes as a result of a directive, they may want to give credit to the therapist for their improvement. However, the therapist should not accept credit for the change. If credit is accepted and the family relapses and returns to their previous dysfunctional behavior, it will be considered the therapist's fault. The therapist can avoid the credit by saying he is surprised that the change occurred and is not sure it will last (Haley & Richeport-Haley, 2003). This will also make the family work harder to maintain the improvement in order to prove to their therapist that it is real.

Evidence Base

Strategic therapists have reported successful research findings with use of strategic techniques (Nugent, 1989; Selvini-Palazzoli, 1986; Wilcoxon & Fenell, 1986). Alexander and Parsons (1973) found strategic therapy superior to other types of therapy when treating adolescent delinquent behavior problems, while Weakland and colleagues (1974) reported strategic therapy superior to nonfamily individual therapies. Stanton and colleagues (1978) found strategic techniques to improve outcomes with black and white lower socioeconomic class male drug addicts. Santisteban and colleagues (1997) found a brief structural/strategic family intervention to improve family outcomes for African American and Hispanic youth diagnosed with conduct or antisocial personality disorder or both.

THE SOCIAL LEARNING APPROACH

Social learning recognizes the importance of family functioning and accepts the mutual impact of interactions of family members, which is shared by a number of other approaches to family therapy. The techniques used in this approach are behavioral and cognitive; and the approach is referred to by other names, including functional family therapy and systemic behavioral family therapy. In addition, other models presented here (i.e., family psychoeducation and family preservation models) make use of cognitive behavioral techniques combined with other techniques. Horne (1999) defines social learning as an education in human relations that takes place within the social environment. Although there is a tendency to think of learning theory as primarily concerned with a group of techniques designed to change behaviors, this is no longer true. Social learning family therapy has evolved as a general set of principles that can be readily applied to a wide variety of human problems (p. 464). It transcends the idea of specific techniques and is currently a method of inquiry for analyzing problems, designing intervention strategies, and evaluating effectiveness (p. 464).

There is no single individual associated with the development of social learning family therapy such as, for example, Minuchin with the structural approach or Haley with strategic therapy. Instead, a number of individuals have made contributions, including Boardman, Patterson, and Falloon; and in social work, Gambrill, Stuart, Barth, and Rose, to mention a few. Early application of social learning theory to family therapy focused on parent training, the treatment of sexual dysfunctions, and behavioral marriage therapy. Families with aggressive children also received attention, with the focus on intervention placed on the child's dysfunctional behavior. Parents and others in the child's environment were trained to act as agents of change by using candy to reward the child for appropriate behavior. This was replaced by the use of a point system that gave the child points for good behavior, and when a given amount of points were received, the child could exchange the points for material things of his choosing. Time-out was used, which meant the child was ignored or isolated for misbehaving (Nichols et al., 2003). In planning intervention strategy, the social learning therapist obtains data with which to determine the conditions under which the behavior in question occurs and the frequency with which it occurs before attempting to change it. This is known as baselining, and it enables the therapist to carry out one of the most important aspects of treatment, which is to measure and monitor treatment progress. Social learning family therapy is under continuous development according to the numerous research studies of it, with successful application to an increasing number of problems reported in the literature. For example, it is now used in work with family members with developmental disabilities, anxiety disorder, depression, and alcoholism, among others (Horne, 1999). Systemic theory has also been incorporated to enable social learning therapists to consider more involved interactional patterns as a basis for change in behavior (p. 472).

Accepted Principles

Families usually come into therapy because of concern about the behavior of a family member who has been identified as disruptive to family functioning. At the beginning of treatment, this individual is the focus of attention. However, further exploration usually reveals that other family members are involved and in some way often unknowingly contribute to the undesirable behavior of the identified disruptive member of the family, usually referred to as the identified patient. The social learning family therapist believes that members of the family behave in an interdependent manner (Horne & Sayger, 1990). These interdependencies are seen as reinforcers of various stimuli and cues provided by different members at different times. In other words, each family member impacts other members and, in turn, is also impacted by them. Therefore, the social learning therapist must understand the reinforcing stimuli provided by all family members and be aware that, to change one member, all members must be changed.

Social learning theory purports that behavior is not innate but instead is a learned activity. There are several ways behavior is learned, including *positive reinforcement, negative reinforcement,* and *accidental learning.*

Positive Reinforcement   Positive reinforcement occurs when family members see particular behaviors as appealing and for this reason those behaviors are encouraged.

Negative Reinforcement   When the stimulus to a behavior is stopped, which in turn leads to an increase in the frequency of that behavior, this is known as negative reinforcement. For example, a child cries because he wants candy, the mother provides the candy, and the crying stops. Giving the child candy then reinforces the mother. However, the child has also been reinforced for the behavior (crying) that the mother wishes to stop because the child has now learned that crying will lead to receiving candy from his mother and will most likely repeat this behavior when candy is again desired. The same negative reinforcement process also works for adults.

Accidental Learning   This type of learning occurs when behaviors develop as a result of unintentional reinforcement or unintentional punishment. The situation in which the child was given candy is an example of accidental learning by unintentional reinforcement.

Reciprocity and coercion are two social reinforcement mechanisms familiar to the social learning family therapist.

Reciprocity   This mechanism is indicative of a social interaction exchange in which two people reinforce each other at an equitable rate, with both maintaining the relationship through positive reinforcement (Horne, 1999, p. 475). In a reciprocal relationship, one partner will most likely receive a reward from the other partner, followed by the recipient's giving of a reward to the partner who gave the first reward.

Coercion   Coercion is shown when both persons exchange distasteful (aversive) stimuli that control the ensuing behavior, which results in negative reinforcement as the aversive reactions are terminated. Coercion in a relationship by one person causes a reciprocal use of coercion by the other person (Horne, 1999).

Companionship with other family members is reinforcing in nondistressed families and results in members being together and engaging in activities that bring them closer. Distressed families may experience high levels of conflict or attempt to stay out of conflictual situations by avoiding each other. Knowledge of the developmental stages of the family is important in social learning therapy. Also, understanding the function of reciprocity in reinforcement and punishment is helpful in determining the source of distress in troubled families.

Role of the Therapist

The social learning approach to working with families emphasizes analyzing problems, formulating strategies for intervention, and evaluating the change that takes place during the therapeutic process. The therapist who has the responsibility of carrying out the three steps in this process must have the necessary skills and training to execute this responsibility. This includes basic interpersonal relationship skills sufficient to establish a therapeutic environment within which family members are comfortable and can feel safe in discussing their most intimate feelings and concerns (Horne, 1999). The therapist must also be an empathic, genuine, caring, and supportive individual who can impart these qualities to family members.

One of the primary roles of the therapist is to define the family's problem in a way that is understandable and amenable to change. This requires a thorough assessment of the difficulties experienced by family members. Observational data can be collected from the family by having various members demonstrate during the interview the ways in which they handle problems and communicate with each other. Another source of information gathering by the social learning family therapist is through use of standardized instruments such as the Marital Adjustment Scale (Locke & Wallace, 1959), the Spouse Observation Checklist (Weiss, Hops, & Patterson, 1973), and the Family Problem Solving Scale (Nickerson, Light, Blechman, & Gandelman, 1976).

Collecting baseline data is essential in assessing progress in social learning therapy. Here the therapist focuses on specific target areas with exactness peculiar to behavioral intervention. For example, the therapist may elicit from family members how many times an individual in question does or does not do what is desired in a given period of time. How many times does the child use vulgar language each day? How many times a week is the husband late for dinner? These data identify the extent of the problem and also establish the norm against which desirable or undesirable behavior is assessed. If, for example, the child begins to use vulgar language only twice a day compared to six times per day prior to therapy, this indicates progress toward eliminating the undesirable behavior. The possession of good relationship-building skills, an accurate assessment of the family problem, and effective use of baseline data will greatly assist the social learning family therapist in carrying out the responsibility with which she is charged. This measurement perspective can be used with a variety of approaches, not exclusively with social learning models.

Techniques

An important part of change efforts in social learning family therapy focuses on teaching parents how to change the behavior of children by using various techniques, including the use of discipline and reinforcement. The method of discipline taught to parents for use with children depends upon the behavior to be changed. The method usually falls into one of the six categories suggested by Horne (1999, p. 487):

1. Withholding attention
2. Grandma's law (Premack Principle: Eat your peas, then you may have dessert.)
3. Natural and logical consequences
4. Time-out
5. Assigning extra work
6. Taking away privileges

Sometimes more than one method of discipline may be used, depending on the nature of the behavior to be changed and the child's cooperation toward this end (Horne, 1999).

Behavioral Rehearsal   This is a technique drawn from learning theory and behavioral therapy. It teaches a client how to handle a specific interpersonal exchange for which he feels unprepared. The client rehearses or practices a specific behavior to be performed in a future interpersonal encounter (Sheafor, Horejsi, & Horejsi, 2000). This is essentially a form of role-playing in which the client practices what he will say to another person with the therapist, who assumes the role of the person in question. The therapist provides feedback to the client, offers suggestions and alternative ways of behaving, and in some cases may demonstrate the behavior that is later imitated by the client. Behavioral rehearsal helps reduce client anxiety and builds confidence.

Contingency Contracting   This technique is usually used with couples after they have been taught to communicate in ways that promote problem solving. It means changing something contingently on changes being made by the other person involved in the relationship. There are two types of contract negotiation used in behavioral family therapy:

1. *Quid pro quo contract.* In this contract, one spouse agrees to make a change in behavior after a prior change is made by the other spouse. Each partner specifies the behavioral changes desired, after which a written list is made and signed by both partners.
2. *Problem-solving training.* This type of contracting is used when problems are too complicated for simple exchange agreements. Negotiations are preceded by a specific definition of problems. When agreement on the definition of a problem is reached, discussion of a solution begins by discussing one problem at a time. Each spouse paraphrases what the other has said and is taught to avoid making inferences about the other's motivation. Verbal abuse should also be avoided, and when defining a problem it is most effective to begin with a positive statement (Nichols et al., 2003).

Reinforcement   Several methods of reinforcement may be used in accordance with a child's needs and interest. For example, a token system may be used with younger children; points or stars are given to reward them for appropriate behavior. When enough tokens are earned, the child may exchange them for a tangible reward such as a toy.

Time-out is also effective with children and may be operationalized by having the child discontinue the undesirable behavior and sit in a corner or be sent to her room. A monetary allowance system usually works well with adolescents.

Marital Counseling   In cases of problematic marital relationships, the social learning family therapist completes an elaborate, structured assessment process. This usually includes interviews and standard marital assessment instruments such as the Locke and Wallace Marital Adjustment Scale (Locke & Wallace, 1959). This instrument consists of 23 questions regarding marital satisfaction. When the assessment is completed, the strengths and weaknesses of the marital relationship and the way rewards and punishments are exchanged between the couple are revealed to the therapist. A low rate of positive reinforcement exchanged is a major contributor to disturbed marital interaction. As a result, the early work with couples should focus on establishing positive behaviors and improving communication. This may be followed by teaching the couple problem solving.

Problem Solving   The steps of problem solving as suggested by Baruth and Huber (1984) are as follows:

1. Discuss only one problem at a time.
2. Paraphrase or clarify communications.
3. Avoid abuse exchanges.
4. Begin with positives.
5. Be specific.
6. Encourage expressions of feelings.
7. Validate feelings.
8. Own mutual responsibilities.
9. Focus on finding solutions.
10. Base final solutions on mutuality and compromise.
11. Make final agreements specific. (pp. 102–04)

As the couple incorporates these steps, progress should be monitored by the therapist. Marital therapy can be provided conjointly with parent training/ family therapy as indicated by Horne (1999, pp. 489–90).

Social learning advocates have developed other skill-building techniques like the problem-solving approach. These include conflict resolution, social skills training, communication training, anger management, and so on (Franklin & Jordan, 1999). These approaches are generally a combination of behavioral and cognitive techniques, including reframing and skills training.

Evidence Base

The cognitive and behavioral techniques from social learning theory have consistently shown positive outcomes. Lambert (2004) reports meta-analysis results that indicate the success of social learning interventions with depression, suicidality, functional impairment, schizophrenia or related disorders, adolescent–parent relationship, cognitive distortion, family environment, family expressed emotion, eating attitudes, family conflict, and marital satisfaction. Research on functional family therapy (FFT), a systemic behavioral model, has a highly convincing evidence base. Jordan and Franklin (1999) review studies indicating a high success rate of FFT used with juvenile delinquents; family functioning, including increased supportiveness and communication; and inhibited sexual desire.

THE FAMILY PRESERVATION APPROACH

The family preservation approach was developed in the unique setting of child protection services (Franklin & Jordan, 1999). This approach developed out of the increasing emphasis toward providing home-based services to families and children involved with the child welfare system. Families accepted into this program are at risk of child placement out-of-home. The practice model is intensive; social workers might spend 12-hour days with a family in their home. But it is also time limited. Demonstration projects in St. Paul, Minnesota, and in Washington State provided the techniques and evaluation; but almost every state in the union has instituted family preservation units in its child protection services divisions. Other service areas also have implemented family preservation services; these include mental health systems and juvenile justice.

Accepted Principles

Families at risk of losing a child for reasons of abuse or neglect are believed to need help in developing nurturing, supportive family environments. Reasons why these families cannot provide this for their children include lack of individual skills and environmental resources. Therefore, the intervention is based on ecological systems, social learning theory, and family empowerment (Franklin & Jordan, 1999).

Ecological Systems   Families involved with the child protection system are believed to have a deficit of support from extended family or from environmental sources. So families are viewed from this ecological systems perspective and assessed accordingly. A goal is to link families to the resources they need to be successful; resources may include food stamps, housing bureaus, schools, health or mental health agencies, daycare, and so forth. Families may be instructed in how to access these services and helped to make initial contacts.

Social Learning Systems   These clients are believed to be in need of life skills training as well. From a social learning family model, families may be taught parenting skills, anger management skills, parent–child conflict resolution, and so forth. Skills learned in the context of the family are believed to generalize to the family members' interactions with other individuals in the community.

Family Empowerment   Finally, family preservation is based on the idea of family empowerment. Families who have been targeted by agencies such as child welfare may believe themselves labeled as "bad," leading to a downward spiral of family and environmental interactions. This approach seeks to build in mechanisms for empowering family members by teaching them the skills they need to know and connecting them with the resources they need to be successfully functioning families. Further, the worker seeks to join with the family to help them develop their own goals for improvement of family life.

Role of the Therapist

The family preservation worker has a variety of roles in offering this home-based approach. Compher (1983) classified family preservation workers as "general case managers, the comprehensive social worker, the in-home team, and the interagency team" (as cited in Franklin & Jordan, 1999, p. 207). He concluded that family preservation workers have the most intensive role as they work with clients around the clock, if needed. They are on call 24 hours a day and may spend many hours each day with the family in their home. Case management and service coordination are used to connect families to services and agencies in the community. Family preservation workers must be able to empower their client families and recognize and build on their strengths. Thus, in addition to being the case manager, the family preservation worker is also a therapist, a teacher, a model, an advocate, and whatever other role may be necessary to help the family.

Techniques

Since family preservation deals with families in crisis at risk of losing a child to foster care, an underlying assumption is that families need both "hard" and "soft" services. In order to understand the full range of services that a client family needs, a thorough assessment is done prior to deciding on other interventions.

Assessment   Jordan and Franklin (2003) reviewed the many risk instruments designed to assess a family's risk of harming their child and the factors that are used to determine risk. Once a family's unique areas of risk are identified, additional standardized measures may be used to more specifically assess and define problem areas. Some of these measures may also be used to track and monitor the family's progress during the intervention.

Task-Centered Techniques   The goal of these techniques is to "resolve immediate crises and teach the family the skills it needs to maintain family integrity independently" (Franklin & Jordan, 1999, p. 208). Connecting the family with needed resources, while at the same time teaching family skills from a social learning family model perspective, increases social supports. Some of these skills were reviewed in the previous section of this chapter and may include parent training, conflict resolution, and anger management.

Evidence Base

Family preservation is a much-studied approach with a positive track record. Social learning theorists such as Patterson (1982) established the relationship between life stresses and social incompetencies in their work with children and families (cited in Franklin & Jordan, 1999). Lambert (2004) cites the positive results of behavioral approaches with families. Family preservation is reported successful, not only in child protective service environments but in juvenile justice and mental health settings as well (Lambert, 2004).

THE FAMILY PSYCHOEDUCATIONAL APPROACH

Family psychoeducational therapy was developed by social workers helping those diagnosed with a mental illness and their families (Franklin & Jordan, 1999). The approach combines education about the nature of the family member's illness with other family techniques. These techniques are administered in a brief framework and may include cognitive-behavioral techniques, social skills training, and other brief family therapy interventions. The approach has a solid research background.

Accepted Principles

Unlike in previous times, families with a mentally ill member are not believed to be the cause of their ill member's disease. Family-blaming theories were developed, some psychodynamic in nature; these asserted that weakened egos and interpersonal relationships, particularly between mother and child, were at fault for the patient's disease. However, the focus on family pathology was not empirically substantiated. Current thinking, supported by empirical research, is that these families are healthy and functional, able to successfully cope with the illness, and able to help their ill member to improve. From this perspective, therapy is needed to increase the family's knowledge of the disease and to improve family members' social interactions. Names associated with the development of this model include Hogarty, Anderson, Reiss, Falloon, and Johnson.

Extensive research has suggested that families high in expressed emotion, that is, high in criticism, hostility, and overinvolvement, contributed to poor outcomes, including relapse of their ill family member. Also, some types of mental illness may result in information processing errors on the part of the patient; thus, communication and conflict resolution techniques are helpful with this population. The model's goals are to increase family understanding of the disease, improve family social interactions with each other and within the community, improve family functioning by reducing family members' expressed emotion and guilt, and increase patient medication compliance.

Role of the Therapist

The role of the therapist in family psychoeducational models is to educate, connect families with community resources, and provide social skills training or other family therapy techniques as needed. Roles needed include case management, advocate, family therapist, and educator. This model may be administered to individual families or to groups of families, so the therapist also needs skills in group work.

Since an important therapist goal is to empower families and help absolve guilt, the therapist must be able to join with families in order to motivate, reinforce, and encourage them. The therapist must be able to model new skills, as well as to design homework assignments for family members to practice away from the therapeutic setting. A nonjudgmental attitude, along with empathy and respect for the family, helps in the joining process.

Techniques

Generally, the family is referred to the therapist while the patient is in the hospital after being diagnosed by a physician or psychiatrist. The therapist begins the intervention at this point, usually with a primary focus on education about the disease. Several structured, manualized models of family psychoeducation have been developed for administration to the immediate family or groups of families (e.g., Falloon et al., 1984). These have various emphases on a few common techniques.

Assessment   Assessment in family psychoeducation focuses on the family's level of skills in areas such as communication and conflict resolution, as well as on the family's social supports. Two areas of primary importance are lack of medication compliance and participation in household activities, as these have been shown to be early warning signs of relapse (Franklin & Jordan, 1999). Both qualitative and quantitative measures may be used. Qualitative techniques such as ecomaps and genograms may help families begin to think about their relationship strengths and weaknesses. Quantitative measures, including standardized measures, can help to specify more exactly areas of concern such as communication skills deficits or parent–child conflict. These measures can also be used to monitor and track outcomes as the treatment progresses.

Education   The educational component of family psychoeducation often begins in the hospital after the patient has been diagnosed and before discharge. Both the patient and the family are usually included in this educational segment. It may be one or more sessions, and it may be administered in groups of families or with the immediate family alone. Families and patients are taught how to cope with the disease in the educational phase, as well as how to recognize early signs of relapse. This phase of treatment is prior to or simultaneous with treatment for other patient and family concerns.

Case Management   The family psychoeducation therapist must be aware of community resources and able to connect the patient and family with these. Examples of services include outpatient treatment, job training, housing, and other "hard" services that the patient may need to live independently. Family members may be helped by social support groups where they meet with families experiencing similar problems.

Family Therapy Techniques   Communication and conflict resolution techniques are usually a part of the treatment plan for families aiming to reduce their level of expressed emotion (i.e., hostility, conflict, and so forth). Problem-solving techniques, marital counseling, and anger control are examples of other components that might be included as families require them. Patients may need social skills training and other life skills training (how to interview for a job, for example), as well as how to manage their medications.

Evidence Base

The evidence base for psychoeducational treatments is strong; they have been shown to be effective in reducing time to relapse and in improving patient and family outcomes (Franklin & Jordan, 1999). Lambert's meta-analysis (2004) shows success of family psychoeducation with affective disorders, major depressive disorder, and anorexia. Lefly concluded that family psychoeducation resulted in positive outcomes for all types of family groups, regardless of background (cited in Franklin & Jordan, 1999, p. 184).

SUMMARY

In this chapter we have discussed six models for family treatment and the assessment and intervention techniques and evidence base of each. The models have in common their system orientation but differ on characteristics such as role of the therapist. Structural, communications, strategic, and social learning approaches were discussed. New in this edition are the social worker–developed family preservation and family psychoeducational approaches.

References

Alexander, J., and Parsons, B. 1973. "Short-Term Behavioral Intervention with Delinquent Families: Impact on Family Process and Recidivism." *Journal of Abnormal Psychology*, 81:219–25.

Ault-Riche, M. 1996. *Women and Family Therapy.* Chapter 1, "A Feminist Critique of Five Schools of Family Therapy." Rockville, MD: Aspen Systems Corporation.

Baruth, L., and Huber, C. 1984. *An Introduction to Marital Theory and Therapy.* Monterey, CA: Brooks/Cole.

Boszormeny-Nagy, I., and Sparks, G. 1973. *Invisible Loyalties: Reciprocity in Intergenerational Family Therapy.* Hagerstown, MD: Harper & Row.

Colapinto, J. 1999. "Structural Family Therapy." In *Family Counseling and Therapy*, 3rd edition, eds. A. Horne and J. Passmore. Belmont, CA: Wadsworth.

Cosse, W. J. 1992. "Who's Who and What's What: The Effects of Gender on Development in Adolescence." In *Gender Issues across the Life Cycle*, ed. Barbara Wainrib. New York: Springer Publishing Co.

Davis, P., Stern, D., and Van Deusen, J. 1977. "Enmeshment-Disengagement in the Alcoholic Family." In *Alcoholism: Clinical and Experimental Research*, ed. F. Seixas. New York: Grune & Stratton.

Dienhart, Anna, and Avis, Judith. 1991. "Men in Therapy Exploring Feminist-Informed Alternatives." In *Feminist Approaches to Men in Therapy*, ed. Michele Bograd. New York: Harrington Park Press.

Falloon, I. 1988. *Handbook on Behavioral Family Therapy.* New York: Guilford.

Falloon, I. R. H., Boyd, J. L., and McGill, C. W. 1984. *Family Care of Schizophrenia.* New York: Guilford.

Ferreira, A. J. 1977. "Family Myths." In *The Interactional View*, eds. P. Watzlawick and J. H. Weakland. New York: W.W. Norton & Co.

Franklin, C., and Jordan, C. 1999. *Family Practice: Brief Systems Methods for Social Work.* Pacific Grove, CA: Brooks/Cole.

Goldstein, M. J., and Milkowitz, D. J. 1995. "The Effectiveness of Psychoeducational Family Therapy in the Treatment of Schizophrenic Disorders." *Journal of Marital and Family Therapy*, 21:361–76.

Haley, J. 1976. *Problem Solving Therapy.* San Francisco: Jossey-Bass.

———. 1980. *Leaving Home.* New York: McGraw-Hill.

Haley, J., and Richeport-Haley, M. 2003. *The Art of Strategic Therapy.* New York: Taylor and Francis, Inc.

Handel, G. 1985. *The Psychosocial Interior of the Family.* 3rd edition. New York: Aldine Publishing Co.

Harkaway, J. E. 1987. *Eating Disorders.* Rockville, MD: Aspen.

Heiss, J., ed. 1976. *Family Roles and Interaction.* Chicago: Rand McNally.

Hess, R. D., and Handel, G. 1985. "The Family as Psychosocial Organization." In *The Psychosocial Interior of the Family*, 3rd edition, ed. G. Handel. Chicago: Aldine Publishing Co.

Horne, A. M. 1999. "Social Learning Family Therapy." In *Family Counseling and Therapy*, 3rd edition, ed. A. M. Horne. Belmont, CA: Wadsworth.

Horne, A., and Sayger, T. V. 1990. *Treatment of Conduct and Oppositional Defiant Disorders of Children.* New York: Pergamon Press.

Jacobson, N., and Margolin, G. 1979. *Marital Therapy: Strategies Based on Social Learning and Behavior Exchange Principles.* New York: Brunner/Mazel Publishers.

Knox, D. 1971. *Marriage Happiness: A Behavioral Approach to Counseling.* Champaign, IL: Research Press.

Knudson-Martin, C. 1994. "The female Voice: Applications to Bowen's Family System Theory." *Journal of Marital and Family Therapy* 20(1):35–46.

Lambert, M. 2004. *Bergin and Garfield's Handbook of Psychotherapy and Behavior Change,* 5th ed. New York: John Wiley & Sons.

Laqueur, H. P., Labrut, H. A., and Morong, E. 1971. "Multiple Family Therapy: Further Developments." In *Changing Families,* ed. J. Haley. New York: Grune & Stratton.

Leeder, E. 1994. *Treating Abuse in Families; A Feminist and Community Approach.* New York: Springer Publishing Co.

Locke, H. J., and Wallace, K. M. 1959. "Short-Term Marital Adjustment and Predication Tests: Their Reliability and Validity." *Journal of Marriage and Family Living* 21:251–55.

Minuchin, S. 1974. *Families and Family Therapy.* Cambridge, MA: Harvard University Press.

Minuchin, S., and Fishman, H. C. 1981. *Family Therapy Techniques.* Cambridge, MA: Harvard University Press.

Minuchin, S., Montalvo, B., Guerney, B., Rosman, B., and Schumer, F. 1967. *Families of the Slum.* New York: Basic Books.

Minuchin, S., Rosman, B., and Baker, L. 1978. *Psychosomatic Families: Anorexia Nervosa in Context.* Cambridge, MA: Harvard University Press.

Nichols, M., Schwartz, R. Z., and Minuchin, S. 2003. *Family Therapy: Concepts and Methods.* 5th edition. New York: Gardner Press.

Nickerson, M., Light, R., Blechman, E., and Gandelman, B. 1976. "Three Measures of Problem Solving Behavior: A Procedural Manual." *ISAS Catalog of Selected Documents in Psychology* (M51190), Winter.

Nugent, W. R. 1989. "Evidence Concerning the Causal Effects of an Ericksonian Hypnotic Intervention. In *Ericksonian Hypnosis: Application, Preparation and Research* (pp. 35–53), ed. S. R. Lankton. New York: Brunner/Mazel.

Okun, Barbara F., and Rappaport, Louis J. 1982. *Working with Families: An Introduction to Family Therapy.* Belmont, CA: Duxbury Press.

Papero, D. V. 1991. "The Bowen Theory." In *Family Counseling and Therapy,* eds. A. Horne and J. Passmore. Itasca, IL: F. E. Peacock Publishers.

Papp, P. 1980. "The Greek Chorus and Other Techniques of Family Therapy. *Family Process* 19:45–47.

Patterson, G. R. 1975. *Families: Application of Social Learning Theory to Family Life.* Champaign, IL: Research Press.

———. 1982. *Coercive Family Process.* Eugene, OR: Castalia.

Rosman, B. L., Minuchin, S., and Liebman, R. 1977. "Treating Anorexia by the Family Lunch Session." In *Therapies for Children: A Handbook of Effective Treatments for Problem Behavior,* eds. C. E. Schaefer and H. L. Millman. San Francisco: Jossey-Bass.

Rosman, B. L., Minuchin, S., Liebman, R., and Baker, L. 1978, November. *Family Therapy for Psychosomatic Children.* Paper presented at the Annual Meeting of the American Academy of Psychosomatic Medicine, Atlanta, GA.

Santisteban, D. A., Coatsworth, J. D., Perez, V. A., Mitrani, V., Jean-Gilles, M., and Szapocznik, J. 1997. "Brief Structural/Strategic Family Therapy with African American and Hispanic High-Risk Youth. *Journal of Community Psychology,* 25(5):453–71.

Satir, V. 1967. *Conjoint Family Therapy.* Rev. edition. Palo Alto, CA: Science and Behavior Books.

Satir, V., and Baldwin, M. 1983. *Satir: Step by Step.* Palo Alto, CA: Science and Behavior Books.

Satir, V., and Bitter, J. 1991. "The Therapist and Family Therapy: Satir's Human

Validation Process Model." In *Family Counseling and Therapy,* 2nd edition, eds. A. Horne and J. Passmore. Itasca, IL: F. E. Peacock Publishers.

Schilson, E. 1991. "Strategic Therapy." In *Family Counseling and Therapy,* 2nd edition, eds. A. Horne and J. Passmore. Itasca, IL: F. E. Peacock Publishers.

Selvini-Palazzoli, M. 1986. "Towards a General Model of Psychotic Family Games." *Journal of Marital and Family Therapy,* 12(4):339–49.

Sheafor, B. W., Horejsi, C. R., and Horejsi, G. A. 2000. *Techniques and Guidelines for Social Work Practice.* Boston: Allyn and Bacon.

Sherman, R., and Fredman, N. 1986. *Handbook of Structured Techniques in Marriage and Family Therapy.* New York: Brunner/Mazel Publishers.

Sluzki, C. E., and Beavin, J. 1977. "Symmetry and Complementarity: An Operational Definition and a Typology of Dyads." In *The New Interactional View,* eds. P. Watzlawick and J. H. Weakland. New York: W. W. Norton & Co.

Stanton, M. D., Todd, T. C., Heard, D. B., Kirschner, S., Kleiman, J. I., Mowatt, D. T., Riley, P., Scott, S. M., and Van Deusen, J. M. 1978. "Heroin Addiction as a Family Phenomenon: A New Conceptual Model." *American Journal of Drug and Alcohol Abuse,* 5:125–50.

Stuart, R. 1980. *Helping Couples Change.* New York: Guilford.

Szapocznik, J., and Kurtines, W. 1989. *Breakthroughs in Family Therapy with Drug Abusing Problem Youth.* New York: Springer.

Watzlawick, P., and Beavin, J. 1977. "Some Formal Aspects of Communication." In *The New Interactional View,* eds. P. Watzlawick and J. H. Weakland. New York: W. W. Norton & Co.

Watzlawick, P., and Jackson, D. D. 1967. *Pragmatics of Human Communication.* New York: W. W. Norton & Co.

Weakland, J., Fisch, R., Watzlawick, P., and Bodin, A. M. 1974. "Brief Therapy: Focused Problem Resolution." *Family Process,* 13:141–68.

Weeks, G. R., and L'Abate, L. 1982. *Paradoxical Psychotherapy: Theory and Practice with Individuals, Couples and Families.* New York: Brunner/Mazel Publishers.

Weiss, R. L., Hops, H., and Patterson, G. R. 1973. "A Framework for Conceptualizing Marital Conflict, A Technology for Altering it. Some Data for Evaluating It." In *Behavioral Change: Methodology, Concepts and Practice,* eds. L. Hamerlynch, L. Handy, and E. Mash. Champaign, IL: Research Press.

Wilcoxon, S. A., and Fenell, D. 1986. "Linear and Paradoxical Letters to the Non-Attending Spouse: A Comparison of Engagement Rates. *Journal of Marriage and Family Therapy,* 12:191–93.

Zeigler-Driscoll, G. 1979. "The Similarities in Families of Drug-Dependents and Alcoholics. In *The Family Therapy of Drug and Alcohol Abuse,* eds. E. Kaufman and P. Kaufman. New York: Gardner.

Beginning Evidence-Based Treatment

This chapter covers several issues regarding family assessment and treatment planning. Information presented helps social workers think through important process questions needed to begin evidence-based treatment and to be effective with families served. One of the areas covered suggests it is important that family therapists never forget the importance of core skills such as relationship building and empathy if they are going to maintain effective helping behaviors with people.

BEGINNING EVIDENCE-BASED TREATMENT WITH FAMILIES

Three questions need to be addressed in the beginning stages of treatment. The first is whether to involve family members in the treatment process; the second is which family members to involve; the third is how family members will be connected to the treatment process. Understanding the family as a system implies that all family members are in some way connected to the problems or whatever happens in the family. Thinking of the family as a system precedes the question of whether to involve other members because the therapist will always keep in mind the effects of change in the person on the family. The question, then, is how much and what kind of help is needed from other family members by the individual being seen, and how much and what kind of help is needed by other family members in accomplishing change.

Family therapists have taken different positions in the past on the totality and frequency of involvement of family members. One position taken was that all family members needed to be present in every session and that if not all were present, the interview would not be held. Rigid adherence to this position often resulted in dropout from treatment. Collins, Jordan, and Coleman (1999) encourage the therapist to make contact with every family member in the beginning phase, seeking facts that establish their distinctiveness. Others take the position of working with family members most able to change, or most motivated, or most willing to participate. While this is not always the person with the presenting problem, it has been shown to result in the disappearance of the problem of the identified patient.

The emphasis is on the potential contribution of the family member to problem solution, as well as on the gain the family member may experience by participation. Family members often interpret the worker's efforts to involve them in treatment as blaming them for the problem. While it may often be true that certain members have helped create the problem, there is no advantage to the establishment of blame or causation, and no efforts are expended in this direction. However, if causation is defined as an interactional sequence, it may be useful for the family to understand the pattern. Whether or not to include children in family sessions can be determined by the presenting problem as well as the family in treatment. If the presenting problem is primarily between the parents, children may be interviewed for information but not included in sessions. Other presenting problems may necessitate the presence of the children in the sessions. Thus, who is included may vary depending on the problem focus at the time. Including young children and others is seen as an important part of family assessment in order to elicit their understanding and insights about the family's functioning and to provide an opportunity to observe how family members relate to each other. Session participants may include, in some cases, people who are not blood family but who play an important role in the family.

Conjoint sessions have advantages that individual sessions cannot offer. Direct observation of family members together provides information not ordinarily produced in family members' telling of how the family operates. Problems in the family's problem-solving and interactional sequences appear during the session and can be immediately noted or addressed. This here-and-now approach allows family members to try out with each other new behaviors suggested by the therapist or to engage in discussion and problem solving with the support and direction of the therapist. Conjoint sessions offer the therapist a greater degree of objectivity, as there is a strong pull from family members to take sides, and they minimize the distortion of information that frequently occurs. A similar advantage occurs for family members who may be distrustful of other family members or the therapist. Conjoint sessions reveal gaps in communication. Different members often perceive family events differently, and often these images and perceptions have not been shared. The exchange of perceptions of events can lead to new definitions and to changes in interpersonal behavior. With the worker's assistance, conjoint sessions can provide a sense of safety and can help reticent members express themselves to others when they have not been able to do so on their own. These sessions can also enable members to confront differences that have been denied or deemed irresolvable.

Individual sessions may be utilized to free members for more involvement in the conjoint session and occasionally to drain excessive emotion that interferes with the progress of the conjoint sessions. Separate sessions should be framed in advance in the context of the conjoint sessions in order to strengthen the individual to deal with content that will be later be brought back into conjoint sessions. This is particularly important because requests by family members for separate sessions often result in revelations of material unknown to the therapist or other family members.

Family members can be involved in treatment constellations other than conjoint sessions. Work on family problems can take place in parent groups, groups for husbands or wives, multiple-family groups, or multiple-couple groups. (These will be referred to at appropriate points in later chapters.)

ASSESSMENT

The initial family assessment is the beginning of the process for families who seek treatment with social workers. It is difficult to separate family assessment from treatment in family therapy in that the two go hand in hand. Therapists assess and intervene simultaneously as they work with families. Many questions come to mind in the preparation for meeting with a new family. Who are members of the family? How will they describe the problem? What do they expect in coming for help? Who should be present at the initial contact with them? What kind of information do I need in order to help? Do they really want help? How can I get their agreement to work with me to solve the problems? How do I get the information needed to understand the way the family works? How do I proceed in my first contact with them?

There is more than one way to proceed and to answer such questions. Different theoretical approaches suggest different ways. This chapter serves to define some of the considerations necessary prior to initial contact. It then describes at length a first-meeting approach taken from our here-and-now orientation, illustrating the types of information that come from this approach. In some instances, additional information about extended family or others in some way connected to the family may be needed. The usefulness of each approach to the worker and to the family will become evident. In addition, there are different methods for gathering information about family functioning. This chapter will focus mostly on interviewing and observation methods that clinicians use in face-to-face work with clients, but it is important to also not forget that there are also a number of excellent standardized assessment and measurement instruments for assessing families. Three well-researched measures that assess family functioning are summarized next. Several other assessment measures are covered throughout this book.

Family Measures

This section offers a quick review of three well-researched family assessment and outcome measures. Other family assessment measures are listed at the end of this chapter.

The Family Adaptability and Cohesion Scales IV (FACES IV)   One of the best researched of all family assessment measures is the Family Adaptability and Cohesion Scales (FACES I, II, III, and IV). FACES I, II, and III measure the first two dimensions of the Circumplex Model: cohesion and adaptability/flexibility. The latest version of the measure, FACES IV (found at www.FACESIV.com), measures communication and family satisfaction. The original Circumplex Model posits a curvilinear understanding of family functioning that emphasizes the need for balance in family relationships. Families falling along extreme dimensions of functioning in cohesion, adaptability/flexibility, or communication are believed to be at risk for dysfunction, while those falling into balanced or midrange dimensions are believed to be better adjusted. For example, in the cohesion dimension, families characterized at the two extremes of enmeshed or disengaged are both considered at risk for dysfunction, while those characterized as balanced between the these two extremes are considered to function well. The same idea applies to the adaptability/flexibility (change) dimension. Families characterized at the extremes of chaotic (too much flexibility and random change, or rigid—not enough flexibility and change) are at risk for dysfunction, and those characterized as balanced are considered to function well. FACES III introduced a linear version of the measure (Franklin & Streeter, 1993).

The FACES assessment measure is a masterpiece in ongoing development. Finally, after repeated difficulties with validity and reliability, a new, improved version of FACES has emerged for use in clinical work. FACES IV is more comprehensive than the previous versions of FACES; the package now includes the six scales from the FACES IV, Family Communication, and Family Satisfaction scales. While FACES IV assesses the cohesion and flexibility dimensions, the Family Communication scale assesses communication (the third dimension of the Circumplex Model) and the Family Satisfaction scale assesses how happy family members are with their family system. In order to use FACES IV, a social worker must use the entire FACES IV Package, which contains 62 items. According to the developers, the FACES IV has six new scales that assess the dimensions of family cohesion and family flexibility from the Circumplex Model. These six scales include two balanced and four unbalanced scales. These scales have very good levels of reliability and validity. There are seven items in each scale, making a total of 42 items in FACES IV. The two balanced scales are called Balanced Cohesion and Balanced Flexibility—similar to FACES II so that results can be linked with past research using FACES. These scores are linear scales so that the higher the score, the more positive it is. The four unbalanced scales assess the low and high extremes of the two dimensions called Disengaged and Enmeshed, for the Cohesion dimension, and Rigid and Chaotic, for the Flexibility dimension. The Life Innovations website for FACES IV provides additional information (http://www.facesiv.com/).

Self-Report Family Inventory   The Self-Report Family Inventory (SFI), developed from the Beavers-Timberlawn Scales, measures family style and competence (Beavers, 2002). The SFI measures two dimensions of family functioning: (1) overall competence, and (2) behavior and emotional style of functioning. The first dimension includes family happiness, optimism, problem solving, and parental coalitions; the second dimension includes conflict communication, cohesion, leadership, and emotional expressions. Family competence helps therapists assess the family's ability to negotiate, function, and deal effectively with stressful situations, whereas behavior and emotional style address the manner and quality of family interaction (Beavers & Hampson, 2000).

The SFI has five domains and may be completed by any family member over the age of 11. The competence axis classifies families into types that fall along a continuum according to their level of functioning: optimal, adequate, midrange, borderline, and severely disturbed. The style axis classifies families according to their quality of interaction: centripetal or centrifugal. Centripetal families turn outward and seek fulfillment in relationships outside the family. Centrifugal families turn inward and seek pleasure and gratification from within the family. Both family competence and style converge to produce levels of family functioning, which are believed to have implications for the types of difficulties children may have in relationship to psychiatric categories. Additionally, when the two dimensions of family competence and family style are combined, nine distinct family groups based on clinical observation and empirical research are diagrammatically defined. Three of these groups are considered functional, while six are problematic and require clinical intervention (Beavers & Hampson, 2000). The validity and reliability of the Beavers Systems Model has been well documented since its initial inception in 1970 (Beavers & Hampson, 2000).

The Family Assessment Measure   The Family Assessment Measure (Skinner, 1995; Skinner, Steinhauer, & Sitarenios, 2000; Steinhauer, 1984), which is based on the Process Model of Family Functioning (Steinhauer, 1984), describes how to conduct family assessments based on seven dimensions: affective involvement, control, task accomplishment, role performance, communication, affective expression, and values and norms. Each of these dimensions is measured at three levels: whole family systems, dyadic relationships, and individual functioning.

The FAM, following 20 years' work in developing the measure, has four self-report components, including the general scale, which is 50 items and

9 subcales; the dyadic relationship scale with 42 items and 7 subscales; the self-rating scale with 42 items and 7 subscales; and the brief FAM with 14 items. The FAM scale yields high alpha values; the general scale = .94; the dyadic relationship scale = .95; and the self-rating scale = .89 (for adults), indicating good consistency reliability (the values for children were similar in these areas) (Skinner et al., 2000). Skinner and colleagues (2000) cite a study by Jacob (1995) that found test-retest reliability to be acceptable: mothers = .57, fathers = .56, and children = .66. The average length of time between testing was 12 days. The literature consistently shows that FAM effectively and efficiently assesses family functioning; the validity has been supported by many studies (Skinner et al., 2000).

TREATMENT PLANNING AND TREATMENT SELECTION

Treatment planning and selection may be predetermined for many clinicians based on their place of employment, but for many clinicians, this step can be challenging. There has been a great deal of focus in recent years on determining evidence-based practice and on providing means for clinicians to deliver the best practice for a particular family. Attempts have been made to enhance treatment effectiveness through treatment planning and treatment selection (Lambert, 2003).

The Psychotherapy Integration (PI) movement involves the search for and promotion of the most effective psychotherapeutic concepts and methods, regardless of the orientation they originated from. Professionals can manifest the PI doctrine through (1) the intentional employment of common factors, (2) theoretical integration, or (3) methodological eclecticism (Bedi, 2001). Since all psychotherapeutic orientations share certain curative factors, professionals seek to maximize exposure of the client to these factors through methodologically eclectic psychotherapy.

Prescriptive psychotherapy falls under the umbrella of methodologically eclectic PI. It encapsulates any methodologically eclectic system of psychotherapy that firmly bases its prescriptive conclusions on empirical rather than theoretical justification. Currently, the predominant emphasis in traditional prescriptive psychotherapy is on the matching of interventions and/or psychotherapeutic orientations to the diagnosis of the clients in treatment. In 1995, the American Psychological Association Division 12's Task Force on Promotion and Dissemination of Psychological Procedures (Society of Clinical Psychology) published a list of 18 so-called "well established, empirically validated" treatments matched up to specific DSM-IV diagnostic categories. Unfortunately, there is evidence that these empirically supported treatments (ESTs) might not be much more efficacious than other psychological treatments. Prescriptive psychotherapists maintain that tailoring interventions to clients further increases the likelihood of positive psychotherapeutic outcome.

The three most prominent and theoretically developed systems of prescriptive psychotherapy are as follows:

1. Multimodal Psychotherapy (Lazarus, 1989; Lazarus, 1992) provides prescriptions based upon an extensive assessment of seven domains of experience.
2. Systematic Treatment Selection (Beutler & Clarkin, 1990) is based upon an assessment of key variables such as problem complexity, coping styles, and personality styles, and involves matching general approaches to clients. For example, externalizers tend to do better with action-oriented approaches, while internalizers do better with insight-oriented therapies.
3. Stage-Appropriate Psychotherapy (Beutler & Clarkin, 1990) is based upon Prochaska and DiClemente's (1992) transtheoretical stages of change. A summary of the stages is presented in Box 3.1. The client's stage of readiness for change is assessed, and approaches are matched to her current stage as it is believed that clients will be most helped when interventions are tailored accordingly. Although results are not always consistent, it appears that the stage strategy often is predictive and can be used to design an intervention (Lambert, 2003, p. 206).

There is research, however, that does not support the superiority of one treatment over another. Project MATCH (Project Match Research Group, 1998), one of the most extensive attempts to match client to treatment, examined the effects of client–treatment matching in a study of treatments for clients with alcohol abuse or dependence. Despite clear and perhaps dramatic differences in philosophies, there were few differences across treatments for all three groups of clients.

When examining the effects of treatment duration within CBT and PI for the treatment of depression, Shapiro and others (1994) found no differences in outcome or rate of change between PI and CBT. When examining these well-designed studies that compare different therapeutic orientations, the findings are consistently small or negligible (Lambert, 2003). The finding of relative equivalence of differing approaches has significant implications for theories regarding the processes of change and the relative importance of theory-specific techniques versus common factors as agents of change. The findings of Wampold (2001) argue against the current trend of identifying empirically supported therapies that purport to be uniquely effective.

The diagnostic categories allow for a great deal of heterogeneity in personality traits to serve as useful predictors or matching variables. The most creative approach to date is to articulate areas of client variability that are likely to have the most powerful effect on treatment process and outcome, and to match therapist behavior, regardless of school of psychotherapy, to the needs of the clients (Beutler, Moleiro, Malik, & Harwood, 2000). Treatments should be connected to the presenting problem that has been targeted for change (Jordan & Franklin, 2003).

BOX 3.1 | Stages of Change

Precontemplation
- Client is not thinking about change.
- Client believes the consequences of the behavior are not serious.
- Clients in this stage may only seek treatment when pressured by others.

Contemplation
- Client recognizes there is a problem but has not committed to making a change.
- Clients in this stage may say they are seriously considering change in the near future.

Preparation
- Client is ready to experiment with making small changes.
- Client may have already attempted to make a change.

Action
- Client is taking action to change.
- Clients in this stage have successfully changed behavior for a period of time.

Maintenance
- Client is maintaining behavior changes over time.
- Client is working to prevent relapse.

Relapse
- Relapse is seen as a normal part of the change process.
- Clients may feel demoralized in this stage.
- Clients may revert to an earlier stage such as precontemplation.
- Treatment during this stage attempts to help client view mistakes as an opportunity for learning.

Source: Norcross, J. C., and Prochaska, J. O. 2002. "Using the Stages of Change." *Harvard Mental Health Letter* 18(11):5–7.

Tasks for the Beginning Phase

The first two tasks of the family social worker in the beginning phase are engaging families in the helping process and assessing the problem with which the family is struggling (Worden, 1994). Engagement involves forming a therapeutic alliance between the social worker and family. As discussed earlier in this chapter, assessment consists of identifying patterns and issues within the family that relate directly to the problem, as well as identifying the connectedness of the family to its social environment.

Engagement and assessment are best accomplished in four steps:

1. Make contact with every family member.
2. Define the problem to include perceptions of all members of the family.
3. Establish goals and clarify an intervention process.
4. Contract with the family.

Engaging the Family in Treatment   Cormier and Cormier (1985) suggest five guidelines that indicate a family or individual may be ready to move on from assessment to treatment: (1) A good client–practitioner relationship exists, (2) the client feels understood, is ready to commit, and is engaging in open communication, (3) an adequate assessment has been conducted, (4) realistic counseling goals are developed, and (5) the client is ready to engage in treatment. These guidelines are useful as the social worker guides the family through the initial assessment and into the first phases of treatment.

The social worker's desire to include a number of family members in the diagnostic process, if not in treatment, influences the procedures used for the first contact. The person who initiates agency contact may be certain only about the need for help but not about the kind of help needed, or may have a specific kind of help in mind that is different from what the agency and the worker have to offer. Negotiation is needed to clarify how expectations of the applicant are or are not congruent with those of the worker or the agency. In the case of the family, there are also differences between family members' perceptions about what is needed. Before family members willingly engage themselves in a treatment process, negotiation among themselves and with the worker as to the purpose, goals, and means of treatment, and the nature of their participation is needed to enable the family to make the shift from applicant to client.

At the beginning of treatment, clients attempt to place workers in a role that meshes with their idea of their own role in the treatment process. This is immensely complicated in family work because each family member attempts to place the worker in a role particularly advantageous to self, a position that may not be at all desirable to another family member. Graham (2003) presents a welcome letter that is mailed to prospective outpatient psychotherapy clients after their initial phone contact. The letter prepares clients for what to expect in therapy and how to participate in their own treatment. It includes problem-solving steps commonly taken by clients during short-term outpatient psychotherapy that includes strategic, solution-focused, and cognitive-behavioral interventions. Using such a letter to prepare clients for therapy has been found to be effective in reducing clients' symptom severity.

Elements of Resistance to Treatment   There are numerous obstacles in the path of engaging family members in treatment. One is the view held by family representatives that one of the members is the problem, not the family as a whole. This barrier to engagement is often very difficult for the family to overcome. The worker will need to take steps to gain acceptance of the need for family participation by the family member who is the contact initiator.

A second obstacle to family participation in treatment is the view that no problem exists. They contact the worker under compulsion from a school, a probation officer, or an employer. They profess no awareness of the reasons for referral, or they see only that others are creating problems for them. The individual identified as the problem may be willing to keep a proffered appointment to comply with the referring person but only for that reason. The family may agree to have the identified person come but sees no need for their participation. The worker, however, may readily sense the need for treatment of the problem and sees the benefits of involvement of the family in treatment.

Work with a family may begin under coercive circumstances. In some situations, the agency or the workers may have the authority to force family members into treatment. Such use of authority may be useful in opening up other possibilities for the family or in considering the consequences of no effort to change. Procedures used by the worker in the initial phases of contact may enable the family to move from participation under a sense of coercion to voluntary participation, with an expectancy of personal and family gain (Cirillo & DiBlasio, 1992).

Because so many families known to social workers are of this type, we will devote considerable space to an explanation of procedures that help in moving the family into the role of client. The method described is the process of engagement by means of conjoint interviews. Other beginnings may be made with families, but the conjoint session has special value in the assessment of family functioning and special usefulness in enabling all family members to see their parts in the family problem-solving process.

Considering that the use of dominant practice models for social work with involuntary clients often alienates rather than engages, De Jong and Berg (2001) describe the use of solution-focused interviewing as a way to engage involuntary and mandated clients. In this way, practitioners can begin the co-construction of cooperation with mandated clients through adopting a not-knowing posture, focusing on and amplifying what clients want and client strengths and successes, and asking relationship questions to generate possibilities for change specific to the mandated context. The "miracle question" offers clients the opportunity to construct a different, more satisfying future by inviting the client to develop a vision for the future that is as vivid and concrete as possible, including definitions of what the client might do differently (de Shazer, 1994). Scaling questions are useful for getting information about many aspects of clients' current lives and future possibilities (Berg & de Shazer, 1993). This way of engaging mandated clients is perhaps more ethical than trying to motivate them in certain directions. It embodies the strengths perspective to helping. In interviews, we discipline ourselves to ask questions with no investment in client outcomes.

The posture does not represent an uncaring attitude toward clients or the welfare of the community but represents an acceptance of the reality that we are working with human beings who make choices. As choice makers, all people's sense of personal dignity and competence are tied to the choices they make. Therefore, we as practitioners can be most useful by inviting clients to co-construct the widest and most informed range of choices possible in their contexts. Client self-determination and respect for human dignity are the worthiest of practice principles and have deep roots in the social work profession.

The Family Encounters the Social Worker   The therapeutic situation evokes certain responses by virtue of the fact that another person is added to the system. Family members calculate how to adjust their responses to account for the new person (the therapist). Each family member has his or her own preferences about what to do and what is needed to cope with the problem. Since the conflicts about possible actions have not been resolved within the family process, there is a natural tendency to seek the support of the worker for one's own position, along with depreciation of the views of others.

These efforts are understandable both in relation to the need of each member to preserve individual integrity and esteem and in relation to the level of caring and trust among family members. There is the expectation that others will not appreciate one's own needs and therefore will not take them into account. Efforts to blame and demand change in others are a defense arising out of this view of others. As these efforts become apparent to the worker, they are also interpretable as efforts to seek the worker as an ally, to strengthen one's own position vis-à-vis other family members. This is revealed with dramatic clarity in some situations when, in separate interviews, individual members are able to be less defensive and accept more responsibility for family problems than they can in conjoint sessions.

The social worker, in response, attempts to establish a caring, understanding relationship with the family members and to value the contributions of each of them. These attempts serve to resist the family pressures to take sides. Family members are forced to take this resistance into account. Failure to take individual responsibility for action is gradually confronted. Family members may counteract the worker's resistance to their usual routines by intensifying their previous efforts; new responses may be found and learned to take the place of the anger and blame.

While the behaviors that family members display during their contact with the worker are manifestations of familiar family routines, they are not fully interpretable in this light. They also should be understood as responsive to the worker's entry into the family system. It is important for the worker to become a part of the family system while at the same time not becoming entangled in its usual routines. The family must be helped to accept the worker's entry into the system and to be responsive to the worker's input demanding change.

The Social Worker's Role with the Family

It has been said of family work that the social worker is in charge of the treatment, but the family members are in charge of their lives. The worker's task in treatment, especially in beginning treatment, is to provide the family with a structure that enables problem solving to take place. The worker actively takes charge of the procedures at this beginning stage. Though the family may appear to have the initiative in the interview, this may be because the worker has asked the members to struggle with a problem in order to see how they go about solving problems. If problem solving does not succeed, the worker interrupts, either to facilitate or move on to other tasks. The degree to which the worker is able to establish control over the process in the session is a measure of the worker's skill. It is also a measure of the family's ability to gain from participation in treatment, and it thus provides diagnostic information about the family's workability and flexibility.

The diagnostic and treatment efforts should help the family members take charge of their lives. In the sessions, the worker requires them to talk about their concerns to the worker and to each other. The worker's requirement that family members engage in different kinds of action in the conjoint sessions vis-à-vis each other sets up new ways of relating that are more productive in problem solving than were their old ways. We expect the family to see the usefulness of the new patterns, learn them, and appropriate them for regular use.

Opening Procedures

The first goal of the initial contact is to acquire a firm understanding of the nature of the problem presented by the family and of the workings of the family system that serve to perpetuate the problem or prevent its solution. A second and equally important goal is to gain the family's agreement to participate in a problem-solving process, since the members do not necessarily come with the readiness to do so. A third goal is to set procedures for change in motion. Family members should be able to leave with beginning confidence that they have been understood, that something new is being offered, and that something positive can happen as a result of agency contact.

The steps we outline are for an initial conjoint session, which includes as many family members as seem necessary to problem solution. Most family treatment begins through contact with one family member. The worker takes a position at first contact that the family needs to be involved. Starting with one person and waiting until later to insist on family participation results in lost time and requires a second start. In the initial contact, whether in person or on the telephone, the worker seeks to learn who the family members are. There is enough exploration of the problem to give the worker some sense of agency appropriateness and family relatedness. But the exploration is brief for two reasons. The problem cannot be adequately understood from one person's reporting, and the image of an alliance between the initiator and the worker needs to be particularly avoided in this phase.

Attention therefore shifts to the need to engage both the initiator of the contact and other family members in the treatment process. The caller is requested to ask other family members to come and to bring them along to an initial session. The value of the information they can provide and of the suggestions they might offer is emphasized. Family members are frequently responsive to this emphasis on the importance of their contributions to problem solving. If they are not responsive, the worker's efforts must focus on the resistance, rather than on the problem presented by the family. If the problem presenter in the initial contact seems resistant, the resistance should be explored. If the problem presenter attributes resistance to other family members, their anticipated reasons and the presenter's intended means for handling their responses can be explored.

If the presenter's means for handling the resistance of other family members seem inadequate, alternative responses may be suggested. The suggestions are, in effect, new inputs into the family system. If the suggestions are adopted, both the behavior of the initial problem presenter and family processes are thereby altered. Treatment of the family has begun. If the resistance is not strong, family members may recognize that each family member's view of the problem is important if it is to be fully understood, and they may respond to the request that all family members participate, at least in the initial exploratory session.

Stage 1: Relieving Initial Anxiety   Once the social worker has succeeded in arranging an in-person meeting with the needed family members, her first task in the initial session is to relate to each family member's feelings about having to be there. The worker's overall objective (as in individual treatment) is to establish a safe, nonthreatening relationship with all persons present. The worker inquires about conversations the family members may have had with each other about the appointment, how it has been explained to them, and how they felt about what they had been told prior to coming. This procedure has both communicative and metacommunicative value. On the communicative level, it elicits information regarding their anxieties about meeting the worker, airing family problems, asking for help, and revealing themselves to other family members. It provides data about the way family members view both the relationship with the worker and relationships within the family. Family members may have communicated little or much about coming. Clear communication may have gone to some members but not to others. They may feel free to speak in the session or wait for cues from others. The procedure's value to the family is that it conveys the worker's intention to regard each person's view as important and permits it to be heard and valued. The individuality and separateness of family members is emphasized, while their value to the problem-solving effort is affirmed. The procedure allows each family member to be heard by other family members. If family members do not spontaneously comment, the worker may ask them if they are aware of each other's point of view or solicit comments on what has been said.

Stage 2: Eliciting Problem Definitions through Questioning   After the family members' anxieties about the interview have been reduced, the social worker can proceed to elicit from each one a statement about the problem or problems that have brought the family to the session. There will likely be differences in statements of the problem. For some families, this may be the first time that different views have been expressed and heard. The worker's presence may create a tolerance for these differences that was not present in the family's own efforts to deal with the problem. The extent of the members' ability to wait for one another's expressions will offer the worker some beginning cues as to the family's ability to listen and to learn.

Frequently, family members may single out one of their number as the problem. The worker gets the clear impression that the identified person is blamed and isolated and finds little support in the family. At this stage, the worker primarily is listening and thinking. Only limited efforts are directed at expanding expressions of feelings or changing feelings or problem definition. The important objective at this time is to hear from everyone.

Family members will not always sit patiently to hear what other members have to say. They may experience difficulty in remaining in a listener status. There are likely to be interruptions and, if the first speaker does not stop, simultaneous talking. In this event, the worker does need to become active to avoid repetition in the session of what the family ordinarily experiences at home. The stage is set for problem solving by disallowing interruptions. At the same time, each participant is assured that his or her point of view will be heard. Strenuous efforts by the worker along these lines may be needed in some families. Even at this beginning stage, the worker's efforts to regulate the conversation may afford the family an experience that they have not had before, and this may enable them to feel that the worker and treatment have something to offer them.

Some family members may be extremely reticent to say anything, much less express an opinion, point of view, or difference. The worker will be aware of halting speech, looking down, and looking to other family members for cues, or avoiding involvement. Such reticence can be as much of an obstacle to problem solving as overactivity. The worker may attempt to draw the individual out during this initial phase of the interview by asking for elaboration or may comment on how the situation makes for difficulty in talking, thereby offering encouragement. These efforts to gain the reticent member's participation become particularly important in the case of the family member whose contributions have not been valued by others. In response to the worker's attitude, other family members may begin to respond differently to the reticent member. The reticent behavior gives diagnostic information about patterns of power, deference, and decision making in the family.

Stage 3: Working toward Problem Consensus   Social workers often see the problem differently from the way the family does, but they still need to start with the family's definition of the problem. The worker sees the problem presented by the family as evidence of failure of problem-solving processes and thus as a symptom of the problem, while the family sees it as the problem. In the procedure we have outlined, the worker's efforts are directed both to solving the problem and to increasing family problem-solving capacity. The following example will illustrate what we mean.

The problem is presented by parents who are concerned with altering the behavior of a child. In such a case, the worker can operate on the premise, likely to be shared by the parents, that the parents have both the prerogative and the responsibility to regulate the behavior of the child. The worker wants to support them in this and to help them with it. Since the family is not asking for help with their problem-solving routines but only for help in correcting this problem, the effort to change problem-solving routines must be focused on these routines as they apply to the presenting problem.

The effort of the worker to establish an alliance with the parents may produce a negative reaction in the child. A positive relationship with all family members must apply to the child as well as the parents. The worker will relate both to the child's feelings about being present and to his definition of the problem. While feelings of anger and blame are likely to be expressed, the worker may also hear the child's wish for approval and understanding from the parents and the desire for a positive relationship with them. If, by the worker's focus on the positive wish instead of the blame, the parents are able to hear something new from their child, a change in family feeling may begin. At a minimum, the child may experience enough of the worker's support and concern to enable him to consent to the helping relationship.

There are also many useful family assessment and measurement tools for assessing family problems, and these measurement instruments can sometimes be used to sort out differences in perceptions about problems in family treatment and to work toward a consensus or focus for the family treatment. For example, the measurement instrument may be used as an objective source of information that helps to externalize the debates by pointing out, for example, that both sides have some issues that might need attention in family counseling. At the same time, there are also some other important areas to consider about their family that they have not yet thought about. The measure can also sometimes say things that the practitioner cannot say about a family without offending the family, or the information on the measure may be externalized away from the practitioner and be viewed as less threatening. Jordan and Franklin (2003) offer reviews of some of the best family assessment measures.

Acceptance of the problem focus defined by the family at the outset is necessary for the family's willingness to participate in treatment. At the same time, the requirement that the family participate emphasizes the family role in finding a solution to the problem. Without the latter requirement, we would expect no change in family organization and a continuation of the problem or problematic behavior. We see this as a healthy shift from the initial problem focus, an increase in the sense of individuality and separateness of the members, which is necessary for a positive sense of togetherness and solidarity.

Stage 4: Focus on Interactional Mechanisms   The fourth stage in the social worker's efforts to engage the family furthers the worker's diagnostic effort. The worker will have gained in understanding from the previous stages about how the family works to cope with its problems. The effort at this stage is more specifically directed at understanding the family's ways of dealing with the presenting problem. This stage can be approached in several ways.

Members' Response to Worker's Questions   One approach is for the worker to inquire of family members how they have responded to the problem, how it has affected them, and what they have tried to do about it. Patterns of involvement and withdrawal, of support and opposition, are evident in differing responses. The worker may comment on the responses to emphasize that each family member does have some connection to the problem, even if he or she has tried to ignore it. This base of connectedness to the problem is the primary incentive for participation in problem solution.

The worker-imposed requirement that each family member hear what the others have to say allows for new information or other members' ideas about a solution to be shared for the benefit of all. The worker specifically draws such reactions and differences to their attention and asks who in the family does what in the face of differences about how to cope, and how each responds to the other's response. Awareness of the difficulty in dealing with differences may ultimately be the basis of agreement to participate in treatment. The wish to do something about how they get along with each other may serve as a common problem definition, a rallying point.

Family Discussion   An alternative approach is to ask the family members to talk with one another about how to solve the problem, while the worker observes what happens when they do. Though the worker may assume that there will be a replay of family operations similar to their usual ones at home, this assumption should be validated. Frequently, family members will confirm that this is the usual routine and express dissatisfaction with the process. Often they will report restraint in their behavior due to the presence of the worker, thus confirming the systems theory assumption that the entry of a new member alters the operation of the system. That may be a positive sign about the treatability of the family, but it is not to be assumed that the restraint will necessarily continue in subsequent sessions.

Communications represent strategies for negotiation and problem solving that have in the past been learned and reaffirmed, and now are apparently in continual use. It is possible that what the worker observes at this point is the simple result of faulty negotiation procedures, such as failure to listen intently or respond relevantly, and what is needed is for the family to learn new negotiation procedures. The family can begin to learn from the worker's efforts to regulate the conversation, beginning with the initial interview.

It may be evident to the worker that family members do not feel very good about each other at this point; negative feelings may be intense with manifestations of undiminished hostility. Struggles for power or control may be revealed, with no one yielding in that struggle or with one family member accepting a completely one-down position without a struggle. Triads may be tightly locked into position. Verbal and nonverbal communications are evidence that those conditions exist. Changing communication modes or routes may be impossible or may not help. Traces of goodwill and the ability to recall positive feelings are important in the willingness of family members to continue both in treatment and in relationships with one another.

Two-Party Discussing   A third alternative approach for Stage 4 is also diagnostic in effect but has a clearer treatment component. The worker may select a specific issue that has been referred to in the discussion and ask an involved pair of family members to work on it. They are asked to talk to each other to try to solve the problem. Other family members are asked to observe. The worker is in a position to observe the interaction of the two parties involved and the behavior of other family members.

Both participants usually direct their efforts at getting the other person to see their own point of view. They may both become wider ranging in their arguments, increasingly insistent and intense, or one of them may become insistent and the other may withdraw. Both may turn to the worker or to the other members of the family for support when their frustration at gaining the understanding of the other reaches a certain level. Noting the strategy that each participant has used in relating to the other and the other's response, the worker may inquire whether they see this description of their interaction as accurate and ask for their estimate of the effectiveness of their actions. In the midst of this awareness of anger and despair, the worker needs to know whether there is also a wish and a hope for change. Some clients may find the possibility of change so inconceivable that they dare not hope for it. The worker's attentiveness to these feelings and accurate description of the participant's interaction conveys understanding and can give rise to hope.

The emphasis is on the immediate experience in the interview rather than on past events, although past events may be the starting point of the discussion. Thus, A might be talking about feeling misunderstood, or hurt, or lonely, or unsupported by B, not only in relation to an earlier event but in the present discussion of the event. B might respond empathetically or in anger, but focus on the present moment's responses makes the issues more alive and less subject to recall's distortions. The intent is to make it possible for family members to feel that their views and feelings have been heard, an experience they have often not had in their own efforts at problem solving.

Whether the effort succeeds at this point or not, it serves as a demonstration of the kind of work that would take place during treatment. While the worker is observing how two family members work on a specific family issue, simultaneous observation of the behaviors of other family members is possible. Other family members may not be able to remain in the observer role; they may become distractors, allies, or peacemakers, or otherwise inject themselves into the negotiations. The reasons for such behavior are many and varied. Children may feel threatened by a too tense exchange between parents and act to draw attention away from the argument and onto themselves. A sibling may identify with the feeling of another child generated in the interaction with a parent. A parent may feel strongly about the behavior of the other parent in relation to a child.

Use of any of these procedures at this stage in the initial contact is likely to be brief because the social worker is seeking primarily to understand how the family is working and to test quickly whether they can respond to worker intervention. At the same time, however, these interventions will be seen as useful, not only in initial contacts but also in ongoing treatment.

Stage 5: Reaching a Treatment Contract   The final stage of the social worker's efforts to engage the family in treatment is achievement of an understanding with the family members about what they want to have changed and what they want from treatment and from the worker. The emphasis shifts from what is wrong to how the family wants things to be, and how the worker can help them get there. The focus is on defining goals and establishing a working contract between the social worker and the family about their ongoing work together. Again, the process is similar to but more complex than that required in individual treatment.

The prior stages of the engagement effort have been preparation for the family to approach this stage, but considerable work remains to be done. The discrepancies in problem statement now must be resolved into a problem definition to which family members can subscribe as one that they are willing to work on. The shift from what is wrong to how they want things to be moves away from complaining to positive, goal-oriented activity. It is not an easy shift to make. The definition of the kind of help needed from the worker is difficult to achieve, since the family has only the present experience with the worker to go by and consequently knows little about what the worker and agency have to offer. Agreement on the problem definition and how the worker will help are both needed.

The worker's effort is directed at achieving a problem definition in harmony with the family's needs and wishes. The worker may see a variety of family problems the family members themselves do not see. He may be aware, for example, that a marital problem exists and that it interferes with the solution of the problem that the family has presented. The worker may make the connection, but the family may not be able to see this as the problem to be solved. If the presenting problem was a child's behavior, the focus at this stage is not on how the parents can get their marriage together but on how they together can cope with the child's problem. The parents may be able to accept the need to join together to help the child, but they may not see the need to work on the marriage in general. While they may subsequently come to see that work on the marriage is needed in order to help their child, the starting point in treatment is with the problem they see and are willing to try to solve.

The worker's emphasis on what the family would like to accomplish in treatment requires the worker to seek responses from family members about what each wants and is willing to do about the problem. A number of difficulties will be encountered in these responses. One is that goals will be stated in terms of the need for someone else to stop doing something or to be different. Not all family members are likely to find such definitions acceptable. The work of the previous stages of the initial contact should have helped to take the edge off some of these tendencies to blame or scapegoat, but it will not have eliminated them. More work is needed to arrive at acceptable definitions.

Another difficulty is that responses from family members may be in global terms. Either the specifics of change do not become clear, or the proposed changes in the family seem so extensive as to appear unattainable. Demands on others and global expectations reflect the continuing difficulty family members have in defining problems or in communicating their needs in a way that others in the family can accept and agree to. If they had other ways of addressing the tasks that the worker now puts to them, they probably would not need treatment. Specific help is needed.

One means the worker has of helping with these difficulties is the ability to restate or reformulate the problem. The worker may use knowledge of the members and of the group acquired earlier in the session. Knowledge about how members see themselves connected to the problem and about their wish to continue as a group may be used to convert negative statements into positive ones, global statements into more specific objectives. Statements about always fighting with each other may be altered to statements such as "I wish that we could talk things over." General unhappiness and dissatisfaction may be converted to a wish for family members to show more appreciation or to get along better.

In rare instances, family members may comment about specific things they themselves can do to improve and may show signs of willingness to do them. The worker may offer formulations that express expectations and goals for the family rather than for individuals or reformulate statements about problems to make them specific rather than global. The general adjustment problem of a family member may be specified in terms such as "planning how things will be when Sally returns home from the hospital" or "what we can do so grandmother won't be so unhappy." Agreement is then sought from members to work to solve these problems and achieve these goals.

Along with the effort to restate goals, the worker draws attention away from individual behavior to focus on the interactive process between members. The worker at this stage also needs to learn what kind of help the family had expected and to define what kind of help she has to offer. The worker's means of helping will, in part, have been demonstrated by her behavior in the interview prior to this point, but these means may be very different from what the family wants. There may be a range of expectations of the worker, from removing a member from the home for placement elsewhere, to straightening out a member; to getting a member to go to school, or to work, or to a doctor; to refereeing family arguments; to helping the family find a way to get along or to talk things over. The worker needs also to convey her own and her agency's capacity to respond to the requests.

The family's response to the worker's evaluations, suggestions, and offers of help provides further data on which to base judgments about family potential for change and responsiveness to helping efforts. The new information and direction serve to upset the family's usual interchanges. The new inputs may be resisted in order to maintain the usual balance, or they may be assimilated in order to promote change.

Whether the family can begin to change or even accept the possibility of change depends on a number of factors, some of which have already been noted. The family's value of family togetherness is one such factor. Even though disaffection and discouragement about the family's situation may be great, there may still be hope that things could be different. Some members, however, may have already lost hope completely, and they cannot be interested in participation in the family. A second factor has to do with the willingness of members to risk. A member's willingness to respond positively to a worker reformulation that says, in effect, "I want you, care about you, and wish to be with you," implies a willingness to risk the possibility that other members may not share those desires. Behind this willingness must lie a strong need and perhaps some confidence that other members do care and share the same wishes. Worker sensitivity can sometimes enable a member to claim ownership of such sentiments when this might not under other circumstances be possible.

Another factor affecting members' consent to participate and willingness to change is the fear that the individual will be lost in pursuing the goals of the group, that he will be unhappily bound to the family and never be free to leave or to grow as an individual. All the procedures described are intended to convey the worker's support for both individuality and connectedness, and not just for a connectedness that keeps the individual inappropriately bound to the family. If, as a consequence of worker activity, the family indicates a willingness to continue in treatment, it is a sign of their capacity to accept outside contributions to their problem solving and perhaps also of the worker's skill in conveying helpfulness and trustworthiness.

We have described in some detail a procedure for assessment and engagement of the family at the time of initial contact. The process need not always be lengthy, however. With some families it will be simple and short; with others it may take several hours. If a clear family and worker agreement does not result, the work may have to be carried over into a second session. Workers may eliminate some stages and still achieve clarity, begin work on a problem, or arrive at a contract with greater efficiency.

A Family Life Chronology (How about Family Assessment?)

Taken in the context of our earlier emphasis on the here-and-now and the lack of emphasis on history, our inclusion of Satir (1983) and the taking of a family life chronology at this point may seem misplaced. Though the effort represents a different approach to treatment, the information obtained can become useful in the ongoing phases of our problem-solving orientation.

The interview begins with learning who the family members are and what they each see as their reason for being present. Questioning about the circumstances that prompted their being here provides the basis for wanting to know basic facts about who is who in the family: names, dates of birth, death, marriage, and who else is in the family. At this point, such questions of fact are relatively unthreatening, seem appropriate to the family, and serve as a means to put the family at ease. However, the process is more than a collection of answers to questions.

The development of the chronology elicits information about relationships between family members, the parents in particular; how they developed; and how others in the family, particularly their parents, felt about them and what else was occurring in their families at the time. The chronology helps to develop images of self and of each other as separate persons, beyond their usual role relationships. Children may, for example, see their parents as persons, not only as harsh rule-makers. Parents can see themselves in the context of the larger family, how they were influenced by parent and sibling behavior, and how this is determining present behavior. Questions relating to births, illnesses, deaths, marriages, and other important family events and about how different family members responded or coped with such events may begin to reveal patterns of coping and possible repetition from generation to generation. The therapist is alert and responsive to the reactions and behavior of other family members to the information being given.

Familiarization with the past may prompt a desire not to repeat patterns. If both parents are in the home, getting the chronology from both may reveal the origins of current differences between them regarding roles or ways of doing things. In the questioning, the therapist serves as a model of communication. The facts are important, but the means of questioning serve to convey respect and to value the contributions of each family member. Questions about, and the presence of, members of several generations enable family members to see themselves in a larger context. As differences and differentness are revealed, the therapist reminds the family that opinions and ways of doing things do not necessarily imply that one is right and the other wrong; they are just different, and they now have a new opportunity to choose how they want things to go.

It should be evident that such an approach does not seek history solely for the sake of facts but is intended to free family members to grow, to be different in their family behavior, and to contribute in a different way to family problem solving. Though Satir put the chronology effort at the beginning of work with the family, it suggests, and is the essence of, a very different approach to treatment. Seen in the context of our approach, additions to the chronology may be sought when new issues arise, such as illness, loss of job or income, or a child leaving home. Family information may help when problem solving around such an issue becomes stuck in disagreement or lack of ideas for how to cope or move.

Therapists in the Bowen (1978) approach to family treatment develop a family *genogram,* a diagram that records much of the same information as does Satir's chronology (McGoldrick & Gerson, 1985). The diagram uses separate symbols for males and females; represents them by generation, giving dates of birth, death, and marriage; and represents whether individuals had a close, intense, or distant relationship. The genogram serves similarly as a record of family membership, history, and events over at least three generations. Here its purpose is slightly different than either ours or Satir's: It is less focused on the presenting problem. Obtaining the data and learning about the family are accompanied by teaching the family about what to look for and how families work. The genogram offers a cognitive grasp of the family's behavior and enables the individual to be more detached, less emotional about family connections, and a separate person, not simply an extension of other members' wishes and intentions. The interest in family history facilitates personal growth and separateness. As we have noted before, change in one member necessitates change elsewhere in the family and may be both welcome and/or threatening.

One other means of recording information about a family and its problems that is needed for assessment and treatment planning is an *eco-map*. The map may initially show members of the current, immediate family, as well as members of the extended family with whom they interact and who might be or become relevant to presenting problem solution. It is less focused on developing a full genogram or chronology. It includes not only family members but other individuals, services, agencies, or resources, and shows whether they are connected in a problematic or a helpful way.

The multicontextual framework (Carter, 1993, as cited in Carter & McGoldrick (1999, Table 1.2, p. 16), is a model of couple and family assessment to assist clinicians in the work of including the relevant issues at all levels of the system in our clinical thinking and treatment. The use of a genogram to identify and track patterns, resources, and problems over the generations cannot be overemphasized. The genogram, a three- or four-generation map of a family, is a major tool for organizing the complex information on family patterns throughout the life cycle (McGoldrick, 1995). Doing a genogram is not a one-session task but a perpetual exploration. Cultural genograms (Congress, 1994; Hardy & Laszloffy, 1995; McGoldrick, Giordano, & Pearce, 1996) map a family's race, ethnicity, migration history, religious heritage, social class, and important cultural issues. A family chronology and a sociogram, a map of the social network of a person or family, are other useful tools to use for family assessment (Carter & McGoldrick, 1999).

Stages of Change

Change is a process that unfolds over time (Hubble, Duncan, & Miller, 1999). The transtheoretical model (TTM) is called a stages-of-change model. It is based on six stages of change and related processes of change that characterize each stage: precontemplation, contemplation, preparation, action, and termination (Prochaska, 1995). Consequently, the model implies ordering or sequence (Sutton, 1996). (See Box 3.1 for additional information.)

In the TTM, change moves in a linear manner. However, cautioned Prochaska (1995), linear progress in the stage model is a relatively rare phenomenon.

The stages-of-change model can be applied to help many more people at each phase of therapy, treatment, or other planned intervention. The five phases include recruitment, retention, progress, process, and outcomes (Hubble, Duncan, & Miller, 1999, p. 232).

With patients in earlier stages of change, therapists can enhance progress through more experiential processes that produce healthier cognitions, emotions, evaluations, decisions, and commitments (Hubble et al., 1999, p. 244). People in precontemplation are likely to have the poorest expectations for change and for therapy. Individuals in this stage will show the poorest outcomes following therapy. They are most at risk of dropping out quickly and inappropriately unless therapists are trained to match strategies to their stage, such as dropout prevention strategies.

Core Qualities Needed by Family Social Workers

Profound differences were discovered in therapists' success with the patients in their case load. Luborsky and others (1985) found that the differences in outcome between therapists could be attributed to a number of interactional variables. Three therapist qualities distinguished the more helpful from the less helpful therapists: (1) the therapist's adjustment, skill, and interest in helping patients; (2) the purity of the treatment she offered; and (3) the quality of the therapist/patient relationship. Reviewers are virtually unanimous in their opinion that the therapist–patient relationship is critical to positive outcome. According to Wampold (2001), there is strong evidence for a "contextual model" of therapy, and this model relies heavily on common factors as agents of change. The common factors most frequently studied are those identified by the client-centered school as "necessary and sufficient conditions" for patient personality change: accurate empathy, positive regard, nonpossessive warmth, and congruence or genuineness (Lambert, 2003).

Research consistently supports the importance of the social worker's capacity to demonstrate empathy, warmth, and genuineness (Beutler, Machado, & Allstetter-Neufelt, 1994). These help the social worker to establish a climate of trust and safety in which family members can begin to view their problems in new ways (Lambert & Bergin, 1994).

Empathy is a core ingredient in establishing and developing relationships with clients. Social workers need to maintain empathy with individuals and respect for the family's way of doing things. Family social work "starts where the client is," even when the client's perspective eventually needs to be challenged (Collins, Jordan, & Coleman, 1999). Empathy can be expressed at different levels of depth and effectiveness. According to Truax and Carkhuff (1967), the highest level of empathy is when the social worker gives accurate responses to all of the client's deeper and surface feelings. The social worker is "tuned in" to the client, making it possible for the two to explore very deeply different aspects of the client's existence. The following procedure has been developed to help in creating empathy statements:

1. "It seems like you feel . . ."
2. Feeling label
3. Place the feeling in a context
4. Make the tense of the feeling *here and now*
5. Check it out for accuracy

Nonpossessive warmth is another important factor in the relationship between the social worker and client. Warmth exists when the social worker communicates with clients in ways that convey acceptance, understanding, and interest in their well-being and make them feel safe regardless of such external factors as the client's problematic behavior, demeanor, or appearance (Sheafor, Horejsi, & Horejsi, 1997). It is largely displayed nonverbally (e.g., Collins et al., 1999, p. 118).

The quality of *genuineness* is perhaps the most difficult to describe. It refers to a lack of defensiveness or artificiality in the social worker's communications with the client. Genuineness is communicated through spontaneity and authenticity, and facilitates building a relationship with the client (Dubois & Miley, 2005).

Guidelines for Effective Interviews   Basic interviewing skills needed by family social workers include the following (Collins, et al., 1999):

- Listening carefully to expressed family meanings
- Being sensitive to verbal and nonverbal communication about desires and goals from each family member
- Recognizing family difficulties related to effective problem solving
- Promoting skills, knowledge, attitudes, and environmental conditions that contribute to effective family coping

The following guidelines can help social workers develop professional relationships with clients (adapted from Kadushin & Kadushin, 1997):

- An interview is deliberate.
- The content of an interview is related to an explicit purpose.
- The family social worker has the primary responsibility for the content and direction of the interview.
- Relationships are structured and time limited.

Family Assessment Measures   Several measures are available to assess family functioning. Some of the best family measures include the following:

- FACES IV (http://www.facesiv.com)
- Index of Family Relations (Hudson, 1982)
- The Family Assessment Measure (Skinner, et al., 2000)

- The McMaster Family Assessment Device (Epstein, Baldwin, & Bishop, 1982)
- The Moos Family Environment Scales (FES) (Moos, 1989)
- The Self-Report Family Inventory (SFI) (Beavers & Hampson, 2000)

FACES IV, The Family Assessment Measure, and The Self-Report Family Inventory are reviewed in this chapter and make excellent tools for assessment and outcome evaluations with families.

SUMMARY

Our concern in this chapter has been to further the understanding of the nature of beginning treatment and the social worker's role in it. Treatment that promotes change in any family member or any set of interactions may be considered family treatment, since it will upset family balance. Conjoint family interviews may be used in treatment but are not synonymous with treatment. A variety of modes of involving family members is possible. Criteria for worker decisions about whom to involve and how to involve them have been suggested.

The social worker's task in the initial stages of contact with family members is twofold. The first task is to come to an understanding of the nature of the problem presented by the family and of the nature of the family's difficulty in solving the problem. This assessment effort is concurrent with the worker's second task of engaging family members in the treatment effort. Engagement is complex because different family members may disagree about both definition of the problem and solutions to it, and they may also differ in their willingness to participate in working at solutions. The section on engaging the family delineates worker activity pertinent to both of these tasks.

While the section on beginning treatment focuses on procedures, we have also considered some of the ways in which the social worker's knowledge about family systems is used in assessment and in the worker's contract with the family for further treatment.

DISCUSSION QUESTIONS

1. Describe two assessment instruments a social worker can use to assess families in the beginning of treatment. What do they measure? Describe some pros and cons of using these types of assessment tools.
2. What does the research tell us about matching clients to treatments?
3. Describe the stages of change and why this information might be useful to know in the beginning stages of treatment.

References

Beavers, W. R. 2002, April 9. *The Beavers System Model of Family Assessment.* Paper presented at the 2002 Conference of the International Academy of Family Psychology. Abstract retrieved May 6, 2003, from http://www.iafpsy.org/

Beavers, W. R., and Hampson, R. B. 2000. "The Beavers Systems Model of Family Functioning." *Journal of Family Therapy* 22(2):128–33.

Bedi, R. P. 2001. "Prescriptive Psychotherapy: Alternatives to Diagnosis." *Journal of Psychotherapy in Independent Practice* 2(2):39–60.

Berg, I. K., and de Shazer, S. 1993. "Making Numbers Talk: Language in Ther-apy." In *The New Language of Change: Constructive Collaboration in Psychotherapy,* ed. S. Friedman. New York: Guilford Press.

Beutler, L. E., and Clarkin, J. 1990. *Systematic Treatment Selection: Toward Targeted Therapeutic Interventions.* New York: Brunner/Mazel.

Beutler, L. E., Machado, P. P. P., and Allstetter-Neufeldt, S. 1994. "Therapist Variables." In *Handbook of Psychotherapy and Behavior Change* (pp. 229–69), eds. A. E. Bergin and S. L. Garfield. New York: John Wiley.

Beutler, L. E., Moleiro, C., Malik, M., and Harwood, T. M. 2000, June. *The UC Santa Barbara Study of Fitting Therapy to Patients: First Results.* Paper presented at the annual meeting of the Society for Psychotherapy Research, Chicago.

Bowen, M. 1978. *Family Therapy in Clinical Practice.* New York: Jason Aronson.

Carter, B., and McGoldrick, M. 1999. *The Expanded Family Life Cycle.* Boston: Allyn & Bacon.

Cirillo, S., and DiBlasio, P. 1992. *Families That Abuse.* New York: W. W. Norton.

Collins, D., Jordan, C., and Coleman, H. 1999. *An Introduction to Family Social Work.* Itasca, IL: F. E. Peacock.

Congress, E. P. 1994. "The Use of Culturagrams to Assess and Empower Culturally Diverse Families." *Families in Society* 75(9):531–40.

Cormier, W. H., and Cormier, L. S. 1985. *Interviewing Strategies for Helpers,* 2nd edition. Monterey, CA: Brooks/Cole.

De Jong, P., and Berg, I. K. 2001. "Co-Constructing Cooperation with Mandated Clients." *Social Work* 46(4):361–74.

de Shazer, S. 1994. *Words Were Originally Magic.* New York: W. W. Norton.

DuBois, B. L., and Miley, K. K. 2005. "Empowering Processes for Social Work Practice." In *Social Work: An Empowering Process* (5th ed., pp. 197–224), eds. B. L. Dubois and K. K. Miley. Boston: Allyn & Bacon.

Epstein, N. B., Baldwin, L. M., and Bishop, D. S. 1982. *McMaster Family Assessment Device (FAD) Manual.* Version 3. Providence, RI: Brown University/Butler Hospital Family Research Program.

Franklin, C., and Streeter, C. L. 1993. "Validity of the 3-D Circumplex Model for Family Assessment." *Research on Social Work Practice* 3(3):258–75.

Graham, G. H. 2003. "Role Preparation in Brief Strategic Therapy: The Welcome Letter." *Journal of Systemic Therapies* 22:1, 3–14.

Hardy, K. V., and Laszloffy, T. A. 1995. "The Cultural Genogram: Key to Training Culturally Competent Family Therapists." *Journal of Marital and Family Therapy* 21:227–37.

Hubble, M. A., Duncan, B. L., and Miller, S. D. 1999. *The Heart and Soul of Change.* Washington, DC: APA Press.

Hudson, W. W. 1982. *The Clinical Measurement Package: A Field Manual.* Chicago: Dorsey Press.

———. 1992. *Index of Family Relations.* Walmyr Assessment Scales. Tallahassee, FL.

Jordan, C., and Franklin, C. 2003. *Clinical Assessment for Social Workers.* 2nd edition. Chicago: Lyceum Press.

Kadushin, A., and Kadushin, G. 1997. *The Social Work Interview.* 4th edition. New York: Columbia University Press.

Lambert, M. J. (Ed.) 2003. *Bergin and Garfield's Handbook of Psychotherapy and Behavior Change.* 5th edition. New York: Wiley.

Lambert, M. J., and Bergin, A. E. 1994. "The Effectiveness of Psychotherapy." In *Handbook of Psychotherapy and Behavior Change* (4th ed., pp. 143–89), eds. A. E. Bergin and S. L. Garfield. New York: Wiley.

Lazarus, A. A. 1992. "The Multimodal Approach to the Treatment of Minor Depression." *American Journal of Psychotherapy* 46:50–57.

Lazarus, M. 1989. "Why I Am an Eclectic." *British Journal of Guidance & Counselling* 17(3):248–58.

Life Innovations. 2004. *Overview of the FACES IV Package.* Retrieved April 4, 2005, from http://www.facesiv.com/

Luborsky, L., McLellan, A. T., Woody, G. E., O'Brien, C. P., and Auerbach, A. 1985. "Therapist Success and Its Determinants." *Archives of General Psychiatry* 42(6):602–11.

McGoldrick, M. 1995. *You Can Go Home Again: Reconnecting with Your Family.* New York: W. W. Norton.

McGoldrick, M., and Gerson, R. 1985. *Genograms in Family Assessment.* New York: W. W. Norton.

McGoldrick, M., Giordana, J., and Pearce, J. K. 1996. *Ethnic and Family Therapy.* New York: Guilford Press.

Moos, R. H. 1989. *Family Environment Scale (FES) Dimensions and Subscales.* Palo Alto, CA: Consulting Psychologist Press.

Norcross, J. C., and Prochaska, J. O. 2002. "Using the Stages of Change." *Harvard Mental Health Letter* 18(11):5–7.

Prochaska, J. O. 1995. "An Eclectic and Integrative Approach: Transtheoretical Therapy." In *Essential Psychotherapies: Theory and Practice,* eds. A. S. Gurman and S. B. Messer, pp. 403–40. New York: Guilford Press.

Prochaska, J., and DiClemente, C. 1992. "The Transtheoretical Approach." In *Handbook of Psychotherapy Integration,* ed. J. C. Norcross, pp. 300–34. New York: Basic Books, Inc.

Project Match Research Group. 1998. "Therapist Effects in Three Treatments for Alcohol Problems." *Psychotherapy Research* 8:455–74.

Satir, V. 1983. *Conjoint Family Therapy.* Palo Alto, CA: Science and Behavior Books.

Shapiro, D., Barkham, M., Ress, A., Hardy, G. E., Reynolds, S., and Startup, M. 1994. "Effects of Treatment Duration and Severity of Depression on the Effectiveness of Cognitive/Behavioural and Psychodynamic/Interpersonal Psychotherapy." *Journal of Consulting and Clinical Psychology* 62:422–534.

Sheafor, B. W., Horejsi, C. R., and Horejsi, G. A. 1997. *Techniques and Guidelines for Social Work Practice.* 4th edition. Boston: Allyn & Bacon.

Skinner, E. 1995. *Motivation, Coping and Control.* Newbury, CA: Sage.

Skinner, H. J., Steinhauer, P., and Sitarenios, G. 2000. "Family Assessment Measure (FAM) and Process Model of Family Functioning." *Journal of Family Therapy* 22(2):190–210.

Steinhauer, P. D. 1984. "Clinical Applications of the Process Model of Family Functioning." *Canadian Journal of Psychiatry* 29:98–111.

Sutton, S. 1996. "Further Support for the Stages of Change Model?" *Addictions* 91:1287–89.

Truax, C. B., and Carkhuff, R. R. 1967. *Toward Effective Counselling: Training and Practice.* New York: Aldine.

Wampold, B. E. 2001. "Contextualizing Psychotherapy as a Healing Practice: Culture, History, and Methods." *Applied & Preventive Psychology* 10(2): 69–86.

Worden, M. 1994. *Family Therapy Basics.* Belmont, CA: Brooks/Cole Publishing Co.

Evidence-Based Intervention Strategies

PART 2

INTRODUCTION

Part II consists of nine chapters focused on intervening with families in order to change dysfunctional patterns of interaction. In this part, the theory and concepts presented in Part I are operationalized in work with specific populations. However, the populations we have chosen to discuss by no means form a definitive group, and their inclusion does not imply preference with regard to other populations seen in family treatment. They simply represent a sampling of the kinds of families and family problems that social workers encounter in contemporary practice. The choices resulted from our own practice experiences, discussions with practitioners in social work agencies, and information provided by students in field work placements. Each chapter has a similar structure: Introduction, Population Description and Definitions, Assessment Issues, Evidence-Based Treatment/Best Practices, Treatment Manual, Case Example, Summary, Questions for Class Discussion, and References.

Chapter 4 addresses the problems of single-parent families and the techniques used in treating this population. The stages through which the family passes in transition from a two-parent to a one-parent family are discussed, together with specific strategies for intervention during the transition period. This chapter also focuses on important assessment criteria for single-parent households, including parental stress and child issues such as poor school performance, feelings of loss, conduct, and other adjustment disorders.

Chapter 5 focuses on the shifting roles of adult children and their aging parents, as well as the difficulties encountered when adult children must take a major role in decision making relative to the welfare of their parents. We look at existing attitudes toward the older members of society and the process of aging as conceptualized in theory. We discuss the significance of earlier parent-child relationships and lifestyles of the parents, and explore problems encountered in engaging the family that is composed of adult children and their parents. The impact of role reversal, spouse–parent relationships, and adult sibling relationships and how to deal with them are also examined. Also examined are the areas of caregiving burden, caregiving roles, and elder abuse.

Chapter 6 addresses the problems of families living in poverty and the techniques for treating this population in contemporary society. The emphasis is on shaping the structure and functioning of these families' needs. The uniqueness of this type of family in relation to communication, rules, and expectations is highlighted. Procedures for intervening with the problem poverty family are discussed, with emphasis on the value of home visits, working with extended-family members, and maintaining a suitable climate for effective intervention. Treatments will focus on multiple levels of social support, housing and other needed resources, children's school performance problems, and parents.

Chapter 7 discusses mental illness in the family and the experiences of family members in coping with this problem. We introduce the use of a psychoeducational approach in treating family and patient, and explain the role of the social worker as the therapist. A list of resources, such as the Alliance for Mental Illness, is included.

Chapter 8 focuses on AIDS and other terminal illnesses. Different classes of chronic illness are identified, including AIDS, pediatric illness, and other adult problems. Evidence-based treatments tend toward the educational models; the new area of health promotions is introduced.

Chapter 9 deals with the treatment of families involved in cases of child abuse and other family violence. We develop an understanding of the abusing parent and of the necessity of addressing the unmet needs of parents who abuse their children. We note the importance of establishing a relationship between worker and parents that attends less to placing blame for the abuse than on assisting change, as well as involving the abused child in treatment. Attention is drawn to violence that may be occurring among other members of the family, especially the parents, and the importance of attending to that as well. Also, emphasis is given to the use of risk factors to inform treatment options as well as to the role of explanations and hypothesis testing in treating traumatized and abused children (Munson, 2004). Other family violence, particularly spouse abuse, will address the debate between experts as to whether gender-specific treatment is superior to conjoint therapy. Promising, though untested, models (Sprenkle, 2005) also are presented.

Chapter 10 describes treatment of families with alcohol- and other substance-abusing members. Much attention is focused on the alcoholism of the adult male. Treatment procedures for alcoholic women and substance-abusing children are also introduced. The chapter includes discussion of the faith-based literature and raises issues about its helpfulness. We talk about Teen Challenge/World Challenge as an example of a faith-based program and discuss how they work with families. Also, we discuss a NIDA study on this program and cite Clay Shorkey's research.

Chapter 11 focuses on the family as it struggles through the process of dissolution, culminating in divorce. The phases of family dissolution and the impact of social forces on the break-up of the family are discussed. A variety of issues that must be addressed by both family members and social workers engaged by them in effecting change are also presented. We offer information on how to help people who choose to divorce, how to set up a structured separation, and how to help people work through emotional divorce. Sprenkle has done some work in this relatively new area of study. Chapter 12 is concerned with remarriage after divorce or widowhood and the adjustment of the reconstituted family created by this union. We view the reconstituted family from a systems perspective and discuss various family patterns. The problems that reconstituted families are likely to encounter, the adjustments necessary for satisfactory functioning, and some suggestions for treatment are included in this chapter. Sprenkle's (2005) phases of divorce adjustment include a post-divorce phase that is discussed here. The Vishers (1990) are probably the best-known name in recommending techniques for stepfamilies; however, much new research has been done since 1990, and that research is described and evaluated. Resources are presented from organizations such as the Stepfamily Association of America. These groups provide educational resources, support groups, and other programs and services.

Evidence-Based Treatment of Families Headed by a Single Parent

The number of families headed by one parent, usually referred to as single-parent families, has increased dramatically. This chapter presents some of the characteristics of single-parent families, assessment issues they present, and strategies for intervention.

POPULATION DESCRIPTION AND DEFINITIONS

"A single-parent family consists of one parent and one or more children. The parent can be either male or female and can be single as a result of the death of a partner, divorce, desertion, or never having been married. A growing number of single parents are single by choice" (Oken, cited in Collins, Jordan, & Coleman, 1999, p. 24). Collins and others (1999) found that 45 percent of all children in the United States live in a single-parent home at some time during their childhood years. Additionally, a concern is that these children exhibit more problems than do children living with two parents; these problems include conduct disorders, attention deficit disorder, poor school performance, and emotional problems (p. 77).

Many reasons have been given for the increase in this form of family organization, including changing views toward marriage and divorce. For example, cohabitation of male and female partners without a legally sanctioned marriage and the bearing of children by single women no longer draw the condemnation of society that was once all but assured. Similarly, divorce is sought and received by legally married couples at an unprecedented rate and without the disapproval such action would have drawn in the not-too-distant past. And the bearing of children by unmarried women and adolescent girls, who are faced with the necessity of functioning as single parents, is a fairly common occurrence. Whether we accept these actions as causative factors or reject them as too simplistic, professionals who provide services to families frequently encounter the family headed by one adult or by an adolescent female.

Because the status of single-parent family is acquired in a variety of ways, it may present different sets of problems. A family headed by one parent may be the result of a divorce; the death of one parent; desertion or disappearance of a parent; or the birth of a child to an unmarried adult or adolescent. The head of the family in each of these situations is usually a female; however, this is not always the case. Included in the one-parent family organization is a relatively new component, the single-parent father. The number of fathers raising children alone has increased in recent years. Some of the increase is believed to be due to the women's movement, which has enabled many women to achieve social and economic benefits commensurate with those available to men. This provides women with ways to define themselves in roles outside the home, unrelated to raising children (Greif, 1986). These advances sometimes place mothers in a more favorable position than fathers to provide economic support for the children at the time of divorce. It is possible, in some cases, that this might impact the courts' decisions in favor of fathers who petition for custody of children. Of course, this is not the only reason fathers receive custody. It is awarded for other reasons, including mutual consent of both parents.

In spite of the growing number of one-parent families, the literature does not reflect the same therapeutic attention to this group as that given to the two-parent family. Next we will review some of the assessment issues to consider in designing a treatment plan, including the route to becoming a single parent, and internal and external systems issues.

ASSESSMENT ISSUES

These families in transition experience several problems. The route to becoming a single parent, and internal and external systems' issues form the basis of our assessment; recommended assessment tools will link up with the interventions presented in the final section of the chapter.

The Route to Becoming a Single Parent

Typical problems experienced by single-parent families are economic difficulties, stress, fatigue, and child adjustment problems; however, level of maternal education appears to ameliorate some of these stressors (Collins et al., 1999, p. 77). The route to becoming a single parent is varied. Those reviewed here include divorce, death of a spouse, and adolescent single parents.

Divorce   The breaking up of a family brings many different reactions from those involved. "Divorce is a life crisis that requires adjustment by all family members" (Collins et al., 1999, p. 74). Parents may engage in disruptive behavior toward each other, impacting the children who frequently blame themselves for the parents' divorce (Thomas & Rudolph, cited in Collins et al., 1999). While the granting of divorce through the court legally terminates the marital relationship, this may not be an accomplished fact. Symptomatic behavior of a child may be indicative of the parents' desire to continue the relationship. This is present in the situation in which divorced parents seem always to find a reason to remain involved around some aspect of a child's behavior or what a child needs from the noncustodial parent. For example, a mother may express her inability to cope with her son's behavior and ask her divorced husband to visit and discipline the boy, which continues a relationship between the parents. Tasks for family members are to make the decision to divorce, plan for the dissolution of the marriage and separation, go through the steps of going to court and divorcing, mourn their losses, and rebuild their lives and relationships with others (Collins et al., 1999).

Death of a Spouse   The process of becoming single through the death of a spouse differs from that caused by divorce. One similarity of the two is that children may be equally traumatized by losing a parent through either divorce or death (Eichler, cited in Collins et al., 1999). However, differences are that widows are less likely to have a dramatic drop in income, are less likely to remarry, and are more likely to keep in contact with in-laws and other supports than are divorced parents (Collins et al., 1999).

Adolescent Single Parents   The adolescent single parent presents a somewhat different picture than the adult single parent. She is almost always still living with her parents and is not faced with problems of divorce or the need to mourn the loss of a husband. Most of her problems are family related, as reflected in the interaction she has with her family en route to a single parenthood. A state of crisis is precipitated by the adolescent's pregnancy. Intense emotion and conflict may surface around this experience, and several solutions to the problems brought on by the pregnancy are likely to be considered, including the possibility of abortion. As the state of crisis gradually subsides and the family becomes more accepting of the pending birth of the child, a more positive attitude will follow. Living arrangements, care for the baby, financial support, and continuing the adolescent's education become the primary focus of attention (Jemail & Nathanson, 1987). As a result of this positive attitude, the adolescent becomes closer to the family and spends more time at home and less time with peers. This change of behavior is rewarded by the family, who sees her as more mature, affectionate, and understanding.

Following the birth of the child, conflict may resurface around issues of childcare. As efforts are undertaken to determine who is responsible for what care, the role of the adolescent single parent is also further clarified. If the family is functioning well, nurturance of the child becomes their primary concern.

However, if the family is not functioning well, family members may detour negative feelings through their interaction with the child (Jemail & Nathanson, 1987). In this case, professional help is usually required to return the family to an acceptable level of functioning.

When working with adolescent single parents and their families, Weltner (1986) suggests that professionals are well advised to use interventions that match the families' particular level of functioning. For example, sometimes a family has difficulty in managing resources, in which case it is unlikely that the basic needs (food, shelter, medical care, etc.) of the adolescent mother and the nurturance needs of her child will be met. The helping professional must then determine who in the existing social network has resources and can assume the executive role in meeting these needs. If no one in the client's social network can meet this requirement, it may be necessary in some situations to seek shelter in a public-supported facility until assistance can be mobilized.

In another situation, the family may be able to meet basic needs but unable to provide structure and the necessary limits. Enabling efforts in this case should focus on clarifying expectations. This might include assigning specific tasks to each family member and assessing the adolescent's developmental level as it relates to her need for structure, limits, and safety. The family should be organized around these needs, which will allow the adolescent single parent to continue her education and contacts with friends.

When the family provides most of what is required to nurture and protect the adolescent single parent and her child but differences and dissatisfactions still exist, professionals should examine the boundary structure within the family. If boundaries are blurred, are too rigid, or show signs of boundary violations, interventions should focus on defending individual and subsystem boundaries and developing generational boundaries where indicated (Weltner, 1982).

Internal Systems Issues

The single-parent family usually passes through a number of predictable phases on the way to readjusting to its new status. Morawetz and Walker (1984) and Korittko (1991) have identified these phases: reaction to a changing family situation, reordering of family members' priorities, settling down to a new lifestyle, separation and parents/children gaining independence, and unresolved mourning. In making the transition to single parenthood, parents experience their own personal problems of adjustment, as do children. This potentially stressful situation may cause parent–child conflict as well.

Parent Problems   Single parents face multiple problems in their attempts to maintain family life for their children. Economic deprivation may be a real problem, as well as other stressors and conflicts. Newly single parents may have varied psychological reactions depending on their feelings about the divorce, ranging from relief to anger, depression or guilt. Granvold (2002) discusses the consequence of divorce on newly single spouses, including dealing with the loss, redefining self, and questioning one's self-worth. He also mentions possible health ramifications, including increased alcohol or drug use, loneliness, oversleep, overexercise, overinvestment of time at work, and all-consuming grief.

Additionally, single parents often experience role overload as they must serve the roles of both parents. Newly single parents may experience multiple stresses while adapting to a new family style. This role overload may be expressed as family disorganization, social isolation, and problems in the parent–child relationship (Holman, cited in Collins et al., 1999, p. 77). Family disorganization may stem from living in new surroundings, requiring adaptation to new environmental conditions. The single parent may not have the economic, personal, or environmental supports he once had to help care for the home and the children. New skills in child and home management may be required.

Social isolation may be experienced by both parent and children, especially if they had to relocate. The social supports the parent once had may no longer be available to provide friendship, advice, and a helping hand. Extended family, as well as friends of the former couple, may feel the need to "take sides" with one parent or the other, particularly if the divorce was particularly bitter. Social isolation may result in depression, anger, or other intrapersonal problems for the parent. Also, if one parent, usually the wife, has not worked outside the home before, she may need help in connecting or reconnecting with the workforce.

Newly single parents who are unhappy and overwhelmed may not be able to parent their children adequately. They may need parent-training assistance or even individual counseling to resolve feelings of loss or guilt that may be affecting their relationship with their children.

Children as a Burden   Morawetz and Walker (1984) report that the dissolution of a marriage may force parents to take on roles different from their accustomed ones. For instance, a mother who has functioned primarily as a homemaker may have to enter the workplace in order to provide for the family. The mother (or father if he is the primary caretaker) may be too overwhelmed and overburdened to fully attend to the needs of the children because of conflicting role demands. The child may turn to some form of maladaptive behavior, such as performing poorly in school, truancy from school, running away from home, or even joining a gang, as a way of expressing his discomfort. When the adaptation to single parenthood is accomplished less traumatically, children may be viewed more positively by the parent and not perceived as a burden. When children's efforts to assist the custodial parent are accepted and rewarded, this can facilitate family adjustment.

For instance, consider the case of an older child who is able to help care for younger siblings. The reward for this activity may be elevation to an adult role in the single-parent family system, which in some ways replaces the noncustodial parent. While a new division of labor is necessary in moving from a two-parent to a one-parent family, allowing a child to fulfill the role of the absent parent must be handled with care. For example, if a child is given added responsibility to compensate for the absence of a parent as a temporary measure and is removed from this position and allowed to return to childhood activities commensurate with her age, it is unlikely that the experience will be seriously damaging. However, if such added responsibility becomes permanent and the child perceives the custodial parent as more needy than herself and moves beyond the caretaker role within the home to confront and respond to problems experienced by the parent from the outside world, the role becomes that of a "parental child." The parental child has abandoned her youth to become overly responsible for the family; she may lack interest in participating in age-appropriate activities and become alienated from peers by this lack of participation. The power of a parental child may also be seen in excessive efforts to control the behavior of siblings and, in some cases, the behavior of the parent with regard to social activities, such as going out with friends and dating (Morawetz & Walker, 1984). Helping professionals will find it very difficult for the parental child to give up the status and power of this position; however, immediate attention should be directed toward decreasing the responsibility of the parental child by returning the parent to the appropriate role of authority and the child to normal association with peers.

External Systems Issues

As seen in the preceding section, newly single parents may be overburdened by their increased responsibilities. This situation may be alleviated or exacerbated depending on external issues such as their economic situation and support systems.

Economic Hardship   Economic hardship is frequently experienced by the single-parent family. This is especially so with female-headed families in the early stages of transition. In an increasing number of cases, the financial well-being of the family is tied to the earnings of both parents. When one parent leaves the home, family income can be seriously diminished. A lack of financial resources can cause a ripple effect with regard to meeting the needs of family members. For example, a custodial parent's inability to provide a child with the necessary resources to continue participating in activities with peers or to purchase clothing in the manner previously experienced can seriously impact the child's feeling of self-esteem. This loss of self-esteem may be reflected in withdrawal behavior, diminished school performance, or disruptive behavior at school and in the home. Additionally, the custodial parent may feel a hardship due to increasing role responsibilities but with less time and less money (Collins et al., 1999). For instance, the single mother who must return to work must maintain the children and the family home, performing the roles of father, mother, primary caretaker, and home manager. With adequate income, some of these problems could be alleviated by the ability to purchase outside help (e.g., cleaning, mowing the lawn). Most single parents do not have this luxury, however.

BOX 4.1	**Cultural Differences**

DeGenova and Rice (2005) review 2000 U.S. Census data to conclude that while all ethnicities are experiencing a rise in single-parent families, African American single-parent families are experiencing far more of this growth than are other groups. Approximately half of all African American children live in one-parent families, compared with 17 percent of Caucasian children and 23 percent of Hispanic children. This phenomenon is due to the high rate of births to unmarried mothers. DeGenova and Rice (2005) cite Smith (1993) and Fine (1992) as attributing this trend to several factors, including poverty, high rates of unprotected intercourse among teens, and African American male unemployment and underemployment. Also, high divorce rates are believed to be a contributing factor (Norton and Moorman, cited in DeGenova and Rice, 2005). The increase in single parenthood, particularly in African American mother–headed families, is problematic because these single mothers experience more poverty and longer spells of welfare receipt than those in other family styles (Franklin et al., cited in DeGenova & Rice, 2005).

Grandparents and Other Support Systems   "Female-headed single-parent families are disproportionately represented among low-income groups" (Collins et al., 1999, p. 77). A lack of sufficient financial resources can also force a financially strapped single parent to return to her family of origin. Although well intentioned, this can lead to additional problems if the grandparents see the mother's return with her children as a sign of weakness and relate to the mother as incapable of carrying adult responsibility. Single parents reportedly experience social isolation, having lost not only their spouse but friends and other supports as well (Collins et al., 1999). If a newly single parent must move to a new house or a new neighborhood, the parent and the children may experience isolation and sadness at the changing environmental situation.

EVIDENCE-BASED TREATMENT/BEST PRACTICES

To sum up the preceding section on issues of newly single parents, Collins and colleagues (1999) list the tasks of this group to help inform our choice of assessment tools and plan for treatment at both the internal and external family systems levels. These tasks are as follows:

1. Resolve feelings of sadness, anger, and loneliness.
2. Cope with stress, fatigue, and role overload without taking it out on the children.
3. Develop time management skills that allow for meeting children's and personal needs.
4. Develop child management skills that do not result in anger directed at the children.
5. Develop adequate social support systems. (pp. 77–78)

Information received in the beginning sessions of therapy with the single-parent family may result in the need to involve the extended family and/or the non-custodial parent in treatment. In some cases, meeting with individual family members may also be appropriately undertaken. However, meeting separately with individual family members must always be undertaken with a great deal of care in order to maintain the proper balance in the therapeutic relationship. After the first interview with the single-parent family, the way in which the therapist proceeds is determined by the existing problems. Also, new problems are likely to surface as interviews continue, and new goals must be established and new interventions undertaken (Haley, 1991). The following are suggested assessment tools, followed by interventions for internal and external family systems problems.

Assessment Tools

An *ecomap* is a good starting place to get a sense of the new single-parent family and the environmental context. An ecomap charts the immediate family members, as does a genogram, but maps important environmental supports, resources, and conflicts around each family member. The practitioner can draw the map while initially interviewing the family. This will help the practitioner to narrow down on specific family issues and then to choose corresponding measurement instruments. Some examples of measures for internal family issues are the Loneliness Rating Scale (Scalise et al., cited in Corcoran & Fischer, 2000, p. 436), the Parent–Child Relationship Inventory (Fine et al., cited in Corcoran & Fischer, 2000, p. 416), and the Social Support Index (McCubbin et al., cited in Corcoran & Fischer, 2000, p. 446). These measures and many others, especially useful for a single-subject approach to practice, may be found in Corcoran and Fischer's *Measures for Clinical Practice,* published in 2000. See Table 4.1 for other examples.

Interventions for Internal Family Systems Problems

Intrapersonal Interventions for the Parent   The single-parent family seeks help in the same manner and for many of the same reasons as the two-parent family. Contact with the therapist is usually initiated by the parent as a result of some type of disruption in the way the family wishes to present itself to the outside world or because someone in the outside world expects a different presentation than that given by the family. The initial contact may come because the parent requires help with his own problems.

Cognitive Therapy for Unresolved Mourning and Post-Divorce Recovery Cognitive techniques such as relabeling, reframing, and goal setting may be employed to help with faulty thinking about the relationship, and for helping the single parent to move forward. The following are examples of themes:

1. Dedicate efforts to the evolution of "possible selves" consistent with the revisioning of one's life.
2. Establish a quality relationship with children.

Table 4.1 | Assessment Instruments

Measure	Description	Reliability	Validity	Source
The Loneliness Rating Scale (LRS)	A 404-item tool measuring affective components of loneliness in two parts: Part A measures the frequency of certain affects and Part B measures the intensity of these.	Internal consistency reliability: .82–.85	Moderate concurrent validity: .25–.46	Fine & Schwebel, 1983
Parent–Child Relationship Survey (PCRS)	A 24-item instrument measuring adults' perceptions of their relationship with their child.	Excellent internal consistency: .89–.94	Good known-groups and predictive validity, discriminates between children of divorced vs. intact families.	McCubbin et al., 1996
Social Support Index (SSI)	Measures the degree to which families find support in their communities.	Very good internal consistency: .82	Good concurrent validity when correlated with a criterion of family well-being, and predictor of resilience and coping.	
The Beck Depression Inventory (BDI)	A 21-item self-administered questionnaire designed to measure depressive symptoms; age range: 13–80; time required: 5–10 minutes.	Test–retest reliability: .48–.86	Content, discriminant, and convergent validity	Beck, Steer, & Brown (1996)
The Hamilton Rating Scale for Depression (HAMD)	A 17-item scale designed to measure the severity of depression symptoms.	Test–retest reliability: .65–.96	Concurrent and discriminant validity	Hamilton (1960)

3. Develop an effective parallel parenting relationship with the ex-spouse.
4. Gain closure on the marriage by grieving and emotionally accepting that it is over.
5. Promote efficacy expectations regarding present and future life satisfaction.
6. Generate rejuvenation goals across various categories of life (e.g., career, hobbies).
7. Seek intimate connectedness with others through clear delineation of partner/relationship qualities, active pursuit, deliberate relationship evaluation, and proactive decision making to terminate or maintain the relationship(s). (Granvold, 2002, pp. 588–89)

Stress and Time Management Granvold (2002) mentions the benefit of stress management techniques during the transition to single parenthood. For instance, he suggests limiting alcohol/drug usage, checking excessive investment in work, deep muscle relaxation, and healthy exercise (p. 588). Time management involves setting goals, delegating responsibilities (e.g., children can help with tasks), developing and making use of outside helpers, and using cognitive techniques to build self-confidence and self-esteem (Jordan & Cobb, 2001).

Parent Training Single parents may have trouble with their children without the second parent available to help with discipline. Corcoran (2002) described components of successful behavioral parent training programs.
1. Training parents in close monitoring of their teen's activities, since lack of supervision has been associated with conduct problems.
2. Teaching parents to have involvement with the school to monitor homework and attendance, activities which were specified on a behavioral contract and subject to rewards and punishments.
3. Teaching parents to give alternative punishments to time-out, including loss of points, restriction of free time, grounding, and work details.
4. Giving parents relevant educational materials (e.g., on topics like ADHD).
5. Adjunctive, supportive intervention to parents was offered to combat depression and lack of social support, which may inhibit effective parent management. (pp. 794–95)

Interpersonal Intervention for the Family and/or the Children   The parent may initiate contact with the therapist to get help for herself; however, this is far less frequent than help-seeking around difficulties experienced by a child. Typical situations include (1) the mother no longer feels able to manage a child's inappropriate behavior, (2) the school pressures the mother to seek help because the child's adjustment within the school is unsatisfactory, or (3) the child's behavior may have brought him into contact with law enforcement agents and the parent must get help if the child is to remain in the home.

Unresolved Mourning   If children have not mourned their losses, once the remaining parent has overcome his resistance to mourning, he will be in a better position to help them. The therapist may then help him become more sensitive to the children's needs and encourage him to talk with them about their feelings of loss and share with them memories of the deceased parent (Fulmer, 1987, p. 35). Nevertheless, mourning alone is usually not enough to bring complete relief of family symptoms. In addition to unresolved mourning, these symptoms have other contributing causes that must be considered. For example, if depression is experienced, medication is likely to be required; delinquent behavior might be helped by strengthening the executive functioning of the parent as head of the family; and if drug abuse is involved, a period of detoxification and group treatment will be needed. These and other measures may be required to restore the troubled single-parent family to effective functioning.

Unresolved Parental Mourning   Reid (2000) reviews the literature related to grief and loss experienced by adults. Treatment suggestions include helping the parent to do the following:

1. Begin to actively mourn the death by confirming its reality; it may help to recount the circumstance surrounding the death.
2. Identify, recognize and express the emotion and pain of grief.
3. Recall memories of the deceased.
4. Reduce stress by repeated mild exposure to grief-inducing stimuli (e.g., pictures) until the distress at exposure decreases.
5. Acquire new living skills, pursue activities, and develop relationships to promote independence (practitioner may use role-play, imagery, etc. to accomplish).
6. If grief is anticipatory (e.g., loved one has been diagnosed with a terminal illness), help each work through feelings about the impending death and loss. (pp.157–58)

Reid also suggests interventions for children experiencing a loss of a loved one. Interventions include helping the child to do these things:

1. Create a memory box.
2. Draw a picture of self with the person who died and the rest of the family, then state feelings based on the picture.
3. Complete a list of what she knows and does not know about the deceased loved one in order to identify and eliminate magical or destructive thinking. (pp.158–59)

Interventions for External Family Systems Problems

Cognitive and ecologically based interventions are helpful with the external systems problems single-parent families experience, for example, trouble with relatives and friends, or need for connections in the larger environment.

Granvold (2002) suggests the use of cognitive techniques to influence the following:

1. Use role-play to strategize informing children, family, and friends regarding the divorce.
2. Use cognitive rehearsal and reframing to facilitate and promote effective relationships with children, family, and friends. (p. 588)

A support group or other support (e.g., career counseling) for the parent may be useful in strengthening his feeling of competence in carrying out the executive functions of the family and reconnecting with the outside environment (Weltner, 1982). Support groups for the entire family or for children or adults grieving the death of a spouse are available as well. Jongsma and Dattilio (2000) have additional treatment suggestions for single-parent families helping their child members:

1. Suggest specific coping mechanisms for dealing with the defined fears and concerns (living with one parent and visiting the other on weekends, having less money to live on, etc.) such as open communication between the parents regarding the children, everyone pledging to sacrifice together financially, or holding periodic family meetings to exchange views.
2. Help the family members to identify support systems in the community as part of a coping mechanism (extended family, church groups, school services, etc.).
3. Hold a separate conjoint meeting with the biological parents to address any resentments or feelings that may be feeding the children's acting-out behaviors.
4. Role-play various social contexts with the children and help them process situations that they may encounter socially that relate to questions about the parents' separation/divorce.
5. Refer the children to support groups for children of divorce in school or through the local church or community. (pp. 262–69)

See Table 4.2 for research studies and Table 4.3 for examples of treatment manuals.

TREATMENT MANUAL

Social Competence Promotion for Youth is a manualized intervention for treatment for troubled youth (LeCroy, 2001). This program includes cognitive development, problem-solving, and social skills training. The social skills training component will be summarized here.

After goals are defined and skills selected by youth participating in the training in a group, the following seven steps are used to teach social skills:

1. The social skill to be taught is presented. The group leader presents the skill and asks if anyone can give an example. After responses are made, the leader provides the rationale for the skill, gives a situation where it might be used, and asks the group members for other reasons why the skill would be a good one to learn. An example is, "What does it mean to resist group pressure?"
2. The social skill is discussed. The group leader gives the steps of the social skill. Using resisting group pressure as an example, the skill steps are good

Table 4.2 | Research Studies

Parenting Treatment	Child/Adolescent Treatment	Adult Treatment	Family-Relationship Treatment
Parent Management (PMT)	Cognitive Behavioral (CBT)	Empirically Validated	Multisystemic Therapy (MST)
Recently divorced mothers (versus controls) experienced positive changes in parenting behaviors, linked with changes in child behaviors (DeGarmo, Forgatch, & Martinez, 1999).	Children receiving treatment (versus controls) showed improvement on multiple measures of anxiety, as well as social problems, aggression, hyperactivity, depression, and distress (Albano & Kendall, 2000).	Empirically validated, well-established treatments exist for a variety of problems, including anxiety and stress, depression, health problems, problems of childhood, and marital discord. Probably efficacious treatments are also listed (Chambless, 1998).	Reviews indicate that the benefits of MST versus other treatments are evidenced on parent and adolescent measures of parent and child psychopathology, family functioning and relationship, rearrest rates, severity of offenses, drug use, and reinstitutionalization. Additionally, MST is shown to be more cost effective than other efficacious treatments, such as functional family therapy, special foster care, and parent problem solving (Burns et al., 2000; Henggeler et al., 1998).

Table 4.3 | Treatment Manuals

Manual Reference	Author's Contact Information
Beck, A. T., Rush, A. J., Shaw, B. F., & Emery, G. 1979. *Cognitive Therapy of Depression*. New York: Guilford.	Cognitive Therapy Training Program Cognitive Therapy Center of New York 3 East 80th Street, New York, NY 10021 Telephone: 212-717-1052
Beck, A., Emery, G., & Greenberg, R. 1985. *Anxiety Disorders and Phobias: A Cognitive Perspective*. New York: Basic Books.	Beck Institute for Cognitive Therapy GSB Building—Suite 700 City Line & Belmont Avenues Bala Cynwyd, PA 19004 Telephone: 610-664-3020
Meichenbaum, D. 1994. *A Clinical Handbook/Practical Therapist Manual for Assessing and Treating Adults with Post-Traumatic Stress Disorder (PTSD)*. Waterloo, ON: Institute Press.	Donald Meichenbaum Department of Psychology University of Waterloo Waterloo, Ontario, Canada N2L 3G1 Telephone: 519-885-1211, ext. 2551
McFarlane, W. R., Deakins, S. M., Gingerich, S. L., Dunne, E., Hornen, B., & Newmark, M. 1991. *Multiple-Family Psychoeducational Group Treatment Manual*. New York: Biosocial Treatment Division, New York State Psychiatric Institute.	http://w3.ouhsc.edu/bpfamily/Detail/McFarlane.html
Sanders, M. R., & Dadds, M. R. 1993. *Behavioral Family Intervention*. Needham Heights, MA: Allyn & Bacon.	Allyn & Bacon 74 Arlinton St., Suite 300 Boston, MA 02116 Telephone: 617-848-6000
Multisystemic Family Therapy for Single Parent and Other Families	Dr. Scott W. Henggeler Family Services Research Center Department of Psychiatry and Behavioral Sciences Medical University of South Carolina 171 Ashley Avenue Charleston, SC 29425-0742 Telephone: 843-876-1800 Fax: 843-876-1808
Social Competence Promotion for Troubled Youth	Dr. Craig LeCroy Arizona State University School of Social Work 340 N. Commerce Park Loop, Suite 250 Tucson, AZ 85745-2700 Telephone: 520-884-5507, ext. 15 Fax: 520-884-5949 craig.lecroy@asu.edu http://ssw-tucson.asu.edu/

nonverbals (eye contact, saying "no," etc.), saying "no" early on, suggesting an alternative to the undesired situation, and leaving.

3. A problem situation is presented and the leader models how to handle it. Members are chosen to help role-play the situation. Members then evaluate and critique the role-play and possibly redo it. A videotaped role-play may be used.

4. Members then do their own role-play. Others observe for nonverbal and verbal behaviors of the actors.

5. Group members rehearse the skill. Rehearsal and guided practice are used. Following a role-play, the leader gives feedback, and the role-play is redone until the actor's behavior is similar to the leader/model's. The goal is overlearning.

6. Group members practice using complex skill situations. This important step adds complexity to the role-plays and asks participants to generate alternate solutions for real-life problems, to select solutions, and to make implementation plans.

7. Finally, training for generalization and maintenance occurs. The more overlearning, the greater the chance of transference to real-life situations. To accomplish generalization, the stimuli are varied. . . . varied models, problems, role-play actors, and trainers all help in this process. Homework is assigned. (pp. 206–10)

CASE EXAMPLE

The client is Bonnie Ford, a 13-year-old seventh grader. She and her mother, Sue, came in for counseling after Sue's divorce from Bonnie's father, Ed. Ed admitted to having an affair when Sue found an unrecognized number on the couple's phone bill. Ed made this confession to Bonnie, too. Since that time, Sue reported being grief stricken, with little energy to get through the day or otherwise deal with her new single-parent status. Bonnie, unsupervised by either of her parents, began leaving her mother's home in the middle of the night to be with friends. Her previously high grades had dropped from an A– average to a C average in two grade periods. Both Bonnie and Sue had participated in grief counseling; Bonnie then participated in Social Competence Training involving three components: cognitive development, problem-solving, and social skills training.

This excerpt of a session is from the social skills training component. This component is done in a group setting; some of the seven steps of the training component will be presented here. Bonnie was one of seven girls participating in the social skills group.

> **LEADER:** Thank you all for working on setting goals and skills that you want to work on in the group. *(Step 1: The social skill to be taught is presented.)* A common goal that everyone here identified is communication, so let's begin there. Some steps of learning good communication are looking the other person in the eye, greeting the other person by name and asking an open-ended question about the person, making a statement to follow up on the person's response,

| BOX 4.2 | **Internet Resources** |

Due to the living nature of the Internet, website addresses often change and thus we have not printed the addresses in this text. Links to the following websites are posted at the Book Companion Site at www.wadsworth.com.

Parents Without Partners Home Page—lists resources and online links to PWP chapters and other helpful organizations, resources, research, and articles for the single parent

Family Health Resources—provides alternative treatments, Ask the Librarian section

Single Spouses.com—parent resources for single parents; links to parenting sites, websites for moms and dads and more; online single-parents community provides support, chats, dating, financial assistance, resources, articles, and fun

Single Parent Resources—justice for children owed child support

Singlemoms.org—resources for single mothers and single fathers; dedicated to providing resources, support, and information to all single parents

Parenting Magazine—offers information and resources such as family fun articles, tips for parents, and articles promoting positive parenting for parents, couples, singles, and teens

Resource Directory for Single Parents—child care is one of the major expenses that single parents face; includes resources with sliding scale fees, reduced rates, and other information

Single Parent Central—Government Resources—includes government resources that might be helpful to the family, including child-care subsidies

A Cup of Joy Single Parent Family Resource Center—provides single-parent family fellowship and resources

Adoption Education Center—provides resources for single parents hoping to adopt

Hunterdon Moms Online—provides single-parent resources and connections

A Single Parents Network—connects the single-parent resources to help single parents make healthy choices

---

asking another open-ended question, making a statement about the conversation, and ending the conversation (LeCroy, 2001). *(Step 2: The social skill is defined and discussed.)* Can anyone give an example of when good communication would be a helpful skill to have? *[Bonnie raises her hand and is called on.]*

BONNIE: The other day, I wanted to meet a new boy in the video store after school, and I didn't know what to say to him. I'm trying to find a new group of friends, since I was getting into trouble with the old group.

LEADER: That's a good example, Bonnie. Communication can be used to meet new people and to say things to others in such a way that they can hear your requests. For example, good communication can help you to resist peer pressure from other kids while not embarrassing yourself and keeping

Single Parent Resource Network—provides information, resources, and networking for single parents and families interested in co-creating community

Focus on Your Child—for the many parents raising children alone; dedicated to the special needs of single moms and dads

Single Parent Resource Sites—located in Houston, Texas, Single Parent Resources provides links to area resources

The Single Parent Resource—The End Notes include resources, survey data, methodology, and information on The Single Parent Resource Scholarship Project

Texas Attorney General—provides resources for single parents

Single Parent Resources/Family Village—provides single-parent resources, including information about Parents without Partners (PWOP)

Parent Soup—provides information on parenting topics

Yahoo! Directory: Single Parents—a single-parent network offering single-parent resources, links, chat, and more

Open Directory Project—a comprehensive site for single parents with feature articles, polls, chats, and links to resources about every aspect of single parenting

The Single Parent Resource—an A to Z manual for the challenges of single parenting

The Single Parent Resource by Brook Noel with Art Klein—twenty-minute sanity savers, including "The Joys of a Discovery Program" and words of wisdom on navigating the single-parent life

Parents Online—resources including movie reviews for single parents

Single Parent Families—the PL Duffy Resource Centre provides resources and an online magazine

Parenthood.com—includes parenting resources, child-care resources, resources for parents of preemies, parenting humor, Christian parenting

TeacherPathfinder.org—site for lawyers, doctors, and single mothers that provides education publications for parents and electronic listings of resources and materials

Westside Pregnancy Resource Center—answers frequently asked questions about single parenting

them as friends. Can anyone think of other reasons why good communication might be helpful?

[Other members respond and their responses are discussed.]

LEADER: Good, everyone. I think you all see the advantages of good communication. Let me give you a problem situation and an example of how to use communication to handle it. *(Step 3: A problem situation is presented and the leader models how to handle it.)* Say, for example, that I'm Bonnie and I want to meet the new kid in the video store. I might handle the situation this way. Bonnie, would you play the role of the new kid? *[With Bonnie as the new kid and the leader as Bonnie, the role-play ensues, with the leader demonstrating the steps of good communication.]*

LEADER [PLAYING BONNIE]: Hello, I'm Bonnie *[leader looks the "new kid" in the eye]*. Your name is Bob, right? My friend Mary said you are new here. Welcome to town! Where did you move here from (open-ended question)?

BONNIE [PLAYING NEW KID]: Yes, I am new here. My family just moved here from Kansas City.

LEADER [PLAYING BONNIE]: Kansas City! That's a nice town. I visited there once with my parents *(follow-up on the person's response)*. How do you like it here so far *(another open-ended question)*?

The session continues with the other steps of the social skills training:

Step 4: Members do their own role-play, then evaluate and critique and redo it.

Step 5: Group members rehearse the skills using rehearsal and guided practice led by the leader. The leader gives feedback. The goal is for the members to overlearn the skills.

Step 6: Group members practice using complex social skills; complexity is added to the role-plays and members generate alternate solutions for real-life problems.

Step 7: Training for generalization and maintenance occurs by overlearning (practicing in session), then the assignment of homework (members are asked to try out their new skill at home and school).

LEADER [ENDING THE SESSION]: Thank you all for your hard work today. Next week, we will learn skills for identifying and dealing with problem situations, like when your friends encourage you to drink at a party. Goodbye, and don't forget to bring your homework sheet next week.

SUMMARY

The single-parent family, except in the case of the unmarried mother, must give up a parent who was once an integral part of the family and adjust to a new life without this family member. The family therapist should have knowledge of the transitional stages through which the single-parent family passes and the behavior its members are likely to display. It should also be remembered when interacting with this family that there is a member who is no longer functioning in the normal capacity of parent but may be having a significant impact on the current functioning of the family. Extrafamilial support, including extended family, is important in the early life cycle of the single-parent family. The losses experienced and the changes that occur in restructuring the family often result in scapegoating or overreliance on a child who may abandon normal childhood activities and assume the role of an adult. These and other issues will confront the therapist who intervenes with the single-parent family. A family system approach that includes establishing appropriate new skills for all involved will be beneficial in solving family problems.

DISCUSSION QUESTIONS

1. What are typical issues faced by single parents?
2. What role do societal forces play in contributing to the problems of single parents?
3. Review some of the typical problems experienced by single parents and match them to the best interventions.

References

Albano, A., and Kendall, P. 2000. "Cognitive Behavioural Therapy for Children and Adolescents with Anxiety Disorders: Clinical Research Advances." *International Review of Psychiatry* 14(2):129–34.

Beck, A. T., Steer, R. A., and Garbin, M. G. 1988. "Psychometric Properties of the Beck Depression Inventory: Twenty-Five Years Later." *Clinical Psychology Review* 8:77–100.

Brestan, E., and Eyberg, S. 1998. "Effective Psychosocial Treatments of Conduct-Disordered Children and Adolescents: 29 Years, 82 Studies, and 5,272 Kids." *Journal of Clinical Child Psychology* 27:180–89.

Burns, B., Schoenwald, S., Burchard, J., Faw, L., and Santos, A. 2000. "Comprehensive Community-Based Interventions with Severe Emotional Disorders: Multisystemic Therapy and the Wraparound Process." *Journal of Child and Family Studies* 9:283–314.

Chambless, D. 1998. "Empirically Validated Treatments." In *Psychologists' Desk Reference*. New York: Oxford.

Collins, D., Jordan, C., and Coleman, H. 1999. *An Introduction to Family Social Work*. Itasca, IL: Peacock.

Corcoran, J. 2002. "Evidence-Based Treatments for Adolescents with Externalizing Disorders." In *Social Workers' Desk Reference* (pp. 793–97), eds. A. Roberts and G. Greene. New York: Oxford University Press.

Corcoran, K., and Fischer, J. 2000. *Measures for Clinical Practice: A Sourcebook.* New York: The Free Press.

DeGarmo, D., Forgatch, M., and Martinez, C., Jr. 1999. "Parenting of Divorced Mothers as a Link between Social Status and Boys' Academic Outcomes: Unpacking the Effects of Socioeconomic Status." *Child Development* 70(5):1231–45.

DeGenova, M. K., and Rice, F. P. 2005. *Intimate Relationships, Marriages, and Families,* 6th ed. Boston: McGraw-Hill.

Fine, M., and Scwebel, A. 1983. "Long-Term Effects of Divorce on Parent-Child Relationships." *Developmental Psychology* 19:703–13.

Fulmer, R. H. 1983. "A Structural Approach to Unresolved Mourning in Single-Parent Family Systems." *Journal of Marital and Family Therapy* 9(3):259–68.

Fulmer, R. H. 1987. "Special Problems of Mourning in Low-Income Single-Parent Families." *Family Therapy Collection* 23:19–37.

Granvold, D. 2002. "Divorce Therapy: The Application of Cognitive-Behavioral and Constructivist Treatment Methods." In *Social Workers' Desk Reference* (pp. 587–90), eds. A. Roberts and G. Greene. New York: Oxford University Press.

Greif, G. L. 1986. "Clinical Work with the Single-Father Family: A Structural Approach." *International Journal of Family Psychiatry* 7(3):261–75.

Greif, G. L. 1987. "A Longitudinal Examination of Single Custodial Fathers: Implications for Treatment." *American Journal of Family Therapy* 15:253–60.

Haley, Jay. 1991. *Problem Solving Therapy*. San Francisco: Jossey-Bass.

Hamilton, M. 1960. "A Rating Scale for Depression." *Journal of Neurology, Neurosurgery and Psychiatry* 23:56–62.

Henggeler, S., Schoenwald, S., Borduin, C., Rowland, M., and Cunningham, P. 1998. *Multisystemic Treatment of Antisocial Behavior in Children and Adolescents.* New York: Guilford.

Horne, A. M., and Passmore, J. L. 1999. *Family Counseling and Therapy.* Itasca, IL: F. E. Peacock Publishers.

Jemail, J. A., and Nathanson, M. 1987. "Adolescent Single-Parent Families." *Family Therapy Collection* 23:61–72.

Jongsma, A. E., Jr., and Dattilio, F. M. 2000. *The Family Therapy Treatment Planner.* New York: John Wiley and Sons, Inc.

Jordan, C., and Cobb, N. 2001. "Competency-Based Treatment for Persons with Marital Discord." In *Structuring Change* (2nd ed.), ed. K. Corcoran. Chicago: Lyceum.

Kissman, Kris. 1992. "Single Parenting: Interventions in the Transitional Stage." *Contemporary Family Therapy* 14(4): 323–33.

Korittko, A. 1991. "Family Therapy with One-Parent Families." *Contemporary Family Therapy* 13(6):625–40.

LeCroy, Craig. 2001. "Social Competence Promotion for Troubled Youth." In *Social Work Practice: Treating Common Client Problems,* eds. Corcoran and Briggs. Chicago: Lyceum Books.

McCubbin, H., Thompson, A., and McCubbin, M. 1996. *Family Assessment Resiliency Coping and Adaptation Inventories for Research and Practice.* Madison: University of Wisconsin Press.

Minuchin, S. 1974. *Families and Family Therapy.* Cambridge, MA: Harvard University Press.

Minuchin, S., and Fishman, H. C. 1981. *Family Therapy Techniques.* Cambridge, MA: Harvard University Press.

Morawetz, A., and Walker, G. 1984. *Brief Therapy with Single-Parent Families.* New York: Brunner/Mazel Publishers.

Munson, C. 2004. "Evidence-Based Treatment for Traumatized and Abused Children." In *Evidence-Based Practice Manual* (pp. 252–63), eds. A. R. Roberts and K. R Yeager. New York: Oxford.

Reid, W. J. 2000. *The Task Planner: An Intervention Resource for Human Service Professionals.* New York: Columbia University Press.

Scalise, J., Ginter, E., and Gerstei, L. 1984. "A Multidimensional Loneliness Measure: The Loneliness Rating Scale (LRS)." *Journal of Personality Assessment* 48:525–30.

Sprenkle, D. H., and Piercy, F. P. 2005. *Research Methods in Family Therapy.* New York: Guilford.

Visher, E. B., and Visher, J. S. 1990. "Dynamics of Successful Stepfamilies." *Journal of Divorce and Remarriage* 14:3–11.

Weltner, J. S. 1982. "A Structural Approach to the Single-Parent Family." *Family Process* 21:203–10.

Weltner, J. S. 1986. "A Matchmaker's Guide to Family Therapy." *Family Networker,* pp. 51–55.

Wescot, M. E., and Dries, R. 1990. "Has Family Therapy Adapted to the Single-Parent Family?" *American Journal of Family Therapy* 18(4):363–72.

Evidence-Based Treatment of Families with Aging Family Members

CHAPTER 5

INTRODUCTION

When we think of the physical structure of a family, the configuration most often visualized is that of parents and children living in the same household. In this family, the parents are the adult members and occupy the hierarchical position that carries with it the executive authority for family operations. However, this is not the only family composition that social workers encounter in professional practice. Some families are headed by only one parent; others include relatives outside the nuclear family, friends of long standing, and so on, all of whom interact with each other in ways that form a functioning unit.

One family makeup with which social workers are familiar consists of elderly parents and their adult children. The members of this family do not usually live in the same household, and executive responsibility for the family system is not necessarily carried by the parents. In fact, the reverse is most often the case. When adult children are involved in planning and providing for their parents' needs, it is usually because the parents are unable to carry this responsibility for themselves. Subsequently, the children, in most cases, occupy the position of final responsibility. This is not to say that the aging parents have no part in the decision-making process, but the adult children assume a major role in assuring a viable existence for their parents.

POPULATION DESCRIPTION AND DEFINITIONS

The number of adults aged 65 and over has grown from approximately 31 million in the 1990 census to almost 35 million in the 2000 census. Adults aged 85 and over represent one of the fastest-growing segments of the population. As the population ages, more adults are caring for their aging parents (U.S. Bureau of the Census, 2000). As a result, family social workers will increasingly need to address family stressors that result from caring for aging parents.

An awareness of the increasing number of older citizens and their need to participate in society in meaningful ways is well established. Yet, underlying attitudes seem to grow out of our well-established belief in individuality, self-reliance, and productivity as symbols of a preferred lifestyle. This lends support to the value placed on youth and leaves little room to reward the accomplishments of the elderly.

A number of stereotypes exist about older persons in our society. Among these stereotypes is the belief by some that they are economically burdensome, are socially undesirable, lack intelligence necessary for learning new skills, are nonproductive, and are susceptible to illness. Yet, research has found most negative stereotypes about the elderly to be untrue. Most of this population are engaged with their families, have frequent contacts with them, and are able to perform in their major activity roles. Thus, social workers and other professionals intervening in situations involving the elderly should be careful not to fall prey to negative attitudes. Instead, they should view the aged as individuals and proceed to meet their needs in the manner most appropriate for each situation.

A family systems approach to working with the elderly will require an understanding of caregivers' experiences. A commonly held belief is that many families institutionalize their elderly family members rather than doing the caregiving themselves. In fact, multigenerational families are the largest providers of care for the elderly in the United States. Less than 5 percent of the elderly live in nursing homes and other institutions, and most caregivers provide care for their family members with no formal assistance (Federal Interagency Forum on Aging-Related Statistics, 2000). For the most part, families have the expectation that they will care for their elderly relatives. Because life spans are longer and the number of the elderly has grown, families are finding many opportunities for reciprocal caregiving (Flori, 2002).

ASSESSMENT ISSUES

In order to work effectively with a family that includes adult children and their aging parents, it is essential to have an understanding of the aging process and how it affects both parents and children. Although growing old is a normal phase in the individual life cycle, it is often the most difficult to accept by the older person who experiences it, as well as by the person's children who witness it. In various ways, aging represents for the elderly an ending process frequently associated with loneliness and dependency. It is also a constant reminder of one's own mortality to younger persons who observe the aging of their elders. Aging adults often experience loss in physical and psychological functioning as well as changes in social supports and family roles. Family treatment will, therefore, need to include an assessment of functioning that addresses all of these areas.

An assessment of an elderly individual and her family should include interviewing the family about their access to public services and resources (Greene, 2000). It is also helpful to conduct a clinical interview to obtain history about recent or past systemic illnesses (acute and chronic); serious injuries, such as head trauma; medication; and substance abuse. Clinicians can ask caregivers to report about the functioning of the elderly member. They may choose to include only one family informant or the entire family, using a family consensus approach, to increase the accuracy of conclusions about the presence of range of cognitive impairments or behavioral changes (Kaszniak, 1996).

Physiological Aging

Physiological aging is a significant part of the life cycle and perhaps the most noticeable process of change among older people. Signs of physiological change may vary to some extent among individuals and are most noticeable as the body begins to be somewhat less efficient in the performance of its customary life-sustaining functions. Among these changes is a gradual dehydration of muscles and other deteriorations that affect the normal functioning of body organs. This is usually accompanied by a loss of physical dexterity and feelings of tiredness. Some increase in blood pressure may also be experienced. Recovery from injuries and the healing of wounds are relatively slower among the elderly. Visual and hearing impairment may occur, together with central nervous system changes that can result in forgetfulness and some decline in mental alertness. While these physiological changes are recognized as part of the aging process, they do not indicate an automatic onset of illness or the need to curtail older persons' performance of major activity roles. To the contrary, most people are able to continue their major activities in spite of physiological aging.

The emphasis of society on a youth culture can impose some limitation on the coping ability of the aged population. Physical attractiveness, strength, and success in competition are highly valued attributes in a youth-oriented culture. However, these attributes diminish with age, and the elderly can no longer compete successfully for rewards that demand these attributes. Skin wrinkles, loss or graying of hair, and other physical indications of aging may also contribute to inferior feelings. Although there is considerable disagreement among researchers and writers with regard to change in the sexual capacity of older people, if there is a decrease in sexual capacity or less enjoyment from the sexual experience, it can cause feelings of depression in aging individuals (Panser et al., 1995).

The elderly themselves are painfully aware of these changes, which come at a time when they are usually involved with fewer people and less frequently than in earlier life. It is well for the social worker to be aware that older people may mourn the loss of physiological functioning in the same manner they experience the loss of a relative, a position, or a status in life. For the elderly, activity is at least one means through which they can maintain contact with the world around them, and good health may be the key to sustained activity.

Although the elderly may experience these losses in physical functioning, aging can be a fulfilling stage of life in which individuals find meaning in their lives. Clinicians need to be aware of the positive aspects of aging as well as the losses that accompany the aging process. Aging can be interpreted as a time in which individuals have opportunities for continued growth and development. Longer life spans are typically seen as a positive development, and aging adults can be encouraged to see themselves as fortunate for having lived for so long (Ronen & Dowd, 1998). Elderly individuals often have an important role in the family because they help to care for grandchildren. Parents often look to their own parents for advice and support in raising their children, and elderly family members can provide a great service by sharing their experiences with parenting.

Psychological Aging

Physical aging is often associated with psychological aging. Physical problems could precipitate negative psychological reactions from the elder, such as depression, insomnia, irritability, and anxiety. Older adults also have to effectively confront the facts that the future is shorter, and physical impairments or limitations may increase. All of this may threaten an elderly person's self worth and could precipitate depression.

Biophysical influences are recognized in the tendency of older people to show a decrease in memory for more recent events, while at the same time demonstrating vivid recall of events and experiences that occurred many years before. This shift in memory to past events usually reflects on a period in the life cycle of aging individuals when they perceived themselves as more successful.

Intelligence and learning receive a good deal of attention from those who study and work with the elderly. It is generally accepted that a close relationship exists between these attributes, but some studies of intelligence show a decline with age, some show no change, and still others show an increase in intelligence among older people. The reason for the disparity may be the measuring processes used. The aged do not share common experiences with the younger groups on whom most tests are standardized. As a result, such tests may not provide an accurate measure of intelligence among the elderly.

Thus, we conclude that a true determination of change in intelligence among older persons has not yet been achieved. In regard to learning, there is little evidence of change in learning itself among the aged. Nevertheless, learning in older people may be affected by interest and motivation in relation to what is to be learned. In other words, the degree of learning may be reduced if the new knowledge or experience is not in keeping with individual interest. Learning scores are also reduced by a slower rate of response, which might be caused by disease or other biological dysfunctions common to the aging process. In summary, there is no support to indicate universal intellectual decline with increasing age (Warner Schaie, Willis, & O'Hanlon, 1994).

There is a common misconception that older individuals are not capable of learning new things and do not want to change. It is important to view aging as just another stage in human development in which individuals can experience continued growth and change (Ronen & Dowd, 1998).

Social Supports

Among the losses experienced by older people, the most inevitable is the breakup of their social network. Elderly adults are confronted with the deaths of many friends and family members who were once important parts of their social network. Retirement brings another disruption in the social network because it brings changes in income, status, and roles. In terms of economic loss, many older people, upon termination of gainful employment, are faced with a change in the standard of living to which they were accustomed. For those who were able to maintain a barely adequate standard of living while fully employed, the loss of income by retirement frequently plunges them into poverty, with all of the psychological implications of this status. For example, the elderly couple who manages to live independently, by careful management of the husband's income, might find themselves needing to depend more upon their children for financial assistance after his retirement. This is likely to interfere with feelings of independence and contribute to a sense of growing insecurity for the older people.

Certain social losses also accompany disengagement from gainful employment. The reality of retirement usually means the end of a number of social and collegial activities such as lunches, attending conferences, union meetings, picnics, and so on. The older person does not easily replace these associations and in many cases may well drift toward a life of increased loneliness.

Although elderly individuals may face losses in social supports, they may gain supports as well. The American Association of Retired Persons (AARP), for example, provides information, resources, and advocacy. Other supports and resources are listed in Box 5.2 at the end of this chapter.

Spirituality

Another dimension useful in assessing a family's needs is the spiritual and existential dimension of health and healing. This area is concerned with questions about the meaning of life. Family traditions, rituals, and love, coupled with participating in religious services, can enhance self-esteem in the elder and create meaning in life. Rituals and traditions add meaning, cohesiveness, and a sense of history to the family system, especially for the elderly family member. A spiritual component may also prove important when dealing with grief and loss issues, whether it is for other family members or the elder (Harway, 1996).

One method that is helpful for assessing spiritual resources is the spiritual genogram. Constructing a spiritual genogram begins, just as a typical genogram, with a diagram of family structure over three generations, including dates of births, marriages, divorces, remarriages, and deaths. The clinician then asks the client to use colored pencils to indicate the spiritual orientation of those listed on the genogram. For example, the space for a grandfather who was Catholic may be colored blue, and the space for the father, who was Baptist, could be colored red, and so on. Clients can also indicate those in the family with whom they have a close spiritual relationship. These spiritual genograms can be important in an assessment of elderly individuals who have a large family network and for whom spirituality plays a large role in their daily lives. The genogram can highlight spiritual resources and facilitate creating a stronger support network for clients because they can easily see those in the family who share their own spiritual beliefs (Hodge, 2001).

Family Functioning

In working with a family caring for an aging member, it is important to assess family functioning. A family assessment can provide an understanding of the complexity of biopsychosocial functioning of the aged person as well as the effect it has on family functioning. The functional-age model of assessment is helpful in understanding the family as a social system, more than just a summation of the individual lives of its members. There is a need to assess the life of the group and treat the family as an organizational structure that is a functioning whole. The social worker should also assess roles within the family and learn how role expectations help define interaction among family members (e.g., who is the caregiver, who is the good child, and who is the bad child?). An assessment may also include understanding how each family member shapes and is influenced by other members' development, and placing the older person's developmental history in a unique family context (e.g., what other crises has the family faced? what and who has solved them?).

Physical problems associated with aging often produce difficulties in relationships in the larger family system. Family members become concerned about the well-being of the aging loved one and are also challenged to have compassion for the expanding needs of the elder family member. This burden is most manifest in the primary adult caregiver because it is she who is expected to be the most responsible for the elder. By providing support and understanding for the primary caregiver combined with giving the caregiver respite from the responsibilities of interacting with the elder (e.g., taking the elder for examinations, tests, etc.), other family members can mitigate some of this burden of the primary adult child caregiver.

Caregiving Arrangements

A study conducted by Chappell (1991) suggests that while elderly individuals perceive a fairly broad network of individuals available to help them in times of need, most elderly persons, in fact, receive help from only one individual. The spouse is more likely to be the caregiver among the married. Some of the many challenges faced by spouses caring for their aging partners include learning new roles, maintaining physical intimacy, and worries about which partner will die first. They may engage in excessive caregiving to appease guilt or feel useful. On the other hand, they may provide inadequate care because they are learning to take on a new role of reversed dependency and are burdened by simultaneous care needs (Lustbader & Hooyman, 1994).

In American families, women are more likely to care for elderly family members than men. Adult children are most likely to be the ones providing care, followed by spouses. Wives typically care for their husbands, while daughters often provide the care for elderly women in the family. The average person will spend four and a half years caring for an elderly family member, and many are caring for the elderly and their children simultaneously (National Alliance for Caregiving & AARP, 1997).

Caregiving for an aging family member is a positive experience for many. Those who have positive beliefs about caregiving find a great deal of satisfaction in being able to care for those who once cared for them. They report finding meaning and satisfaction in caregiving (Flori, 2002). Social supports affect caregiver well-being. Caregivers have greater life satisfaction, lower stress, and fewer health problems when they have positive relationships with others. When multiple family members share their responsibilities and provide overnight respite care, families are less likely to institutionalize family members.

Relationships

An assessment should include exploring the relationship that exists between adult children and their parents. The social worker will find it useful to obtain some sense of the kind of parent–child relationships experienced during the developmental stages of the adult children, and how this relationship developed over the years. If the adult children shared a relationship with their parents during the early years that provided for growth and was experienced as satisfactory, the current relationship is likely to be sufficiently strong to make constructive problem solving a successful undertaking. On the other hand, if the earlier relationship was characterized by conflict and this conflict was not resolved, efforts to work with parent and child at a later time are likely to be very difficult. This past unresolved conflict may return and interfere with the adult child's ability to help the parents and the parents' ability to accept help from the child.

Role Reversal

In working with aging parents and their adult children, it is important to understand the role shifts that occur between them. This shift in roles between the two generations may be considered *role reversal*. In other words, the elder who has carried the accustomed role of protector and provider for the child at an earlier point in time now gives up this role to the adult child and becomes the receiver of these benefits.

The literature reflects some disagreement about the concept of role reversal. Some authors do not accept role reversal as an appropriate definition of what takes place when the adult child assists, protects, and provides for the parent who is unable to plan appropriately and provide for her own needs. For example, Brody (1990) believes that role reversal is a destructive concept and suggests that its use be discontinued. Jarvik (1990) argues that use of role reversal should not be abandoned by professionals until something else is found that reflects the purpose and utilization currently supported by role reversal.

The term *role reversal* is controversial because the aged parent does not make a complete psychological transition from the adult role to that of a child, nor does the adult child completely transfer from the role of child to that of a parent. The fact that both have long experience and emotional investment in their previous roles makes a complete psychological transition of roles unlikely. Yet the adult child is frequently required to assume responsibility in relation to the aged parent that is normally associated with the parental role, and, to this extent, parent and child are operating in a role-reversal position, which can result in conflict for both participants. Consider the situation in which the adult child is required to make decisions that will affect the way the parent is to live for the remaining years of life. The child, especially one who has experienced a good relationship with the parent, is likely to perceive such action as causing the parent pain and will have a great deal of difficulty accepting the responsibility for making such decisions. In this context, the concept of role reversal denotes a shift in role responsibility within the aged parent/adult child relationship.

In our experience, role reversal frequently takes place amid a great deal of resentment on the part of parents, and much guilt is often evidenced by children. The parents are likely to view the takeover by children as another loss, which is met with a struggle to maintain as much control as possible over their own lives. On the other hand, children often perceive their actions in assuming decision-making power over their parents as degrading the persons for whom they have the greatest respect. Most children feel strongly that it is their duty to honor their parents with respect, rather than promoting within them feelings of helplessness by taking over control of their lives. The fact that this shift in roles comes at a time in the life cycle of the parents when they are less able to regain the decision-making function in their lives, and thereby may remain dependent upon the adult children, is likely to increase the burden of guilt for these children.

Problems can occur for adult children in spite of their intellectual aware-ness of the parents' needs. Although children may realize that their parents are unable to function independently and a shift in roles may be necessary, they frequently need help in accepting the change on an emotional level. Parents may also need help in handling their feelings in relation to depending upon the children.

At the time added responsibility is brought on by the needs of aging par-ents, many adult children are still very much involved with their own nuclear families. For example, some may still have children in school or just begin-ning their careers who look to them for help at the same time as the elderly parents. It is also likely that many of these second-generation adults will be deeply involved in their own careers, and this, too, will claim a good deal of their attention. Role shifts involving aged parents under these conditions pre-sent the adult children (second generation) with quite a dilemma. In some cases they may need direct help in sorting out and establishing priorities that will allow them to continue functioning in their various roles. When there are also problems in relationships between these extended family members, the social worker must understand the nature of the conflict and determine where changes are needed and can be realized.

Conflicts and Disagreements

Disagreements between children may be encountered in work with the multi-generational family. These disagreements may arise from misunderstanding, lack of information, rivalry between children, and so on. When failure to agree centers around information deficits, often the situation can be corrected through improved processing and sharing of information among family members.

When rivalry between the children is involved, however, the problem is much more difficult. Not only are the principals in the rivalry situation adults but many are also parents of adult children to whom the rivalry is likely to have been passed. When this is the case, the third generation may be involved in the problem. A tremendous amount of energy has usually been invested by the second-generation adults in various forms of competition and differences over the years. As a result, their responses are influenced by a lifetime of thoughts, feelings, and experiences based on these unresolved rivalries. When these adults are seen in relation to problems involving aged parents, they are likely to have relatively fixed positions. Each child is interested primarily in working his own will successfully. The struggle between these adult children can easily reach the level where the parents' needs become secondary to the children's need to prevail.

In such situations, each side may seek additional support and gain momentum as the struggle continues. Spouses and children frequently become involved in the conflict, and sometimes other relatives and friends lend their support to one of the sides. The following case summary reflects the difficulty that can be encountered when disagreement about planning for an elderly parent is based on rivalry between adult children.

> The client, a frail man of 75 years, was brought to the Adult Consultation Clinic by his daughter, who explained her difficulty in continuing to maintain him in her home. As a result, she was seeking help in planning for a new living situation for her father. The father did not take kindly to the possibility of residing in a special-care facility and wanted to contact a son with whom he thought he could live. The daughter was obviously distressed at the mention of her brother's involvement but gave in to her father's wishes. Soon after the father's contact with his son, the son called the clinic to arrange an appointment and requested that all consideration of his father's entering a residential facility be discontinued.
>
> In the following weeks, several members of this extended family were involved. The tug of war between the son and daughter was readily seen. Charges and countercharges relative to respective efforts to gain control of the client's finances and other properties were heard from both. Each pulled in other relatives who were sympathetic to their respective views, and these relatives were as firmly fixed in their opinions as the children. Although the son could not arrange for his father to live with him and presented no alternative plan, he could see his sister getting her way and maintaining an advantage with their father. He suggested the possibility of court action to protect what he perceived as his own interests, and his sister was also willing to battle with him through court proceedings. It was obvious that the aged father's needs were being ignored as the struggle intensified between the children, and the extended family's energies were now also being spent in the contest.

The social worker must keep in mind the needs of the aged parents and refrain from becoming completely consumed in the struggle between the children. This kind of struggle usually neutralizes efforts to plan for the parents, and significant change in the rivalries between the children is likely to require long-term intervention. Therefore, in the interest of the parent, it may be necessary to address the children's struggle only after an acceptable outcome has been realized on behalf of the parent. In this case, the focus of intervention is removed from the children's struggle with one another to the needs of the parent and what can be done in this regard.

Conflicts and disagreements may also develop between adult children and their parents as they interact on behalf of the parents. Consider the following situation where parents insisted on compensating the efforts of children by doing something for them in return. When this was discouraged, the parents became even more determined to repay them in some way. They insisted on helping with housekeeping chores, paying for groceries at the market, and so on. Finally, having become thoroughly annoyed with the parents' behavior and realizing no improvement in their efforts to curtail it, the children sought professional help.

When the adult couple was seen by the social worker, it was decided that further use of direct confrontation with the parents was not likely to improve the situation. It was therefore suggested that they should try something different. The new strategy was not only to allow the parents to help with chores but to find something for them to do. And when they insisted on paying for groceries, they were to be allowed to do so. After repeated experiences with this new attitude on the part of the children, the parents felt they were being unfairly used and refused to perform chores or go to the market with the children. As a result, the adult children regained control over what they considered their responsibility, and the parents gave up the need to repay the children for their willingness to help them.

Role of the Spouse

It is also important to understand the roles of the spouses of adult children when aging parents are included in the family group, both relationships between this adult pair and relations between the spouse and the parent. If the adult child and spouse enjoy a satisfactory relationship, work involving the aged parent will most likely proceed without representing a serious threat to the relationship of this subsystem. However, when the spouse relationship is characterized by disagreement and tension, the strain of involvement with the aging parent is likely to escalate the conflict. The resulting struggle between the spouses will interfere with the social worker's efforts to intervene on behalf of the elderly parents. If, in addition to a good relationship between the adult child and spouse, relations between the spouse and the parent-in-law are also good, the intervention process usually proceeds without major conflicts or disruptions, and outcomes are likely to be acceptable to all concerned.

When there is conflict between the spouse and the elderly parent, the work to be done will be difficult. This conflict creates the likelihood of disruption in other family relationships, especially between adult child and spouse and sometimes between the adult child and the parent, as the reciprocal aspects of relating within the family system take over. In most situations, these types of relationships are readily identified, and the strategies social workers commonly use in dealing with relationship problems are usually sufficient.

Nevertheless, the fact that problems can develop out of what appear to be satisfactory relations between adult children and spouses should not be overlooked. This outcome is not uncommon, especially in cases where one of the principals in the relationship has adapted to a deficit in the functioning of the other, and this adaptation is taxed by closer involvement with an extended family member, such as an aging parent. For example, consider the spouse who over the years has adapted to the necessity of meeting the dependency needs of the husband or wife and gives the appearance of enjoying a satisfactory relationship. When the parent is brought into the picture, the role of this spouse may be required to expand to the point of meeting the needs of not one but two dependent people. This is especially so if the aged member needs assistance with routine maintenance or in the area of decision making. The dependent spouse will usually have trouble carrying executive responsibility relative to these needs of the parent, as indicated by the following case summary:

> Mr. and Mrs. J had been married for 15 years without children when Mr. J's father came to live with them. Mrs. J was the strong member of this marital pair, and her authority and overall assertiveness in relation to family matters were accepted by Mr. J, who preferred to remain in the background. It soon developed that the aging father required a great deal of supervision with regard to his behavior and personal hygiene but was resistive to any effort to control his activities. The burden of responsibility increased considerably for the wife, as she found her husband unable to provide any direction for his father. In various ways, he deferred decision making and care for the aging parent to his wife. When they were unable to work this out, Mrs. J asked for help. Although she was very fond of her father-in-law and had not objected to his moving in with them, she had not anticipated the problems he brought into their lives, especially her husband's reactions to his father's needs. In retrospect, Mrs. J could see that she had, in some ways, been a mother to Mr. J but was unwilling to add a new baby at this stage of her life.
>
> This situation represented a real threat to the marital relationship, and this relationship was crucial in meeting the needs of the aging father. The social worker chose to focus on the interactions between the marital pair as it related to roles, expectations, and so on. While alternative plans for Mr. J's father were discussed, neither spouse wished to have him placed outside of their home, and Mr. J was gradually able to take on some of the responsibility for his father.

Encounters of this type clearly indicate the importance of the role assumed by the adult child's spouse and the necessity of understanding the spouse's relationship within the family unit. Social workers will find it very useful, in working with families in which elderly parents are members, to pay special attention to the spouse without kinship ties to the parents. If this individual experiences conflict in existing family relationships or is unwilling to accommodate the intervention process, the realization of desired outcomes from such activity will be difficult.

Elder Abuse

Clinicians working with the elderly and their families need to be aware of elder abuse, including physical and emotional abuse of the elderly family member. Elderly individuals who are abused are three times more likely than others to die within three years. As awareness of elder abuse has increased, a growing body of literature has also developed, providing many resources for assessment and intervention. Elder abuse is defined as intentionally causing harm or increasing risk of harm, failure to meet that person's needs, or failure to protect the person from harm. Types of abuse include physical, psychological, or sexual abuse; neglect; and exploitation of the individual's material resources. Clinicians working with the elderly should be aware of risk factors for elder abuse, which include a conflictual or stressful living situation, social isolation, mental illness, alcohol misuse, financial dependence upon the elderly family member, and the presence of dementia in the elderly family member (Lachs & Pillemer, 2004).

Assessing for elder abuse within a family is difficult because injuries are common among the elderly. Frequently missed medications could be a sign of forgetfulness or of abuse. Rapid weight loss could be a result of neglect or of illness. Although screening for abuse is difficult, clinicians should be aware of signs that are often associated with elder abuse, including skin lesions, bruises, welts, fractures, signs of dehydration, social withdrawal, and families who infantilize the elderly member. When abuse is suspected, a clinician can begin a discussion about elder abuse by talking about safety in the home. Abusers are likely to withdraw from treatment if they feel they are being confronted. An empathetic and nonjudgmental approach can help prevent losing contact with the family (Lachs & Pillemer, 2004).

Few interventions for elder abuse have been evaluated, so there is little knowledge about the best treatments. Potentially helpful interventions include providing respite services, psychotherapy for caregivers, increasing the family's support system to alleviate some of the caregiver burden, adult day care, and involvement of law enforcement and adult protective services. Working within multidisciplinary teams is helpful for ensuring that the family's medical and psychological needs are met, and that the family is connected to appropriate community resources (Lachs & Pillemer, 2004).

Assessment Tools

A variety of tools are available to assess for a wide range of issues relevant to work with elderly individuals and their families:

- Ecomaps and spiritual genograms
- Memory and Behavior Problems Checklist, a 31-item measure for memory and behavior problems (Zarit, Orr, & Zarit, 1985)
- The Zarit Burden Interview, a 22-item measure that assesses for caregiver distress (Zarit, Reever, & Bach-Peterson, 1980)

Because depression and anxiety are common among the elderly, it may be helpful to include measures that assess for symptoms of these disorders. Measures that have demonstrated strong reliability and validity include the following:

- The Beck Depression Inventory
- The Hamilton Rating Scale for Depression
- The State Trait Anxiety Inventory

Table 5.1 provides more information about relevant assessment instruments.

Although the assessment issues and tools described here can be helpful in assessing family functioning in many areas, it is important to remember that cultural differences can greatly influence perceptions about caregivers and caregiver stress. Box 5.1 provides an overview of some of these cultural differences.

Table 5.1 | Assessment Instruments

Measure	Description	Reliability	Validity	Source
Memory and Behavior Problems Checklist	A 24-item measure completed by the caregiver to measure behavior problems associated with dementia	Internal consistency reliability is .95 (Allen et al., 2003)	Convergent validity (Teri et al., 1992)	Allen et al., 2003
Wechsler Memory Scales-III	A battery of scales designed to measure components of memory	Internal consistency reliability is .74–.93 (Sullivan, 2000)	Effectively differentiates between clinical and normal populations (Fisher et al., 2000)	Franzen & Iverson, 2000
Geriatric Depression Scale	A 30-item measure used to screen for depression in older adults	Internal consistency reliability is .83–.89 (Bell & Goss, 2001)	Correctly identified depression in 88% of cases (Bell & Goss, 2001)	Bell & Goss, 2000
The Beck Depression Inventory (BDI)	A 21-item self-administered questionnaire designed to measure depressive symptoms; age range: 13–80; time required: 5–10 minutes	Test–retest reliability is .48–.86	Content, discriminant, and convergent validity	Beck, Steer, & Brown, 1996

Measure	Description	Reliability	Validity	Source
The Hamilton Rating Scale for Depression (HAMD)	A 17-item scale designed to measure the severity of depression symptoms	Test-retest reliability is .65–.96 (Kobac et al., 1990)	Concurrent and discriminant validity (Maier et al., 1988)	Hamilton, 1986
State Trait Anxiety Inventory	A 20-item self-report inventory that measures transitory as well as stable anxiety traits	Internal consistency reliability is .88–.93 (Spielberger et al., 1983)	Content and concurrent validity	Spielberger et al., 1983
UCLA Loneliness Scale	Designed to measure feelings of loneliness and social isolation	Internal consistency reliability is .89–.94 (Russell, 1996)	Content and convergent validity (Russell, 1996)	Russell, 1996
Zarit Burden Interview	A 22-item measure of caregiver distress	Internal consistency reliability is .88–.91 (Hassing, 1985; Gallagher et al., 1985)	Convergent validity (Derogatis et al., 1970)	Zarit, Reever, & Bach-Peterson, 1980
Revised Ways of Coping Checklist	A structured interview to measure coping of family caregivers (Vitaliano, Russo, & Carr, 1985)	Coefficient alpha is .75–.88	Evidence supports construct validity	Vitaliano, Russo, & Carr, 1985

BOX 5.1 | **Cultural Differences**

Many aspects of the experience of aging are similar across cultures. Wishing not to be a burden seems to be a vital issue for seniors generally (Matsuoka, 1999). Working with families caring for an elderly individual requires an understanding of cultural differences regarding the aging process, caregiving, and perceptions of caregiver burden. Cultural definitions of the self, for example, may influence coping. Some non-Western cultures define the self as embedded in social roles and families and communities rather than individuals. People from non-Western cultures are, therefore, less likely to perceive that they have individual control of situations and more likely to view circumstances as determined by fate, God, spirits, and the social group (Aranda & Knight, 1997).

Asian Americans are more likely to be providing care for their older relatives than other ethnic groups, followed by Hispanic Americans and African Americans. A smaller percentage of Caucasians provide care to their elderly relatives than other ethnic groups. Results from an AARP survey (2001) indicate that African Americans were more likely to feel stressed by caregiving than other ethnic groups, while Asian Americans indicated that they felt guilt about not doing enough.

Aranda and Knight (1997) provide insight about important cultural factors that may influence treatment with Latinos. Although Latino elders report higher levels of impairment and a greater need for community-based services than the general population, the literature suggests that older Latinos underutilize community-based, long-term care services (Green & Monahan, 1984; Wallace & Lew-Ting, 1992). Latino older adults may require higher levels of informal community care but are less able to access and afford long-term care services when needed.

According to Valle, Cook-Gait, and Tazbaz (1993), Latino social networks are likely to be large, composed of multigenerational households, extended family, and nonkin "family," including personal care workers. However, Latinos are

EVIDENCE-BASED TREATMENTS/ BEST PRACTICES

A growing number of research studies demonstrate the effectiveness of treatments such as cognitive behavior therapy for elderly clients or caregivers suffering from depression or anxiety. However, there is a great need for research on the effectiveness of family therapy models with this population. In spite of this lack of research, there are a few studies on promising family treatment approaches, although no one approach has been shown to be more effective than the others (Flori, 2002). Table 5.2 provides a list of research studies that have evaluated family therapy techniques with families caring for an aging adult. Since there are so few studies evaluating family therapy approaches, the table also includes research evaluating individual therapy approaches with elderly individuals or their caregivers.

less likely to talk about their situation or share their private feelings, obtain professional help, or inform others of problems with their caretaking situation. They also rely more on their faith or prayer in coping with problems.

Cultural differences also affect perceived burden and stress among caregivers. Caucasian caregivers report higher levels of caregiver stress, burden, and depression and less strongly held beliefs about filial support than other caregivers (Connell & Gibson, 1997). African American caregivers of Alzheimer's patients report less subjective burden and greater caregiving satisfaction than Caucasian caregivers (Lawton, Rajagopal, Brody, & Kleban, 1992).

Caregivers from different cultural backgrounds differ in making decisions to institutionalize an elderly family member. Latino caregivers may delay institutionalization significantly longer than Caucasian caregivers of elderly family members with dementia (Mausbach et al., 2004). African American families may be less likely than Caucasians to institutionalize a cognitively impaired family member (Morycz, Malloy, Bozich, & Marz, 1987).

Elderly individuals from different cultures differ in their preferences about who should be the primary caregiver. Filial piety in East Asian families has deep historical roots in Confucianism (Okada, 1988). As a result of this rich and powerful tradition, understanding the elderly Asian patient requires appreciation of the Confucian background that has influenced cultural development in China, Korea, and Japan. Due to the influence of Confucian ethics on family caregiving practices in China and other Asian cultures, the elder son is obligated to ensure care for aging parents (Okada, 1988). Although the son is often the preferred caregiver in traditional Japanese culture, Japanese Canadians are more likely to prefer that a daughter be the primary caregiver. A strong preference for children as preferred caregivers was more prominent among first-generation than second-generation Japanese Canadians (Matsuoka, 1999).

Research demonstrates that family therapy approaches such as those displayed in the table are most effective when included as part of a multicomponent intervention. For example, treatment that includes family therapy, individual therapy, and psychoeducation, along with linkages to respite care and support groups, have the most beneficial effects on caregivers' well-being (Flori, 2002).

Two family therapy approaches that are well suited to work with families caring for an aging individual are *psychoeducation* and *solution-focused therapy*. Table 5.3 provides a list of treatment manuals that are helpful for learning about these approaches in detail.

Psychoeducation is reviewed in detail in Chapter 7, which focuses on families affected by mental illness. It can be helpful for families caring for aging parents for similar reasons. Families are believed to be more effective caregivers when they are educated about their aging parent's situation. Psychoeducation

Table 5.2 | Research Studies

Solution-Focused Therapy	Psychoeducation	Cognitive Behavior Therapy	Multicomponent Intervention
Elderly clients who received solution-focused therapy experienced significant improvements in GAF scores (Dahl, Bathel, & Carreon, 2000).	Caregivers who participated in psychoeducation group intervention experienced significant improvements in knowledge and coping resources (Schwiebert & Myers, 1994). Participants in a one-day psychoeducation group experienced improvements in self-reported physicality, aging symptoms, socialization, and depression (Mullen, 1998).	Elderly clients participating in CBT experienced significantly greater improvement than those receiving supportive counseling on measures of anxiety and depression (Barrowclough et al., 2001). Elderly clients participating in a group CBT intervention experienced improvements in depressive symptoms (Cappaliez, 2001). Depressed caregivers of elderly relatives experienced improvements in depressive symptoms after participating in individual CBT (Gallagher-Thompson & Steffen, 1994).	A meta-analysis of evaluations of the REACH program, which includes family therapy, psychoeducation, skill-building, and environmental components, indicates that the program effectively reduces depressive symptoms (Gitlin et al., 2003).

Table 5.3 | Treatment Manuals

Manual Reference	Author's Contact Information
Chevalier, A. J. (1995) *On the Client's Path: A Manual for the Practice of Brief Solution-Focused Therapy.* Oakland, CA: New Harbinger.	Unavailable
McFarlane, W. R., Deakins, S. M., Gingerich, S. L., Dunne, E., Hornen, B., & Newmark, M. (1991). *Multiple-family psychoeducational group treatment manual.* New York: Biosocial Treatment Division, New York State Psychiatric Institute.	http://w3.ouhsc.edu/bpfamily/Detail/McFarlane.html
Family Psychoeducation for the Implementing Evidence-Based Practices Project. (Family Psychoeducation Workbook.)	http://www.mentalhealth.samhsa.gov/cmhs/communitysupport/toolkits/family/workbook/default.asp
Gleason-Wynn, P. (2003). "Psychoeducation with Caregivers of Older Adults." In *Clinical Applications of Evidence-Based Family Intervention* (pp. 297–344), ed. J. Corcoran. New York: Oxford.	http://www.baylor.edu/social_work/index.php?id=000747

for these families may be provided primarily to caregivers rather than to the entire family or groups of families (Gleason-Wynn, 2003). The approach includes the following steps:

1. Joining with the family, developing rapport and empathy
2. Providing an explanation of the psychoeducational approach
3. Education on dementia and management of behavioral symptoms associated with aging
4. Information on caregiver stress and coping strategies
5. Education on depression and cognitive-behavioral strategies
6. Information on community resources for in-home and long-term care, including nursing home placement

Chapter 7 provides a sample treatment manual and case example of a psychoeducational approach.

Another approach that is helpful with families caring for an aging parent is solution-focused therapy (Bonjean, 2003). Dahl, Bathel, and Carreon (2000) found that solution-focused therapy improved aging family members' global assessment of functioning scores and self-reports of well-being. Because the approach focuses on the strengths and resources of clients, it can be helpful in

reducing feelings of loss in the aging process and tendencies to focus on negative aspects of aging. Misconceptions that aging adults cannot change may
lead clinicians to opt for interventions aimed at maintenance rather than
change. It is important for clinicians to acknowledge the advantages of aging
in working with elderly adults. Clinicians should approach aging individuals
with the assumption that they have strengths and resources they can use to
learn new things and increase their quality of life. Clinicians can help aging
individuals to accept the changes that come with aging while recognizing the
positive aspects of living a long, healthy life (Flori, 2002).

The solution-focused social worker forms a relationship with the client
that will serve as the context for finding solutions that fit for the client. The
client defines goals and is assisted in examining any exceptions to the situation she has identified as a problem. The social worker adapts to the client's
language, world view, and values.

Solution-focused social workers work to demonstrate great respect for
the client and belief that the client is the expert in resolving her problem. They
assume that clients have the knowledge, strength, skills, and insights to solve
their own problems (Berg, 1994). Four underlying assumptions guide solution-
focused therapy sessions:

1. Every client is unique.
2. Clients have the strength and resources to find solutions to problems.
3. Change is constant, and small change can lead to bigger changes.
4. Since it is not possible to change the past, concentrate on the present and
   future. (Lipchik, 2002)

TREATMENT MANUAL

A review of the main techniques of solution-focused therapy and descriptions of
sessions provides an understanding of how the approach draws on client
strengths to achieve goals quickly. Franklin and Biever (1997), as cited in Franklin
and Moore (1999), outline the steps in a typical first session in solution-focused
therapy. These techniques have been applied here to work with elderly individuals and their caregivers.

I. A Conversation between the Social Worker and Client to Find Out about the Client's Life

This conversation is helpful for engaging with the client and understanding the
problem-solving strategies the client has used, successes and failures around
the presenting problem, motivation, and resources (Berg, 1994). The social
worker takes the position of "not knowing" by laying aside assumptions about
the definition of the problem and its potential solutions (Berg, 2002).

In working with a family caring for an elderly relative, this conversation
can help the social worker understand the strengths and resources of the elderly individual along with the family's approach to caregiving. The family

may communicate, for example, who takes on the bulk of the caregiving duties and how the other family members help out. The conversation can also provide a sense of the family's resources, which can help the social worker anticipate the level of stress the primary caregiver is experiencing.

II. Gather a Brief Description of the Problem and the Context of the Problem

The social worker allows the client to define the problem and helps the client to change the focus of the discussion from the problem to potential solutions. Through externalizing the problem, the social worker encourages clients to view their problems as existing separately from themselves, which is helpful in developing confidence that they can overcome their problems (Franklin & Moore, 1999).

The social worker who is working with a family caring for an elderly relative will help the family to change the focus of the conversation from the problems and stressors that brought them into therapy, such as the emotional stress the caregiver is experiencing, to a discussion about the family's resources and the strategies they have used to care for each other as well as they have. For an elderly family member who feels a sense of loss because of decreased physical abilities or social supports, the social worker can draw attention to the important role the family member still has in the family. Many compliments are used during this conversation to help the family see their strengths and that they care about each other. Otherwise, they would not have come to the therapy session.

III. Use Relationship Questions

Relationship questions ask the client how others, such as children or a spouse, would perceive the presenting problem. They help the social worker understand the client's beliefs about others' perceptions of the problem. These questions are helpful to identify who is involved in the problem situation and any potential resources. Relationship questions can be useful in clarifying the roles of each family member. Who does most of the caregiving? Who is most likely to help the primary caregiver? Who feels particularly close with the aging family member? Who are the primary supports for each family member? These questions can help the social worker discuss the supports and strengths the family has in relation to each other.

IV. Track Exceptions to the Problem

Exception questions ask about times when the presenting problem could have happened but didn't and are helpful in shifting clients' focus away from the problem to times when the problem was not present or less severe. In discussing times when the problem was absent and how they avoided the problem, clients may feel they already have the skills and knowledge to find solutions (de Shazer, 1985; Berg, 1994). In working with a caregiver who feels that no one else in the family is sharing the responsibility for caring for an elderly family member, for example, a social worker might ask if there was ever a time when other people in the family helped more or when the caregiver felt more supported by her family.

V. Scale the Problem

Scaling questions are often used to assess self-esteem, perceptions of hopelessness, and progress toward meeting goals. These questions involve rating something on a scale from 0 to 10, with 0 being the worst/lowest and 10 being the best/highest. Scaling is a helpful technique that can be used with a wide range of clients because it is easy to understand. It may be especially helpful when clients are having difficulty seeing any progress (Sklare, 1997; Berg, 1994).

A social worker could use scaling with caregivers or elderly family members to help them track their own progress toward meeting their goals. A caregiver who feels a great deal of stress could be asked to rate her ability to manage that stress on a scale from 1 to 10, with 1 meaning that she could not manage the stress at all and 10 meaning that she could manage the stress with no difficulty. By asking this question of the caregiver each week, the social worker can see whether the caregiver is changing in her ability to manage stress. During weeks in which the caregiver changed the scale rating, the social worker can ask what specifically brought about the change. What did the caregiver do differently that week? What did the family members do differently?

VI. Use Coping Questions

Coping questions involve asking clients how they have been able to cope with a problem previously. The social worker listens for strengths and resources in the client's definition of the problem and uses these in formulating coping questions (Berg, 1994). Again, using the example of the caregiver experiencing a great amount of stress, the social worker can ask whether there were times when she was better able to cope with the stress of caring for an elderly family member. Typically, there have been times that the caregiving job has been easier and less stressful. By asking the caregiver to talk specifically about her behaviors and those of her family during those times, the family can develop goals that are likely to draw on resources they have used before.

VII. Ask the Miracle Question to Develop Solutions

The miracle question can help clients formulate specific goals. The client is asked to imagine what life would be like if the problem disappeared. This removes focus from the presenting problem, engenders hope, and helps clients define treatment goals in their own terms. The miracle question may also reveal ways that a solution is already occurring in their lives (Berg, 1994).

The miracle question can be helpful for stressed caregivers as well as aging family members wrestling with feelings of loss. An elderly family member who no longer feels that he plays an important role in the family can use the miracle question to clarify what it would look like if he did feel important. The social worker might ask, for example, "Let's say that you go to bed tonight and a miracle happens while you are sleeping. A miracle happens and you now have a very important role to play in your family, but you do not know the miracle has happened because you have been sleeping. What would you notice when you wake up in the morning that would let you know this miracle had happened?" The client's answers will be used to define goals for treatment that will help him feel that he is an integral part of his family.

VIII. Negotiate the Goal for Change

Solution-focused goals are specific, attainable, and defined in clients' terms so that they will be motivated to accomplish them. If the client defines a harmful goal, the social worker may ask questions about the desired outcome of the goal instead of the goal itself. This can encourage the formulation of a positive goal that can achieve the desired result (Sklare, 1997).

In the previous example in which the social worker asks the miracle question to an elderly family member who no longer feels that he is an important part of his family, the social worker would proceed to help the client identify small, achievable goals. Clients are likely to select a goal that is ambiguous and difficult to achieve. For example, the client might say that he wants to feel appreciated again. The social worker will then ask him to explain exactly what that would look like. The social worker continues to ask the client to be more specific in his answers and define small behavioral tasks that the family can work toward. Instead of saying he would like to feel more appreciated, he would define his goal as spending some time each week preparing dinner, washing dishes, or caring for the children. A goal for the family might be to express their appreciation by explicitly thanking him for washing the dishes and explaining how his help has made their day easier. These goals are small and achievable, and they are defined by the client.

IX. Taking a Session Break

At the end of each session, the social worker takes a short break, composes a reflection on the session (a summary of main points, compliments, and suggestions for noticing, thinking about, or trying certain behaviors), and shares it with the family (Bonjean, 1997). The social worker also delivers compliments to the clients based on the content of the session and may assign a behavioral homework task. The task will often involve asking clients to do more of the behaviors the client has identified as helpful. Conversely, the social worker will tell clients to do something different when they have tried the same behavior repeatedly without success (Berg, 1994).

Compliments that may often be given to a family caring for an elderly relative would include talking about how devoted the family has been to their aging relative and to each other and that they are showing their commitment to help by coming to the therapy session. Most family caregivers put a great deal of time and emotion into caring for family members, even though they may feel guilty for not doing more, so the social worker can compliment them on a number of generous behaviors.

The following section provides a case example of the first solution-focused therapy session with a caregiver for an elderly parent.

CASE EXAMPLE

This is the first session with a woman who is caring for her mother, who has recently had a stroke.

SOCIAL WORKER: So, tell me what brings you here today.

MARY: My mother has not been doing well. She had a stroke a couple of months ago and requires a lot of care. My father has had a really hard time dealing with all of this, so I have been spending a lot of time with them, helping out with Mom. She can't feed herself, use the bathroom, or bathe by herself. It all happened so suddenly and I've been feeling very overwhelmed. Every day, I get to the house early in the morning and I'm there until she goes to sleep at night. By the end of the day, I'm just a nervous wreck. I cry all of the time. It's just so hard to see her like that. And my dad seems so depressed—he cries a lot—and I'm worried about what all of this will do to his health, too.

SOCIAL WORKER: I see. You have really been helping out a lot. You're there every day? Your parents are very lucky to have you for a daughter. You've been doing this for two months now?

MARY: Yes, pretty much every day since she came home from the hospital after the stroke.

SOCIAL WORKER: So, how are you able to do this every day? How are you able to get out of bed so early and take care of your mom every day when it has clearly been difficult for you—making you a nervous wreck?

MARY: You know, it's just that I love my parents very much—I love my mom and she has always been there for me. I want to be there for her too, but it's just been very hard. I miss my mom the way she was.

SOCIAL WORKER: You are a loving, devoted daughter. I can see that. Even though it is so difficult for you, you are there every day. Are there days when it is not so difficult to go and help your mom?

MARY: Some days are definitely easier than others.

SOCIAL WORKER: What makes those days a little easier?

MARY: It's a lot easier on days when my sister is there to help out. She works full time so she can't be there a lot. It's also easier when my dad isn't so out of it.

SOCIAL WORKER: On the days when your dad isn't out of it, what is he doing instead?

MARY: On those days, he interacts with my mom more. He will talk to her and go for a walk with her.

SOCIAL WORKER: What do you think your dad would say about the situation with your mom?

MARY: I think he would say that he has lost the partner he knew. My mom is so different now. She can hear what you're saying and can nod her head, but she really can't speak. He would say that he misses talking with my mom and going to the movies.

SOCIAL WORKER: What would he say about you?

MARY: He would probably say that I help out a lot and that he feels bad that I am spending so much time there. He tells me that all the time. But, when I see how broken up he is most of the time, I can't imagine leaving him to deal with all of this on his own.

SOCIAL WORKER: So I'm going to ask you a question that will sound a little strange. Let's imagine that one morning, you go to your parents' house to take care of your mother and all of these things that make it difficult for you when you go there to care for your mother, all of these things are gone. Your mother still has all of the difficulties from her stroke, but all of the difficulties you have had in caring for her are gone. How would you know that they were gone when you walked into your parents' house?

MARY: Well, my dad would be out of bed when I got there in the morning, and he wouldn't be crying.

SOCIAL WORKER: What would he be doing instead of crying?

MARY: He would greet me at the door. He would smile and tell me good morning and he would have made coffee like he used to before Mom had the stroke. He would have gotten Mom out of bed and dressed, and we could all sit at the table together. My dad would be able to watch me feed my mom without getting upset, and maybe he would even feed her himself.

SOCIAL WORKER: What would your dad notice was different about you?

MARY: He would notice that I didn't look like I'd been crying.

SOCIAL WORKER: What would he see instead?

MARY: I would be smiling and talking with Mom a lot, asking her how she was feeling, even if she couldn't answer, telling her stories. I would be talking more with my dad, too.

SOCIAL WORKER: What else would you notice that would help you know that the difficulties you have been having are gone?

MARY: My sister would be there. We would be able to stop talking about how hard it is to see my mom so disabled.

SOCIAL WORKER: What would you be talking about instead?

MARY: We would be able to talk about how lucky we are that she is still alive and that we are all able to help her, since she has always been there for us. We would be able to all sit together and talk about other things?

SOCIAL WORKER: What are some of those other things?

MARY: Well, we used to talk about how work was going for my sister, my dad's garden, how my kids are doing in school—my oldest son is a junior in college and is majoring in sociology, so we talk a lot about his progress and what he wants to do when he graduates. We would talk about Thanksgiving and what we are going to make for dinner and who is going to be there.

SOCIAL WORKER: Who is going to be there for Thanksgiving?

MARY: My daughter and my son, my sister and her husband, my dad. Since my mom has had the stroke, her sister and husband and kids are coming, too, so it will be a bigger group than usual.

SOCIAL WORKER: That's wonderful that everyone can come together for Thanksgiving. You must have a very caring family.

After discussing what the solution would look like, the social worker takes a short break. When she returns, she gives Mary compliments about her devotion to her parents and the wonderful care she provides for her mother. She then reviews specific aspects of the solution that can be used as goals. For example, one solution that Mary described was to talk more with her sister and father about her children, her sister's career, and her dad's garden. Talking more about these topics can become a goal for Mary and her family.

SUMMARY

With the steady increase in the elderly population in the United States, many adult children are seeking help in planning for their aging parents. We have presented in this chapter some guidelines for understanding the aging process and how it affects older people, as well as treatment strategies that are helpful with this population. Some of the problems encountered in working with adult children and elderly parents have been examined, and suggestions for intervention have also been discussed.

The guidelines given for understanding and working with this family group are based on the culture and traditional values existing in the United States. While some of the strategies and techniques are applicable to work with immigrant populations, social workers who engage in work with such groups should consider the cultural values to which they adhere and the unique position the elderly may hold as a result of their age. Awareness by social workers of their own attitudes toward older people will reduce the possibility of inappropriate input and enhance the likelihood of successful therapeutic outcome.

BOX 5.2 | Internet Resources

Due to the living nature of the Internet, website addresses often change and thus we have not printed the addresses in this text. Links to the following websites are posted at the Book Companion Site at www.wadsworth.com.

Resource Locators
> **Family Caregiver Alliance, National Center on Caregiving**
>
> **Benefits Checkup**—helps thousands every day to find programs for people ages 55 and over that may pay for some of the costs of prescription drugs, health care, utilities, and other essential items or services
>
> **Eldercare Locator**—a nationwide directory-assistance service designed to help older persons and caregivers locate local support resources for aging Americans to help them remain independent in their own homes
>
> **Senior Sites**—a source of nonprofit housing and services for seniors
>
> **Directory of Web and Gopher Sites on Aging**
>
> **GeroWeb**—an online resource for researchers, educators, practitioners, and others interested in aging and older individuals
>
> **National Academy of Elder Law Attorneys**—a search engine for locating an elder law attorney
>
> **National Association of Professional Geriatric Care Managers**—a non-profit, professional organization of practitioners whose goal is the advancement of dignified care for the elderly and their families

Federal Government Agency Websites
> **Administration on Aging**
>
> **Centers for Disease Control and Prevention**
>
> **Centers for Medicare and Medicaid Services**
>
> **Department of Veterans Affairs**
>
> **Medicare**
>
> **Social Security Online**
>
> **National Center for Health Statistics: Aging Activities**
>
> **National Institute of Health**
>
> **National Institute of Mental Health**
>
> **National Institute of Neurological Disorders and Stroke**
>
> **National Organization for Rare Disorders**

Caregiver Resources
> **Arch National Respite Network and Resource Center**
>
> **Caregiver.com**
>
> **Faith in Action Volunteer Caregivers**

DISCUSSION QUESTIONS

1. Describe some strengths you would likely find in an elderly family member and caregivers.
2. Describe three solution-focused therapy techniques that could be used to change the conversation from a discussion about a problem to a discussion about the solution.
3. Describe three areas that are important in an assessment of an elderly family member or caregiver.

References

AARP. 2001. *In the Middle: A Report on Multicultural Baby Boomers Coping with Family and Aging Issues*. Washington, DC: Authors.

Allen, R. S., Burgio, L. D., Roth, D. L., Ragsdale, R., Gerstle, J., Bourgeois, M. S., Dijkstra, K., and Teri, L. 2003. "The Revised Memory and Behavior Problems Checklist—Nursing Home: Instrument Development and Measurement of Burden among Certified Nursing Assistants." *Psychological Aging* 18(4):886–95.

Aranda, M. P., and Knight, B. G. 1997. "The Influence of Ethnicity and Culture on the Caregiver Stress and Coping Process: A Sociocultural Review and Analysis." *The Gerontologist* 37(3):342–54.

Barrowclough, C., King, P., Colville, J., Russell, E., Burns, A., and Tarrier, N. 2001. "A Randomized Trial of the Effectiveness of Cognitive-Behavioral Therapy and Supportive Counseling for Anxiety Symptoms in Older Adults." *Journal of Consulting & Clinical Psychology* 69(5): 756–62.

Beck, A. T., Steer, R. A., and Brown, G. K. 1996. *Manual for the Beck Depression Inventory*, 2nd edition. San Antonio, TX: The Psychological Corporation.

Bell, B. D. 1976. *Contemporary Social Gerontology*. Springfield, IL: Charles C. Thomas, Publisher.

Bell, M. A., and Goss, A. J. 2001. "Recognition, Assessment, and Treatment of Depression in Geriatric Nursing Home Residents." *Clinical Excellence for Nurse Social Workers* 5(1):26–36.

Berg, I. K. 1994. *Family-Based Services: A Solution-Focused Approach*. New York: W. W. Norton and Company, Inc.

———. 2002. *Interviewing for Solutions*, 2nd edition. Pacific Grove, CA: Brooks/Cole.

Bonjean, M. J. 1997. "Solution-Focused Brief Therapy with Aging Families." In *The Aging Family: New Visions in Theory, Practice, and Reality* (pp. 81–100), eds. T. D. Hargrave and S. M. Hanna. New York: Brunner/Mazel.

———. 2003. "Solution-Focused Therapy: Elders Enhancing Exceptions." In *Mental Wellness in Aging: Strengths-Based Approaches* (pp. 201–35), eds. J. L. Ronch and J. A. Goldfield. Baltimore: Health Professions Press.

Botwinick, J. 1973. *Aging and Behavior*. New York: Springer Publishing Co.

Brody, E. 1990. "Role Reversal: An Inaccurate and Destructive Concept." *Journal of Gerontological Social Work* 15:15–22.

Burgess, E. W. 1954. "Social Relations, Activities, and Personal Adjustment." *American Journal of Sociology* 59:52–60.

Cappeliez, P. 2001. "Presentation of Depression and Response to Group Cognitive Therapy with Older Adults." *Journal of Clinical Geropsychology* 6(3):165–74.

Chappell, N. 1991. "Living Arrangements and Sources of Caregiving." *Journal of Gerontology: Social Sciences* 46:51–58.

Connell, C. M., and Gibson, G. D. 1997. "Racial, Ethnic, and Cultural Differences in Dementia Caregiving: Review and Analysis." *The Gerontologist* 37(3):355–64.

Dahl, R., Bathel, D., and Carreon, C. 2000. "The Use of Solution-Focused Therapy with an Elderly Population." *Journal of Systemic Therapies* 19(4):45–55.

Derogatis, L. R., Lipman, R. S., Covi, L., Richels, K., and Uhlenhuth, E. R. 1970. "Dimensions of Outpatient Neurotic Pathology: Comparison of a Clinical Versus an Empirical Assessment." *Journal of Consulting and Clinical Psychology* 34:164–71.

Derogatis, L. R., and Spencer, P. 1982. *Administration and Procedures: Brief Symptom Inventory Manual.* Baltimore: Johns Hopkins University Press.

De Shazer, S. 1985. *Keys to Solutions in Brief Therapy.* New York: Norton.

Federal Interagency Forum on Aging-Related Statistics. 2000. *Older Americans 2000: Key Indicators of Well-Being.* Accessed March 8, 2005, from http://www.agingstats.gov/chartbook2000/Older-Americans2000.pdf

Flori, D. C., Ledbetter, M. F., Cohen, N. J., Marmor, D., and Tulsky, D. S. 2000. "WAIS–III and WMS–III Profiles of Mildly to Severely Brain-Injured Patients." *Applied Neuropsychology* 7(3):216–32.

Flori, D. E. 2002. "Clinical Update: Caring for the Elderly." *Family Therapy Magazine* 1(4):36–42.

Franklin, C., Biever, J., Moore, K., Clemons, D., and Scamardo, M. 2001. "The Effectiveness of Solution-Focused Therapy with Children in a School Setting." *Research on Social Work Practice* 11(4):411–34.

Franklin, C., and Moore, K. C. 1999. "Solution-Focused Brief Family Therapy." In *Family Practice: Brief Systems Methods for Social Work* (pp. 105–42), eds. C. Franklin and C. Jordan. Pacific Grove, CA: Brooks/Cole.

Franzen, M. D., and Iverson, G. L. 2000. "The Wechsler Memory Scales." In *Neuropsychological Assessment in Clinical Practice: A Guide to Test Interpretation and Integration,* ed. G. Groth-Marnat. New York: Wiley.

Gallagher, D., Rappaport, M., Benedicy, A., Lovelt, S., and Silver, D. 1985. "Reliability of Selected Interview and Self-Report Measures with Families' Caregivers." Paper presented at the Annual Scientific Meeting of the Gerontological Society of America, New Orleans.

Gallagher-Thompson, D., and Steffen, A. M. 1994. "Comparative Effects of Cognitive-Behavioral and Brief Psychodynamic Psychotherapies for Depressed Family Caregivers." *Journal of Consulting and Clinical Psychology* 62(3):543–49.

Gitlin, L. N., Belle, S. H., Burgio, L. D., Czaja, S. J., Mahoney, D., Gallagher-Thompson, D., et al. 2003. "Effect of Multicomponent Interventions on Caregiver Burden and Depression: The REACH Multisite Initiative at 6-Month Follow-Up." *Psychological Aging* 18(3):361–74.

Gleason-Wynn, P. 2003. "Psychoeducation with Caregivers of Older Adults." In *Clinical Applications of Evidence-based Family Intervention* (pp. 297–344), ed. J. Corcoran. New York: Oxford.

Green, V. L., and Monahan, D. J. 1984. "Comparative Utilization of Community Based Long-Term Care Services by Hispanic and Anglo Elderly in a Case Management System." *The Journals of Gerontology* 39:730–35.

Greene, R. R. 2000. *Social Work with the Aged and Their Families,* 2nd edition. New York: Aldine de Gruyter.

Hamilton, M. 1960. "A Rating Scale for Depression." *Neurosurgery and Psychiatry* 23:56–62.

Hargrave, T. D., and Hanna, S. M. (eds.). 1997. "Integrating the Process of Aging and Family Therapy." In *The Aging Family: New Visions in Theory, Practice, and Reality* (pp. 81–100). New York: Brunner/Mazel.

Harway, M. 1996. *Treating the Changing Family: Handling Normative and Unusual Events.* New York: John Wiley & Sons, Inc.

Havinghurst, R. J., and Albrecht, R. 1953. *Older People.* New York: Longmans Green.

Hodge, D. R. 2001. "Spiritual Genograms: A Generational Approach to Assessing Spirituality." *Families in Society* 82(1): 35–48.

Jarvik, L. 1990. "Role Reversal: Implications for Therapeutic Intervention." *Journal of Gerontological Social Work* 15: 23–34.

Kaszniak, A. W. 1996. "Techniques and Instruments for Assessment of the Elderly." In *A Guide to Psychotherapy and Aging: Effective Clinical Interventions in a Life-Stage Context* (pp. 163–219), eds. S. H. Zarit and B. G. Knight. Washington, DC: APA.

Kobak, K., Reynolds, W. M., Rosenfeld, R., and Greist, J. H. 1990. "Development and Validation of a Computer Administered Version of the Hamilton Depression Rating Scale." *Psychological Assessment: A Journal of Consulting and Clinical Psychology* 2:56–63.

Lachs, M. S., and Pillemer, K. 2004. "Elder Abuse." *Lancet* 364 (9441):1263–72.

Lawton, M. P., Rajagopal, D., Brody, E., and Kleban, M. H. 1992. "The Dynamics of Caregiving for a Demented Elder among Black and White Families." *Journal of Gerontology: Social Sciences* 46:181–89.

Lipchik, E. 2002. *Beyond Techniques in Solution-Focused Therapy.* New York: Guildford Press.

Lustbader, W., and Hooyman, N. R. 1994. *Taking Care of Aging Family Members: A Practical Guide,* Revised and expanded ed. New York: The Free Press.

Matsuoka, A. K. 1999. "Preferred Care in Later Life among Japanese Canadians." *Journal of Multicultural Social Work* 7(1/2):127–48.

Mausbach, B., Coon, D. W., Depp, C., Rabinowitz, Y. G., Wilson-Arias, E., Kraemer, H. C., Thompson, L., Lane, G., and Gallagher-Thompson, D. 2004. "Ethnicity and Time to Institutionalization of Dementia Patients: A Comparison of Latina and Caucasian Female Family Caregivers." *Journal of the American Geriatrics Society* 52(7):1077–84.

Morycz, R. K., Malloy, J., Bozich, M., and Marz, P. 1987. "Racial Differences in Family Burden: Clinical Implications for Social Work." *Gerontological Social Work* 10:133–54.

Mullen, R. P. 1998. "An Assessment of the Effects of the Psychoeducational Workshop on Minor Depression for Enrollees in a Hospital-Based 55Plus Program." *Dissertation Abstracts International Section A: Humanities & Social Sciences* 59(6-A):1869.

National Alliance for Caregiving and AARP. 1997. *Family Caregiving in the U. S.: Findings from a National Survey.* Washington, DC: Authors.

Okada, T. 1988. "Teachings of Confucianism on Health and Old Age." *Journal of Religion and Aging* 4(3–4):101–107.

Panser, L., Rhodes, T., Girman, C., et al. 1995. "Sexual Function of Men 40 to 79 Years: The Olmsted County Study of Urinary Symptoms and Health among Men. *Journal of American Geriatrics Society* 43:1107–11.

Ronen, T., and Dowd, T. 1998. "A Constructive Model for Working with Depressed Elders." *Journal of Gerontological Social Work* 30(3/4):83–99.

Russell, D. W. 1996. "UCLA Loneliness Scale (Version 3): Reliability, Validity, and Factor Structure." *Journal of Personality Assessment* 66(1):20–40.

Schwiebert, V. L., and Myers, J. E. (1994). "Midlife Care Givers: Effectiveness of a Psychoeducational Intervention for Midlife Adults with Parent-Care Responsibilities." *Journal of Counseling & Development* 72(6):627–32.

Sklare, G. 1997. *Brief Counseling That Works: A Solution-Focused Approach for School Counselors.* Thousand Oaks, CA: Corwin Press, Inc., Sage Publications.

Spielberger, C. D., Gorsuch, R. L., Lushene, R., Vagg, P. R., and Jacobs, G. A. 1983. *Manual for the State Trait Anxiety Inventory.* Palo Alto, CA: Consulting Psychologists Press.

Sullivan, K. A. 2000. "Examiners' Errors on the Wechsler Memory Scale-Revised." *Psychological Report* 87:234–40.

Teri, L., Truax, P., Logsdon, R., Uomoto, J., Zarit, S., and Vitaliano, P. P. 1992. "Assessment of Behavioral Problems in Dementia: The Revised Memory and Behavior Problems Checklist." *Psychological Aging* 7(4)622–31.

U.S. Bureau of the Census. 2000. *Current Population Reports. Population Profile of the United States.*

Valle, R., Cook-Gait, H., and Tazbaz, D. 1993. *The Cross-Cultural Alzheimer/ Dementia Caregiver Comparison Study.* Paper presented at the 46th Scientific Meeting of the Gerontological Society of America in New Orleans, LA.

Vitaliano, P., Russo, J., and Carr, J. E. 1985. "The Ways of Coping Checklist— Revision and Psychometric Properties." *Multivariate Behavioral Research* 20:3–26.

Wallace, S., and Lew-Ting, C. 1992. Getting By at Home: Community-Based Long-Term Care of the Elderly." *The Western Journal of Medicine* 157:337–44.

Warner Schaie, K., Willis, S., and O'Hanlon, A. 1994. "Perceived Intellectual Performance Change over Seven Years." *Journal of Gerontology* 49:108–18.

Williams, J. M. 1987. *Cognitive Behavior Rating Scales: Manual, Research Edition.* Odessa, FL: Psychological Assessment Resources.

Zarit, S. H., Orr, N. K., and Zarit, J. M. 1985. *The Hidden Victims of Alzheimer's Disease: Families under Stress.* New York: New York University Press.

Zarit, S. H., Reever, K. E., and Bach-Peterson, J. 1980. "Relatives of the Impaired Elderly: Correlates of Feelings of Burden." *Gerontologist* 20:649–55.

Evidence-Based Treatment of Families with Multiple Problems, Including Income Loss and Poverty

CHAPTER 6

INTRODUCTION

Families with multiple problems have historically received help from social workers; they present challenging problems for social work intervention. The needs of these families require intervention at several levels, including the family systems as well as environmental systems levels. Families experience multiple sources of internal and external stress as they attempt to solve problems such as child behavioral and family relationship problems (Jordan & Franklin, 2003; Harris & Franklin, 2004). In Chapter 6 we take a look at multiproblem families and their descriptions, followed by assessment and treatment issues and approaches.

POPULATION DESCRIPTION AND DEFINITIONS

Not all families with multiple problems are poor, nor are all poor families beset with the multiplicity of problems that are a frequent consequence of income loss and poverty. But we begin by noting some of the connections between poverty status and families' multiple problems, including family system and environmental problems. Our approach to the multiproblem family is consistent with the systems approach outlined in earlier chapters; we view the family as an organized system of interacting subsystems engaged in varying ways and degrees with external systems. Events in other systems are seen as influencing internal family relationships, and vice versa.

The behavior of external systems is viewed as particularly important in the internal operations of multiproblem poor families; especially in the ways family members engage each other in seeking to have their needs met, to gain cooperation, to establish order, to negotiate differences, or to otherwise regulate family activity. Attention is paid to the way that current problems evoke and reinforce unproductive modes of problem solving and relating.

ASSESSMENT ISSUES

Income Loss

Despite increasing economic advantages for some Americans during the last decade, the poorest segment has grown poorer. The gap between the richest and the poorest of Americans continues to widen (The Center on Budget and Policy Priorities, 2000). Many multiproblem families have been poor for lengthy periods of time. Additionally, data from the National Survey of America's Families (Brennan et al., 1999) indicates that white Americans are improving on indicators of well-being while minority Americans are more likely to live in deep poverty or 50 percent below the poverty line.

Studies of families that have been economically self-sufficient and unexpectedly experience income loss provide a beginning understanding of the difficulties that families in longer-term poverty may experience. Sales' (1995) study of recently unemployed workers points to the kinds of economic resources needed by them and their families. The longer unemployment persists, the greater the percentage of families who have exhausted their unemployment benefits, their savings, earnings, borrowing, and private charity resources, and help from family and friends, and who become dependent on government programs. Sales notes, as have others, that economic resources serve to buffer the effects of unemployment on workers and their families.

The strains become evident in the correlation of periods of high unemployment in the economy with the general increases in rates of alcoholism, crime, and mental illness. Typically in our society, individuals gain a sense of status and worth from employment even if they do not like the particular work they do. Loss of work and of economic self-sufficiency affects both the worker and the family. "Extreme poverty and homelessness can affect people's feelings about themselves, make some people 'crazy' and leave many more feeling helpless, powerless and despairing; and can lead to substance abuse as an escape from misery" (Parnell & VanderKloot, 1991, p. 187).

Workers may lose status and authority within the family as well as outside. They react to the loss of employment and economic support with feelings of shame, humiliation, worthlessness, anger, anxiety, depression, and, in some instances, free-floating hostility, increased drinking, paranoid ideas, depression, and thoughts of suicide. Other family members may experience similar feelings (Borrero, 1979). Further, conflicts arise among family members as a result of the lack of financial resources and debate concerning how the fewer resources should be allocated. Also, roles may change when additional members of the family seek to produce income. The unemployed worker may take on unaccustomed functions within the family. The resulting stress may be accompanied by increased drinking and physical abuse, creating further problems for all members.

Liem and Liem (1988) looked at factors other than money that might buffer the stress of loss of employment. In general, the emotional climate in the home and the wife's positive performance of household, child-rearing, and marital responsibilities eased the stress for the unemployed husband. The family role performance of the newly unemployed workers (in this case, husbands) was an early casualty, preceding negative changes in the wives' performance of family roles. Husbands and wives reported significantly less cohesion and more conflict than did spouses in a comparison group. Norms for performance in family roles did not change, but performance deteriorated with the lengthening of unemployment.

Other Family Problems

Other family problems—truancy, delinquency, alcohol or other substance abuse, incest, physical abuse, neglect, separation, or divorce—may be present or may be exacerbated by the lack of economic resources. And they may stand in the way of coping effectively with the economic aspects of life.

Clearly, there is a relationship between poverty and the problems of the families we will be discussing, but it is also clear that not all of their problems are attributable to poverty. In defining their goals with the family, social workers need to distinguish which problems are due to situational distress. Family members experience withdrawal, alienation, developmental delays, learning disorders, and frequent emergencies (Williams, 1994). In addition to the usual life cycle stresses, they are likely to experience the disruptions of imprisonment, addictions, mental illness, poor health, frequent loss and/or change of employment, and change in family responsibilities and roles due to any of these (Williams, 1994). Adolescent family members may experience "violence, behavioral problems, substance abuse, HIV infection, pregnancy, and homelessness" (Harris & Franklin, 2004, p. 312), as well as school problems. Women may have experienced domestic violence (Reid, 2000).

Wood, Valdez, Hayashi, and Shen (1990) note that expenditure of a disproportionate share of family income on housing was a factor in families becoming homeless and that homeless compared to housed poor families reported more spouse and child abuse, more drug and mental health problems, and weaker support systems. Neighborhoods are deteriorating, and strong community organization, standards, and values are frequently not available to provide needed supports for the family when help is sought

(Aponte, 1991; Jenkins, 1990). Family energy is consumed with the task of dealing with multiple control agencies and their disparate requirements.

Internal Family System Operations   The nature of the problem poverty family's boundaries, rules, communications, and identity follows from the nature of the family's relationships to external systems. The negative nature of the relationships with external systems for these families has been defined; there is little in them to offer either adult or child a sense of positive meaning or affirmation. As breadwinners or as clients of an income maintenance program, adults feel depreciated and find no status; children receive minimal affirmation or recognition for their efforts in school. Consequently, for gratification of personal needs, each member turns to other family members. The need to seek all gratifications within the family places undue stress on internal family operations. Unsatisfactory patterns develop and persist as long as the family's position in the community persists. Jordan and Franklin (2003) review some of the key issues.

Boundaries   Family boundaries define the various subsystems in the family structure (see Chapter 2). The marital pair first forms a marital subsystem, which may become a parental subsystem. Family operations and strength depend in large measure on the ability of the adults to form a strong bond with each other. Satisfaction in their own relationship derives from that bond, as does the ability to support each other in child rearing. In problem poverty families, however, the relationships between the adults are characterized by distance, conflict, and transience. They interact with each other primarily as parents, minimally as spouses.

Some evidence of the difficulty in parental bonding is the fact that up to 60 percent of poor families are headed by female single parents. For a variety of reasons, the adult pair is not available to each other or their children as a parental pair. In these instances, the maintenance of a separate household has fallen on the mother. Her income is less and the demands on her are greater.

While communicational and interactional problems (which we will describe shortly) are primary sources of the inability to form a strong marital bond, the structural outcomes must also be considered. When relationships do not work, partners may withdraw from them, psychologically or physically or both, and the withdrawal may be temporary or permanent. Or they may engage in overt conflict, verbal or physical or both. In families with children, a parent may withdraw from the parenting function as well as from the spouse role. Withdrawal from the parenting function represents the relinquishment of parental leadership. The role of the withdrawing spouse/parent may thus become more that of a child than of a parent. The usual generational lines are crossed.

A second form of generational boundary violation may occur when the failure of marital bonding results in conflict that cannot be contained within the bounds of marriage. A parent may seek a member of the child generation as an ally, sometimes to gain support for self, sometimes as a means of attack against the spouse. If both parents have remained in the home or are significant for the child, the child is placed in an untenable position between them.

The parental child, as we have labeled this usually older child in Chapter 2, who responds to this boundary breakdown by moving to comfort or support one of the parents increases his isolation from the other parent. Thus, he deprives himself of the support of the other parent and may thereby accentuate the conflict between the parents. He may seek to reconcile parental differences, a function that places him more in the parent generation, or he may actually take on parental functions. Or he may develop other emotional, physical, or behavioral symptoms because of this uncomfortable positioning. Cues from the parents will suggest to the child the ways in which he is needed. The breakdown in parental leadership is manifest also in those instances in which children move into parenting roles with other children. Such movement may be prompted by the parent, and it gains parental approval. While it often results from parental conflicts or default, it may in other instances often be necessary for a child to perform in the role of a parent, as for example when work, illness, or errands leave both parents unavailable. (This becomes even more likely in single-parent families.) An older child may take on a child-caring role with younger siblings during after-school hours, before the parents return home from work. Or a child may be asked to undertake extra household tasks during an illness of one of the adults. Troubles may arise when parents have not provided sufficient direction.

An older girl was left in charge of several siblings who began fighting with each other. Having no instructions from the parents about what to do about this behavior, she separated them and did not allow them to play together until the parents returned home. The younger siblings complained to the parents who, in turn, chided the girl for her actions. No instructions were offered about what to do if the behavior recurred. The girl was left with negative feelings toward her siblings for causing her trouble and toward her parents for not supporting or directing her. The younger siblings were likewise left with angry feelings and a reduced need to be cooperative.

In these circumstances, the parents failed to provide a clear, unambiguous structure within which the parenting child and the other children could relate, leaving cause for disagreement and fighting. Where parental leadership is clear, all children will know their limits and responsibilities during a parent's absence.

The likelihood of a child's becoming a parental child seems greater in problem poverty families than in other families. The parents' poor position in the outside world, as we have suggested, leaves the parents with reduced need satisfaction, self-esteem, and status within the family. These factors combine to reduce parental assertiveness and leadership. Seeking affirmation and status, they may more readily seek a child as an ally or yield to the wishes of a child, especially when these needs are not met by a spouse who may have similar needs and may be unable to meet the other's needs. Furthermore, the tendency to rely on parental children increases in single-parent families, which many of these families are.

Rules   Closely related to a lack of structure evidenced in generational boundaries and parental leadership is a lack of clear and consistent norms and rules
for behavior. In problem poverty families, parental responsibilities in setting
limits to behavior often are not fulfilled. What is a limit today may not be a
limit tomorrow or even 10 minutes from now. A limit defined by one parent
may not be held to by the other parent. Behavior is regulated by injunctions
on a particular piece of behavior but with no further explanation about why
it should be stopped, about circumstances under which it is permitted, or
about what desirable behavior should be substituted. Children consequently
have no consistent guides for behavior that they can internalize and thereby
become self-regulating, either in the parents' presence or away from them.
Parents are constantly required to regulate the activity of the children, leaving
them totally enmeshed and absorbed in childcare and less free to meet their
own needs. They feel overburdened and overwhelmed.

The parents' abdication from regulation or their total withdrawal from
the family, either temporary or permanent, leaves relationships disrupted and
reinforces the sense of inconsistency and instability. Parental behavior in this
area is also attributable, at least in part, to the parents' limited status outside
the family and their own and family members' reactions to that status. Where
the parents have themselves been raised in similar families, these behaviors
are learned in their families of origin.

Such interaction of course interferes with the growth and development of
the children and the parents. The process does not allow for individuation
and separation of family members but instead keeps them dependent upon
and bound to one another. It is a kind of being "stuck" together that is very
different from being able to see oneself as an individual; it is an individual
who takes satisfaction and enhances his identity out of belonging to the family. The "stuck togetherness" is similar to the situation of enmeshment
described by Minuchin and Montalvo (1967) and to the undifferentiated family situation described by Bowen (1978).

Similar but less often described is the lack of clear expectations and rules
about marital behavior. Dissatisfaction with marital relations may result. Adults
may think of themselves primarily as parents and devote little attention and
effort to their roles as spouses. Frequently, spouses are unsure of themselves as
males or females. They become aware of their spouse's expectations primarily
when they fail to meet them, not through transactions that result in explicit definitions of what is expected and desired. Complaints are frequent; the freedom
to say what "I want, need, or would like" is lacking, as is the means for expression. As in parent–child relationships, it is easier for spouses to learn what is not
wanted than to learn what is wanted. Role performance cannot be achieved
with confidence. Since role expectations are not clearly defined, the interpersonal process leaves spouses feeling insecure and lacking in self-affirmation.

Communications   When clear and consistent rules for behavior are lacking,
communications are likely to be dysfunctional to family stability and problem
solving. Communication is characterized by interruptions, simultaneous

talking, topic changes, and unclear meanings. Members do not really listen to each other and frequently do not really expect to be heard. When others respond, it is often to make a counterpoint of their own, rather than to respond to what has been said. Voices escalate in volume in an effort to be heard, and in the noise, affect rather than content is communicated. The verbal message is lost and is not responded to. Interaction reveals affect and feelings rather than information and ideas, and the interpersonal aspect of the message predominates over the content aspect. In some instances, limitations of language ability affect the ability to achieve understanding and solution of a problem. The families are thereby impoverished in their attempts to generate information and solutions to problems. On the other hand, positive, clear communications in low-income Spanish-speaking families, for example, have been shown to enable reduced difficulty on the part of asthmatic children in managing their asthma attacks (Clark et al., 1990).

These characteristics of communication in poverty families, as contrasted to other problem families, differ in intensity, not in kind. Intense need and seeking on the part of family members are implied. In such families, consequently, efforts at problem solving by means of verbal communication are unproductive. Nothing in the family changes so long as communications operate in this manner. Furthermore, the members' frustration with one another and their sense of isolation are increased. They get no sense of being listened to and really heard. They do not obtain understanding, self-affirmation, or nurture from the unresponsiveness or arguments of others. The communications thus reflect family relationship and structure. The isolation or lack of support within the structure that one or more members may feel becomes evident through the lack of supportive communications and the volume of negative messages directed at them. Members feel isolated from other family members or fear that others are allied against them. For example, when a child communicates as though she were a parent, one of the parents may feel as if the other parent and the child are allied against him. Or parent communication may seem to derogate a spouse in favor of a child.

Thus, the communicative effort at both the content and the relationship levels serves to perpetuate the unsatisfying relationship rather than to change it. A homeostasis is reached, and problem solving does not occur. Family structure is maintained in its disabling form. The family system is stable (morphostatic) but in a form that gradually leads to less rather than more effective functioning.

Identity, Integration, and Solidarity   A number of writers have attested to the importance of a sense of family identity in family coping and problem solving. In our view, this is both consequence and cause of the problems of family functioning. The image that members hold of the family as a group has meaning for the individual and is important for individual growth and role-taking within the family. The image may take various forms, such as "the people I live with," an image that suggests a feeling of disconnectedness and of not belonging or being valued by others. Or the image may be "the family that I belong to," an image that suggests a sense of cohesion and belonging, really a valued part of the group. Rabinowitz (1969) observes that it is this sense of being a group that is lacking in poor, multiproblem families:

Researchers participating in the Wiltwyck study were struck by how little these families seem to be recognized by their members as groups of people who belong together. Parents seem to disassociate themselves from each other and from their children. They seldom have conversations with each other or with a child. "Both enjoyment of family life and any positive valuing of family relationships are notably absent" (Minuchin et al., 1967, p. 180). Although they maintain a family form, they do not develop a family consciousness.

Having a sense of the family and of belonging to it is as important to individual functioning as is the sense of separateness of self. But it is difficult to develop a positive image of the family in the midst of the structural and communication deficits found in poverty families. The modes of coping with problems and of handling relationships have served to drive members apart rather than to promote a sense of unity and harmony. The family's material status also has its effect. It becomes easy, when material necessities and the means for acquiring them are lacking, to doubt, argue, and blame, and over time to come to feel alienated and apart from the group. The group, in turn, holds insufficient meaning or value for the individual, since it is not a source of nourishment or support. Members are not likely to be committed to preserving it or making an effort to improve it.

We have observed the opposite effects in certain cases, however. In some families, the children are able to become upwardly mobile. Such families seem to be characterized by a family theme, defined by the parents or other parenting figures, which conveys that though the external world is hostile, the family can succeed if everyone joins together. Goals of survival and achievement are emphasized. Parental leadership is strong, and rules are explicit and clearly enforced. Long-term family survival is given priority over immediate individual goals. Staying together and working together are essential to survival. Under these circumstances, individuals can achieve and advance despite poverty. The individual is enhanced through the esprit de corps of the family group. In some instances, however, the individual may experience a sense of rigidity and overcontrol, and have difficulty achieving individuality or separateness from the group.

Lack of Environmental Supports

"Millions of American families have not been able to absorb the economic shock of the last few years. Loss of employment, escalating drug abuse and violence, physical and social deterioration of neighborhoods, and reductions in social services and entitlements have virtually paralyzed communities. Many families have become powerless to meet their basic needs without stable communities to support them" (Williams, 1994, p. 48).

Kantor, Peretz, and Zander (1984) cite the impact of poverty on reducing the chances for the children of these families to attain good health, educational achievement, and economic self-sufficiency. Because their lives are often disrupted by emergencies and other unpredictable events, they frequently suffer from exhaustion and hopelessness, lowered school performance, and reduced social contact. Poverty and limitation of choice often lead to unplanned pregnancy, protracted dependency, and ongoing poverty. The pain and isolation inherent in a lifestyle of poverty may create a limitation of perspective, of the representation of the world, and of what might be possible in it. It is therefore necessary to connect the client with the world in some way that gives a richer set of choices.

For poor families, external systems have such a powerful impact because they are dependent on them for survival. In a stable environment, it is normally sufficient to address the individual/family unit, assuming a degree of constancy and stability in the larger systems sphere. This is not a realistic assumption in the urban centers of the United States. We can no longer deny that our institutions are not adequately performing the functions for which they were designed. Historically, part of the solution to the fiscal crisis has been to target social programs for cuts and to blame the poor for their poverty (Parnell & VanderKloot, 1991).

All of these difficulties suggest the need for varieties of services and treatment for the family. Unfortunately, the unemployed population appears to resist traditional counseling services (Sales, 1995, p. 492). Serving them requires methods that meet their needs for resources as well as help with internal issues.

The problems of family functioning in poverty-level families will not be resolved without some change in the family's poverty status. Income maintenance by itself does not appear to be a sufficient solution, however. It has long been known that while unemployment is clearly disruptive to marriages (Bishop, 1980), the provision of income maintenance, either in the form of AFDC or a negative income tax, has also increased the rate of marital dissolution. Thus, though the provision of income is necessary for family functioning, some changes in family functioning must also occur if the family is to be extricated from the perpetuation of individual and family problems, and from poverty status. Further, adequate external system supports, such as those described next, are essential to motivate change in poverty families and to forestall the repetition of present patterns in succeeding generations. Extrication from the poverty status rests not only with the family but also with a change in the perspectives of the external systems that affect it. We are concerned with facilitating change at both levels.

External System/Family System Operations Jenkins (1990) notes that compared to the power of the state, poverty-level families are powerless. There is the need to be clear about the system level at which intervention needs to occur. At the societal level, policies and programs that allow each family the needed income for basic necessities should be in place, should be comprehensive, and should provide service in the many facets of their lives in which need may occur (Conte, 1983; Halpern, 1991; Schorr, 1991).

Further, negative attitudes and sometimes outright hostility toward the poverty family may be manifested by the public, by agencies, and by workers. Middle-class values lead to expectations of certain responses from the family and to disparagement and rejection when the family does not manifest these responses. The feedback to the family depreciates the family's image of itself and of its individual members. When the family is lacking in self-enhancing feedback from the outside world, the esteem of family members for each other suffers. Self-esteem, useful as a source of strength and motivation, is diminished, and the burden of promoting it is left totally to the already overburdened family. Another negative impact that external systems have on the poverty family is the existence of policies that divide families rather than bring them together. In some states, policies are still in effect that provide support for mother and children when father is not there but do not support them when he is present but unable to provide financial support. This serves to divide the family and inhibit family strength and growth.

Other agency policies that divide and fragment the family are services to the physical or mental health needs of some family members but not of others, or attentiveness only to the physical or mental health of a family member without attention to the family circumstances that affect health.

Agencies that require the family to conform to agency policy operate as though the family is an extension of the agency, subject to its bidding. Instead of providing support to the family's own problem-solving efforts, the policies of agencies and the actions of workers often serve to inhibit the capacity for independent thought and action. In conceptual terms, the family loses its boundaries as a separate system and becomes incorporated as part of the agency system, thus increasing rather than decreasing its dependency. Families known to more than one agency may find themselves faced with contradictory requests, which may result in breakdown of family structure or family boundaries. Family interaction with other, less official or public systems may operate similarly. The extended family, the siblings or parents of the adult family members, sometimes provides little or no support. In poverty families, these persons are often psychologically or materially not in a position to be supportive and are themselves in need of support. When a relationship exists, extended family members often see the members of the poverty family as people to be controlled, directed, or drawn upon for their own support. Consequently, the inputs to the family system from the extended family leave it diminished in capacity for independent operation.

Extended family members, however, can be helpful in providing supports, sometimes financially and materially, sometimes in services such as childcare or homemaking during illness. Stack (1974) has noted the particular means of helpfulness of kin and kin-like networks. When such relationships are tenuous, family members can sometimes be helped to strengthen them, to their own gain.

Often problem poverty families simply lack connection with the outside world. Friendships are meager or nonexistent. Encounters with institutions such as churches, schools, and health services are dreaded and avoided. The potential for connectedness, interest, and self-affirmation is not available. This avoidance of systems is particularly problematic when school-age children are in the family. Children from transient families may be behind in school or be targets of ridicule from other children due to their lack of appropriate wardrobe and accessories. Parents who do work may not have the resources to provide after-school care for their children, leaving little ones alone at home to fend for themselves. Children in this situation are referred to as latch-key children.

In these and other ways, external systems can affect the processes operative within the family and leave its members alienated, depreciated, distrustful, and hostile toward the outside world. They are thus more intensively dependent on one another for affirmation and rewards, and are subject to heightened interpersonal tension. Fewer exchanges with external systems mean that family members often lack awareness of the standards and expectations of the outside world. There is a lack of knowledge of what may be available to them or how to make use of what is available. Agencies sometimes even operate to make such information inaccessible to family members. Therefore, problem poverty families often lack the repertoire of appropriate knowledge and behaviors available to them. The family system has in effect been closed off to inputs from the outside world that could be potentially helpful in solving the family's problems. Because of deficits of information and skills, contacts with social institutions often end in failure and disappointment. Thus, a negative interaction occurs between the poverty family and external systems. Over time, relationships deteriorate unless processes are set in motion that alter the behaviors of either the family or external systems, or both. The failure to achieve the desired positive connections must be attributed to the stance of the outside world and to the family's limitations. New behaviors initiated by the family or by the external systems affect the interaction between them and offer hope of improvement in the family and in its relationship with the outside world. If new information and resources are made available, the family has to be able to respond to make effective use of them. It may need assistance in learning to respond to the altered situation, since its responses have been tailored for the external systems as they had been behaving. Treatment, therefore, must contain a substantial element of advocacy to change external systems. In other instances, the limitations in the family's knowledge and coping skills should be the focus of treatment.

Learning how and where to find and acquire better housing, employment, daycare, educational and health services, and competence in relating to the people they have to meet in the process are among the knowledge and skills areas needed (Ziefert & Braun, 1991). The benefits of these services and the acquisition of skills in relating to the people involved will alter transactions with the outside world. The emphasis on here and now and what is to be done, which is reflective of family treatment in general, is a particularly useful orientation with this stressed group of families.

EVIDENCE-BASED TREATMENT/BEST PRACTICES

All too often, social workers and other helpers have concluded that reality problems such as income, housing, and health care must be solved before obvious problems of individual and family coping can be addressed. Our approach addresses both aspects concurrently, not sequentially. It is necessary to focus simultaneously on both the internal and external family issues, as well as on the way in which the family manages its relationship with those realities. Solutions to the very real problems of employment, housing, health care, and job and school performance are achieved when the family works together at the solutions. Interactions between family members that encourage or discourage, help or hinder, and speed or slow progress are a concurrent focus of family work.

Assessment Tools

Chapters 8 and 9 in Jordan and Franklin (2003) describe techniques for assessing families, especially those with multiple problems. Genograms and other maps may be used with families to begin to understand their multiple problems in a systemic way. Then, family systems measures such as the FACES III (Olson, 1986) can help to assess family boundary and other issues. Other family issues, such as communication, problem solving, and family relationship, may be measured by rapid assessment instruments (RAIs) in Corcoran and Fischer (2000). RAIs are brief and easy to administer, as well as designed for use with the single-subject design approach mentioned in Chapter 3. The Corcoran and Fischer book also includes measures of social supports and other environmental scales to assess the external problems of these multiple problem families, such as need for housing, support groups, and so forth.

A problem-solving orientation in intervening with families is consistent with an emphasis that has long existed in some places in social work (Perlman, 1957). The social worker has the dual task of achieving solutions to a problem and increasing the problem-solving capacity of the persons being served. Next we will emphasize the means for developing the problem-solving capacity of the family group as we suggest interventions for both the internal and external systemic problems that multiple-problem families experience.

Internal Family Interventions

Internal family interventions seek to improve the relationship functioning of the family. The focus here is on family communication training, structural family therapy, and in-home treatment.

Family Communication Training When family communication patterns are faulty, they do not result in decisions to change or undertake new action. Things are left hanging when attention is diverted or there is overt disagreement and no way to resolve it. As the family persists in its unproductive ways, positive feelings shared among members dissipate. The worker's role in regulating the family's communications must therefore be an active one.

BOX 6.1 | Cultural Differences

Data from the National Survey of America's Families (Urban Institute, 2000) indicates that Caucasian Americans are improving on indicators of well-being while minority Americans are more likely to live in deep poverty or 50 percent below the poverty line. Though most poor people are Caucasian, minorities are disproportionately represented in the group below the poverty line.

The reasons for poverty in African American families include the interplay between chronic unemployment, discrimination, and a decline in marriage rates with a corresponding increase in single-parent teen mothers.

Lambert (2004) reports communication training and partner-assisted problem solving as effective with general life stresses and problems (pp. 399–400). He also reports support of communication training for families with anxiety problems in either general situations or those involving an alcoholic member. Specific techniques used were cognitive behavioral mood management training, individual communication training, and communication training with a family member or close friend participating (Lambert, 2004, pp. 422–23).

Family Structural and Other Family Systems Interventions   Interventions in structure are designed to do several things. They serve to support the adults as parents who can provide the direction and structure needed by the children for adequate socialization and emotional growth. This implies that there will consequently be less need for the children to function as parents or for generational boundaries to become unclear and diffuse. Interventions in this area also seek to strengthen the marital relationship, if there is one, or to provide the single parent with some source of satisfaction of the need for growth and emotional support outside of the relationship to the children.

Structural and other family systems interventions show promise for effectively helping families. "Models like . . . behavioral couple therapy, emotionally focused couple therapy, functional family therapy, and multisystemic therapy have demonstrated effectiveness for a wide range of clients with various clinical problems and can be replicated in local communities (Lambert, 2004, p. 638). Franklin and Jordan (2002) cite a number of effectiveness studies (p. 258) that claim the following family models as having the best evidence to support their efficacy: behavioral, functional, psychoeducational, multisystemic, and structural family therapies. These models reportedly have well-developed clinical protocols, procedures, and treatment manuals.

A number of techniques from these models may be used with families (Corsini & Wedding, 2005, pp. 391–93), including the following:

Reframing is a technique used to relabel families' problem behavior by relabeling it as a positive. A rebelling teenager is reframed as striving for independence.

Table 6.1 | Assessment Instruments

Measure	Description	Reliability	Validity	Source
Family Adaptability and Cohesion Scale (FACES III)	A 20-item measure of family structure, specifically family cohesion and adaptability	Fair internal consistency with .77 for cohesion and .62 for adaptability	Good face validity and fair known-groups validity	Olsen, 1985
The Beck Depression Inventory (BDI)	A 21-item self-administered questionnaire designed to measure depressive symptoms; age range: 13–80; time required: 5–10 minutes	Test-retest reliability ranges from .48–.86	Content, discriminant and convergent validity	Beck, Steer, & Brown, 1996
Family Problem-Solving Communication	A 10-item questionnaire designed to measure the two dominant family communication patterns: incendiary and affirming communication (the way families cope with hardship and catastrophes)	Excellent internal consistency with alpha of .89	Good concurrent validity	McCubbin et al., 1996
Social Support Index	A 17-item scale designed to measure degree to which families find support in their communities	Very good internal consistency with alpha of .82	Good concurrent validity	Hamilton et al., 1986

Enactment, a role-playing technique, instructs families to act out their problem in the therapy session. The practitioner then may intervene on the spot with structural or other modifications to more successfully resolve the problem.

Circular questioning is a technique used by practitioners to get at differing family members' perceptions of the same issue. For instance, the same question is asked of every family member. Family members' awareness is increased about others' views and how the problems originated, allowing them the opportunity to create new solutions.

Cognitive restructuring may be used to reveal family members' unrealistic expectations or beliefs. Once the faulty beliefs are out in the open, the practitioner may help to replace these with more profitable thinking.

The *miracle question* is a technique used to help family members operationalize their problem and outcomes. For example, they may be asked to describe what life would be like if they woke up tomorrow morning and life was perfect.

The behavioral approaches "emphasize learning skills through a four-step process: (1) therapists' modeling the skill, (2) clients' role-playing and practicing the skill in session, (3) clients' being assigned homework to continue practicing the skill in their daily lives, and (4) therapists' gaining feedback from clients about their success in learning the skills and adjusting the training to accommodate individual differences when learning is not successful" (Franklin & Jordan, 2002, pp. 258–59).

In-Home Treatment   Beginning in-home treatment may be guided by a set of principles, the first being to "start where the client is." In finding "where the family is," it is particularly important to identify the needs and goals of family members as they often don't see the need for treatment or change. Family members need to be able to see what is in it for them, especially in those instances in which the referral was because of the actions of only one of them.

A second principle is to work with the family as a group; the third principle is to work at the client families' home or at least be available for work at home. A significant corollary is that, even though these families do not see themselves in need of counseling or therapy, therapeutic change efforts do not have to wait until the family's material or service needs have been met.

In the worker's efforts during beginning stages to join the family and establish a good working relationship, it is important to remain aware of the harsh realities confronted by poor families. Workers' willingness to help families deal with these realities by seeking to understand their living conditions, cultural patterns, value systems, and goals needs to be conveyed. Gwyn and Kilpatrick (1981) emphasize this as being of particular value in working with poor black families. Sherman (1983) also stresses the effort of the worker and family to identify, clarify, and achieve goals that are important to the family in dealing with both material and interpersonal problems. Developing tasks related to these roles and building skills needed to complete the tasks are important aspects of the worker and family's agenda. These activities serve both to solve problems and increase family problem-solving ability. Worker bridging and advocacy with school systems, for example, conveys willingness to help with practical issues while also developing the family's ability to handle them (Aponte, 1976). Respecting family autonomy in setting goals and in seeking their active participation gradually decreases the likelihood of the unresponsiveness described previously. Rabin, Rosenberg, and Sens (1982) found that efforts to create an atmosphere of familiarity were particularly helpful in establishing a working relationship with the family. Workers attempted to become known as family members through informality and the sharing of personal experiences and feelings, including anger. They also made extensive efforts to know the resources, practices, and values of the community and to become known in it. These efforts enabled families to be in more positive contact with the world beyond themselves and to reduce their sense of isolation.

In-home services usually include clinical services (counseling) , skills training (anger management), and concrete services (food, housing) (Walton, 2002, p. 286). We will discuss this model again in Chapter 9 when we describe use of an in-home approach for families involved with the child welfare system.

Child Treatment   Although parents tend to avoid organizations like schools, the schools can be a major source of support for at-risk populations, such as homeless or latch-key children. Lambert (2005) reviews interventions that are well designed, empirically sound techniques for helping that include: cognitive-behavioral skills training approaches, cognitive-behavioral school interventions, problem-solving models, and group modality and brief treatment models (pp. 314–18). The treatment manual in this chapter is from this group of interventions (see Table 6.3).

Intervening with External Systems: Broker and Advocate

Agency System   As the "hard to reach" label often applied to this group of families attests, the traditional approaches in family agencies, mental health services, and public social services have not been successful in meeting their needs or gaining participation in treatment efforts. First of all, it is necessary to conceptualize the problems as those of the family in order for the staff to "think family" in looking at the presenting problem. The approach we are putting forth envisions work with all members of the family, frequently in conjoint sessions, and often in the home (although sometimes in the office). Success in engaging the family requires that workers relate to family-defined needs and concerns including material ones, rather than those of the worker or referral source. And, given unpredicted occurrence of new or unanticipated problems, the traditional once-a-week, by-appointment approach must yield to telephone or in-person availability as needed.

While these strategies have been used with a variety of families, their use with poverty families is especially necessary for successful engagement. In these aspects of beginning the treatment and continuing throughout the treatment effort, the worker acts to meet real needs, both material and psychological, while also working to develop trust, to teach and educate by instruction and demonstration, and to alter structure and interrupt dysfunctional interactive processes between family members. Such activity implies not only special efforts, orientation, and attitudes on the part of workers but also a special commitment of agency purpose and resources that is not always required in treatment of other families.

Worker and Time Investment   Different combinations of workers and allocations of time have been utilized in engaging multiple-problem families. So often their needs are immediate, or problems occur simultaneously with several family members, or agencies to which one or another member is known have conflicting expectations. They feel themselves to be in crisis. With all that is happening, one person cannot be responsive to all aspects of their lives.

In some instances, attempts to work with the family begin as endeavors to coordinate the efforts of agencies that have been working with different members of the family, with each agency having expectations for family participation, some of which may be confusing. A meeting of representatives of all agencies with the family leads to a designation of a therapy team, clarifies for the family what is known about them, and serves to define the goals of the family. This has been found to be particularly useful in enjoining participation in treatment in cases of child abuse and neglect in which the parents do not acknowledge the violence (Cirillo & DiBlasio, 1992). This may be followed, in some instances, by a multiple-impact approach. A team of professionals schedules a full day or more for its initial meeting with the family, generally at an office. The several therapists meet together with the entire family. As they become clearer about the problems, who is affected by them, and the roles of various family members, different members of the team meet separately with subsets of family members, such as parents or children, for further assessment and work on specific aspects of the problem or on particular relationships. At some point, the team meets separately to clarify their understanding and to formulate a plan and/or make recommendations.

In other instances, contact begins with the family bringing a problematic family member to the agency or clinic with the request to treat or change that individual. Sufficient time is spent with the patient and the family to understand the circumstances that prompted the family action and how the individual's behavior affects and is affected by other family members, and to develop an initial plan for treatment that relates to the problems and offers help for all affected members.

In another variation of worker time investment, the worker moves into a heavier time commitment in the home. The therapist is responsible only for three or four cases and spends a day or more weekly in contact with the family, assisting in location of resources, medical care, and housing, as well as promoting joint activities and helping to resolve conflicts inside the family and relationships outside of it. That much time with the family offers a good opportunity to observe family operations and to promote constructive methods specific to the situations that arise.

Therapist Attitudes   Social workers need a substantial degree of self-awareness and self-examination about their similarity to and difference from the poverty family with regard to their own family experience, social class, and ethnic and cultural background (Aponte, 1991). The tendency of workers to judge the family solely on the basis of their own life experience needs to be replaced by efforts to see the family in its social context. An attitude of positive regard for the family is essential, one that assumes that they are doing the best they know how, given their situation, but need help in finding more useful ways (Parnell & VanderKloot, 1991). Similarly, workers need to be aware of the family's consciousness of their difference from the worker and the ways in which this is a barrier to the worker's attempt to join with the family.

Problem poverty families often exhibit behaviors that test the worker's attitudes, interest, and concern. Previous experience with workers may enhance the family's doubts about the worker's interest, reliability, and concern. Such behavior decreases over time as workers persevere and family members become convinced of the worker's interest and dependability.

Work with the Extended Family   The client family may have at some point turned to extended family for help with material needs or other problems with the result that extended family capacity to help may be exhausted or never have been available. The reverse is often the case, with extended family problems adding to those of the client family. Problems of mental illness, substance abuse, and marital relationships of siblings or their parent generation require involvement, investment of time and, often, taking sides. Getting these extended family persons connected to sources of help becomes necessary to relieve the client family. The finding that extended family is not always a resource is supported by Lindblad-Goldberg and Dukes (1985) in a study of single-parent black families known to a community clinic and a comparable group of nonclinic families. In terms of reciprocity of emotional support, clinic mothers felt they provided significantly more emotional support than they received from all network members, especially family members. The same was true of instrumental needs.

In other instances, the problem is more one of conflicted relationships. The parent or parents have not separated and are overconnected to families of origin. They are still struggling with issues of control or being cared about and find themselves unable to maintain their separateness from parents or siblings. Material dependence may inhibit individuation and achievement of psychological independence.

The situation of Mrs. B is illustrative. She was separated from her husband, who was extremely controlling. She had no special job skills and had never had outside employment. She was referred by the school because of her second son's loud talking and foul language in school and at home, where she found him hard to control. At first contact, she and her three children were living with and dependent upon her parents. Her mother had always been overprotective of her, as demonstrated by Mrs. B's report that her mother had accompanied her to the school bus stop until she was in high school. She continued to operate in this controlling manner with Mrs. B and was directive with the children as well. Mrs. B had never become fully independent of her mother, and grandmother was competing for the role of mother, the role of grandmother being nonexistent in this instance. The children reported that they felt like Ping-Pong balls between their mother, who was trying to handle parental responsibilities, and grandmother. Treatment for the family included helping Mrs. B to find ways to enter the job market, to find separate housing once she got work, to provide structure for the three children, and to be firm with her mother that she was responsible for the children's care and discipline, and that she (grandmother) would not have this responsibility but would be called upon for counsel and advice. Reconciling conflicts with extended family may serve to reduce isolation in addition to providing other types of support for families who need it.

Developing Community Networks   Where family networks are small, other networks in the community may serve as connections and support. Delgado and Humm-Delgado (1982) identify natural support systems in the Hispanic community in addition to the extended family; religious institutions, social clubs, and folk healers. Researchers emphasize the importance of the therapist becoming aware of the resources of the cultural and ethnic community by attending their meetings and learning to know individuals in them and what they are doing (Franklin & Jordan, 1999; Piazza & delValle, 1992). Members of client families can respond to members of their cultural community. They need to hear the complexity of the family's story within the context of society's stories in a way that simplifies the story for ordinary, daily family life (Franklin & Jordan, 1999; McGill, 1992). Learning the cultural story helps in showing how others have dealt with similar problems and connects them to persons in their own group who might be helpful.

In addition to connectedness to community in the ways just discussed, facilitating connectedness to community institutions and services is a core element in assisting these families. The bridging effort often requires the worker to accompany one or more family members to new locations to establish contacts with the workers providing those services or with members of other families who are participating. Since some family members may be more ready than others to participate, the worker must direct attention to the way some members undermine the efforts of others to relate to new services or individuals.

The family's increasing openness to these new relationships may be attributed to the trust they acquire in the worker. It is also, in part, a function of the restructuring of the relationships and communication processes. The family's use of these resources offers more natural support for the family and may reduce over time the amount of worker investment required.

In the systems frame of reference, only part of the family's isolation and lack of positive relations in the community may be attributed to the family itself. We have suggested that the operations of external systems often work to the direct disadvantage of the family through policies that divide the family or restrict the resources available to it. In addition, agencies sometimes work at cross purposes, further undermining the performance of individual members and the integrity of the family group.

Family members may learn, when they don't know how, to relate to external systems in ways that produce advantages for them. But direct worker intervention is often needed to help loosen interpretations of restrictive policies or to coordinate when policies of different agencies are at cross purposes. The worker's interpretation to agencies of the functioning and needs of the family is one direct way of intervening. Case conferences with several agencies are often needed. Joint conferences between the family members and workers from several agencies may also be helpful. These are particularly significant when a given agency is acquainted with only part of the family and is unaware of or does not understand significant aspects of the family situation. The effort of the family worker is to orient all personnel involved to the family as a whole.

Additionally, practitioners need knowledge of the "public policy process, how legislators create policy, and where in that process intervention can take place" (Segal, Gerdes, & Steiner, 2004, p. 379). Worker brokerage on behalf of the family brings full circle the range of interventions with poverty problem families. Though we have directed our attention primarily to work with the family itself and to the need to participate with the family in engaging agencies, we do not thereby minimize the importance of the worker's role of broker and advocate for the family.

See Table 6.2 for a summary of research studies on the interventions mentioned here.

TREATMENT MANUAL

Reid (2000, pp. 166–68) discusses the tasks of helping homeless clients in his book *The Task Planner*. Though the treatment plan provided here is not totally operationalized, it provides a step-by-step plan for helping homeless clients.

GOALS:

Provide client with:
1. job training
2. life skill
3. employment resources

TASK MENU:

1. Apply for social services and emergency shelter. Practitioner's role: (1) Homeless clients may be experiencing low self-esteem and inability to identify or verbalize their basic needs. They need help from the practitioner in identifying those basic needs, such as food or transportation. (2) Female, homeless clients may have experienced violence at home or on the streets. This should be addressed and appropriate resources provided. (3) Lists of available resources should be provided for clients. These may include resources for health care, shelter, financial aid, legal aid, employment and job training, and housing. These lists should also include

Table 6.2 | Research Studies

Family Communication	Child Treatment	Systems Intervention
PREP, a skills-based relationship enhancement program, is being studied with high-risk couples (minorities and those who are economically disadvantaged). It was previously shown to improve communication and relationship satisfaction in controlled studies (Stanley et al., 2002).	Children receiving an eight-week problem-solving intervention at school improved significantly over the control group on variables including school attendance and grades (Harris & Franklin, 2004). Children receiving CBT treatment (versus controls) showed improvement on multiple measures of anxiety, as well as social problems, aggression, hyperactivity, depression, and distress (Albano & Kendall, 2000).	Reviews indicate that the benefits of MST versus other treatments are evidenced on parent and adolescent measures of parent and child psychopathology, family functioning and relationship, rearrest rates, severity of offenses, drug use, and reinstitutionalization. Additionally, MST is shown to be more cost effective than other efficacious treatments, such as functional family therapy, special foster care, and parent problem solving (Burns et al., 2000; Henggeler et al., 1998).

sleep-off stations, drug and alcohol services, abused women's shelters and services, immigrant services, and self-help groups such as Alcoholics Anonymous.

2. Obtain documents. Practitioner's role: Clients may have lost documents needed to obtain a job or other services, such as a social security card. They may need help applying for these.
3. Compose a resume. Practitioner's role: Help clients put together a resume by providing samples or copies. Then assist the client in putting together her own resume that builds on her strengths.
4. Practice interviewing skills. Practitioner's role: Help the client by role-playing with her a typical job interview. Give corrective feedback and use repeated practice until the client feels comfortable.
5. Use stress inoculation. Practitioner's role: Help the client by preparing her for the stress to be expected in job and other situations.
6. Secure appropriate clothing. Practitioner's role: Help the client find clothing appropriate for job training or interview situations.
7. Apply for job or training program. Practitioner's role: Help the client find and apply for appropriate jobs and programs. She may need help with the paperwork and other details of applying.

See Table 6.3 for a listing of available treatment manuals.

Table 6.3 | Treatment Manuals

Manual Reference	Author's Contact Information
Multiple-Family Psychoeducational Group Treatment Manual McFarlane, W. R., Deakins, S. M., Gingerich, S. L., Dunne, E., Hornen, B., & Newmark, M. 1991. *Multiple-Family Psychoeducational Group Treatment Manual.* New York: Biosocial Treatment Division, New York State Psychiatric Institute.	http://w3.ouhsc.edu/bpfamily/Detail/McFarlane.html
Behavioral Family Intervention Sanders, M. R., & Dadds, M. R. 1993. *Behavioral Family Intervention.* Needham Heights, MA: Allyn & Bacon.	Allyn & Bacon 75 Arlington St., Suite 300 Boston, MA 02116 Telephone: 617-848-6000
Taking Charge: A Cognitive-Behavioral Life Skills Curriculum for Adolescent Mothers. Harris, M., & Franklin, C. 2004. "Evidence-Based Life Skills for Pregnant Adolescents in School Settings." In *Evidence-Based Practice Manual,* eds. A. Roberts & K. Yeager. New York: Oxford.	Oxford Press 198 Madison Ave. New York, NY 10016 http://222.oup-usa.org
PREP, Prevention and Relationship Enhancement Program Stanley, S., Markman, H., & Jenkins, N. 2002. *Marriage Education and Government Policy: Helping Couples Who Choose Marriage Achieve Success.* Denver, CO: PREP.	PREP Inc. P.O. Box 4793 Greenwood Village, CO 80155-4793 Telephone: 800-366-0166 http://www.prepinc.com/main/prep_team.asp

CASE EXAMPLE

Star Evans came to the clinic after being referred from the homeless shelter. She had been living on the streets for the past year; she had been staying in the shelter for the last three weeks at night, ever since the weather turned colder. Star, age 22, had her two children with her: Max, age 3; and Millie, age 1 1/2. The children's father, Ron, left Star when she was 8 1/2 months pregnant. He moved to another state and had had no contact with his children since he left town.

> **THERAPIST:** Hello Star. It's nice to meet you. My, your children are so well behaved!

> **STAR:** Thank you, and it's nice to meet you, too.

THERAPIST: I know that the shelter referred you here today, so I'm guessing there are some needs you and the children have that maybe I can help out with, like clothes, a place to live.

STAR: Yes, I do need some help, but I don't want to ask for too much. It would seem selfish.

THERAPIST: Don't worry about that—we want to help you and the children to have a more stable situation.

STAR: OK. Where do we start?

THERAPIST: Let's talk about what your needs are; the ones that are *not* getting met? (Step 1: Help the client to identify her needs.)

STAR: It's hard to live on the street with two babies. I would like some help with them. Maybe then I could apply for a real job. Also, it can be scary sometimes, and I worry for our safety. I would like to get a job, but I need childcare before that can happen. And . . .

THERAPIST: Maybe you would like to take a look at this list of resources to help you think of what is missing for you, Max, and Millie. (Step 1: Have a list of resources available.)

STAR: This does help! We need food, baby formula, diapers, and a place to stay. We need a washer and dryer, good clothes, daycare for the children so I can work. Those are some of the most important ones right now.

THERAPIST: To get a job, you must have some form of identification. Do you have a driver's license or other picture ID?

STAR: No, I lost them about six months ago in the park when I was trying to catch Max. He ran away from me while I was feeding the baby.

THERAPIST: That is something we can help with. (Step 2: Obtain documents.)

THERAPIST: Our agency can help with an apartment; we have a program with HUD and you qualify. We also have a pantry with food and clothing that will be a start until you can get on your feet. Oh, and the apartments have washers and dryers there for residents to use, and a playground for the children. (Step 6: Secure appropriate clothing.)

STAR: What about the daycare and a job for me? Is it hopeless?

THERAPIST: No, Star, it is definitely not hopeless; we just need to connect to the correct person. I would like to call the Rehabilitation Office while you are here so that you can speak with Mrs. Jones. She can set up an interview for you to meet with her and go over some issues about childcare and getting a job. Their office can arrange for job training, provide childcare, and so forth. (Step 7: Apply for job or training program.)

STAR: That sounds great!

THERAPIST: After we talk with Mrs. Jones, we could work on getting together a resume for you. Could we go over some of your recollections of your schooling, other training, and work history? (Step 3: Help client write a resume.)

| BOX 6.2 | **Internet Resources** |

Due to the living nature of the Internet, website addresses often change and thus we have not printed the addresses in this text. Links to the following websites are posted at the Book Companion Site at www.wadsworth.com.

Habitat for Humanity—addresses the needs of some 2 billion people worldwide living in poverty housing. More than 1 billion live in urban slums, and that figure is expected to double by 2030. Many of these people earn less than US$2 per day.

Ford Foundation—goals are to strengthen democratic values, reduce poverty and injustice, promote international cooperation, and advance human achievement.

HollandSentinel.com—works one-on-one with families to identify problems, set goals, problem solve, and establish and develop empowering strategies for escaping poverty.

PoliticsWatch.com—watches services for children and their families, with specific mention of programs that specifically target child poverty. It aims to seriously tackle the root problem of poverty.

Homeless Resources

BPHC-HCHIRC—provides Health Care for the Homeless Information Resource Center

Massachusetts Homeless Resources—provides information for and about the homeless and their service providers

US Department of Housing and Urban Development (HUD)—provides support and information for states dealing with homelessness

Marin Community Resources—Homelessness—Links to resources and services for the homeless in Marin county; sponsors Adopt A Family

Homeless Resources (Seattle Crisis Resource Directory)—provides resources particularly useful to homeless women

Harmony's Home Page: Homeless Resources & Humanitarian Links—provides information on human rights, ACLU, homelessness, animal rights, homeless resources, free speech, activism, immigrants, job opportunities, mental illness, and charities

Minneapolis.about.com—resources for the homeless, including locations of shelters and places providing free meals; lists homeless resources for some of the warmer states

SUMMARY

This chapter has focused on a rehabilitative approach to families with severe problems. It is encouraging to note the increasing numbers of family support programs that serve families in an educational mode designed to assist families before functioning becomes so problematic. Much in the manner of settlement

Other Internet Homeless Resources at http://nch.ari.net/otherhomeless .html—Internet resources on homelessness, including tips for finding free public access to the Internet and describes online resources for homeless persons

Children Living in Poverty/Latch-Key Children

Women, Children in Poverty—resources for women and children living in poverty

NCCP | National Center for Children in Poverty—identifies and promotes strategies that prevent child poverty in the United States and that improve the lives of low-income children and families

www.Campaign2000.com—reports on the more than 1.1 million children living in poverty, including reports on the release of data for child poverty in 2000

Teenpregnancy.org—reports on teen pregnancy data and the proportion of children under 6 living below 100% of the federal poverty line

BBC News | UK |—reports that four million children are living in poverty and that poor mothers are more likely to have premature babies

The Mavens' Word of the Day—reports on the origin of the phrase "latch-key children"

Aboutourkids.org—reports about latch-key children

FCD/ecitizen.gov—reports about family and community development, including latch-key children, teens, and youth

People.Virginia.edu—provides a Parenting Stress Index for use with latch-key children, measuring items like satisfaction with child-care arrangements, effects on adaptation to parenthood, and so forth

AFSCME.org—report of a conference on latch-key children in Las Vegas, 1992

Parentkidsright.com—Dr. Marilyn Heins reports on parenting strategies regarding latch-key kids

The National Crime Prevention Council—reports on latch-key children

AffordableMonitoring.com—reports on alarm systems to monitor latch-key children

North America Missing Children Association (NAMCA)—index of missing children and advice on runaway children

houses of an earlier era, programs have been initiated to relate to childhood education and health concerns. They are, however, focused on the entire family and strive to "enhance family stability, develop parental competencies, and promote the healthy development of children" (Lightburn & Kemp, 1994; Roberts & Greene, 2002).

Family support programs tend to be neighborhood oriented in order to provide easy access. They assume members have strengths that can be developed and do not focus on deficits of the families. Educational groups for fathers, mothers, children, or combinations of family members offer learning, times of celebration, and times to work together. Activities serve to foster family cohesion, as well as understanding of family roles and role performance, and to make new acquaintances and thus mitigate social isolation.

DISCUSSION QUESTIONS

1. Think of a family you know who is in danger of becoming homeless. What would be some of the important assessment issues for this family?
2. Thinking of the same family as in Question 1, what treatments would you recommend?
3. What are some of the societal issues that need to be addressed in order to eliminate homelessness?

References

Albano, A., and Kendall, P. 2000. "Cognitive Behavioural Therapy for Children and Adolescents with Anxiety Disorders: Clinical Research Advances." *International Review of Psychiatry* 14(2): 129–34.

Alexander, J. F., and Parsons, B. 1973. "Short-Term Behavioral Intervention with Delinquent Families." *Journal of Abnormal Psychology* 81:219–25.

Aponte, H. 1976. "Underorganization in the Poor Family." In *Family Therapy: Theory and Practice* (pp. 432–88), ed. P. Guerin. New York: Gardner Press.

———. 1991. "Training on the Person of the Therapist for Work with the Poor and Minorities." *Journal of Independent Social Work* 5(3–4):23–39.

Bandler, R., and Grinder, J. 1975. *The Structure of Magic*, Vol. I. Palo Alto, CA: Science and Behavior Books.

Beck, A. T., Steer, R. A., and Brown Garbin, M. G. 1988. "Psychometric Properties of the Beck Depression Inventory: Twenty-Five Years Later." *Clinical Psychology Review* 8:77–100.

Bishop, J. H. 1980. "Jobs, Cash, and Marital Instability: Review and Synthesis of Evidence." *Journal of Human Resources* 15(3):301–34.

Borrero, M. 1979. "Psychological and Emotional Impact of Unemployment." *Journal of Sociology and Social Welfare* 7:916–34.

Bowen, M. 1978. *Family Therapy in Clinical Practice*. New York: Jason Aronson.

Brennan, N. J., Holahan, J., Kenney, G. M., Rajan, S., and Zuckerman, S. 1999. *Snapshots of America's Family's Variations in Health Care across States*. Washington, DC: Urban Institute.

Burns, B., Schoenwald, S., Burchard, J., Faw, L., and Santos, A. 2000. "Comprehensive Community-Based Interventions with Severe Emotional Disorders: Multisystemic Therapy and the Wraparound Process." *Journal of Child and Family Studies* 9:283–314.

Center on Budget and Policy Priorities. 2000. "Poverty Rate Hits Lowest Level since 1979 as Unemployment Reaches a 30-Year Low." CBPP News Release retrieved October 2004 from http://www.cbpp.org/9-26-00pov.htm

Cirillo, S., and DiBlasio, P. 1992. *Families That Abuse*. New York: W. W. Norton & Co.

Clark, N., Levison, M., Evans, D., Wasilewski, Y., Feldman, C., and Mellins, R. 1990. "Communication within Low Income Families and the Management of Asthma." *Patient Education and Counseling* 15:191–210.

Conte, J. 1983. "Service Provision to Enhance Family Functioning." In *Child Welfare: Current Dilemmas, Future Directions*, eds. B. G. McGowan and W. Meezan. Itasca, IL: F. E. Peacock Publishers.

Corcoran, K., and Fischer, J. 2000. *Measures for Clinical Practice: A Source Book*. New York: The Free Press.

Corsini, R. J., and Wedding, D. 2005. *Current Psychotherapies*, 7th edition. Belmont, CA: Brooks/Cole.

Delgado, M., and Humm-Delgado, D. 1982. "Natural Support Systems: Source of Strength in Hispanic Communities." *Social Work* 27(1):83–89.

Franklin, C., and Jordan, C. 1999. *Family Practice: Brief Systems Methods for Social Work*. Belmont, CA: Brooks/Cole.

———. 2002. "Effective Family Therapy: Guidelines for Practice." Chapter 45 in *Social Workers' Desk Reference* (pp. 254–63), eds. A. Roberts and G. Greene. New York: Oxford.

Gwyn, F., and Kilpatrick, A. 1981. "Family Therapy with Low Income Blacks: Tool or Turnoff." *Social Casework* 62(5):259–66.

Halpern, R. 1991. "Supportive Services for Families in Poverty: Dilemmas of Reform." *Social Service Review* 65:343–63.

Hamilton, H, Patterson, J., and Glynn, T. 1986. "Social Support Index (SSI)." In *Family Assessment: Resiliency, Coping and Adaptation. Inventories for Research and Practice* (pp. 357–89), eds. H. McCubbin, A. Thompson, and M. McCubbin. Madison: University of Wisconsin.

Harris, M. B., and Franklin, C. 2004. "Evidence-Based Life Skills Interventions for Pregnant Adolescents in School Settings." In *Evidence-Based Practice Manual: Research and Outcome Measures in Health and Human Services* (pp. 312–23), eds. A. R. Roberts and K. R. Yeager. New York: Oxford University Press.

Henggeler, S., Schoenwald, S., Borduin, C., and Rowland, M. 1998. *Mulitsystemic Treatment of Antosocial Behavior in Children and Adolescents*. New York: Guilford.

Jenkins, H. 1990. "Poverty, State and the Family: A Challenge for Family Therapy." *Contemporary Family Therapy* 12(4):311–25.

Jordan, C., and Franklin, C. 2003. *Clinical Assessment for Social Workers: Quantitative and Qualitative Methods*, 2nd edition. Chicago: Lyceum Books.

Jordan, C., Hunter, S., Rycraft, J., and Vandiver, V. 2004. "Assessing Families Who are Multistressed." In *Clinical Assessment for Social Workers: Quantitative and Qualitative Methods* (2nd ed., pp. 313–83), eds. C. Jordan and C. Franklin. Chicago: Lyceum Books.

Kagan, R., and Shlossberg, S. 1989. *Families in Perpetual Crisis*. New York: W. W. Norton & Co.

Kantor, D., Peretz, A., and Zander, R. 1984. "The Cycle of Poverty: Where to Begin." In *Family Therapy with School Problems*, ed. Barbara Okun. Rockville, MD: Aspen Systems Corp.

Lambert, M. 2004. *Bergin and Garfield's Handbook of Psychotherapy and Behavior Change*. New York: John Wiley and Sons.

Liem, R., and Liem, J. 1988. "Psychological Effects of Unemployment on Workers and Their Families." *Journal of Social Issues* 44(4):87–105.

Lightburn, A., and Kemp, S. 1994. "Family Support Programs: Opportunities for Community-Based Practice." *Families in Society* 75(1):16–26.

Lindblad-Goldberg, M., and Dukes, J. 1985. "Social Support in Black, Low-Income Single-Parent Families: Normative and Dysfunctional Patterns." *American Journal of Orthopsychiatry* 55(1):42–58.

McCubbin, M., McCubbin, H., and Thompson, A. 1996. "Family Problem Solving Communication (FPSC)." In *Family Assessment: Resiliency, Coping and Adaptation. Inventories for Research and Practice* (pp. 639–86), eds. H. McCubbin, A. Thompson and M. McCubbin. Madison: University of Wisconsin.

McGill, D. 1992. "The Cultural Story in Multi Cultural Family Therapy." *Families in Society* 73:339–49.

Minuchin, S. 1965. "Conflict Resolution Family Therapy." *Psychiatry* 28:278–86.

Minuchin, S., and Montalvo, B. 1967. "Techniques for Working with Disorganized Low Socio-Economic Families." *American Journal of Orthopsychiatry* 37:880–87.

Minuchin, S., Guerney, B., Rosman, B., and Schumer, F. 1967. *Families of the Slums*. New York: Basic Books.

Montalvo, B., and Gutierrez, M. 1983. "A Perspective for the Use of the Cultural Dimension in Family Therapy." In *Cultural Perspectives in Family Therapy*, ed. Celia Falicov. Rockville, MD: Aspen Systems Corp.

Olsen, D. 1985. "Circumplex Model VII: Validation Studies and FACES-III." *Family Process* 25:337–51.

Olson, D. H., and Tiesel, J. 1993. *FACES III: Linear Scoring and Interpretation*. St. Paul: University of Minnesota, Family Social Science.

Parnell, M., and VanderKloot, J. 1991. "Mental Health Services, 2001: Serving New America." *Journal of Independent Social Work* 11(2):183–203.

Perlman, H. 1957. *Social Casework*. Chicago: University of Chicago Press.

Piazza, J., and delValle, C. 1992. "Community-Based Family Therapy Training: An Example of Work with Poor and Minority Families." *Journal of Strategic and Systemic Therapies* 11(2):53–69.

Rabin, C., Rosenberg, H., ad Sens, M. 1982. "Home Based Marital Therapy for Multi-Problem Families." *Journal of Marital and Family Therapy* 8(4):451–62.

Rabinowitz, C. 1969. "Therapy for Underprivileged Delinquent Families." In *Family Dynamics and Female Sexual Delinquency*, eds. O. Pollack and A. Friedman. Palo Alto, CA: Science and Behavior Books.

Reid, W. 2000. *The Task Planner: An Intervention Resource for Human Service Professionals*. New York: Columbia University Press.

Roberts, A., and Greene, G. 2002. *Social Workers' Desk Reference*. New York: Oxford.

Roberts, A., and Yeager, K. 2004. *Evidence-Based Practice Manual*. New York: Oxford University Press.

Sales, E. 1995. "Surviving Unemployment: Economic Resources and Job Loss Duration in Blue Collar Households." *Social Work* 40(4):483–94.

Satir, V. 1983. *Conjoint Family Therapy*, 3rd edition. Palo Alto, CA: Science and Behavior Books.

Schorr, L. 1991. "Children, Families and the Cycle of Disadvantage." *Canadian Journal of Psychiatry* 36:437–41.

Schuerman, J., Rzepnicki, T., and Littel, J. 1994. *Putting Families First*. New York: Aldyne-deGruyter.

Segal, E. A., Gerdes, K. E., and Steiner, S. 2004. *Social Work: An Introduction to the Profession*. Belmont, CA: Brooks/Cole.

Seitz, V., Rosenbaum, L. K., and Apfel, N. H. 1985. "Effects of Family Support Intervention: A Ten-Year Follow-Up." *Child Development* 56:376–91.

Sherman, R. 1983. "Counseling the Urban Economically Disadvantaged Family." *American Journal of Orthospychiatry* 40: 413–25.

Stack, C. 1974. *All Our Kin*. New York: Harper & Row.

Stanley, S., Markman, H., and Jenkins, N. 2002. *Marriage Education and Government Policy: Helping Couples Who Choose Marriage Achieve Success*. Denver, CO: PREP.

Walton, E. 2002. "Family-Centered Services in Child Welfare." Chapter 51 in *Social Workers' Desk Reference* (pp. 283–89), eds. A. Roberts and G. Greene. New York: Oxford.

Whittaker, J., Kinney, J., Tracy, E., and Booth, C. 1990. "Reaching High-Risk Families." Chapter 3 in *The Homebuilders Model*. New York: Aldyne-deGruyter.

Williams, B. 1994. "Reflections on Family Poverty." *Families in Society* 75: 47–50.

Wood, D., Valdez, R. B., Hayashi, T., and Shen, A. 1990. "Homeless and Housed Families in Los Angeles: A Study Comparing Demographic Economic and Family Function Characteristics." *American Journal of Public Health* 80(9):1049–52.

Ziefert, M., and Braun, K. 1991. "Skill Building for Effective Intervention with Homeless Families." *Families in Society* 72(4):212–19.

Evidence-Based Treatment of Persistent Mental Disorders

CHAPTER 7

INTRODUCTION

Social work treatment with severe and persistent mental disorders has included direct services to mentally ill individuals and work with their families. In addition to feeling overwhelmed, confused, guilty, and helpless, families have often felt they were being blamed for the mental disorders of their family members. This blame was even worse for family members who happened to have a mental disorder themselves. Recent research does not support the view that families are the cause of mental illness. Although mental illness maybe transmitted genetically, family relationships are not responsible for the creation of any particular mental disorder. In the past, however, mental health professionals, including social workers, fell into the faulty assumptions of viewing family communication patterns and relationship problems as causing mental illness. In particular, problems in relationship functioning (i.e., boundaries, cohesion, and conflict) and communication were identified as causing persistent mental disorders such as schizophrenia, for example.

While these problems are often present in families who have a mentally ill member, they are not unique to families of persons with severe and persistent mental illness, and relationship and communication problems have often been observed in families of clients with other diagnoses or presenting problems. Unhealthy family relationships and communication patterns are the family's response to crisis, stress, and mental illness, and these patterns can adversely affect the client's adjustment or recovery. The good news, however, is that families can learn more appropriate communications and coping patterns, and family members can acknowledge that their responses to the mental illness have solved neither their family members' difficulties nor their own. Thus, the family can learn how to cope with the difficult behavior they encounter in their mentally ill family member, and in response, this helps the mentally ill family member's improvement as well. This chapter reviews prevalence, assessment, and best evidence-based treatments for major depressive disorder, bipolar disorder and schizophrenia. It further illustrates in some detail treatments for schizophrenia using an evidence-based, multifamily group treatment manual and a case study.

POPULATION DESCRIPTION AND DEFINITIONS

Schizophrenia

Schizophrenia is a disorder that affects families across many different countries and cultures. The occurrence of schizophrenia among adults is between .5 percent to 1.5 percent, and the range of new cases reported annually varies between .5 to 5 cases per 10,000 people. Individuals born in urban areas are at higher risk than those born in rural areas. Rates of schizophrenia are higher for individuals who have a family history of schizophrenia (DSM-IV-TR, 2000). The typical age of onset for schizophrenia is the mid 20s for men and late 20s for women. Affected individuals may develop symptoms abruptly or gradually, although symptoms typically develop slowly over time. Although many individuals living with schizophrenia experience more severe symptoms as the illness progresses, others may experience symptoms sporadically with periods of remission.

The Diagnostic and Statistical Manual (DSM-IV-TR) identifies the symptom characteristics and behaviors of a general type of schizophrenic illness as well as several subcategories in which certain characteristics of the general type are predominant. Symptoms of schizophrenia are classified as positive or negative symptoms. Symptoms are positive if they represent an excess or distortion of normal functions, such as delusions, hallucinations, disorganized speech, and disorganized behavior. Negative symptoms indicate a loss or diminution of normal functions, such as flattened affect or alogia, which is indicated by brief, empty responses to questions such that the person may appear to have poor fluency. Symptoms that occur early in the course of the disorder may include social withdrawal, a decreasing interest in school or work, poor hygiene, and an increase in unusual behavior or angry outbursts. Basic characteristics also include delusions, hallucinations, incoherent thinking, flat affect, and catatonia, which is indicated by a decrease in reactivity to the environment, sometimes appearing as stupor with the individual maintaining a rigid posture and resisting efforts to be moved.

Individuals with schizophrenia are diagnosed with one of five different subtypes based on symptoms presented in their most recent evaluation. Subtypes may change over time. *Paranoid* type is characterized by hallucinations and delusions that are persecutory or grandiose, and they are typically organized around a common theme. The *disorganized* type of schizophrenia is characterized by disorganized speech and behavior as well as flat or inappropriate affect. Delusions and hallucinations are not organized around a coherent theme. An individual diagnosed with *catatonic* type schizophrenia may present with physical immobility characterized by catalepsy, indicated by stupor or a waxy flexibility in which a posture may be held for long periods and movements are slow, or by excessive motor activity that is not influenced by external stimuli. Catatonic type may also be characterized by a rigid posture, bizarre postures or grimacing, repetition of a word or phrase spoken by another (echolalia), and repetitive imitation of another's movements (echopraxia). When an individual is diagnosed with *undifferentiated* type, her symptoms meet the criteria for schizophrenia but not the criteria for paranoid, disorganized, or catatonic type. *Residual* type schizophrenia is used for individuals who have had at least one episode of schizophrenia but currently do not have prominent positive symptoms such as delusions or hallucinations.

Mood Disorders

Mood disorders include the depressive disorders and bipolar disorders, which are characterized by a combination of depressive and manic episodes. *Major depression* is a common and serious depressive disorder that is more common than either schizophrenia or bipolar disorder. Symptoms of major depression include a depressed mood that lasts for most of the day nearly every day, diminished interest in almost all activities, significant weight loss or weight gain or change in appetite, insomnia or hypersomnia, psychomotor retardation or agitation, feelings of worthlessness or excessive guilt, diminished ability to concentrate, recurrent thoughts of death, and suicidal ideation. Among women, 10-25 percent will develop major depression during their lifetime, and 5 to 12 percent of men will develop the disorder (DSM-IV-TR, 2000).

Dysthymic disorder is characterized by a chronically depressed mood for most of the day for the majority of days during the past two years or longer. As many as 75 percent of those diagnosed with dysthymic disorder will be diagnosed with major depressive disorder within five years. Approximately 6 percent of the population will develop the disorder during their lifetimes, and women are two to three times more likely to develop the disorder in adulthood than men are (DSM-IV-TR, 2000).

Approximately .4 to 1.6 percent of adults will develop *bipolar I disorder* during their lifetimes. Among adolescents, 10 to 15 percent of those who experience recurrent major depressive episodes will develop bipolar I disorder. The prevalence of bipolar I disorder is approximately .5 percent of adults. The disorder affects men and women differently, with men tending to experience more hypomanic episodes and women experiencing more depressive episodes. Rapid cycling, indicated by at least four episodes of a mood disturbance during the last 12 months, is more common among women. Bipolar disorder is classified as bipolar I or bipolar II, which are distinguished by the presence of a depressive episode. Bipolar I disorder is characterized by at least one manic episode. Symptoms of a manic episode may include persistently elevated, expansive, or irritable mood; grandiosity; decreased need for sleep; flight of ideas and racing thoughts; distractibility; psychomotor agitation; and engaging in pleasurable activities that are likely to have negative consequences, such as spending excessive amounts of money in a short period of time. Bipolar II disorder is characterized by the presence of a depressive episode and a hypomanic episode. In order to meet the specifier for the diagnosis for rapid cycling, the client must have experienced rapid cycling of four mood disturbance episodes during the last 12 months (DSM-IV-TR, 2000).

ASSESSMENT ISSUES

Schizophrenia

Many measurement instruments are available to assess for symptoms of schizophrenia. Table 7.1 presents a list of measures commonly used for assessment and treatment of severe persistent mental illnesses, along with reliability and validity information. Measures available to clinicians include highly structured and semi-structured interview schedules, such as the Schedule of Affective Disorders and Schizophrenia (SADS), the Diagnostic Interview Schedule, and the Structured Clinical Interview for the DSM-IV. Valid and reliable rating scales such as the MMPI and the Milan are also available to assess for symptoms of mental illness. Other scales can be used to measure changes in symptoms. These include the Scale for the Assessment of Negative Symptoms, the Scale for the Assessment of Positive Symptoms, the Brief Psychiatric Rating Scale, and the Psychiatric Symptom Assessment Scale.

Mood Disorders

Many of the measures mentioned for their use with schizophrenia are also used for assessing symptoms of mood disorders. These include the Structured Clinical Interview for the DSM and the Schedule for Affective Disorders and Schizophrenia as well as the MMPI and Milan scales. The Multiple Problem Screening Inventory (MPSI) is a self-administered assessment that includes subscales for assessing symptoms in many areas including depression. There are several assessment measures specifically designed for assessment of depression. The Beck Depression Inventory is the most widely used measure for depression in adults. It consists of 21 items and was designed to be consistent with the DSM-IV-TR. The measure is self-administered and can be completed in 5 to 10 minutes (Beck, Steer, & Brown, 1996). The Hamilton Rating Scale for Depression is designed to be completed by the practitioner and is typically used when the practitioner has strong evidence that the client has a depressive disorder. Like the Beck Depression Inventory, it is designed for use with adults. Another measure used to assess for depression is the Center for Epidemiological Status Depression Scale, Revised (CES-D-R). This measure has been used successfully with clients of varying ages, ethnicities, and cultures (Beals, Manson, Keane, & Dick, 1991).

Assessing the Impact on the Family

Relationships between families affected by mental illness and mental health practitioners have often been compromised by the historical view that families caused or exacerbated the symptoms of the family member suffering from mental illness. In the case of schizophrenia, psychoanalytic theorists defined dysfunctional familial relationships and the "schizophenogenic" mother as causes of schizophrenia, which resulted in families feeling that they were being blamed for the illness (Franklin & Jordan, 1999).

Families affected by mental illness face periods of crisis brought by the onset of symptoms or the return of symptoms. They raise questions about hospitalization and how the family should respond. In the case of schizophrenia, the problems of thought and perception, severe withdrawal from contact, and the bizarre and assaultive behaviors cause problems of adaptation and coping in families. Family members experience stress and difficulty in knowing how to stop or control their response to behaviors. Families often experience feelings of grief and loss similar to that of losing a child (MacGregor, 1994). They report feelings of shame and guilt, efforts to shield the client and themselves from public view, and the resulting isolation from family, friends, and the larger community and its institutions. Other family members report feeling tied down and not able to live their own lives. They experience a financial drain, which is no small part of the situation (Lowyck, et al., 2004).

Family members use a variety of means to cope with their stressful situation (Fox, 1992). They may deny, explain away, hide, control, or attribute client behavior to calculated deviousness or to contrariness. They readily recognize that their efforts to deal with client behaviors have been unsuccessful in controlling the behavior, with no possibility of eliminating it. In some instances, family members' responses seem to exacerbate the unwelcome behavior, with the circular interaction resulting in regression, even to the point of hospitalization.

Family members may have difficulty understanding the complex nature of schizophrenia and its social impairments. They may lack skills to cope effectively with acute and chronic symptoms of schizophrenia and find it difficult to express feelings, both negative and positive, especially toward the family member with schizophrenia. Families may need problem-solving skills to reduce tension and may limit social contacts outside the family because of the stigma attached to a diagnosis of schizophrenia (Falloon, 1999).

In addition to assessing the family member for symptoms he is experiencing, it is also important to conduct an assessment of the family's functioning and coping skills, as well as communication skills. Ecomaps are useful in assessing the family's social supports, and role-playing can help the practitioner observe the family's patterns of communication and problem solving. Hudson and Nurius (1994), Jordan and Franklin (2003), and Corcoran and Fisher (2000) also discuss techniques that are helpful in assessing the functioning of families with a mentally ill member and present measurement instruments. Measures of family coping and caregiver burden, such as the

Table 7.1 Assessment Instruments

Measure	Description	Reliability	Validity	Source
Self-Administered Questionnaires				
Brief Psychiatric Rating Scale	An 18-item scale designed to measure changes in symptoms of schizophrenia and depression.	Reliability coefficients range from .64–.8 for subscales	Confirmatory factor analysis supports a good fit for measuring four subscales	Overall & Gotham, 1962
Brief Assessment of Cognition in Schizophrenia (BACS)	A brief questionnaire that assesses for cognitive impairments closely associated with schizophrenia.	Mean reliability coefficients range from .86–.92	Assesses major constructs of cognition and is sensitive to cognitive changes over time	Keefe et al., 2004
The Beck Depression Inventory (BDI)	A 21-item self-administered questionnaire designed to measure depressive symptoms; age range: 13–80; time required: 5–10 minutes.	Test-retest reliability ranges from .48–.86	Content, discriminant, and convergent validity	Beck, Steer, & Brown, 1996
The Hamilton Rating Scale for Depression (HAMD)	A 17-item scale designed to measure the severity of depression symptoms.	Test-retest reliability ranges from .65–.96 (Kobac et al., 1990)	Concurrent and discriminant validity (Maier et al., 1988)	Hamilton, 1986
Center for Epidemiological Status Depression Scale, Revised (CES-D-R)	A 20-item measure designed to assess for symptoms of depression.	Internal consistency reliability ranges from .85–.90	Evidence supports convergent validity	Radloff,1977
Minnesota Multiphasic Personality Inventory - 2 (MMPI-2)	Self-report measure of adult personality and psychopathology; can be administered to those age 16 and older and requires an 8th-grade reading level.	Test-retest reliabilities range from .58–.92 (Butcher et al., 1989)	Evidence supports predictive validity (Grove et al., 2000)	Lubin, Larsen, & Matarazzo, 1984

The Millon Clinical Multiaxial Inventory - III (MCMI-III)	A 175-item true-false self-report measure used for diagnosing Axis I and Axis II disorders.	Test-retest reliabilities range from .66–.95	Evidence supports predictive validity	Millon, Davis, & Millon, 1997
Family Assessment Revised Ways of Coping Checklist	A structured interview to measure coping of family caregivers.	Coefficient alpha ranges from .75–.88	Evidence supports construct validity	Vitaliano, Russo, & Carr, 1985
Interview Schedules Schedule of Affective Disorders and Schizophrenia (SADS)	A semi-structured interview schedule for assessing psychopathology in adults; special training required for administration; time required: 1½–2 hours.	Test-retest reliability ranges from .52–.88	Discriminant, convergent, and predictive validity	Spitzer & Endicott, 1978
Schedule of Affective Disorders and Schizophrenia for School Age Children (K-SADS)	A semi-structured interview schedule for assessing psychopathology in children; special training required; time required: 3 hours.	Test-retest reliability ranges from .55–1.00	Discriminant, convergent, and predictive validity	Kaufman et al., 1999
Diagnostic Interview Schedule	A structured interview schedule that assesses for the presence of major psychiatric disorders; time required: 60–90 minutes.	Test-retest reliability ranges from .37–.46	Correctly identified diagnoses of interviewees approximately 75% of the time	Robins, Cottler, Bucholz, & Comptom, 1996
Structured Clinical Interview for the DSM-IV	A semi-structured interview schedule for assessing psychopathology; special training required; time required: 45–90 minutes.	Test-retest reliability ranges from .35–1.00	Demonstrated validity according to "best estimate of diagnosis" (Basco et al., 2000; Kranzler et al., 1995)	First, Spitzer, Gibbon, & Williams, 1995

BOX 7.1 | **Cultural Differences**

Cultural differences are important to consider in assessing symptoms of schizophrenia. Ideas that are classified as delusions in one culture may be defined as normal in others. Some religions define visual or auditory hallucinations as a normal part of religious practice. There are also cultural differences in emotional expression, eye contact, and body language. A flat affect in one culture may be defined as appropriate emotional expression in another. Because of these cultural differences, some ethnic groups may be overdiagnosed with schizophrenia. For example, there is some evidence that African American and Asian American individuals are diagnosed with schizophrenia more often than individuals from other racial and ethnic groups. There may also be cultural differences in symptoms of those diagnosed with schizophrenia. Catatonic behavior, for example, is less common among those diagnosed in the United States than among those diagnosed in non-Western countries (DSM-IV-TR, 2000).

Revised Ways of Coping Checklist, can also be helpful in assessing the family because caregiving and the potential burden that goes along with that task is a big part of helping families with a mentally ill family member.

Although these techniques are helpful in assessing and treating families affected by mental illness, it is important to be aware of culture difference in the presentation of mental disorders and their impact on families. Box 7.1 summarizes some relevant cultural issues.

Cultural differences also exist in the experience of depression. In some cultures, individuals with depression may be more likely to complain of somatic symptoms, such as headaches and fatigue, than feelings of sadness. Individuals from one culture may think that depression is a serious disorder that requires treatment, whereas those from another culture may feel that the symptoms are not serious at all (DSM-IV-TR, 2000).

Practitioners who are aware of culture differences can tailor treatments to better meet the needs of their clients. Bae and Kung (2000) have suggested the need for a culturally sensitive model because many Asian families are caring for mentally ill relatives. Practitioners should have an understanding of the stigma attached to seeking help outside the family and cultural expectations toward clinicians and treatment. The therapist may also need to assess the level of acculturation and tailor the treatment accordingly. Home-based interventions are helpful when families are anxious about seeking help from outsiders and about the stigma associated with mental illness. Home-based sessions also provide the chance to observe the dynamics and interactions of the family in a more natural setting. During engagement, the practitioner should provide an orientation to service to reduce any discrepancies between the practitioner's and family's expectations of treatment and outcome. These expectations should be actively discussed and negotiated, which may include explaining the role of the mental health worker and stages of treatment. Asian

Americans are reluctant to admit emotional or psychological difficulties to people outside the immediate family. Therapeutic interventions involve deeper revelations of emotional vulnerability and familiar conflicts, so multifamily psychoeducational groups may not be appropriate. Asian Americans often prefer directive and structured approaches rather than treatment that is affective, reflective, and insight-oriented (Berg & Jaya, 1993; Sue & Sue, 1990).

Like Asian American families, Hispanic families have special needs when it comes to psychotherapy interventions. Even though Hispanic families from different countries of origin have different values, Bean, Perry, and Bedell (2001) suggest engaging the family with warmth in the first session. It may be helpful to assess for level of acculturation and gather information on the family's immigration experience when relevant. If the family believes in folk medicine, it may be important to collaborate with folk healers. Demonstrating respect for the father figure is important because of his central role in the family. In families with a strong hierarchical structure, the practitioner may need to interview the children separately so that children can express without directly challenging the authority of their parents. It is important to appreciate the wide range of family structures and not to misinterpret a culturally normative relationship as pathological.

Provide the family with concrete suggestions that they can quickly implement; Bean, Benjamin, and Bedell (2002) have studied African American families in treatment and suggest guidelines that have emerged from the treatment literature and may be helpful for work with African American families. Some of these guidelines suggest addressing the issue of racism and its effects in their lives as well as concerns about having a non-African American therapist, if relevant. It is important to join with the family before gathering sensitive information. If the family is religious, it may be appropriate to involve the family's religious leader or to use scriptural metaphors in treatment. Maintaining a broad definition of family when assessing family structure and roles and respecting differences in family structure is critical.

Expressed Emotion

Expressed emotion (EE) is a measure of family environment based on the family members' style of communication about a mentally ill family member. It is important to consider when conducting an assessment of family functioning because it has been linked to relapse rates among individuals with severe and persistent mental illness (Butzlaff & Hooley, 1998). The Camberwell Family Interview (CFI) is a semistructured interview schedule used to assess expressed emotion in families (Muesser et al., 1993). The interview is conducted using the schedule and is audiotaped. The interview is then scored according to the number of critical comments made during the interview; statements of rejection about the person with the mental illnes; and overinvolvement, characterized by exaggerated emotional responses, self-sacrificing behavior, overprotection of the person with mental illness inappropriate for the person's age, and poor boundaries between the person with mental illness and family members.

EE is defined as having two components: expression of criticism and hostility, and emotional overinvolvement. An example of criticism and hostility are statements like "stop acting crazy," "you are ruining my life," "I wish you had never been born," and "start acting right or else." These statements are delivered in a hostile tone or contemptuous tone. Statements such as these often involve a desperate attempt on the part of family members to get the mentally ill family member to behave better. Emotional overinvolvement, on the other hand, involves tiptoeing around the client, being fearful, and making excuses for her behavior or doing for her tasks she can do for herself, and so on. Ratings of criticism and hostility have been made with a variety of instruments, including direct observation of family interaction. Some have taken into account not only the content of what has been said but also tone of voice and speed of talking. Attempts that include overprotection of the client include self-sacrifice and emotional upset on the part of the family member. Both the emotional expression and the overprotection are seen as the family member's responses to client behavior. They arise out of the anxiety and stress family members experience, as well as the insufficient social support that is available (Fosler, 1993).

Fox (1992) reminds that instead of attributing blame to the family for high expressed emotion, workers should direct attention to the feelings that arise out of the client's behavior and its stress on the family. Even though the expressions may be attributed to family concern or caring, negative consequences seem to follow. While family therapists have often encouraged open and direct communication of both positive and negative feelings and expectations to other family members, more recent thinking and practice have cast doubt upon such an approach to treatment. The mentally ill client's inability to process information, just described, suggests that both the nature and amount of communication and expressed emotion by family members need regulation in order to be helpful. In other words, family members need to learn to control their fears, anger, and hopeless emotions around their mentally ill family members. A lot of emotional ventilation and expression of strong emotions does not help mentally ill family members, but instead it is important to create a more secure and safe family environment to help manage the behavior problems of mentally ill persons.

Kuipers, Bebbington, Pilling, and Orbach (1999), in their review of research on expressed emotion, report a number of studies that show high EE as a factor in the client's relapse. Other studies have indicated that family intervention as a part of the overall treatment program reduces the relapse rate. Questions remain about whether one of the two components of EE is more significant than the other, in what ways it is related to the family's coping resources, and whether it is high primarily during acute episodes of the illness or was an ongoing part of family life either before or after hospitalization.

Although much of the research on expressed emotion has focused on its effect on individuals with schizophrenia, a growing body of research demonstrates that EE increases relapse rates for those with mood disorders (Butzlaff & Hooley, 1998). A meta-analysis examining the impact of expressed emotion on relapse rates found 27 studies that examined the relationship between

EE and relapse rates in schizophrenia. All but three of the studies found a significant positive relationship between the amount of expressed emotion and relapse rates. In the case of mood disorders, the meta-analysis included six studies, all of which demonstrated a relationship between high expressed emotion and higher relapse rates. The effect sizes were larger in the studies examining mood disorders, suggesting expressed emotion may be a stronger predictor of relapse rates for mood disorders than schizophrenia (Butzlaff & Hooley, 1998).

Practitioners can use psychoeducation to help families understand the impact of expressed emotion on a family member with mental illness, as in the following case example:

> A social worker is beginning treatment with a Mexican American family in which the adult son, Bill, is diagnosed with schizophrenia. Bill's mother and sister attend the first session along with Bill. During the course of the interview, Bill's mom is very emotional and explains that she wants to protect Bill from people who might take advantage of him. She insists that either she or his father accompany him when he leaves the house, and he is not allowed to talk on the phone. She explains that he cannot be independent because he needs assistance. Bill's sister tells the social worker that their mother treats Bill like a young child, cooking every meal for him and cleaning up after him. She says that her mother spends her entire day caring for Bill. The mother responds by saying that she wouldn't spend all of her time caring for Bill if he weren't so disabled. During the interview, Bill becomes increasingly agitated and has difficulty sitting still.
>
> The social worker explains to the mother and sister that certain ways of communicating may place too much stress on Bill. She says that she notices Bill has become agitated during the interview, especially when the mother refers to needing to care for him because of his disabilities. The social worker explains that expressing intense emotions and talking openly about caregiving burdens are consistent with high expressed emotion and are often associated with relapse in people living with mental illness. She then asks Bill's mother and sister to discuss their daily routine without using Bill as the reason for their behavior.

EVIDENCE-BASED TREATMENT AND BEST PRACTICES

Although medication is an important component in the treatment of individuals with schizophrenia and mood disorders, a review of the literature indicates that family intervention is also an effective tool to improve functioning (Barbata & Avanzo, 2000; Huxley, Parikh, & Baldessarini, 2000). Characteristics common to most evidence-based family treatments are the inclusion of the client in some of the treatment, long treatment duration, and the provision of information and education in a supportive setting (Barbata & Avanzo, 2000). Successful interventions also discourage blaming of family members, supporting medication compliance, and improving communication and social supports (Lauriello, Bustillo, & Keith, 1999). Table 7.2 provides a list of meta-analyses that examine evidence-based psychosocial treatments for schizophrenia and mood disorders.

Table 7.2 Meta-Analyses of Evidence-Based Treatments

Schizophrenia	Mood Disorders
Adams, C. E. (2000). *Psychosocial Interventions for Schizophrenia.* Effective Health Care Bulletin. NHS Centre for Reviews and Dissemination, University of York: York. Bustillo, J. R., Laurillo, J., Horan, P., and Keith, S. J. 2001. "The Psychological Treatment of Schizophrenia: An Update." *American Journal of Psychiatry* 158:163–75. Butzlaff, R. L., and Hooley, J. M. 1998. "Expressed Emotion and Psychiatric Relapse: A Meta-Analysis." *Archives of General Psychiatry* 55:547–52. Dixon, L., Adams, C., and Lucksted, A. 2000. "Update on Family Psychoeducation for Schizophrenia." *Schizophrenia Bulletin* 26:5–20. Gottdiener, W. H., and Haslam, N. 2003. "A Critique of the Methods and Conclusions in the Client Outcome Research Team (PORT) Report on Psychological Treatments for Schizophrenia." *Journal of the American Academy of Psychoanalysis and Dynamic Psychiatry* 31(1):191–208. Gould, R. A., Mueser, K. T., Bolton, E., Mays, V., and Goff, D. 2001. "Cognitive Therapy for Psychosis in Schizophrenia: An Effect Size Analysis." *Schizophrenia Research* 48:335–42. Krabbendam, L., and Aleman, A. 2003. "Cognitive Rehabilitation in Schizophrenia: A Quantitative Analysis of Controlled Studies." *Psychopharmacology* 169(3/4):376–83. De Mari, J. J., and Streiner, D. 1994. "An Overview of Family Interventions and Relapse on Schizophrenia: Meta-Analysis of Research Findings." *Psychological Medicine* 24:565–578.	Bower, P., Byford, S., Barber, J., Beecham, J., Simpson, S., Friedli, K., et al. 2003. "Meta-Analysis of Data on Costs from Trials of Counseling in Primary Care: Using Individual Client Data to Overcome Sample Size Limitations in Economic Analyses." *British Medical Journal* 326 (7401):1247–50 Bower, P., Rowland, N., and Hardy, R. 2003. "The Clinical Effectiveness of Counseling in Primary Care: A Systematic Review and Meta-Analysis." *Psychological Medicine* 33(2):203–15. Casacalenda, N., Perry, J., and Looper, K. 2002. "Remission in Major Depressive Disorder: A Comparison of Pharmacotherapy, Psychotherapy, and Control Conditions." *American Journal of Psychiatry* 159:1354–60. Cuijpers, P. 1998. "A Psychoeducational Approach to the Treatment of Depression: A Meta-Analysis of Lewinsohn's 'Coping with Depression' Course." *Behavior Therapy* 29(3):521–33. Ellis, P. M., and Smith, D. A. 2002. "Treating Depression: The Beyond Blue Guidelines for Treating Depression in Primary Care. 'Not So Much What You Do But That You Keep Doing It.'" *Medical Journal of Australia* 176(supp):S77–S83. Gregory, R. J., Schwer Canning, S., Lee, T. W., and Wise, J. C. 2004. "Cognitive Bibliotherapy for Depression: A Meta-Analysis." *Professional Psychology: Research & Practice* 35(3):275–80. Haby, M. M., Tonge, B., Littlefield, L., Carrer, R., and Vos, T. 2004. "Cost-Effectiveness of Cognitive Behavioural Therapy and Selective Serotonin Reuptake Inhibitors for Major Depression in Children and Adolescents." *Australian & New Zealand Journal of Psychiatry* 38(8):579–81.

Mojtabai, R., Nicholson, R. A., and Carpenter, B. N. 1998. "Role of Psychosocial Treatments in the Management of Schizophrenia: A Meta-Analytic Review of Controlled Outcome Studies." *Schizophrenia Bulletin* 24:569–87.

Pilling, S., Bebbington, E., Kuipers, E., Garety, P., Geddes, J., Orbach, G., et al. 2002. "Psychological Treatments in Schizophrenia: I. Meta-Analysis of Family Intervention and Cognitive Behavior Therapy." *Psychological Medicine* 32:763–82.

Pilling, S., Bebbington, E., Kuipers, E., Garety, P., Geddes, J., Orbach, G., et al. 2002. "Psychological Treatments in Schizophrenia: II. Meta-Analyses of Randomized Controlled Trials of Social Skills Training and Cognitive Remediation." *Psychological Medicine* 32:763–82.

Pitschel-Walz, G., Leucht, S., Bauml, J., Kissling, W., and Engel, R. R. 2001. "The Effect of Family Interventions on Relapse and Re-Hospitalization in Schizophrenia: A Meta-Analysis." *Schizophrenia Bulletin* 27:73–92.

Rector, N. A., and Beck, A. T. 2001. "Cognitive Behavior Therapy for Schizophrenia: An Empirical Review." *Journal of Nervous and Mental Disease* 189:278–87.

Twamley, E. W., Jeste, D.V., and Lehman, A. F. 2003. "Vocational Rehabilitation in Schizophrenia and Other Psychotic Disorders: A Literature Review and Meta-Analysis of Randomized Controlled Trials. *Journal of Nervous and Mental Disease* 191(8):515–23.

Kho, K. H., van Vreeswijk, M. F., Simpson, S., and Zwinderman, A. H. 2003. "A Meta-Analysis of Electroconvulsive Therapy Efficacy in Depression." *Journal of ECT* 19(3):139–47.

Lam, R. W., and Kennedy, S. H. 2004. "Evidence-Based Strategies for Achieving and Sustaining Full Remission in Depression: Focus on Meta-Analyses." *Canadian Journal of Psychiatry* 49(supp. 1): 17S–26S.

Lawlor, D., and Hopker, S. 2001. "The Effectiveness of Exercise as an Intervention in the Management of Depression: Systematic Review and Meta-Regression Analysis of Randomised Controlled Trials." *British Medical Journal* 322:763–67.

McDermut, W., Miller, I. W., and Brown, R. A. 2001. "The Efficacy of Group Psychotherapy for Depression: A Meta-Analysis and Review of the Empirical Research." *Clinical Psychology: Science and Practice* 8:98–116.

Michael, K. D., and Crowley, S. L. 2002. "How Effective are Treatments for Child and Adolescent Depression? A Meta-Analytic Review." *Clinical Psychology Review* 22(2):247–69.

Thompson, C. 2002. "Light Therapy in the Treatment of Seasonal and Non-Seasonal Affective Disorders: A Meta-Analysis of Randomised Controlled Trials." *Journal of Affective Disorders* 68:89.

Townsend, E., Hawton, K., Altman, D. G., Arensman, E., Gunnell, D., Hazell, P., et al. 2001. "The Efficacy of Problem-Solving Treatments after Deliberate Self-Harm: Meta-Analysis of Randomized Controlled Trials with Respect to Depression, Hopelessness and Improvement in Problems." *Psychological Medicine* 31:979–88.

Wampold, B., Minami, T., Baskin, T., and Tierney, S. 2002. "A Meta-(Re) analysis of the Effects of Cognitive Therapy Versus 'Other Therapies' for Depression." *Journal of Affective Disorders* 68:59–65.

Westen, D., and Morrison, K. 2001. "A Multidimensional Meta-Analysis of Treatments for Depression, Panic, and Generalized Anxiety Disorder: An Empirical Examination of the Status of Empirically Supported Therapies." *Journal of Consulting and Clinical Psychology*

Family Psychoeducation

Family psychoeducation is an intervention that has been used successfully to work with families affected by severe and persistent mental illness. This approach has been used successfully as a treatment for schizophrenia (Pilling et al., 2002), depression (Holden & Anderson, 1990; Schwartz & Schwartz, 1993), and bipolar disorder (Brennan, 1995). Research demonstrates that such programs are effective when offered to single families as well as multiple family groups.

One approach to psychoeducation for working with families affected by schizophrenia was developed by Anderson, Hogarty, and Reiss (1980). The approach was derived to a large extent from structural family therapy techniques, such as joining with the family and enhancing boundaries with the family system. The approach begins with the therapist building a strong working alliance with the family. The therapist develops an understanding of the family's resources and past attempts to cope with the illness, as well as establishes expectations about the treatment through contracting. The therapist provides the family with a survival skills workshop during which they receive current information about the illness and treatment. Throughout treatment, the therapist emphasizes the family's strengths. The approach assumes that boundaries are necessary to create barriers to stimulation that may exacerbate symptoms of schizophrenia. The therapist engages with the family and communicates empathic acceptance of the family's suffering, burdens, and frustrations in caring for the family member with schizophrenia.

Education about the illness typically includes providing information about symptoms and the course of the illness, such as the fact that schizophrenia is a lifelong illness, medication, and coping strategies. Providing information about schizophrenia and its treatment, along with research evidence supporting relevant treatments, is an important component of the approach as well. The therapist helps families understand how to create a positive psychosocial environment for reducing symptoms, such as creating a quiet environment and simple daily routines (Hogarty et al., 1991). Sessions include discussion of early warning signs of relapse, strategies for living together, medication compliance, and client resumption of responsibility.

Developing social and community support for families is an important component of psychoeducation. Social supports may include other families who are affected by mental illness, extended family, or supporting friends. Community supports may include church groups or vocational programs. Vocational rehabilitation is an important part of therapy and focuses on engaging clients in a larger social network. Social skills training may be important for strengthening these support networks. Social skills can help clients to form relationships and interview for a job. Social skills training includes modeling of the skills by the practitioner, the client's rehearsal of skills followed by feedback from the practitioner, and further rehearsal of skills (Collins, Jordan, & Coleman, 1999).

Goals of psychoeducational treatment include increasing the quality of life for family members, reinforcing generational boundaries, decreasing the likelihood of overinvolvement with the client, and helping family members make individual social connections outside the home. During the final stages of treatment, the family works on renegotiating the contract and continues to focus on original goals. When clients experience a level of stability and comfort with their present life situation, they may choose the option of maintenance sessions rather than either ongoing therapy or termination (Hogarty et al., 1991).

Multicomponent Psychoeducation

A model of family psychoeducation that includes behavioral strategies was developed by Falloon, Boyd, and McGill (1984). The approach combines psychoeducational workshops with behavior management and problem-solving skills. Research suggests that this approach combined with medication treatment is highly effective in preventing the recurrence of psychotic symptoms for clients diagnosed with schizophrenia (Hahlweg & Wiedermann, 1999). The approach includes techniques for assessment, intervention, and ongoing review. The treatment consists of three months of weekly in-home family therapy sessions followed by six months of biweekly therapy sessions. Monthly sessions may then be maintained for up to two years.

The therapist conducts a behavioral analysis of the strengths and needs of each family member and the family unit as a whole. Single-family treatment sessions are held in the home and include education about mental illness and strategies for improved communication, as well as development and rehearsal of problem-solving techniques. The therapist is guided by the strengths perspective and assumes that each family member is functioning at his or her best.

The therapist begins treatment with a detailed systematic analysis of family behavior that includes identifying the following:

1. Specific assets and deficits of individual family members
2. Assets and deficits of the family group as a whole
3. The role that specified "problem" behaviors play in the overall functioning of the family unit

Other behavioral assessment procedures include journal recording, family self-observation, and direct observation.

During educational workshops, families learn to reframe mental illness as a problem in living. They also learn the determinants of illness behaviors, symptoms, and impairments. The therapist provides information about social learning principles, which emphasize learning through imitation and reinforcement. Reinforcing small steps in the desired direction is used to shape behavior. The family learns how to use contracting to negotiate meeting each others' needs. The therapist can also teach the family about medications and how to recognize the warning signs of relapse.

During behavioral communication skills training, families practice communicating positive and negative feelings. Inappropriate communication and inadequate expression of feelings are addressed as well. While families rehearse typical interactions, the therapist provides constructive feedback, coaching, modeling of appropriate behaviors, and positive reinforcement. The therapist also encourages family members to provide feedback, suggest alternative modes of expression, and praise each other for progress.

This phase develops an understanding of what level of activity and responsibility families can reasonably expect of the client, and how to communicate their expectations clearly with a minimum of emotion and intrusiveness. Family members might rehearse possible communications in the family groups. By this point in the treatment program, some clients and family members may meet together with the worker regulating the communication to discuss client and family expectations. Clients have a similar need to learn new ways of communication. Though enhancement of client–family communication is desirable, the new experience may be difficult.

Among the essentials of needed communication are clarity about what each person intends to convey and also to whom in the family the message is addressed, and checking that the receiver of the message has correctly understood and has an opportunity to give response. The focus on the "how" of communication may be done in relation to specific problems, such as what the discharge plan will be. Marley (1992) calls these aspects elucidating, naming, differentiating, and consensual validation. He also identifies disagreement among therapists about how to relate to psychotic communications, as in the incident in the previous case example, but points to the value to both client and family at some point in the process of attempting to understand their meaning.

Another facet of the work at this stage focuses on problem-solving and skill development (Falloon, 1999). Problem-solving training begins with defining the problem, generating and evaluating alternative solutions, and selecting the best strategy for working through a problem. Families also review previous efforts to solve problems. Family problems other than those engendered by the client's illness are likely to become evident over time in these problem-solving sessions. Splits between family members, particularly marital disagreements and the side-taking of one parent with the client against the other, are revealed. Siblings of the client or parents may also participate on one side or the other. It is initially necessary to focus on and resolve disagreements as they affect the client, either postponing or shifting to separate sessions a direct focus on problems in the marriage or other issues.

Psychoeducational Multifamily Groups

Multifamily group treatment engages the members of the family and their social support network as partners in the client's treatment and rehabilitation. The goal is to help the client with schizophrenia attain full symptomatic recovery and achieve as rich and full participation in the usual life of the community as possible. Research demonstrates that this approach has more positive outcomes than standard care in managing negative symptoms of schizophrenia (Voss, 2003). Negative symptoms—such as lack of goal-directed behavior, for example, versus positive symptoms like hallucinations—do not respond as well to conventional antipsychotic medications, so this is a particularly promising finding. In studies comparing psychoeducation in single-family groups and multiple-family groups, the multiple-family groups had significantly lower relapse rates (McFarlane, 1994; McFarlane, Link, Dushay, & Marchal, 1995).

The program's format is similar to the single-family model and includes four major stages:

1. Joining with individual clients and families
2. Conducting an educational workshop for families
3. Preventing relapse through the use of problem-solving groups attended by both clients and families
4. Pursuing vocational and social rehabilitation in the same multifamily groups

The therapist forms an alliance with the family while providing information about schizophrenia and guidelines for managing the illness. The family practices solving problems associated with the illness. The approach assumes that the family is functioning normally until clearly proven otherwise and that a better outcome for the ill member is most likely when the family makes compensatory adjustments in its daily life.

Interventions may include creating family management guidelines, problem solving, working on social and vocational rehabilitation, enhancing interpersonal boundaries, and beginning the social network building process. *Self-triangulation* is a technique that involves serial individual and family interviewing in which the therapist intentionally interposes herself between the members of different families, directing interaction through herself, and inhibiting interaction between families or individuals. The therapist may interact with individuals within a family or may focus on the family as a whole. For example, if a family member is having difficulty maintaining appropriate boundaries with the family member who has a mental illness, the therapist may place the two family members so they are not sitting next to each other, or the therapist may stand between them so they cannot rely on each other in discussing their situation.

Group interpretation involves taking a complementary position to the entire group in order to lay ground rules, to share personal reactions, to point out commonalities in the families or in subgroups, to set group themes, and to make conventional group interpretation. *Cross-family linkage* helps to foster therapeutic interaction between families, such as sharing feelings, open feedback, and a creative search for solutions and opportunities. *Interfamily management* enhances and reinforces interfamily contacts and promotes the process of quasi-natural social network development. (MacFarlane, 2002). The next section of this chapter provides a sample treatment manual for the first three sessions of psychoeducation that includes multifamily groups, and a case example that illustrates the use of some psychoeducational techniques used in the first multifamily group session. Because families who are caring for a relative with mental illness may have few social supports, participating in a group with other families who are experiencing the same challenges can help family members feel supported.

Case Management

The efforts of the families described in the previous paragraphs imply the existence of a variety of needs on the part of clients with chronic disorders and the demand for a variety of services to meet them if clients are to remain in the community. In early contacts, it falls to the social worker to inform the family of available services and of their particular usefulness, and to facilitate connection to them. Over time, the family may be helped to take on some of the effort of coordinating with and connecting to the needed services in order to work out the best plan of care.

Unfortunately, many of the services are expensive, and questions have been raised about cost effectiveness. Community and family care have been considered better for client adjustment but can be expensive. The result has been a shift in emphasis from producing a care plan of maximum benefit to containment of costs by reducing eligibility for services or limiting the extent of care provided. The need to provide relatively inexpensive services has brought about changes in the services provided to families with a mentally ill relative. For example, a plan of care for a relative with mental illness that once included a range of community services, such as residential treatment, may now include only a limited range of services that are less expensive (Belcher, 1993). These changes in the length of stay for inpatient care may place profound limits on the extent of assistance social workers can provide to families and clients during the hospitalization phase (Ettner & Hermann, 1998; Farley, 1994). Shortened time limits restrict both the time a worker has to engage the family in a treatment plan and the extent of the family's involvement in it. Primary attention is of necessity directed to planning for discharge and what happens after that.

In these circumstances, the availability of a network of other services to meet client and family needs becomes crucial. While short-term hospitalization can serve as crisis intervention, continuing service is needed to enable family and client to handle ongoing understanding and decisions about medications, activity level, work, and interpersonal and social contact. Community care requires support services such as day hospitals, sheltered workshops, and alternatives to family housing; however, development of these resources has not kept pace with the emphasis on deinstitutionalization. Social work's concern for client and family extends to these aspects of care as well.

Today, a large number of resources are available on the Internet for gathering information about mental disorders, their treatment, and supports that are available to families. Also, a number of organizations provide advocacy for families caring for a relative with mental illness. The National Alliance for the Mentally Ill (NAMI), for example, is a nonprofit advocacy organization for those living with mental illness, and their family and friends. Their mission is to improve the quality of life for all those affected by mental illness. On its website, NAMI provides information about mental illness, resources for those affected by mental illness, and information about becoming involved with advocacy for those affected by mental illness. A list of resources for families is provided in at the end of this chapter in Box 7.3.

Medication

Evidence-based treatment for mental illness integrates pharmacotherapy and psychosocial interventions. While social workers cannot prescribe medication, their knowledge of its importance and effects is vital. They can facilitate family and client awareness in this area and help them to devise means of ensuring

Table 7.3 | Effective Treatments for Schizophrenia

Disorder	Effective Family Interventions	Psychopharmacology	Other Treatment Strategies
Schizophrenia	Psychoeducation, psychoeducational multifamily groups, behavioral and cognitive behavioral intervention	*Conventional Antipsychotics*: Thorazine (Chlorpromazine) Mellaril (Thiridazine) Trilaton (Perphenazine) Stelazine (Trifluoperazine) Prolixin (Fluphenazine) Prolixin D (Fluphenazine) Haldol (Haldoperidol) Orap (Pinozide) Navane (Thiothixene) Moban (Molindone) Loxitane (Loxipine) *Atypical Antipsychotics*: Clozapine Respiradone Olanzapine	Intensive case management, day treatment, residential treatment, employment support programs
Bipolar	Cognitive behavioral, interpersonal, psychoeducation	Tegretol (carbamazepine) Eskalith/Lithobid (lithium) Depakote/Depakene (valproic acid)	Intensive case management, electro-convulsive therapy
Depression	Cognitive behavioral, interpersonal, psychoeducation	Zyban (Wellbutrin) Buspar (buspirone) Celexa (citalopram) Norpramin (desipramine) Prozac (fluozetine) Luvox (fluvoxamine) Tofranil (imipramine) Remeron (mirtazapine) Serzone (nefazodone) Pamelor/Aventyl (nortriptyline) Paxil (paroxetine) Risperidal (risperidone) Zoloft (sertraline) Desyrel (trazodone) Effexor (vanlafaxine)	Electro-convulsive therapy

that schedules will be kept. Social workers may see the client and/or the family more frequently than the prescribing physician, especially during the client's stay in the community. They need, therefore, to acquire knowledge of and ability to observe effects and side effects, as well as client symptoms and behavior, that may be indications of client need for change in type or amount of medication (Bentley, 2000; Hiratsuka, 1994). The most commonly prescribed medication for schizophrenia is haloperidol, although other medications, such as respiradone, olanzapine, and clozapine, are frequently prescribed as well (Schatzberg & Nemeroff, 2001). Table 7.3 displays the medications often prescribed for schizophrenia, depression, and bipolar disorder.

Although medication is a critical component in effective treatment of individuals with schizophrenia, family treatment plays an equally important role because families are extensively involved in care provision. Pharmacological treatment is more successful when combined with effective family interventions. Given the extremely difficult client behaviors and the levels of anxiety, burden, confusion, and lack of knowledge and ability to cope effectively, the need on the part of family members for professional assistance is great.

In order for social workers to be effective in the family treatment of severe and persistent mental disorders, they must work with a broad knowledge-base across many systems of care and use both a systems and psychoeducational framework. Box 7.2 highlights critical components needed for effective treatment, and we next present an evidenced-based family treatment manual.

TREATMENT MANUAL

The Center for Mental Health Services (CMHS) at The Substance Abuse and Mental Health Services Administration (SAMHSA) provides guidelines for providing psychoeducational multifamily groups that are based on evidence-based approaches developed by Anderson Hogarty, and Reiss (1980) and McFarlane (1994). Families participate in a single-family psychoeducation session first. After the individual family workshop, the families join a multiple-family group psychoeducation program, which is lead by a facilitator and cofacilitator (Center for Mental Health Services, 2004).

The individual family workshop begins with welcoming the participants and thanking them for coming. The facilitator also provides an overview of the treatment process, explaining that the group members will learn about mental illness and strategies for coping. The facilitator also explains that, although the first session includes only one family, they will be meeting with a group of families on a regular basis.

Single-Family Workshop

After allowing time for information interaction among the group members and facilitators, as well as introductions, the facilitators follow the following format:

I. Facilitators provide information about the phenomenology, etiology, course, and outcome of the illness. The information should include a discussion of biochemical theories, genetic theories, socio-cultural theories, and family theories, as well as the private and public experience of schizophrenia. This section should take approximately 1 hour.
II. A 15-minute break
III. Medication: The facilitators present information about medication used to treat schizophrenia, explaining how each medication works, its benefits, and its side effects. This segment should take about 30 minutes.
IV. Other Treatments: The facilitators then discuss other treatments, including family psychoeducation and multifamily groups, social skills training,

BOX 7.2	**Core Ingredients for Family Treatment for Severe and Persistent Mental Disorders**

Family Treatment and Collaboration

Despite the variation in family treatment approaches, researchers report lower relapse and rehospitalization rates when family work is part of the treatment protocol (Atwood, 1990; Falloon et al., 1985; McFarlane, 1983; East, 1992). It is important to see the family as interested, as a resource, and as collaborators in helping, definitely not as culprits in causing the illness.

Reductions in High Expressed Emotion

Reductions in high EE have been shown to reduce the risk for relapse (Kuipers & Bebbington, 1988; Miklowitz et al., 1989). These efforts also enable families to feel better about the service they get for themselves and the client by being more knowledgeable about the illness (Posner, Wilson, Kral, Lander, & McIlwraith, 1992).

Information and Education

By becoming well-informed about the nature of the illness and the available medical treatment, social workers can undertake the education of the family about the illness (Walsh, 1988). This includes the medication management of these illnesses and the potential side effects of those medications.

Family Relationship and Skills Development

Social workers need to be in possession of skills in working with the family, including skills for handling family communication in a new way that promotes separateness, reduces overinvolvement/intrusiveness, lowers the level of affect, and promotes problem solving. Also in the repertoire of needed skills is the ability to work with groups of families in multifamily groups to promote learning and social support.

Case Management, Advocacy, and Resource Development

Social workers need skills for helping families in mental health systems and with members of treatment teams like physicians, psychologists, and nurses. The ability to help family and client establish and maintain contact with other agency support systems and other social networks is also of considerable importance. Work with these families is long term, but the mark of success is maintaining them in the community; this requires work with multiple systems, including maintaining financial and community resources needed to promote social rehabilitation, and the necessary social supports to prevent relapse.

day treatment, vocational rehabilitation and supported employment, and psychotherapy. This segment also includes information about managing the illness and maintaining health, including a discussion of diet and stress management. This segment takes about 45 minutes.

V. A 1-hour lunch break

VI. The Family and Schizophrenia: The facilitators discuss the client's needs and the family's needs as well as common family reactions to schizophrenia and common problems. This section includes information about the family's needs and reactions to the illness as well as common problems encountered by the families. The facilitators introduce family guidelines, which lay out the expectations of family members participating in the group. The guidelines include the following:

- Go slow.
- Keep it cool. It's okay to express enthusiasm and disagreement, but keep it toned down.
- Give each other space.
- Set limits with each other.
- Ignore what you can't change.
- Keep it simple. Express yourself simply and calmly.
- Follow doctor's orders.
- Carry on business as usual. Maintain normal family routines and stay in touch with family and friends.
- No street drugs or alcohol.
- Pick up on early signs. Note changes in symptoms and consult with your family.
- Solve problems step by step.
- Lower expectations. Use your personal experience to compare this month to last month rather than last year.

A handout listing the guidelines should be given to each family member.

VII. Wrap up: The facilitators address questions, provide a description of the multifamily group process, and end with some time for informal interaction.

Multifamily Group Sessions

The First Multifamily Group Session   In the joining session, families learn that they are expected to meet with five to eight other families for 1 1/2-hour meetings every other week for at least six months, and then monthly for as long as families find it helpful.

The goal of the first group is for practitioners and family members to get to know each other. Chairs should be arranged in a circle or around a table so everyone can easily see and hear each other, and refreshments should be available to encourage relaxed interactions before and during the group. Facilitators should say at the start of the session that it is all right to move around, get a drink, or go to the bathroom whenever necessary. Participants should be made to feel they can leave the room whenever necessary.

The facilitator explains that this session will be used to help the families get to know each other. He asks family members to talk about themselves and their families, focusing on their strengths and refraining from discussing problems associated with mental illness for the current session. The facilitator begins in order to provide a model for the rest of the group. Then, the practitioner turns to the next person and continues around the circle, thanking each one after her contribution. The second practitioner sits halfway around the circle and takes her turn to speak.

The Second Multifamily Group Session   This group will focus more on how the mental illness has changed the lives of the people in the group. The cofacilitators should state clearly that the focus of the evening is "how mental illness has changed our lives." In this session, the goal is to continue building trust among group members. This meeting is intended to help participants quickly develop a sense of a common experience of having a major mental illness or having a relative with a disorder. This session is important for building a strong group identity and sense of relief.

After welcoming members to the group and directing them to the refreshments, one facilitator outlines the agenda for the meeting and explains that the group will begin with 15 minutes of informal discussion followed by each family member talking about how he or she has been affected by mental illness.

It is important to begin groups by socializing. The facilitators should encourage participation by modeling, pointing out connections between people and topics, and asking questions. They should also join in the discussion, if appropriate. Facilitators should gently discourage interrupting, monopolizing the conversation, criticizing, complaining, and speaking for others.

After socializing, the facilitators proceed to the topic for this meeting, explaining that in this meeting everyone will have the opportunity to discuss ways in which mental illness has affected their lives. A facilitator begins by sharing a personal story. Since group members will follow the facilitators' examples, facilitators should share as much as possible about their own professional and personal experiences. Facilitators may want to share a story about a friend or family member with mental illness or talk about how they have been affected by treating people with serious mental illnesses.

Because group members will be discussing difficult experiences, facilitators should encourage them to express any feelings that arise, such as anxiety, confusion, fear, guilt, anger, sadness, and grief. After each person has briefly shared his story, the cofacilitator should thank him. This is a good time to point out any similarities to another group member's experience and help them realize they are not alone. The leaders also remind group members that the next meetings will include working on solving problems like the ones expressed in this meeting. It is important to be optimistic and send people home with the sense that the group can and will help them.

At the end of the group meeting, the facilitator should remind members of the time and date of the next meeting. There should be 10 minutes or so to socialize before concluding the group. Facilitators should promote socializing at the end of the group and tie conversations into concrete topics, like weekend plans, recent movies seen, holiday plans, and so on. The purpose of the socializing is to reacquaint people with the art of small talk and to gain confidence in making interpersonal contacts.

Table 7.4 | Treatment Manuals

Manual Reference	Author's Contact Information
Anderson, C. M., Reiss, D. J., and Hogarty, G. E. 1986. *Schizophrenia and the Family.* New York: Guilford.	http://w3.ouhsc.edu/bpfamily/Detail/Anderson.html
Falloon, I. R. H., Boyd, J. L., and McGill, C. W. 1984. *Family Care of Schizophrenia: A Problem Solving Approach to the Treatment of Mental Illness.* New York: Guilford Press.	http://w3.ouhsc.edu/bpfamily/Detail/Falloon. html
Miklowitz, D. J., and Goldstein, M. J. 1997. *Bipolar Disorder. A Family-Focused Treatment Approach.* New York: Guilford Press.	http://psych.colorado.edu/~clinical/miklowitz/
Spaniol, L., Zipple, A. M., Marsh, D. T., and Finley, L. Y. 2000. *The Role of the Family in Psychiatric Rehabilitation: A Workbook.* Sargent College of Health and Rehabilitation Sciences, Boston University. Boston: Center for Psychiatric Rehabilitation.	http://www.bu.edu/cpr/about/profiles/leroys. html
Barrowclough, C., and Tarrier, N. 1992. *Families of Schizophrenic Clients: Cognitive Behavioral Intervention.* London: Chapman & Hall.	http://w3.ouhsc.edu/bpfamily/Detail/Barrowclough.html
Kuipers, E., Leff, J., and Lam, D. 2002. *Family Work for Schizophrenia: A Practical Guide.* 2nd edition. London: Gaskell Press.	http://w3.ouhsc.edu/bpfamily/Detail/Kuipers. html
McFarlane, W. R., Deakins, S. M., Gingerich, S. L., Dunne, E., Hornen, B., and Newmark, M. 1991. *Multiple-Family Psychoeducational Group Treatment Manual.* New York: Biosocial Treatment Division, New York State Psychiatric Institute.	http://w3.ouhsc.edu/bpfamily/Detail/McFarlane.html
Family Psychoeducation for the Implementing Evidence-Based Practices Project. (Family Psychoeducation Workbook. Available at http://www.mentalhealth.samhsa.gov/cmhs/communitysupport/toolkits/family/workbook/default.asp	http://www.mentalhealth.samhsa.gov/cmhs/communitysupport/toolkits/family/workbook/default.asp

CASE EXAMPLE

A tall, well-groomed 28-year-old man was brought to the emergency room by a police officer because he hit another man in his apartment building and tried to take his mail. He told the police and hospital staff that his name was Bill Bradford. He then told the hospital social worker that, despite the fact that all of his identification cards bore the name Bill Bradford, his real name was Tom Williams. He explained that he was on a secret mission for the CIA to catch people stealing others' mail. He said that the man he hit was trying to steal the mail of a neighbor who had won the lottery. He explained that he communicates with his CIA supervisors via a high-frequency radio stashed in his bag. They could also communicate with him through a chip implanted in his head, so he could hear them talking to him at any time. He said that secret agents from Russia are trying to capture and kill him because he has been tracking a Russian criminal who was stealing the mail of high-level CIA operatives. The client confided that the "real" Bill Bradford was, in fact, dead, and he had assumed his identity in order to hide from the Russian secret agents. He explained that staying in one place for too long was very risky because the Russian agents would find him and kill him. A call to "Tom Williams's" family confirmed that his real name was Bill Bradford. His mother, father, and sister agree to meet with the social worker.

Interviews with Bill's family reveal that they are frustrated with Bill's behavior and do not understand how he has developed such detailed delusions. In addition to being frustrated by constant complaints about Bill's behavior from neighbors, they are unsure whether to challenge his paranoid beliefs for fear that he will become angry and violent. In addition to ensuring that Bill sees a psychiatrist and has the appropriate medication, the social worker decides to include the family in a psychoeducational multifamily group that she is leading with a fellow social worker as a cofacilitator. The family agrees to attend.

The first meeting begins with introductions and efforts to make the families more familiar and comfortable with each other. The Bradford family is eager to learn about the other families' experiences and to express their frustrations about living with Bill. The social worker begins by welcoming all of the families and inviting them to have some refreshments. She also explains that family members should feel free to help themselves to refreshments at any time during the meeting. After about 15 minutes of informal conversation, the facilitator says she would like to begin and says, "We are going to spend some time getting to know each other during this session. Each of us will have a chance to tell the rest of the group about themselves. I know that you may all be eager to talk about the challenges of mental illness, and we are going to get to that in our second group meeting. However, for now, let's talk about other things that are important in your life, especially the things you and your family are proud of. I'll begin. I am a social worker who has been working here at the Family Services Center for about three years now. I'm married and have two children, who are 8 and 10. They are growing up very quickly. I also have two cats. My family is close even though I and my husband both work full time. Last weekend we went for a picnic at the state park, one of our favorite outings. My older daughter came back with a bad case of poison ivy, but she is dealing with it very well—and using it as an excuse to eat ice cream every night before going to bed. Now, Mrs. Bradford, would you like to tell everyone a little about yourself and your family?"

Mrs. Bradford begins to talk about her family and says that she is most proud of her children. They are both incredibly intelligent and had both graduated from college with honors. She explains that this is one reason that Bill's behavior has been so upsetting to her, because it was such a dramatic change. In order to guide the conversation away from a discussion about mental illness, the social worker says, "I know that has been difficult for you. We're going to get into these difficulties more during the next session. Why don't you tell us more about the strengths that make your family unique?"

The session moves along with family members from each family talking a little about themselves. Occasionally those within a single-family group become involved in a side conversation. When this happens, the facilitator says, "I am very interested in what Mr. Jones has to say, but I'm having a little difficulty hearing him when more than one person is talking." At one point in the group, one family member interrupts another while she is telling her personal story. The facilitator gently corrects this behavior by saying, "That's interesting. Let's allow Jane to finish her story and hear what she has to say about that. Then, we'll get back to your point."

The facilitator thanks each group member for his or her contribution after speaking. After everyone has finished speaking, the facilitator concludes the group by saying, "Thank you all for coming tonight and taking the time to get to know each other. I know we are moving slowly, but don't get frustrated. In our next session we are going to talk more about our experiences with mental illness. Please take some time to chat and have some refreshments before you leave."

SUMMARY

In this chapter, we have covered prevalence, assessment, and family treatment issues for three persinentent mental disorders: schizophrenia, major depressive disorder, and bipolar disorders. Nothing we have described suggests the possibility of cure for persistent mental disorders like schizophrenia, major depressive disorder, and bipolar disorder because these disorders are known to be both persistent and lifelong mental disorders. Even though social workers are conducting family treatment with these families, the psychoeducational family approach described in this chapter does not center on cure but rather on the hope that recurrence of the most severe symptoms and disturbing behaviors can be averted, and that rehospitalization may be avoided so that clients can remain in the community. Associated with these primary goals is the specific family treatment goal for families to acquire methods of coping with the stresses they experience due to mental illness, better methods of relating with

---

BOX 7.3 | **Internet Resources**

Due to the living nature of the Internet, website addresses often change and thus we have not printed the addresses in this text. Links to the following websites are posted at the Book Companion Site at www.wadsworth.com.

General Mental Health:
National Alliance for the Mentally Ill
National Institute of Mental Health
National Mental Health Association
President's New Freedom Commission on Mental Health
Psychiatric Rehabilitation Consultants
SAMHSA's National Mental Health Information Center

Bipolar Disorder:
Practice Guideline for Treatment of Clients with Bipolar Disorder from the American Psychiatric Association
Boston University's Center for Psychiatric Rehabilitation
The Depression and Bipolar Support Alliance (DBSA)

Depression:
Families for Depression Awareness
Major Depression—Practice Guideline for the Treatment of Clients with Major Depressive Disorder, 2e, American Psychiatric Association
National Foundation for Depressive Illness, Inc.

Thought Disorders:
Health Place.com: Thought Disorders Community

---

one another, and problem-solving skills that will improve both their family functioning and the functioning of their mentally ill family member. This chapter has presented best evidenced-based treatments for schizophrenia, major depressive disorder, and bipolar disorder, and has illustrated in some detail treatments for schizophrenia using a multifamily group treatment manual and a case study.

DISCUSSION QUESTIONS

1. Explain expressed emotion and its effect on those living with mental illness and their families.
2. Describe a hypothetical family and explain how you could use an ecomap to provide important assessment information for that family.
3. Explain the advantages of including multiple families in a psychoeducation program.

References

Anderson, C. M., Griffin, S., Rossi, A., Pagonis, I., Holder, D. P., and Treiber, R. 1986. "A Comparative Study of the Impact of Education Versus Process Groups for Families of Clients with Affective Disorders." *Family Process* 25:185–205.

Anderson, C. M., Hogarty, G. E., and Reiss, D. J. 1980. "The Family Treatment of Adult Schizophrenic Patients: A Psychoeducational Approach." *Schizophrenia Bulletin* 6:490–505.

Anderson, C. M., Reiss, D. J., and Hogarty, G. D. 1986. *Schizophrenia and the Family*. New York: Guilford.

Atwood, N. 1990. "Integrating Individual and Family Treatment for Outclients Vulnerable to Psychosis." *American Journal of Psychotherapy* 44(2):247–55.

Bae, S.-W., and Kung, W. W. M. 2000. "Family Intervention for Asian Americans with a Schizophrenic Client in the Family." *American Journal of Orthopsychiatry* 70(4):532–41.

Barbato, A., and Avanzo, B. D. 2000. "Family Interventions in Schizophrenia and Related Disorders: A Critical Review of Clinical Trials." *Acta Psychiatrica Scandinavica* 102:81–97.

Basco, M. R., Bostic, J. Q., Davies, D., Rush, A. J., Witte, B., Hendrickse, W. A., et al. 2000. "Methods to Improve Diagnostic Accuracy in a Community Mental Health Setting." *American Journal of Psychiatry* 157:1599–1605.

Beals, J., Manson, S. M., Keane, E. M., and Dick, R. W. 1991. "Factorial Structure of the Center for Epidemiologic Studies-Depression Scale among American Indian College Students." *Psychological Assessment* 3(4):623–27.

Bean, R. A., Benjamin J. P., and Bedell, T. M. 2002. "Developing Culturally Competent Marriage and Family Therapists: Treatment Guidelines for Non-African-American Therapists Working with African-American Families." *Journal of Marital & Family Therapy* 28(2):153–64.

———. 2001. "Developing Culturally Competent Marriage and Family Therapists: Guidelines for Working with Hispanic Families." *Journal of Marital & Family Therapy* 27(1):43–54.

Beck, A. T., Steer, R. A., and Brown, G. K. 1996. *Manual for the Beck Depression Inventory*. 2nd edition. San Antonio, TX: The Psychological Corporation.

Belcher, J. R. 1993. "The Tradeoffs of Developing a Case Management Model for Chronically Mentally Ill People." *Health and Social Work* 18(1):20–31.

Bellack, A. S. 1992. "Cognitive Rehabilitation for Schizophrenia: Is It Possible? Is It Necessary?" *Schizophrenia Bulletin* 18(1):43–50.

Bentley, K. 2000. *Social Worker & Psychotropic Medication: Toward Effective Collaboration with Mental Health Clients, Families, and Providers*. New York: Thomson Learning.

Berg, I. K. and Jaya, A., 1993. "Different and Same: Family Therapy with Asian-American Families." *Journal of Marital & Family Therapy* 19(1):31–38.

Boyd-Franklin, N., and Shenouda, N. T. 1990. "A Multi-Systems Approach to the Black Inner-City Family with a Schizophrenic Mother." *American Journal of Orthopsychiatry* 60(2):186–95.

Brennan, J. 1995. "A Short Term Psycho Educational Multiple Family Group for Bipolar Clients and Their Families." *Social Work* 40(6):737–743.

Butcher, J. N., Dashlstrom, W. G., Graham, J. R., Tellegen, A., and Kraemmer, B. 1989. *Minnesota Multiphasic Personality Inventory-2 (MMPI-2): Manual for administration and scoring*. Minneapolis: University of Minnesota Press.

Butzlaff, R. L., and Hooley, J. M. 1998. "Expressed Emotion and Psychiatric Relapse: A Meta-Analysis." *Archives of General Psychiatry* 55:547–52.

Center for Mental Health Services. 2004. *Evidence-Based Practices: Shaping Mental Health Services toward Recovery: Family Psychoeducation.* Retrieved September 24, 2004, from http://www.mentalhealth. samhsa.gov/cmhs/communitysupport/ toolkits/family/workbook/default.asp.

Collins, D., Jordan, C., and Coleman, H. 1999. *An Introduction to Family Social Work.* Itasca, IL: Peacock.

Corcoran, K., and Fisher, J. 2000. *Measures for Clinical Practice: A Sourcebook.* 3rd edition. New York: The Free Press.

Diagnostic and Statistical Manual-IV-TR. 2000. Washington, DC: American Psychiatric Association.

East, E. 1992. "Family as Resource: Maintaining Chronically Mentally Ill Members in the Community." *Health and Social Work* 17(2):93–97.

Ettner, S. L., and Hermann, R. C. 1998. "Inpatient Psychiatric Treatment of Elderly Medicare Beneficiaries." *Psychiatric Services* 49(9):1173–79.

Falloon, I. 1983. "Behavioral Family Interventions in the Management of Chronic Schizophrenia." In *Family Therapy in Schizophrenia,* ed. William McFarlane. New York: Guilford.

Falloon, I., Boyd, J., and McGill, C. 1984. *Family Care of Schizophrenia.* New York: Guilford.

Falloon, I., Boyd, J., McGill, C., Williamson, M., Razani, J., Moss, H., et al. 1985. "Family Management in Prevention of Morbidity of Schizophrenia." *Archives of General Psychiatry* 42:887–96.

Falloon, I. R. 1999. "Optimal Treatment for Psychosis in an International Multisite Demonstration Project." *Psychiatric Services* 50(5):615–18.

Farley, J. 1994. "Transitions in Psychiatric Inpatient Clinical Social Work." *Social Work* 39(2):207–12.

Ferris, P., and Marshall, C. A. 1987. "A Model Project for Families of the Mentally Ill." *Social Work* 32(2):110–14.

First, M. B., Spitzer, R. L., Gibbon, M., and Williams, J. B. W. 1995. *Structured Clinical Interview for DSM-IV Axis-I Disorders.* New York: Columbia University.

Fischer, J., and Corcoran, K. 1994. *Measures for Clinical Practice: A Sourcebook.* 2nd edition. New York: Free Press.

Fosler, M. 1993. *The Relationship between Selected Family Factors and Schizophrenia.* Unpublished Doctoral Dissertation, University of Maryland at Baltimore.

Fox, P. 1992. "Implications for Expressed Emotion within a Family Therapy Context." *Health and Social Work* 17(3):207–13.

Franklin, C., and Jordan, C. 1999. *Family Practice: Brief Systems Methods for Social Work.* Pacific Grove, CA: Brooks/Cole.

Grove, W. M., Zald, D. H., Lebow, B. S., Snitz, B. E., and Nelson, C. 2000. "Clinical Versus Mechanical Prediction: A Meta-Analysis." *Psychological Assessment* 12:19–30.

Hahlweg, K., and Wiedermann, G. 1999. "Principles and Results of Family Therapy in Schizophrenia." *European Archives of Psychiatry and Clinical Neuroscience, Supplement 4,* 108–15.

Haley, J. 1967. "Toward a Theory of Pathological Systems." In *Family Therapy and Disturbed Families,* eds. I. Boszormenyi-Nagy and G. Zuk. Palo Alto, CA: Science and Behavior Books.

Hamilton, M. 1986. "The Hamilton Rating Scale for Depression." In *Assessment of Depression* (pp. 143–152), eds. N. Sartorius and T. A. Ban. Berlin: Springer-Verlag.

Hatfield, A. 1983. "What Families Want of Family Therapists." In *Family Therapy in Schizophrenia*, ed. William McFarlane. New York: Guilford.

Hiratsuka, J. 1994. "Working with Medicine on the Brain." *NASW NEWS* (February).

Hogarty, G. E., Anderson, C. M., Reiss, D. J., Kornblith, S. J., Greenwald, D. P., Ulrich, R. F., et al. 1991. "Family Psychoeducation, Social Skills Training, and Maintenance Chemotherapy in the Aftercare Treatment of Schizophrenia. II. Two-Year Effects of a Controlled Study on Relapse and Adjustment." *Archives of General Psychiatry* 48(4):340–47.

Holden, D., and Anderson, C. M. 1990. "Psychoeducational Family Intervention for Depressed Clients and Their Families." In *Depression and Families: Impact and Treatment* (pp. 57–84), ed. G. I. Keitner. Washington, DC: American Psychiatric Press.

Holden, D. F., and Lewine, R. R. 1982. "How Families Evaluate Mental Health Professionals, Resources, and Effects of Illness." *Schizophrenia Bulletin* 8(4):626–33.

Hudson, W. W., and Nurius, P. S. 1994. *Controversial Issues in Social Work Research*. Boston: Allyn and Bacon.

Huxley, N. A., Parikh, S. V., and Baldessarini, R. J. 2000. "Effectiveness of Psychosocial Treatments in Bipolar Disorder: State of the Evidence." *Harvard Review of Psychiatry* 8(3):126–40.

Johnson, H. 1987. "Biologically Based Deficit in the Identified Client: Indications for Psycho-Educational Strategies." *Journal of Marital and Family Therapy* 13(4):337–48.

Jordan, C., and Franklin, C. 2003. *Clinical Assessment for Social Workers*. 2nd edition. Chicago: Lyceum Press.

Kaufman, J., Birmaher, B., Brent, D., Rao, U., Flynn, C., Moreci, P., et al. 1999. "Schedule for Affective Disorders and Schizophrenia for School-Age Children—Present and Lifetime Version (K-SADS-PL): Initial Reliability and Validity Data." *Journal of the American Academy of Child and Adolescent Psychiatry* 38(9):1065–69.

Keefe, R. S. E., Goldberg, T. E., Harvey, P. D., Gold, J. M., Poe, M. P., and Coughenour, L. 2004. "The Brief Assessment of Cognition in Schizophrenia: Reliability, Sensitivity, and Comparison with a Standard Neurocognitive Battery." *Schizophrenia Research* 68(2/3):283–87.

Kobak, K. A., Reynolds, W. R., Rosenfeld, R., and Greist, J. H. 1990. "Development and Validation of a Computer Administered Hamilton Depression Rating Scale." *Psychological Assessment* 2:56–63.

Kotcher, M., and Smith, T. 1993. "Three Phases of Clozapine Treatment and Phase-Specific Issues for Clients and Families." *Hospital and Community Psychiatry* 44(8):744–47.

Kranzler, H. R., Kadden, R. M., Burleson, J., Babor, T. F., Apter, A., and Rounsaville, B. J. 1995. "Validity of Psychiatric Diagnoses in Clients with Substance Use Disorders—Is the Interview More Important Than the Interviewer?" *Comprehensive Psychiatry* 36:278–88.

Kuipers, E., Bebbington, P., Pilling, S., and Orbach, G. 1999. "Family Intervention in Psychosis: Who Needs It?" *Epidemiologia e Psichiatria Sociale* 8(3):169–73.

Kuipers, L., and Bebbington, P. E. 1988. "Expressed Emotion Research in Schizophrenia: Theoretical and Clinical Implications." *Psychological Medicine* 18:893–909.

Lauriello, J., Bustillo, J., and Keith, S. J. 1999. "A Critical Review of Research on Psychosocial Treatment of Schizophrenia." *Biological Psychiatry* 46:1409–17.

Leff, J., and Vaughn, C. 1980. "Interaction of Life Events and Relatives Expressed Emotion in Schizophrenia and Depressive Neurosis." *British Journal of Psychiatry* 136:146–53.

Leff, J., Kuipers, L., and Berkowitz, R. 1983. "Intervention in Families of Schizophrenics and Its Effects on Relapse Rate." In *Family Therapy in*

Schizophrenia, ed. William McFarlane. New York: Guilford.

Lourie, I., and Katz-Leavy, J. 1991. "New Directions for Mental Health Services for Families and Children." *Families in Society* 72(3):277–85.

Lowyck, B., De Hert, M., Peeters, E., Wampers, M., Gilis, P., and Peuskens, J. 2004. "A Study of the Family Burden of 150 Family Members of Schizophrenic Patients." *European Psychiatry* 19(7):395–401.

Lubin, B., Larsen, R. M., and Matarazzo, J. 1984. "Patterns of Psychological Test Usage in the United States, 1935–1982." *American Psychologist* 39:451–54.

MacGregor, P. 1994. "Grief: The Unrecognized Parental Response to Mental Illness in a Child." *Social Work* 39(2):160–66.

Maier, W., Phillipp, M., Heuser, I., Schlegel, S., Buller, R., and Wetsel, H. 1988. "Improving Depression Severity Assessment—I. Reliability, Internal Validity, and Sensitivity to Change of Three Observer Depression Scales." *Journal of Psychiatric Research* 22:3–12.

Marley, J. A. 1992. "Content and Context: Working with Mentally Ill People in Family Therapy." *Social Work* 37(5):412–17.

McFarlane, W. 1983. "Multiple Family Therapy in Schizophrenia." In *Family Therapy in Schizophrenia,* ed. William McFarlane. New York: Guilford.

McFarlane, W. R. 1994. "Multiple Family Groups and Psychoeducation in the Treatment of Schizophrenia." *New Directions in Mental Health Services* 62:13–22.

———. 2002. "An Overview of Psychoeducational Multifamily Group Treatment." In *Multifamily Groups in the Treatment of Severe Psychiatric Disorders,* ed. W. R. McFarlane. New York: Guilford Press.

McFarlane, W. R., Link, B., Dushay, R., and Marchal, J. 1995. "Psychoeducational Multiple Family Groups: Four Year Relapse Outcome in Schizophrenia." *Family Process* 34:127–44.

Miklowitz, D., Goldstein, M., Doane, J., Nuechterlein, K., Strachan, A., Snyder, K., et al. 1989. "Is Expressed Emotion an Index of a Transactional Process? Parents Affective Style." *Family Process* 28:153–67.

Millon, T., Davis, R., and Millon, C. 1997. *MCMI-III Manual.* 2nd edition. Minneapolis, MN: National Computer Systems.

Muesser, K. T., Bellack, A. S., Wade, J. H., Savers, S. L., Tierny, A., and Haas, G. 1993. "Expressed Emotion, Social Skill, and Response to Negative Effect in Schizophrenia." *Journal of Abnormal Psychology* 102:339–51.

Overall, J. E., and Gotham, D. R. 1962. "The Brief Psychiatric Rating Scale." *Psychological Reports* 10:799–812.

Pilling, S., Bebbington, E., Kuipers, E., Garety, P., Geddes, J., Orbach, G., et al. 2002. "Psychological Treatments in Schizophrenia: I. Meta-Analysis of Family Intervention and Cognitive Behavior Therapy." *Psychological Medicine* 32:763–82.

Posner, C. M., Wilson, K. G., Kral, M. J., Lander, S., and McIlwraith, R. D. 1992. "Family Psycho Educational Support Groups in Schizophrenia." *American Journal of Orthopsychiatry* 62(2):206–18.

Radloff, L. S. 1977. "The CES-D Scale: A Self-Report Depression Scale for Research in the General Population." *Applied Psychological Measurement* 1:385–401.

Robins, L. N., Cottler, L. B., Bucholz, K. K., and Comptom, W. 1996. *The Diagnostic Interview Schedule (Version IV).* St. Louis, MO: Washington University School of Medicion.

Schatzberg, A..F., and Nemeroff, C. B. 2001. *Essentials of Clinical Psychopharmacology.* Washington, DC: American Psychiatric Association.

Schwartz, A., and Schwartz, R. 1993. *Depression: Theories and Treatments.* New York: Columbia University Press.

Spitzer, R. L., and Endicott, J. 1978. *Schedule for Affective Disorders and Schizophrenia—Change Version.* 3rd edition. New York: New York State Psychiatric Institute, Biometrics Research.

Stein. J. A., Nyamathi, A., and Kington, R. 1997. "Change in AIDS Risk Behaviors among Impoverished Minority Women after Community-Based Cognitive-Behavioral Outreach Program." *Journal of Community Psychology* 25:519–33.

Sue, D. W., and Sue, D. 1990. *Counseling the Culturally Different.* 2nd edition. New York: Wiley.

Tessler, R. C., Fisher, G. A., and Gamache, G. 1992. *The Family Burden Interview Schedule.* Amherst, MA: Social and Demographic Research Institute, University of Massachusetts.

Vitaliano, P., Russo, J., and Carr, J. E. 1985. "The Ways of Coping Checklist:

Revision and Psychometric Properties." *Multivariate Behavior Research* 20:3–26.

Voss, W. D. 2003. "Multiple Family Group (MFG) Treatment and Negative Symptoms in Schizophrenia: Two-Year Outcomes." *Dissertation Abstracts International: Section B: The Sciences & Engineering, Vol 63(11-B),* 5541.

Walsh, Joseph. 1988. "Social Workers as Family Educators about Schizophrenia." *Social Work* 33:138–41.

Willis, Mary. 1982. "The Impact of Schizophrenia on Families: One Mother's Point of View." *Schizophrenia Bulletin* 8(4):617–19.

Treatment for Families with Chronically and Terminally Ill Members (Using HIV/AIDS as an Example)

CHAPTER 8

INTRODUCTION

Family togetherness and family adaptability are both severely tested at times of illness of a family member. Even brief illnesses or periods of incapacity due to accidents make explicit or implicit demands to shift responsibility, allocate time differently, temper wants in favor of others' needs, and adjust the image of other family members as persons and role takers, if only for a short period of time. Short-term adjustments may or may not be easily made, and they are dependent not only on the way the family has been organized but also on the stage of the family life cycle at which the illness occurs, on the ways in which illness has been handled in the past, and on the type and causes of the present illness and its meaning to the family. Additionally, there is a growing body of research indicating the family not only is influenced by a member's illness but the family can influence the course of the disease in return.

Long-term illnesses make all the same demands for adaptability. In addition, they require accommodation to the changes that might be taking place due to the advance of the family life cycle or those due to changing stages or phases of the illness. The need to cope with the long term may not only exacerbate the stress of the illness itself; it may also result in reinforcing family patterns that were dysfunctional for family members or make for difficulty in moving to new patterns that allow for members' growth and life enhancement.

Families with differing membership composition—traditional nuclear, single parent, extended, remarried, gay or lesbian—will all have adaptability tasks specific to their membership. So will a network of relationships with people who may not be blood relatives but who may be considered family in specific instances. Each type of family group will have different needs for services and resources as well as changing, ongoing relationships with the health care team. Further, the role and position of the stricken member is a significant variable in the family's response. We will next describe types of chronic illness, followed by assessment issues and intervention suggestions.

POPULATION DESCRIPTION AND DEFINITIONS

We intend, thereby, to provide the reader a general framework for thinking about family functioning and ways of helping in a variety of chronic illness situations for both adults and children. Families with members who have Acquired Immune Deficiency Syndrome (AIDS) will be a special focus.

Rolland (1987) offers a classification of types of chronic illnesses. They can be grouped according to three dimensions: by nature of onset, by difference in course, or by degree of progression and ultimate outcome. Some illnesses are sudden in onset, with ready recognition that something is different and that drastic, immediate, and long-term adaptation on the part of the patient and the family will be necessary. Accidents with handicapping results may have similar impact. The family may experience this as a crisis, having had no opportunity to prepare for change nor to prior experience with similar circumstances. In other instances, the onset is gradual, giving patient and family time to integrate the significance of the illness and to plan.

The course of illness is not the same in all instances. In some cases, the course may not be constant, with periods of remission or relapse. In other instances, signs of illness are constant. They may proceed to a fixed level of disability or worsen progressively. They may ultimately be fatal, or life shortening, or primarily incapacitating and limiting. According to these categories, the onset of AIDS is gradual, but its course is progressive and ultimately fatal.

The time span from initial infection with the Human Immunodeficiency Virus (HIV) to the appearance of the first manifestations of AIDS may be as long as 10 years. But, as will be shown later, although the time span from first symptoms to death is relatively short in most AIDS cases, some patients are living beyond the anticipated time, a circumstance that creates its own issues for patient and family. Awareness of such change in timing and progression may come first to the patient and vary among family members, suggesting yet another complication in family adaptation.

ASSESSMENT ISSUES

Sprenkle (2002) cites the growing body of research on the role of the family in influencing the course of the disease of their ill member. He asserts that numerous studies (i.e., Berkman, in Sprenkle, 2002, p. 312) have established that family social support to their ill member is health promoting, with emotional support being the most important type of support. Other studies have established the importance of a positive marital relationship to promote health (Kiecolt-Glaser & Newton, in Sprenkle, 2002, p. 313). "Married individuals are healthier than the widowed, who are in turn healthier than either divorced or never-married individuals" (Sprenkle, 2002, p. 313). However, Sprenkle summarizes the studies: "These findings suggest that loss of a spouse has the greatest health effects on men, but the impact of poor marital quality may be greater for women" (2002, p. 313).

Sprenkle goes on to report on a recent review of the research on families and health (Weihs, Fisher, & Baird, in Sprenkle, 2002, p. 313), which identifies key family protective factors that include family closeness and connectedness, caregiver coping skills, mutually supportive relationships, clear family organization, and direct communication about the illness. Risk factors included conflict or criticism, psychological trauma related to the disease, external stressors, family isolation, disruption of developmental tasks by the disease, and rigidity or perfectionism.

Adult Chronic Illness

Families with a chronically ill member become unbalanced in that they allow the illness to take over and dominate the family to the detriment of other family tasks and activities. A multifamily psychoeducational group intervention has been used to help regain balance in families experiencing HIV/AIDS, adult cancer, and end-stage renal disease (Gonzalez et al., in Sprenkle, 2002, p. 324).

Hypertension is an adult illness experienced by many, and adherence to a medication regimen has been shown to be critical. Educating spouses about their ill partner's disease results in improved treatment adherence, lowered blood pressure, and lowered mortality (Earp et al., in Sprenkle, 2002, p. 324). Emotional support by a spouse to the partner after a heart attack has been demonstrated to significantly improve survival rate (Berkman, in Sprenkle, 2002, p. 324). Few interventions for cardiac rehabilitation have been developed or tested. The challenge for patients diagnosed with noninsulin dependent diabetes is to reduce weight: adhere to a special diet, exercise, and medication routine; and monitor blood sugar. Studies show that those patients who have a participating spouse show improvement on several indicators, including diabetic control (Gilden et al., in Sprenkle, 2002, p. 325).

Other adult diseases where family involvement has been shown to be a factor include smoking, weight loss, and poor nutrition/cardiovascular risk. Though studies show that family interventions can promote healthy behaviors, no studies have shown the superiority of family over individual interventions in these areas (Sprenkle, 2002). An area with more research backing is that of family caregivers of elderly family members diagnosed with dementia or Alzheimer's. A meta-analysis of 78 studies showed that intervention, particularly psychoeducational intervention, improved the outcomes for caregivers. They need intensive interventions, which include skills training and problem-solving help (Sorensen et al., in Sprenkle, 2002, p. 319).

Children with Chronic Illness

Healthy family functioning has been shown to be associated with positive child outcomes in children with chronic diseases. Patterson (in Sprenkle, 2002, p. 320) identified nine positive family characteristics that are associated with good child outcomes for children with chronic illness. These include: "balancing the illness with other family needs; maintaining clear boundaries, developing communication competence, attributing positive meaning to the situation, maintaining family flexibility, maintaining family cohesiveness, engaging active coping efforts, maintaining social supports, and developing collaborative relationships with professionals" (p. 320).

Sprenkle concludes that family interventions are likely to improve outcomes with families experiencing a severe illness but that mild illness is unlikely to benefit from family interventions. He summarizes the status of the child and health literature: ". . . family interventions for childhood illnesses clearly demonstrate health benefits for asthma, diabetes, and cystic fibrosis, and show promise for reducing the psychosocial morbidity associated with cancer and cardiac surgery" (2002, p. 623).

HIV/AIDS

One of the first questions asked by both patient and family about illness, chronic or not, is what caused it? How did the patient get it? Can I get it? We will look at sources of infection, as well as phases of illness.

Years of uncertainty and misinformation about causes of HIV/AIDS fostered intense anxiety and were a genuine basis for fear. Eventually, the accumulation of data about who became infected with the Human Immunodeficiency Virus (HIV) and subsequently became ill permitted an understanding of how it was spread. A recent report of the Centers for Disease Control (1994) shows that, for adolescent and adult males of all races/ethnic groups, the chief source of exposure is through sexual activity with other men. The next highest number of cases comes through sharing of needles in injected drug use. Substantially smaller percentages of males are infected through heterosexual contact with injecting drug users or are hemophiliacs who have been recipients of contaminated blood transfusions.

For adolescent/adult women, the chief source of infection is injected drug use, or heterosexual contact with an infected injected drug user or with a bisexual male. This is true for most racial/ethnic groupings except for Asian/Pacific Islanders and American Indian/Alaskan natives, where heterosexual contact is a more frequent source of infection than injected drug use.

Also, small numbers of cases are hemophiliacs or others who have received transfusions of contaminated blood.

For children under age 13, male and female, the main source of exposure is a mother with (or at risk for) HIV infection, with small numbers being hemophiliacs transfused with contaminated blood.

For both patient and family, the means of acquisition of HIV/AIDS poses problems in coping with this chronic illness that are not present, at least to the same degree, in most other chronic/terminal illnesses. Other patients and families may not be eager to disclose the presence of chronic illness; they may question whether something they had been doing could account for the illness, but generally they do not have to deal with factors that are considered to be stigmatizing and that put them at risk of rejection and ostracism, as do homosexuality and intravenous drug use.

Phases of Illness

One similarity in the effects and demands on families for all chronic illnesses is that they have specific time phases to which family members have to adapt. While the phases may not be identical, the importance of recognizing phase-specific issues and adapting to them is.

Crisis: Diagnosis   The person with HIV/AIDS (PWA), no matter who in the family the person is, and the rest of the family have similar problems after the diagnosis of the illness is established. Prediagnosis time is filled with uncertainty, speculation, and anxiety. One may have expected the worst; another possibly refused to think about it. At diagnosis, some uncertainty may be lifted, but the future is altered, and it appears bleak.

Disclosure: Why? Why Not and to Whom?   But now, at this transition, with whom can the information be shared? If the PWA is gay and has handled that with parents, their response to news of this illness is still an unknown. If parents don't know of the homosexuality (or suspect only drug use), is it worth the hassle of telling them? Even more critical, how will the partner react? If the PWA is a parent, should the children be told? What will be the spouse's response if the PWA is infected through extramarital sex or drug needle sharing? And when the family knows, whom can they tell or talk to? With whom can they share the burden and pain?

In many situations of chronic, disabling, or terminal illness, the family has been told or knows the diagnosis before the patient. Among medical personnel, excepting those who sometimes doubt the virtue of informing the patient, there is general consensus that both patient and family should be aware so that they can be open and free in sharing feelings and making plans. And in the case of HIV/AIDS, the patient generally knows first.

Many factors enter into the decision about when and to whom to disclose. They include the patient's own feelings and the anticipation of family members' reactions. Feelings of denial, shame, guilt, and anger, as well as fear of stigma, rejection, and of the burden and pain ahead are experienced by both patient and family. Kaplan (1988) notes that many patients have bought into the cultural view that the disease is a retribution for deviance; this is certainly true for many families. Anger on the part of the patients may be prompted by loss of the ability to perform a job and loss of other resources, and may be directed at those through whom the infection was acquired and at self for failing to protect himself or herself. Arguing and fighting may be prompted by the patient's feeling of guilt for having exposed a partner and perhaps an effort to get the partner to leave before the partner becomes infected.

Stuhlberg and Buckingham (1988) note anger reactions from parents and from partners, both heterosexual and homosexual, toward the implied unfaithfulness in acquiring the disease. Anger can be at both the illness and its consequences, as well as at the patient's drug abuse or homosexuality.

Whether the PWA talks and to whom in the family will depend on the degree to which family communications have been open, and on family coalitions of which he or she has or has not been a part. Some therapists believe that if the patient has not been able to communicate with and be a part of the family prior to diagnosis, the likelihood of establishing a positive connection at this stage is very slim or doomed to turmoil or further disappointment. The disadvantages of secrecy may outweigh the advantages of disclosure (Mohr, 1988). Others argue that, because HIV/AIDS is so debilitating, demanding, and disheartening for the patient and caregivers, it is too much of a burden to be carried alone and that family should know. Active attempts should be made to involve them.

The importance for both family and patient of being informed and able to talk about the situation can hardly be overemphasized. Otherwise, they will be in the position of playing games with each other and being denied the needed mutual support that can come from open and honest communication. The definition of family should, therefore, be broad and include the couple, whether gay or heterosexual, the family of origin, friendship networks, and the family of caregivers.

On the side of openness is the fact that many families are already connected. Frequently they are ready to provide care, even though they may still be unaccepting of the gay or substance-abusing lifestyle. Lack of readiness to acknowledge the patient's gay relationships sometimes may lead to efforts by the family of origin to exclude gay partners from the caring team, an effort that would deprive the patient of a close, important relationship. Such a situation calls for therapeutic help in resolving the conflict. Tiblier, Walker, and Rolland (1989) report an instance of bringing together in therapy a gay son and his uncommunicative Irish family at the time of disclosure. In the encounter, the son was able to relieve his mother of a sense of guilt over his gayness and illness and allow her to express her sadness over the years of distance in their relationship.

Family Role in the Decision about Disclosure   Finally, it is the patient's choice to disclose or not to disclose. Help in making the choice and in anticipating the difficult times ahead may be needed. Rolland (1987) advocates inquiry into the family's experience and history with illness and the ways each family member has responded. Using the framework of a genogram (McGoldrick & Gerson, 1985), it becomes possible to see not only the types of illness situations with which the family has had to cope but also each member's feeling about them, their ability to take on added responsibility, and shifts in relationships.

A genogram might reveal, for example, a past experience of parents' initial ability to properly shift their focus of caring to a child during a lengthy illness. They may, at the same time, have had appropriate expectations and not done for the child what the child could do for self. An alternate outcome could also be possible. A closeness may have developed between mother, as primary care-taker, and son in the caretaking relationship that continued beyond the illness and resulted in the father's feeling not only left to the side but also somewhat hostile to the son. This represents a failure to return to the normal family life cycle at termination of an illness. Mother's genogram might reveal that she had an overly responsible caretaking role in her family of origin. Father's genogram could reveal that males did not, for whatever reason, alter their family roles in time of illness. Such information may provide the patient who now has HIV/AIDS with a basis for understanding what reception in the family the disclosure of HIV/AIDS might encounter. At a later stage, it might help to understand a certain amount of unhappiness generated in the care of the patient.

Family Readiness for Caregiving   Assessment of the family's ability, willingness, and readiness to help is important (McDonell, Abell, & Miller, 1991) and requires discussion between them and the patient. Discussion will reveal who is closest to the patient, who cannot or does not want to be involved, and what time, energy, and resources are available. Therapists also need to help the family be clear about what resources and services may be needed, what they will need to do for the patient, and what the patient can do for self. Family members' perceptions of the situation should also enter in, including their fear of stigma and isolation, and their assessment of their own and the patient's ability to cope. Their ties to religious and other outside groups and the way they view mutual ties also enter in to the assessment of the family's caretaking capacity.

While family contact and investment are desirable, families may overinvolve themselves. Some families feel that they must devote themselves entirely to the patient, that to do otherwise would be selfish and uncaring (Schwartz & Schwartz, 1977). Such family behavior may be the result of feelings of guilt or the manifestation of a chronic family enmeshment. The family may tend also to take charge and make decisions for the patient rather than together with the patient, unless the staff, as we have suggested, make an active effort to include both family and patient in developing a care plan. Brown and Furstenberg (1992) draw attention to the need in this instance to empower the patient by restoring him or her to a more active role in decision making.

Angry feelings expressed by both patients and families are common. These may be directed at each other or at the medical staff, accompanied by demands that they do or not do something. Particularly in cases in which HIV/AIDS is transfusion acquired, the anger toward medical staff is understandable

(Gallo-Silver, Raveis, & Moynihan, 1993). In other instances, the anger is displaced onto persons from the patient's frustration and need to blame, out of feelings of helplessness and hopelessness, and as a result of the patient's life situation. Alternately, the anger may be a reflection of unresolved relationship issues in the family.

Chronic Phase   How to lead a semblance of a "normal" life along with the anticipation of death is an ongoing concern, whether facing an enduring disability or an earlier end to life. Return to prediagnosis "normalcy" will not be possible, perhaps not even desirable. Even with months or years left before the time of death, it is easy to succumb to the feeling that life is over, that there is no more living to be done. "How to get through life feeling alive" becomes the issue. Repeated hospitalizations increase the sense of burden and despair. On the other hand, a return home may serve to evoke hope and/or the reality that it is not over yet. The emotional roller coaster contributes greatly to everyone's stress. The need to pull together may become unduly binding and stifling (Penn, 1983), or come at a time in the family life cycle when a loosening of family connectedness would otherwise be occurring (Rolland, 1987) and when members increasingly seek more of a life of their own.

In the orientation of a gay mental health center, the focus on death is combated with displays of love, affection, compassion, and humor, such experiences as the patient might still be able to have (Walker, 1988). In a later report, Walker (1991) emphasizes the creation of a supportive atmosphere for staff as well as patient and family by shifting focus from the dying patient to the living family. Patients and families may set goals about the kind of experiences they would still like to have, as well as the kind of living they would like to do and is within their capacity to have.

Jue (1994) reports that in 1988, 15 to 20 percent of HIV/AIDS patients lived for three years after diagnosis. Such patients took responsibility for making things happen and did not just wait for things to happen to them. They had short-term goals, such as doing volunteer work, going places they had always wanted to see, and developing relationships with others with whom they could share experiences and really be themselves. In all illnesses, treatment programs that involve patient and family in decision making empower them (see Brown & Furstenberg, 1992) to advocate for themselves and reduce the feeling that things are beyond their control.

With patients who are living longer, there is the necessity of setting new short-term goals. Other patients become jealous, and the longer-life patient may experience some guilt at surviving. Some of these longer-living patients, feeling good about their longevity, also feel pressure not to draw attention to their longevity so as not to undermine the continuing need to find new means of treatment.

Drug-abusing patients who continue to abuse create special problems for their families. In their continuing battle with their habit, they have, in many instances, been in recurrent contact with family. At times parents withdraw, feeling they have done enough. Some parents feel responsible and tend to blame themselves for the drug habit and the illness acquired through needle sharing. The patient may continue to use drugs and to deny or avoid facing the HIV/AIDS aspect of his or her situation and, in a worst-case scenario, may view continued usage as a means to hasten the end. Alcohol abuse, a problem widely encountered in the gay community, may similarly complicate relationships and the family's ability to continue to care for the patient.

The provision of information and the efforts to connect the ill person and family just discussed are inherent parts of an ecosystemic view. Beyond these family ties and those with the medical care staff, widening the connections to sources of support are also important. Family groups may make connections to sources of support and have been found to be useful. Mayers and Spiegel (1992) report that in a pediatric AIDS treatment unit, family groups were helpful when the patient and family needs for service and direction began to overwhelm staff as well as the families themselves. Groups helped to deal with denial and social isolation of the families to allow for expression of feelings and to provide support in general.

Jiminez and Jiminez (1992) report that while Latino families are accustomed to caring for chronically ill members, including patients with HIV/AIDS, special factors make for difficulty in doing so. Latinos account for over 15 percent of HIV/AIDS cases, but they make up only 8.5 percent of the U.S. population. However, many Latinos have no health insurance, so they do not get medical care early and are more likely to suffer complications. Moreover, families are often already caring for elderly members and lack the resources for home-based care. These authors advocate income support for care-providing families as well as a community organization effort to develop resources and help the families cope with their isolation due to attitudes about HIV/AIDS.

Terminal Phase and Mourning   Family and patient may not be at the same place in their readiness to deal with approaching death. The patient may have arrived at acceptance that all has been done that could be done, but family members may feel that the patient is giving up too easily and may urge the patient to submit to yet another form of treatment. A review with family and patient of what is possible and definable as appropriate may help in achieving a sense of resolution.

Patients at this stage of readiness to die may or may not desire constant company. Being alone is not the same as being lonely; patients may know that family is with them even if they are alone. Some may simply wish to withdraw; others may even prefer being alone because they lack the energy or don't want to be seen in their debilitated condition.

The dying AIDS patient is typically a younger member of the family, rather than older, as in the case of many chronic and terminal illnesses. Parents are left to review their role as parents. They may feel a sense of guilt, a need to rescue (as has often been true of the parent of the drug-addicted patient), or a need to be with the patient constantly. Alternately, their strenuous efforts in caregiving may leave them in need of support and assistance in letting go. Partners of gay patients may have similar experiences.

| BOX 8.1 | **Cultural Differences** |

Congress (2002) reports that ethnic families have varying beliefs about health, disease, and treatment that impact the provision of services. Immigrant families may use non-traditional care (e.g., faith healers, shamans). Families may have cultural taboos against telling family business to outsiders (i.e., the therapist). There may be one decision maker, head of the household whom everyone defers to.

Black families see care provision for sick and elderly family members as a family responsibility (Bonuck, 1993). The definition of family is broad and includes an extended kin network, as in the network definition previously advocated for the AIDS network. Black families are less inclined than white families, generally, to seek substitute care for persons with chronic illness (Dungee-Anderson & Beckett, 1992). At the same time, feelings of anger or shame that are evident in the general community response to HIV/AIDS create stress for black family caretaking, as does the disapproval of homosexuality.

Special techniques, such as Congress's (2002) culturagram, may be used to identify the unique beliefs and values about health. This will allow the therapist to design a treatment plan to fit the needs of the family within the context of the evidence-based/best practice options available.

Grieving on the part of survivors is also different in the AIDS death. Gay partners may or may not be able to find support from their family of origin. And parents and siblings may not have a community to mourn with them, especially if they have maintained secrecy about AIDS or any aspect of it in their contracts at work or other social networks. See Box 8.1 for information specific to cultural issues.

EVIDENCE-BASED TREATMENTS/BEST PRACTICES

We will look at some possible assessment tools for this population of the chronically and terminally ill family member. Finally, we will suggest some interventions for prevention of HIV/AIDS, as well as interventions appropriate for different disease stages.

Assessment Tools

As stated earlier, genograms have been used both for assessment and treatment of this population. For assessment, genograms are helpful in identifying relationships between family members, as well as to provide therapeutic insight into family dynamics driving members' behaviors (both positive and negative). Typically, three problem areas have been the focus of measurement for those experiencing health problems: stress, substance abuse, and caregiver burden. Quality of life also is sometimes used. Typical standardized measures used include Mackay and Cox's Stress-Arousal Checklist, the Spoth and Dush

Adult Health Concerns, Leigh and Stacy's Alcohol Outcomes, Skinner's Drug Abuse, Zarit and colleagues' Caregiver Burden, Jacob and colleagues' Chronic Pain, and Abell's Willingness to Care (found in Corcoran & Fischer, 2000). See Table 8.1 for more information about measures for use in assessment.

Additionally, six areas of client functioning are important to consider in an assessment with family members experiencing a chronic illness: psychological adjustment, disease status, family context, school or work adjustment, peer relationships, and developmental issues (Jordan & Scannapieco, in press).

Psychological Adjustment   Standardized measures with high reliability and validity may be used to measure the psychological adjustment of the ill person and his family members. These include the Hudson's scales, which measure the emotional health of the ill individual and other family members. Examples include depression, self-esteem, impulsivity, eating behaviors, coping skills, and so forth.

Disease Status   Campbell (in Jordan & Scannapieco, in press) suggests that interventions for assessing the impact of chronic diseases, diabetes, asthma, or hypertension, for example, may be measured by use of physiologic measures. Examples are glycosylated hemoglobin, pulmonary function testing, and blood pressure. In the case where no physiologic measure exists, self-reports of symptoms or disability, or adherence to medical treatment may be measured.

Family Context   Positive family support versus critical or conflictual family is an important issue. Hudson's Index of Family Relationships may be used to assess overall family functioning (Fischer & Corcoran, 2000). The Conflict Tactics Scale is an example of a measure of family conflict (Corcoran & Fischer, 2000). Critical interactions with family members are known to worsen the ill family member's outcomes.

School/Work Adjustment and Peer Relationships   Fischer and Corcoran (2000) reproduce scales appropriate for use in measuring school issues, including adjustment. One example is the Hare Self-Esteem Scale, which measures the child's self-esteem in three areas: home, school, and with peers. Other scales in the book measure behaviors thought to be indicators of success in school and work settings, including problem solving, level of social support, and alcohol beliefs (Corcoran & Fischer, 2000).

Child Development Issues   Traditionally, testing administered by psychologists has been used to assess children's development levels. Examples of scales often used include the Bayley Scales of Infant Development, the Stanford-Binet Intelligence Scale, the Kaufman Assessment Battery for Children, the McCarthy Scales of Children's Abilities, the Wechsler Preschool and Primary Scale of Intelligence, the Leiter International Performance Scale, the System of Multicultural Pluralistic Assessment, Bender-Gestalt, and the Peabody Individual Achievement Test (Mash & Terdal, 2001).

Family Functioning   Assessment and measurement of family functioning should include interpersonal as well as contextual variables. Those discussed here include: financial burden, family and social impact, personal strain, developmental issues, and mastery.

Financial Burden   Corcoran and Fischer (2000) provide scales for helping to assess family issues, including finances and other family maintenance behaviors. These include the Family Inventory of Resources for Management, the Family Crises-Oriented Personal Evaluation Scales, the Family Responsibility Index, and the Family Inventory of Life Events and Changes.

Family and Social Impact   Important areas to consider for family and social impact include family relationship issues, especially critical and hostile behaviors. Examples of scales that help to measure family functioning are the Index of Family Relations, the Conflict Tactics Scale, the Family Adaptability and Cohesion Evaluation Scale, and the Parental Nurturance Scale (Corcoran & Fischer, 2000). To assess social impact, scale examples are the Network Orientation Scale and the Perceived Social Support Scales (family and friends versions) (Corcoran & Fischer, 2000).

Personal Strain   Stress responses with a corresponding need for coping skills are to be expected when the family is experiencing a child's health problem. Examples of scales to measure both personal and family stress and coping are the Adolescent Coping Orientation for Problem Experiences, the Adolescent-Family Inventory of Life Events and Changes, the Family Hardiness Index, the Impact of Event Scale, the Index of Clinical Stress, the Hopelessness Scale for Children, and the Reasons for Living Inventory (Corcoran & Fischer, 2000).

Family Developmental Issues   Families differ in their response to members' issues, in part due to family developmental issues such as relationship between parents and children, between child and siblings, and between family and extended family. Some appropriate scales for measuring the quality of these relationships are Parent-Child Relation, Child's Attitude About Parents, Index of Brother and Sister Relations, and Family-of-Origin Scale (Corcoran & Fischer, 2000).

Mastery   Mastery has to do with how well the child and other family members are able to do for themselves and feel good about their level of achievement. Examples of scales include the Separation-Individuation Process, the Ascription of Responsibility Questionnaire, the Belief in Personal Control Scale, the Family Empowerment Scale, and the Internal Control Index (Corcoran & Fischer, 2000).

See Table 8.1 for an excerpt of some of these scales and their reliability and validity information.

Table 8.1 | Assessment Instruments*

Measure	Description	Reliability	Validity	Source
Stress Arousal Checklist	A 30-item measure that assesses respondent's stress and arousal reports	Data not available	Known-groups validity, consistency	Mackay et al., 1985
Index of Alcohol Involvement	A 25-item instrument designed to measure the degree of magnitude of problems of alcohol abuse	Excellent internal consistency, alpha is .0	Very good factorial and construct validity	MacNeil, 1991
Caregiver Strain Index	A 13-item instrument to measure the strain among caregivers of physically ill and functionally impaired older adults	Very good internal consistency, with an alpha of .86	Fairly good construct validity	Robinson, 1983
Life Satisfaction Index-Z	An 18-item instrument designed to measure the life satisfaction of older people	No data	Some degree of concurrent validity, known-groups validity	Neugarten et al., 1961
Index of Family Relationships	A 25-item scale designed to measure problems family members have in their relationships	Excellent internal consistency with a mean alpha of .95	Known-groups validity, good construct validity	Hudson, 1992
Conflict Tactics Scale	A 15-item instrument designed to measure three conflict tactics used by family members: reasoning, verbal aggression, and violence	Internal consistency of .42 to .96	Concurrent validity and construct validity is well established	Straus & Gelles, 1990

* In Corcoran and Fischer, 2000. *Measures for Clinical Practice*, 3rd edition. New York: Free Press.

Interventions/Health Promotion Strategies

The assessment tools section identifies measures used to assess chronically ill individuals and their families, to select the appropriate treatment, and to monitor client progress throughout the intervention process. Campbell (2002) reviewed examples of health promotion strategies from exemplary programs. Three types of medical family therapy, a model of family therapy designed to help families with a member who is experiencing a health problem, were reported: family education and support, family psychoeducation, and family therapy.

The *family education and support model* provides information and emotional support to families with a member experiencing a health problem. The group leader may be a professional or a peer counselor who has experienced the same illness as the family.

The *family psychoeducation model* provides education and support as do the other models, plus therapy for family relationship issues that might arise as a consequence of the chronic illness. The leader may be a family therapist or other facilitator.

The *family therapy model*, performed by a qualified family therapist, provides only therapy for relationship issues. Health aspects are not discussed, as the illness may be explained as resulting from dysfunctional family relationships.

Keeping these three models used in health promotions in mind, we will now look at several model programs for health promotions as described in Lambert (2004):

Psychoeducational: Coping with Depression Course for Adolescents

Kazdin reported on a coping-with-depression course for adolescents that assumes a cognitive and behavioral explanation of the depression. The treatment is cognitive behavioral; clients are taught to recognize the cognitive features of their depression (i.e., negative thinking), to substitute positive thoughts, to elicit positive reinforcement from the environment, and to use specific social skills. The treatment is presented in a psychoeducational framework so that the stigma of being in treatment is reduced. The adolescents receive training in a group; parents receive group training as well. They are taught to support the new skill acquisition of their children.

The process of therapy includes brief assessment focused on skills and a 16-week group course followed by booster sessions offered at four-month intervals for a two-year period. Empirical research on this approach shows decreased depression for adolescents, especially for younger males. The parent group has not been shown to add to the basic intervention, but studies are continuing.

Family Therapy: Multisystemic Therapy for Antisocial and Delinquent Adolescents (MST)

Kazdin (2004) reports on Henggeler's approach to intervening with and altering behavior that is embedded. Treatment may focus on multiple systems (parents, peers, school, etc.) where the youth has problems. Risk factors (i.e., parental discipline, child communication skills, etc.) are an assessment focus and help to determine the appropriate intervention. Interventions are individualized and multifaceted, and may include marital therapy, skills training, contingency management, and so forth.

The goals of treatment are "to help the parents develop the adolescent's behaviors, to overcome difficulties that impede the parents' ability to function as parents, to eliminate negative interactions between parent and adolescent, and to develop or build cohesion and emotional warmth among family members" (Kazdin, 2004, p. 558). Kazdin reports strong evidence for MST. In addition to the child's relationships with parents and others and reducing child psychopathology, the approach is known for its cost effectiveness.

HIV/AIDS Prevention   "Cognitive behavioral treatment (CBT) has been used both to reduce risk for HIV infection and to reduce distress following notification of HIV status" (Kelly & Murphy, and Hollon & Beck, in Lambert, 2004, p. 477). See Treatment Manual later in this chapter for an example.

Practitioner Issues   Family therapists at every stage of work with the chronically ill are challenged in their reactions to patient and family behavior. They know the patient's pain and experience stress from it. They are confronted with their inability to restore the patient to health. In many instances, there has been a long-term relationship, and, at the time of death, workers experience a sense of loss much as they would with the loss of members of their own family. Sometimes a patient has been cast in the role of a family member with whom there is unfinished business. In such an event, inappropriate expectations or anger may be directed at a patient for failure to follow a medical regimen or for behavior that exacerbates illness, such as continued drug use on the part of the HIV/AIDS patient. Or a relative may be resented for being either not caring enough, for doing too much, for being overdemanding of staff, or for being overcontrolling of the patient. Nor are therapists immune to a tendency to blame the patient for their illness.

In the case of HIV/AIDS, therapists are confronted with the important issue of sexual behavior in its various forms. They need to be comfortable talking about sex and sexual behavior. Their fears about contagion need to be calmed. Attitudes about substance abuse and toward gay and lesbian sexuality will certainly surface, and negative therapist attitudes are likely to interfere with the patient's freedom to raise issues as well as with the family's ability to move toward a responsive relationship with the patient. Large numbers of chronically ill persons are poor, are representative of minority groups, and may have been denied early access to needed care. In service to the chronically ill, and especially with the HIV/AIDS families, sexist and racist attitudes in the individual therapist and in the service provision network need to be surfaced and combated. See Table 8.2 for details about research studies in this area.

Table 8.2 | Research Studies

Health Promotion Strategies/ Family Psychoeducation	Educational: Self-Management Model for Chronic Illness
Campbell (2002) reviewed the research on health promotion strategies for children and families. His review indicates that family interventions, particularly family psychoeducational approaches, are superior to other types of interventions in promoting health. Campbell suggests that these family-oriented interventions improve the mental and physical health of all family members and are cost effective as well; many have proven effectiveness for some types of problems while showing promise for others. He concludes: "Family interventions for childhood disorders, especially diabetes and asthma, are effective in improving medical . . . as well as psychosocial outcomes. Not surprisingly, family interventions are most effective at each end of the life cycle when much of the care is provided by family caregivers" (p. 331). Campbell goes on to assert that the limitations of the research include too few observational and intervention studies on families and health, as well as too few family researchers and clinicians involved in the study of this area of practice.	This model teaches clients, particularly those with chronic illness, to perform the care necessary to maintain and control their illness. The techniques of this approach are from the behavioral (operant conditioning) and cognitve behavioral approaches, and are empirically established as efficacious. These techniques may include but are not limited to self-monitoring, self-instruction, relaxation, and imagery. Self-efficacy is often used as the outcome measurement. The process of self-management is a six-step process: goal selection, information collection, information processing and evaluation, decision making, action, and self-reaction. Empirical studies of self-management approaches report success in use of self-management skills, reduced medication use, improved exercise, and cognitive and physical symptom management (Creer et al., 2004, pp. 726–727).

TREATMENT MANUAL

Reid (2000) reviewed some interventions for HIV/AIDS prevention including the following:

- Learn about HIV/AIDS.
- Assess your risk.
- Consider a monogamous intimate relationship with a like-minded partner.
- Learn skills to negotiate safe sex.
- Always use protection during sexual encounters.
- Do not share needles.
- Practice safe sex and partner with those who also take these precautions.
- Consult an expert if you believe you have been exposed. (pp. 164–165)

Crisis: Diagnosis

As mentioned previously, cognitive behavioral therapy has been used to reduce distress in patients and families following diagnosis. An extensive program of CBT has been found to protect participants against distress following notification, as well as to produce better preservation of immune system functioning among infected individuals. Experiential therapy has shown some promise in early studies of providing the same results (Lambert, 2004). "Treatment protocols used in group models to treat HIV/AIDS focus on psychosocial factors (stress, psychological distress, coping, and social support). Most last three to four hours and rely on a single session. . . . others rely on more traditional group formats (17 sessions)" (Lambert, 2004, p. 663).

Chronic Phase

During the chronic phase, the ill family member with HIV/AIDS may experience related diseases such as cancer. Lambert (2004) cites research supporting the use of group treatment for changes in emotional distress and coping skills; improvements in anxiety and depression were seen. Lambert (2004) notes that "significant, yet smaller improvements result in quality of life and patient knowledge . . . and that mixed support exists for effects on immune system functioning, disease recurrence, and survival rates" (p. 663). Cwikel and Behar (in Lambert, 2004, p. 663) found the middle stage of the disease to be the best time for psychosocial intervention.

Terminal Phase and Mourning

Sheard and Maguire (in Lambert, 2004) found the greatest effect from depression to be in the final or terminal stage of the illness. CBT and support groups outperformed waitlist patients on measures of depression, anxiety, hostility, and somatization (Kelly & Mulder, in Lambert, 2004, p. 663).

Reid (2000) offers guidelines for helping patients and their families through the grief and loss experience. If the grief is anticipatory, that is, the loved one has been diagnosed with a terminal illness, the treatment goal is to help the family talk through their feelings about the impending loss. Reid (2000) continues, "It is important not to dwell excessively on death/loss issues. Once some resolution has been achieved, try to enjoy the present and preserve pleasurable routines as long as possible. If there is hope for a miracle cure, indulge yourself in it and don't worry about being in 'denial'. As the end nears, reminisce about satisfactions in the relationship" (p. 158).

After the loved one is gone, Reid (2000) suggests interventions for the grieving family and friends:

1. Mourn the death by acknowledging it and realizing its finality.
2. Express the emotions associated with the pain of losing the deceased.
3. Talk about the positive and negative memories of the loved one.
4. Use exposure techniques for any unresolved grieving.
5. Turn to new activities to move on from the grieving experience. (pp. 157–158)

Table 8.3 | Treatment Manuals

Manual Reference	Author's Contact Information
Adult	
"Psychodynamic Therapy with the HIV-Infected Client." Position Papers. 2005 Position Statement on HIV Disease. Canadian Psychiatric Association. Found at http://www.cpa-apc.org/Publications/Position_Papers/HIV.asp	Dr. Peter DeRoche Mount Sinai Hospital 600 University Avenue Toronto, Canada Telephone: 416-586-4595
Martin, 1993. "Psychodynamic Management of Chronic Headaches." *Psychological Management of Chronic Headaches.* New York: Guilford.	Guilford Press 72 Spring Street New York, NY 10012 Telephone: 212-431-9800 www.guilford.com
Jehu, D. 1979. *Sexual Dysfunction: A Behavioural Approach to Causation, Assessment and Treatment.* New York: Wiley.	Wiley and Sons Customer Care Center—Consumer Accounts 10475 Crosspoint Blvd. Indianapolis, IN 46256 Telephone: 877-762-2974 Fax: 800-597-3299 http://support.wiley.com
Family	
Multiple-Family Psychoeducational Group Treatment Manual. McFarlane, W. R., Dunne, E., Luken, E., Newhart, M., McLaughlin-Toran, J., Deakins, S., & Horen, B. 1993. "From Research to Clinical Practice: Dissemination of New York State's Family Psychoeducational Project." *Hospital and Community Psychiatry* 44:265.	William McFarlane, MD Maine Medical Center 22 Bramhall Street Portland, ME 04102 (Multiple Family Psychoeducational Groups)

CASE EXAMPLE

John and Danny came into the clinic for relationship counseling. During their first session the week before, the therapist discovered that the couple were not in a mutually exclusive relationship and that they were both participating in high-risk behaviors (such as multiple partners, unprotected sex, and so forth). The couple had agreed to talk with the therapist at the second session about their lifestyle choices and sexual relationship.

THERAPIST: I'm glad you both came back today. I would like to start by talking about the ways in which HIV can be transmitted. As I am talking, please feel free to raise any questions you may have. The most common routes of transmission are unprotected sexual intercourse with an infected partner, sharing needles that are not sterilized, and maternal-child transmission. (Step: Learn about HIV.)

DANNY: We both have been worrying about the danger to us since one of our friends recently passed away. He had been living with AIDS for about three years.

THERAPIST: I know you said last week that you both have been experimenting with other partners. Did I hear that correctly?

JOHN: Yes, and we haven't used any protection either. Do you think we should be tested? (Step: Assess client's risk level.)

THERAPIST: Yes, I think it might be helpful for you to reassure yourselves or to know what the situation is. And have you two thought about entering a mutually exclusive relationship? With just the two of you? I remember that you said last week that you've been together for the last four years and that you feel like you have a pretty strong relationship. (Step: Explore the possibility of a monogamous relationship.)

DANNY: We have talked about that before but do not feel ready to settle down with just each other to that extent yet.

JOHN: I agree with that.

THERAPIST: Well then, another option you might consider is for me to help you develop some strategies . . . some ways of talking to potential partners, so that you can protect yourselves while not interrupting the potential encounter or upsetting your partner.

(Step 4: Develop skills to avoid unsafe sexual encounters.)

DANNY: That might be a good idea. I never know what to say. It's embarrassing.

JOHN: I think it would be a good idea, too.

THERAPIST: And we can talk about some other ways of protecting yourselves, for example use of protection that offers the most safety to you, such as protective latex barriers (Step: Use protection during sexual encounters.) or learning other ways of satisfying yourself and your partner besides intercourse.

JOHN: When can we start?

SUMMARY

We have discussed issues related to assessing and treating children and adults with chronic illnesses. We have drawn attention to concerns specific to HIV/AIDS sufferers at various stages of illness, along with the issues that their families and lovers need to confront at each stage. Acknowledgment of

BOX 8.2 | Internet Resources

Due to the living nature of the Internet, website addresses often change and thus we have not printed the addresses in this text. Links to the following websites are posted at the Book Companion Site at www.wadsworth.com.

Adults

ATHealth—focuses on the treatment of adult patients with chronic illnesses

Aging and Adult Website—contains information about chronic diseases such as chronic fatigue syndrome and mental health/illness

Health and Social Work—information about chronic illness

Irish Health

Adult Chronic Pain Management Services in Primary Care—provides information on medications for managing nonmalignant chronic pain, managing illness, and education

ClinPsyDoc—useful reference lists and websites relating to chronic illness in older adults

Adolescent/Young Adult Medical Practice—discusses the role of arts and spirituality in the lives of adult survivors of chronic illness

Children

Child and Adolescent Mental Health—discusses psychological and developmental complications of chronic illness

Children and Chronic Illness—promotes resilience in youth with chronic illness, provides tools for kids who cope with chronic conditions, and serves as a guide for parents with a child who has cancer

Kids Can Cope

Caring for Children with Special Needs—offers strategies for inclusion and building your relationship with the child in ways other than rules regarding the child's illness

---

the presence of chronic illness is difficult for a variety of diagnoses; the stigma attached to HIV/AIDS due to the means of its acquisition makes the initial stages especially difficult for both patient and family. Conflicts between patients, biological family, and the patient's lover and other significant others complicate the situation, defining an important area of work with all of them. Long-term relationships of therapists with these families require therapists to evaluate their own attitudes about the disease and the set of relationships, and to deal with the ending of the relationship when the patient dies.

Brave Kids—thousands of resources for children with special needs

Pain and Chronic Illness—addresses pain management in chronic illness and premature death

The American Academy of Child and Adolescent Psychiatry—facts for families with a child living with chronic illness

Child and Family Services

AIDS/HIV

The Body: The Complete HIV/AIDS Resource—covers every aspect of HIV and AIDS from the medical to the social, and hosts over 70 top AIDS groups; free interactive Q & A

AIDS Education Global Information System (AEGiS)—Enhanced Site—frequently asked questions: What do you know about HIV?

HIV InSite Gateway to HIV and AIDS Knowledge—breaking information on antiretroviral drugs and research

UNAIDS: The Joint United Nations Programme on HIV/AIDS—background and information on UNAIDS program

AIDSinfo—HIV/AIDS Information—deals with HIV/AIDS treatment, prevention, medical research, climical trials, drugs, treatment guidelines, vaccines for patients

CDC-NCHSTP-Divisions of HIV/AIDS Prevention (DHAP) Home Page—mission is to prevent HIV infection and reduce the incidence of HIV-related illness and death

AIDS/HIV at About.com—a guide to AIDS/HIV that includes a free newsletter

AIDS.ORG—a nonprofit worldwide AIDS organization harnessing the power of the Internet in the battle against HIV

AIDS/HIV—covers every aspect of HIV and AIDS from the medical to the social, and hosts over 70 top AIDS groups

DISCUSSION QUESTIONS

1. Role-play a client situation in which family members must be told that a member has been diagnosed with HIV/AIDS.
2. How would you go about doing an assessment on an adult client who has just been diagnosed with a chronic illness? Does the type of illness determine treatment, and if so, how?
3. Is treatment of a child with a chronic illness different from that of treating an adult with a chronic illness? If so, what are the differences?

References

Berger, R. M. 1990. "Men Together: Understanding the Gay Couple." *Journal of Homosexuality* 19:31–49.

Bonuck, K. A. 1993. "AIDS and Families: Cultural, Psychosocial and Functional Impacts." *Social Work in Health Care* 18(2):75–89.

Boykin, F. F. 1991. "The AIDS Crisis and Gay Male Survivor Guilt." *Smith College Studies in Social Work* 61(3):147–259.

Brown, J., and Furstenberg, A. 1992. "Restoring Control: Empowering Older Patients and Their Families During Health Crisis." *Social Work in Health Care* 17(4):81–101.

Buckingham, S., and Van Gorp, W. 1994. "HIV-Associated Dementia: A Clinician's Guide to Early Detection, Diagnosis, and Intervention." *Families in Society* 75(6):333–45.

Caldwell, S. 1991. "Twice Removed: The Stigma Suffered by Gay Men with AIDS." *Smith College Studies in Social Work* 61(3):234–46.

Campbell, T. L. 2002. "Physical Disorders." Chapter 11 in *Effectiveness Research in Marriage and Family Therapy,* ed. D. H. Sprenkle. Alexandria, VA: AAMFT.

Cates, J., Graham, L., Boeglin, D., and Tielker, S. 1990. "The Effect of AIDS on the Family System." *Families in Society* 71:195–201.

Centers for Disease Control. 1994. *HIV/AIDS Surveillance Report* 5(4):8–11.

Congress, E. 2002. "Using the Culturagram with Culturally Diverse Families." Chapter 10 in *The Social Worker's Desk Reference,* eds. A. Roberts and G. Greene. New York: Oxford.

Corcoran, K., and Fischer, J. 2000. *Measures for Clinical Practice: A Sourcebook.* New York: Free Press.

Dane, B., and Simon, B. 1991. "Resident Guests: Social Workers in Host Settings." *Social Work* 36(3):208–12.

Dicks, B. 1994. "African American Women and a Public Health/Social Work Challenge." *Health and Social Work* 19(3/4):123–41.

Dungee-Anderson, D., and Beckett, J. 1992. "Alzheimer's Disease in African American and White Families: A Clinical Analysis." *Smith College Studies in Social Work* 62(2):154–68.

Gallo-Silver, L., Raveis, V. H., and Moynihan, R. T. 1993. "Psychosocial Issues in Adults with Transfusion Related HIV Infection and Their Families." *Social Work in Health Care* (18)2:63–74.

Giddens, B., Ka'opua, L., and Tomaszewski, E. P. 2002. "HIV/AIDS Case Management." Chapter 93 in *Social Workers' Desk Reference,* eds. A. Roberts and G. Greene. New York: Oxford.

Goshros, H. L. 1992. "The Sexuality of Gay Men with HIV Infection." *Social Work* 37(2):105–09.

Griffith, J., and Griffith, M.. 1987. "Structural Family Therapy in Chronic Illness." *Psychosomatics* 28(4):202–05.

Hare, J. 1994. "Concerns and Issues Faced by Families Headed by a Lesbian Couple." *Families in Society* 75:27–35.

Icard, L. D., Schilling, R. F., El-Bassell, N., and Young, D. 1992. "Preventing AIDS among Black Gay Men and Black Gay and Heterosexual Male Intravenous Drug Users." *Social Work* 37(5):440–45.

Jiminez, M., and Jiminez, D. 1992. "Latinos and HIV Disease: Issues, Practice and Policy Implications." *Social Work in Health Care* 17(2):41–51.

Jordan, C., and Franklin, C. 2003. *Clinical Assessment for Social Workers: Quantitative and Qualitative Methods.* Chicago: Lyceum.

Jordan, C., and Scannapieco, M. (in press). "Health Promotion and Mental Health: An Integrative Approach." In *Health Promotions,* ed. V. Vandiver. New York: Oxford.

Jue, S. 1994. "Psychosocial Issues of Long-Term AIDS Survivors." *Families in Society* 75(6):324–32.

Kaplan, L. 1988. "Aids and Guilt." *Family Therapy Networker* (January/February):40–41, 80 ff.

Kazdin, A. 2004. "Psychotherapy for Children and Adolescents." Chapter 12 in *Bergin and Garfield's Handbook of Psychotherapy and Behavior Change* (5th ed.). New York: John Wiley and Sons.

Keller, D. and Rosen, H. 1988. "Treating the Gay Couple within the Context of Their Families of Origin." *Family Therapy Collections* 25:105–19.

Lambert, M. 2004. *Bergin and Garfield's Handbook of Psychotherapy and Behavior Change,* 5th edition. New York: John Wiley and Sons.

Macklin, E. 1988. "AIDS: Implications for Families." *Family Relations* 37:141–49.

Macks, J. 1988. "Women and AIDS: Counter-Transference Issues." *Social Casework* 69:340–47.

Mash, E. J., and Terdal, L.G. (eds.) 2001. *Assessment of Childhood Disorders.* New York: Guilford Publications.

Mayers, F., and Spiegel, L. A. 1992. "A Parental Support Group in a Pediatric AIDS Clinic: Its Usefulness and Limitations." *Social Work in Health Care* 17(3):183–91.

McDonell, J., Abell, N., and Miller, J. 1991. "Family Members Willingness to Care for People with AIDS: A Psychosocial Assessment Model." *Social Work* 36(1):43–53.

McGoldrick, M., and Gerson, R. 1985. *Genograms in Family Assessment.* New York: W. W. Norton & Co.

Mohr, R. 1988. "Deciding What's Do-Able." *Family Therapy Networker* (January/February):34–36.

Morales, E. 1989. "Ethnic Minority Families and Minority Gays and Lesbians." *Marriage and Family Review* 14(3–4): 217–39.

Penn, P. 1983. "Coalitions and Binding Interactions in Families with Chronic Illness." *Family Systems Medicine* 1(2):16–25.

Polikoff, N. 1986. "Lesbian Mothers, Lesbian Families: Legal Obstacles, Legal Challenges." *Review of Law and Social Change* 14(4):907–14.

Reid, W. 2000. *The Task Planner.* New York: Columbia University Press.

Robinson, B., Walters, L., and Skeen, P. 1989. "Response of Parents to Learning That Their child Is Homosexual." *Journal of Homosexuality* 18(1–2): 59–80.

Rolland, J. 1987. "Chronic Illness and the Life Cycle: A Conceptual Framework." *Family Process* 26:203–21.

Rotheram-Borus, M. J., and Koopman, C. 1991. "Sexual Risk Behavior, AIDS Knowledge, and Beliefs about AIDS among Predominantly Minority Gay and Bisexual Male Adolescents." *AIDS* 3(4):305–12.

Schwartz, R., and Schwartz, A. 1977. *Visiting the Hospitalized Cancer Patient.* Chicago: University of Chicago Medical Center.

Serovich, J. M., and Greene, K. 1993. "Perceptions of Family Boundaries: The Case for Disclosure of HIV Testing Information." *Family Relations* 42(2):193–97.

Sheinberg, M. 1983. "The Family and Chronic Illness: A Treatment Diary." *Family Systems Medicine* 1(2):26–36.

Sprenkle, D. 2002. *Effectiveness Research in Marriage and Family Therapy.* Alexandria, VA: AAMFT.

Stuhlberg, I., and Buckingham, S. 1988. "Parallel Issues for AIDS Patients, Families and Others." *Social Casework* 69: 355–65.

Taylor-Brown, S. 1992. "Women Don't Get AIDS: They Just Die from It. *Affilia* 7(4):96–98.

Tiblier, K., Walker, G., and Rolland, J. 1989. "Therapeutic Issues When Working with Families of Persons with AIDS." In *Aids and Families,* ed. E. Macklin. New York: Haworth Press.

Tolley, N. 1994. "Oncology Social Work, Family Systems Theory, and Workplace Consultations." *Health and Social Work* 19(3):227–30.

Walker, G. 1988. "An AIDS Journal." *Family Therapy Networker* (January/February):20–32.

———. 1991. "Pediatric AIDS: Toward an Ecosystemic Treatment Model." *Family Systems Medicine* 9:211–27.

Woody, R. 1993. "Americans with Disabilities Act: Implications for Family Therapy." *American Journal of Family Therapy* 21(1):71–78.

Child Abuse and Other Family Violence

CHAPTER 9

INTRODUCTION

Scenes of violence greet us every day in America as we watch the news on television, read newspaper headlines, or receive the latest news bulletin on our laptop computers. There is little doubt that we live in a violent society. We see the assaults upon individuals, the murders that have taken place that day, children shooting other children in school yards. Our own children sometimes fear going to school or want to arm themselves for self-protection. This chapter discusses family violence and suggestions for its assessment and treatment at both the family and community levels.

POPULATION DESCRIPTION AND DEFINITIONS

We would like to think that home and family would provide a haven from such fears and dangers. Unfortunately, homes are not always the safe haven we would like them to be. Children are physically and sexually abused by parents, and parents are assaulted and sometimes murdered by their children; children are physically and sexually abused by their siblings; adult children abuse aging parents; husbands batter their wives; and sometimes the opposite is true. Levinson (1989) finds evidence of many forms of family violence in cultures around the world, of which wife beating and physical punishment of children are the two most common. Adult women are the family members most likely to be the recipient of violence. Aside from the widespread resort to violence in society at large, what can account for its occurrence at home? What is it about the family, the persons in it, their ways of interacting, their connection to the outside world that leads to violence in one form or another or directed to one individual or another? If we can come to understand it, can we also do something that will intervene and stop it?

Following are the generally accepted definitions that we will use for the various categories of child and other types of violence (DeGenova & Rice, 2005):

> Spouse abuse and child abuse are more limited and specific terms than family violence; they usually refer to acts of violence that have a high probability of injuring the victim. An operational definition of child abuse, however, may include not only physical assault that results in injury but also malnourishment, abandonment, neglect (defined as the failure to provide adequate physical and emotional care), emotional abuse, and sexual abuse (Finkelhor & Araji, 1986; Hodson & Skeen, 1987). Sexual abuse by a relative is incest (J. A. Nelson, 1986). Spouse abuse may include not only battering but sexual abuse and marital rape as well. (p. 381)

This section has a focus on physical violence directed toward children. But we begin by noting violence elsewhere in the family, between other sets of family members, and also by noting the factors that frame our analysis and approach to treatment for violent families generally and abused child families in particular.

Pervasiveness of Family Violence

Van Soest and Bryant (1995) have concluded from their study that social workers have attended primarily to violence within the family and have not shown wider concern about the broader base of violence at the institutional and structural-cultural level. At the latter level, "conventional values and everyday social relations form a collective way of thinking which in the United States is white supremacy and patriarchy that becomes part of both individual and societal psyches" (p. 551), ultimately revealing itself "in an easy acceptance of the use and threat of violence as a form of social control and the solution to problems" (p. 552). Such a wider societal view supports rather than retards the occurrence of violence within the family.

Feminist therapists "view all forms of violence, particularly that within the family as an act of power, control, and domination that are products of a patriarchal social order. Violent men are exercising control over their partners and children that they and society historically have defined as legitimate. They do so because they feel entitled to assault and victimize" (Leeder, 1994, p. 2). We concur, given the widespread occurrence of violence in our society, that there is broad social approval for violence in and outside the family. The sanction may have roots in addition to the feminist position just cited.

Stanley and Goddard (1993) confirm the idea that more than one family member may be abused at a given time or may experience physical and sexual abuse at the same time. Also, a child may be abused by a sibling as well as a parent. In their study, the abused children themselves demonstrated violence or aggressive behavior toward siblings or other children. The tendency to separate in our thinking and in practice the forms of violence and the persons who experience it from consideration of the whole family may mean that the current method of intervention in child abusive families is less than efficient, or worse, is incorrect.

Avis (1992, p. 228) draws attention to an array of statistics that lead us to the unavoidable conclusion that male violence and abuse directed against women and children is extremely common; incest, sexual assault, and wife abuse are understood as intrinsic to a system of male supremacy, the most overt and visible forms of control wielded by men as a class over women, implicitly sanctioned by the culture. While not disagreeing that much family violence is attributable to males, Erickson (1992) does caution against attributing violent behavior to all males. Consistent with this view, sexual abuse and rape are seen not solely as sexual acts but more as coercion and the use and abuse of power.

A closer look at some of the linkages suggests that battered women often give their abusers full-time attention in a futile effort to control the level of violence, or they respond by withdrawing from the family, including the children, in an effort to protect themselves (McKay, 1994). Women also try to deflect their partner's rage from their children onto themselves. Sometimes they over-discipline in the hope that the children will behave in their father's presence and forestall attacks upon them, an explanation that helps to account for some of the abuse of children administered by women. The complexities of interaction make for difficulty at times in predicting who will be victim and who will be perpetrator.

We also point out that the resort to violence has been attributed to the family's socioeconomic status or immediate situational stress, to the personality or character of the abuser, and to the personality of the victim. Each of these may be seen as cause in combination with the others and may be the basis of an interactive process culminating in violence. For example, a couple stressed by recurring illness find their patience waning. One makes a blaming remark to the other, provoking a cycle of angry accusations and counteraccusations, ending only when one physically attacks the other. This sort of explanation of the occurrence of violence implies reciprocity of participation, including the victim's contribution to his or her own abuse. While we see that the "victim's" characteristics or behavior may be a factor in violent occurrences, this is not the same as equal responsibility for it.

Also implied is an equality of power on the part of wives and husbands, or more generally of females and males, and sometimes of children vis-à-vis their parents. A feminist point of view has some relevance here (Bograd, 1990). Feminists have considered family therapy approaches that focus on such circular processes to be biased against women. Feminist theorists have offered power imbalance as the basis upon which conjugal violence is built (Dobash & Dobash, 1979). Russell (1984) similarly sees the power imbalance as the basis for sexual abuse. Such an explanation, while it may be useful in understanding male violence, both sexual and physical directed toward

women and children, and may offer understanding of women's countervio-
lence to men, may not by itself be sufficient to explain the violence of women
toward their children.

Definition of Abuse

Having said that violence in the family goes in many directions and is closely
connected to violence toward children, we define the child-abusing family as
one in which children are subjected to nonaccidental physical injury. Given
this brief definition, we are limiting or excluding extended discussion of other
forms of violence in the family.

Our discussion of sexual abuse is accordingly limited. While it is clearly
damaging to the child victim and may be seen as an expression of the power
imbalance in favor of males, as is the sexual abuse of the children's mothers,
many other dynamics enter in and would take our discussion beyond our
space limitations.

Another excluded topic is abuse that is not physical but is administered
verbally and is psychological in effect. This does not fall within most statu-
tory definitions, however much it may concern helping professionals.
Psychological abuse includes a broad range of parent-child interactions and
results in a variety of outcomes for children.

Neglect also is not considered child abuse, although the separation of
abuse situations from neglect situations is not always easy, as neglect readily
appears to abuse the child. The issue is most clearly demonstrated in "failure
to thrive" children, who may suffer physical ills due to parental neglect. While
some of the family dynamics that lead to neglect may appear similar to those
found in families of physically abused children, our attention will be on the
physically abused child.

Within the physical abuse category there can be great variation. Physical
abuse ranges in severity from surface bruises or injuries, to internal injuries,
to death. In frequency, it may be confirmed on the basis of a single incident or
of repeated incidence over extended periods of time prior to actual reporting.
Thus, both "mild," single incidents and severe, repeated incidents are reported
and confirmed as physical abuse. The dynamics of specific cases may be
described within this range of differences, but the same set of dynamics clearly
does not apply to all cases.

Other elements complicate the effort to discuss the dynamics of abuse situations. The abuse of one child involves different conceptualizations of family
processes than the abuse of several children in the same family. In some situations, abuse is inflicted by a sibling rather than a parent. Parents are also
involved in the dynamics of such a situation but in a different way than when
the parent inflicts the injury directly. Other forms of violence may not be unrelated to situations in which the child is abused. Sometimes spouses abuse each
other. Though there may be common family processes in all these forms of
family violence, we will not attempt to account for all of them. Our discussion focuses on physical violence directed at children by parents.

ASSESSMENT ISSUES

Next we will review some issues to be considered in doing a thorough assessment on families experiencing violence. We will look at characteristics of children and family members, including siblings.

A Model for Understanding the Occurrence of Violence toward Children

A natural reaction to child abuse is to wonder how a parent could behave in such a destructive way toward a child who is helpless or at least relatively powerless in the relationship with the parent. One common theory holds that a parent who injures a child must be emotionally unbalanced or mentally disturbed. In this linear, cause-and-effect relationship, the disturbed parent's behavior is traced to internal psychological conflict due to a deprived and destructive childhood of her own. Typically, the abusing parent was an abused child. As we shall see, there is merit to this position, but it does not by itself explain the occurrence of abuse. Why does violence occur at some times and not at others, and why is one child in a family injured when others are not?

The characteristics of the abused child are another element in a model that seeks to account for abuse. Children who are sickly, unresponsive, aggressive, developmentally disabled or delayed, or otherwise unrewarding to the parent have been more subject to abuse than other children.

In addition to the cultural, economic, and social situation of the family that impinges on family functioning, stresses that are situational and transient may also contribute to the occurrence of abuse. Some crises in families that have been found to be in evidence in studies of abusive families include unwanted or unexpected pregnancies, large family size, loss of family members through death or desertion, marital stress, illness, role changes, loss of income, and other more immediate stresses such as criticism or disappointment.

Bolton and Bolton (1987) and Belsky (1980) organize their review of the research and writing on family violence, including wife battering and "granny bashing," around this same three-factor frame: the disturbed parent; sickly, unresponsive children; and family stresses. Pecora (in Jordan & Franklin, 2003, p. 327) uses the same set of factors to understand child maltreatment, calling it an ecological integration. We concur with this framework, though our discussion of the situational elements will focus mainly on the relationships and interaction between family members. Violence does not occur just because the three elements are present; a further negative cycle of interactions emanates from these beginnings and leads to the resulting physical violence.

The following sections draw on the existing literature to identify data and events that are needed for understanding the various elements and the interactions among them. We offer our conceptualization of the process that occurs and identify treatment methodology that has been developed to disrupt the negative processes and to promote the well-being of the abused child, siblings, and parents.

Characteristics of the Abuser

The catalog of characteristics of the parents who abuse their children is lengthy. While it is a given that child abuse and other kinds of family violence occur in families of all social classes, and the number of cases in upper classes may be underreported, the stresses of lower-class living result in greater frequency of occurrence. Since social class may be viewed as a characteristic of both the parent and the social situation, it may be that social situational stresses rather than personality characteristics are the significant aspect that contributes to the perpetration. Both need to be evaluated. This caution would certainly be appropriate in viewing the higher rates of both spouse and child abuse in the black community, as reported by Hampton (1991). Hampton comments that higher rates may be due to changing cultural attitudes about which acts of violence are appropriate for use on children. In any event, the social conditions under which black families need to survive must be considered.

Osnes and Stokes (1988) report that abusive parents have been shown to be socially isolated. They also interact less with their children than other parents do. And they have been seen as relying on their children to gratify their dependency needs, having unresolved interpersonal conflict, lacking in preparation for parenting, having a high need for dominance and control, and lacking in personal and social skills (Bolton & Bolton, 1987). In other studies, abusive parents have been seen as anxious, depressed, untrusting, impulsive, and tending to have a distorted view of their children, projecting on them their own negative attributes. Parents who abuse their children have frequently themselves been found to have been deprived, subject to parental violence, and suffering from an intense need for love and acceptance.

Attempts to identify personality characteristics that distinguish maltreating parents have been inconsistent and difficult to translate into practice. The reality, however, is that behavioral differences in maltreating parents are now known to be more a function of complex, situationally specific variables than of any personality element operating within the individual (Bolton & Bolton, 1987, p. 56).

Swinford et al. (in DeGenova & Rice, 2005, p. 386) found that abused children who have adolescent adjustment problems have an increased likelihood of perpetrating violence as adults. The practitioner must be alert to the possibility that, in the case of a perpetrator's history of abuse, partial learning has taken place and violence mediating strategies may not be available to individuals based upon learned or observed patterns in their childhood. And though as practitioners we may feel empathy for abusers out of knowledge of their life experiences, the perpetrator is still responsible for the abusive behavior.

Characteristics of the Abused Child

A whole array of characteristics of abused children has been reported (Jordan & Franklin, 2003; Berry, 1999). Children of both sexes and all ages are abused. Male and female children are abused in about equal numbers. Some studies report that more younger children than older children are abused, but it is not clear that this is generally true because many investigations have focused on younger children. Thus, sex and age, as characteristics of the child, do not appear to be factors in vulnerability. Birth order or sibling position may be a factor. Only-child, oldest-child, or youngest-child positions have all been identified in various studies as more subject to abuse.

DeGenova and Rice (2005) summarize the research on the characteristics of abused children. They conclude that certain patterns of child behavior are apt to be at high risk for abuse. Children who are difficult for the parents to care for, for whatever reason, are more subject to being abused by the parents. Such difficult child characteristics include the prematurely born child, the restless or fretful child, and the disabled child. These unresponsive children impose greater demands on, and offer fewer satisfactions to, the parent. Additionally, when parents have too many children to care for or there is a lack of emotional bond between parent and child, the child is more likely to be abused. Also, children in a home with one or more nonbiological parents are at greater risk of being abused. Physical illness appears to make children more subject to abuse. Jean-Gilles and Crittenden (in DeGenova & Rice, 2005) found siblings of abused children to be adversely affected as well.

It appears that child characteristics do not by themselves account for the occurrence of abuse and certainly do not in all instances evoke a negative response. We do nevertheless conclude that most research studies that measure the abusive parent's perception of the abused child indicate that most abused children are seen as more difficult by their parents.

Bolton and Bolton's (1987) comprehensive review of studies regarding the characteristics of physical or sexual abuse victims notes that no one characteristic is identifiable as a common factor in a majority of cases. Furthermore, it becomes impossible to determine whether a given characteristic, such as poor self-esteem or defensiveness, existed prior to or appeared after the abuse. Bolton and Bolton reach a similar conclusion with regard to conjugal violence.

Family Interactions

The particular characteristics of parent and child in child abuse situations set up conditions for a relationship that is likely to be unsatisfying to either of them (Franklin & Jordan, 1999; Berry, 1999). For example, a small child who is sickly and in need of a great deal of care and attention is likely not only to be unsatisfying to the parents but also to place additional demands on them. Parents who in their own development lacked both needed nurturance and a clear understanding of their needs may find the neediness of the child overwhelming, and this may result in unresponsive neglect or an aggressive response. In either case, the child may respond with more of the same crying and parent-requiring behavior rather than less of it, resulting in more of the same response from the parent. In other instances, the infant may not possess any particular difficult physical or mental characteristics, but the circumstances of birth or some other element that elicits a negative image of the infant in the mind of the parents may prompt the negative parental response.

By reference to the situational aspect, we draw attention to the interaction between the abusive parent and the child; the interaction between parenting figures, whoever they may be; and the way these figure into the abuse. Collins, Jordan, and Coleman (1999) list five overlapping conditions that are correlates of child abuse; they qualify this by stating the correlates are not limited to only these five. The conditions are (1) isolation from family and friends, (2) negative interactions within the family, (3) inappropriate expectations of the children, (4) high rates of stress, and (5) lack of parenting skills.

Cirillo and DiBlasio (1992) look beyond these relationships to the entire set of relationships, including past and present relationships with families of origin. They use the term "games," which refers to the roles that the various family members play in a particular set of relationships. Given a particular set, the abuse may be an expression of anger toward the spouse or a particular child and simultaneously a signal given by the abuser of a sense of unfitness for parenting. The following paragraphs will provide examples.

Gaensbauer and Sands (1980) report an in-depth study of parental and professional staff reactions to child behaviors such as social and affective withdrawal, lack of pleasure, unpredictability and inconsistency, shallowness of affect, ambivalence, distress, and anger. Staff became aware of their own reactions to the child behavior as similar to that of parents. Both they and the parents countered the child with their own tendencies toward withdrawal, unpredictability, anger, and other responses. Clearly, the child's behavior serves as a stimulus to parental action.

Kadushin and Martin (1981) offer further insight into the parent-child interaction. In an extensive and detailed review, they document the bidirectionality of parent-child interaction. Their own research on abuse incidents showed that behavior on the part of the child had precipitated the abusive incident, prior to which the parent had tried to deal with the behavior in other ways. "Parents were described as reacting to crying, disobedience, hostility or some other behavior of the child in nine out of ten of the incidents" (p. 114). In their view, children respond selectively—sometimes positively, sometimes negatively—to parent behavior. Parent behavior is contingent upon child behavior as well as the other way around. "The feedback from each party in the interaction has consequences for each, which, over a period of time, establishes the patterns of behavior which characterize the relationship" (p. 149). This is not to say that the child "causes" the abuse, because this is only one of many factors operative, but it does suggest that new interaction patterns could be helpful in precluding further abuse.

For an infant, the behavior cannot in any sense be thought of as premeditated but only as an expression of the needs of the child and thus an unwitting contribution to the situation. Older children have their own ways of expressing their need for a positive parental response. Both their withdrawn and unresponsive behavior, as well as their aggressive behavior, may be means of seeking such a response, but neither is likely to be perceived by the parents as rewarding their own need for a positive response from others. When they respond negatively to the child's behavior and thereby fail to meet the child's needs for a positive response, the parents also do not dispose the child to friendly behavior in return. The negative response of each to the other becomes more extreme, until violence to the child results or something else happens to interrupt this sequence. In older children, violence toward the parent may also, in some instances, be a consequence.

The dyadic interaction of parent and child does not take place in isolation from other forces and events. A number of factors contribute to its occurrence and perhaps occasionally to its interruption. Among the more significant of these situational factors is the relationship between the parents. The dyadic interaction of a single parent and child could fit the description in the previous section. Also, we recognize that the burdens of parenting fall heavily and differently on single parents. Chapter 4 addresses the issues of single-parent families.

Siblings

There is amazingly little documentation of the position of siblings of the abused child in the occurrence of violence. In some instances, siblings are also abused, sometimes worse than the child whose abuse was first reported. If the abused child is removed from the home, another child is sometimes scapegoated by being singled out for abuse. In other cases, a sibling may ally himself with the parent in attacking a child or even become the means of the parent's attack on the child, similar to the way a spouse can be provoked to attack a child. And a sibling who is neither victim nor perpetrator may live in fear that what happened to the abused child may also happen to him and may doubt the parents' love. In some instances, siblings feel they are somehow responsible for the abuse, and they should have protected the abused child. Whatever their role, their participation in the family will be affected. Treatment also should attend to these various aspects of the siblings' experience, both to enable their own growth and to improve the functioning of the family group.

External Family Systems Issues

Other external persons and situations may be a source of stress for the family and contribute to the abusiveness of the situation. These include unique situational elements, such as parental illness and lack of extended family support.

Other Situational Elements   Illness in the parents, like illness in the abused child, can be a factor in abuse. Parents who are ill are limited in ability to meet the child's needs and may be frustrated because they are deprived of meaningful roles, either within the family or outside it. Illness or disability sometimes deprives parents of a meaningful role outside the home as breadwinner and thrusts them into a more direct but unaccustomed child-caring role when the spouse goes to work. Their inabilities to adapt to the illness or disability, plus the thrust into the undesired role, serve to upset whatever balance in relationships existed prior to the illness. Underlying or together with all of these factors may be the frustrations in some families brought about by poor housing and limited resources.

Losses of relationship also appear to be a significant situational element. Losses may be barely discernible, as when the nonabusing parent leaves the house or is unavailable when needed or desired by the child-caring parent. Other losses may be more obvious. The withdrawal of a boyfriend from a relationship or the separation of a spouse can serve to undermine the parent's ability to respond positively to a child. Family change and instability both appear as situational elements contributing to abuse.

Illness and losses might be manageable if the family had other supports. But DeGenova and Rice (2005) report that abusive families are isolated, including isolation from social agencies to which they had in the past gone to seek to have their needs met. There is in such situations little relief from child-caring responsibility, or any support when other stresses such as illness, change of housing, loss of employment, or intrafamily conflicts occur. DeGenova and Rice's (2005) review confirms the impact of current life stress in abuse families:

> Economic distress is associated with both physiological distress and psychological distress, and it has far-reaching effects on families. It increases the possibility of divorce because of lower levels of consensus, poorer communication, disharmony, and stress in the relations between spouses and between parents and children. (p. 391)

The combination of limited parental coping capacity, the care-requiring characteristics of the child, the tenuously balanced relationships between pairs of triads of family members, and situational stress appear to set the stage for abuse of the child. In some instances, material means may discourage violence by allowing relief through the hire of child-care services or by making the parent feel rewarded with treats or purchases. Such relief is not available to the economically deprived family. Nor does such relief always serve to avoid violence, as is evident in more affluent families in which abuse occurs. In other instances, a responsive environment in the form of an empathetic circle of friends or a caring extended family might be helpful. But where these are not available or helpful, other means of treatment are necessary. Box 9.1 discusses some information about the additional impact of culture.

EVIDENCE-BASED TREATMENTS/BEST PRACTICES

Interdisciplinary treatment teams and concrete services are both useful and necessary in work with abusive families. Our discussion of treatment will draw on the model proposed previously for understanding the occurrence of violence toward children and the interactions between these elements: characteristics of the child, characteristics of the parents, and the situational effects of the environment in which the interactions take place.

| BOX 9.1 | **Cultural Differences** |

Domestic violence has been found in all socioeconomic groups and ethnic groups (Hampton et al., in DeGenova & Rice, 2005). Lower socioeconomic group families (disproportionately from minority groups) are reported for child abuse more than middle- or upper-class families are; however this may be due to underreporting from the middle and upper classes. Similarly, "very young, single, poor parents are particularly prone to child abuse, since their immaturity and inexperience and inability to cope create feelings of helplessness and anger that they are not able to control" (Young & Gately, in DeGenova & Rice, 2005, p. 385).

Assessment Tools

The state-of-the-art assessment for this population consists of risk assessment instruments that may be classified into four types: matrix, empirical predictor, family assessment scales, and the Child At Risk Field (CARF) (Pecora, in Jordan & Franklin, 2003). The *matrix model* rates severity of risk to the child; the *empirical model* looks at risk factors in order to predict abusive behavior; *family assessment scales* look at child and family functioning; and *CARF* identifies risk factors from an ecological perspective. The accuracy, reliability, and predictability of these models is still being debated. We prefer the behaviorally oriented family assessment scales, particularly the ones with high reliability and validity coefficients. Jordan and Franklin (2003) list some of the most commonly used scales, including Abidin's Parenting Stress Index, Straus et al.'s Parent-Child Conflict Tactics Scale, and the National Committee for Prevention of Child Abuse's Parenting Program Evaluation Manual (p. 330). See Table 9.1 for assessment tools.

Internal Family Systems Interventions

Given the violence that has occurred in the family, initial contacts present problems for both the family and the worker. Some of the family's feelings and behavior may be attributable to the explanations given by the referral source and to the family's prior experiences with workers and agencies. Anxiety and defensiveness are sure to be present, along with some degree of hostility as well as a possible underlying sense of guilt and fear of having children removed from the home. The worker, uncertain of the level of aggressiveness that might be expressed and concerned about the continuing danger to the abused child, may anticipate hostility. Both the worker's horror at the abuse and anger at someone who would harm a child are feelings that, if not resolved, could interfere with seeing the parents as persons with their own needs and developing a working relationship with the whole family.

All of the worker's skills in achieving contact, a working relationship, and a definition of the problem(s) to be solved will be called upon. Either by

Table 9.1 | Assessment Instruments*

Measure	Description	Reliability/Validity	Source
Family Awareness Scale (FAS)*	This 14-item questionnaire measures family competence as defined by the Beavers-Timberlawn model. Families studied included a child in out-of-home placement.	The FAS has very good internal consistency (alphas = .85–.88), and some degree of concurrent validity.	Green et al, 1985
Family Attachment and Changeability Index 8 (FACI8)	Measures family functioning, particularly of African American youth in residential treatment and their families.	The FACI8 has good internal consistency with a range of .73 to .80 for the subscales. Validity is reported as good in predicting program completion and placement.	McCubbin et al., 1996
Family Assessment Device (FAD)	This 60-item questionnaire measures family functioning, including problem solving, communication, roles, affective responsiveness, affective involvement, and behavior control.	The measure has some degree of concurrent and predictive validity. Subscale reliability reports range from .72 to .92.	Epstein et al, 1983

Family Adaptability and Cohesion Evaluation Scale (FACES-III)	FACES-III is a 20-item questionnaire that measures family cohesion and adaptability.	The measure has fair internal consistency, .68, and good stability; .83 for cohesion and .80 for adaptability.	Olson, 1986
Child's Attitude Toward Father (CAF) and Mother (CAM) Scales	Two 25-item scales that measure problems children have with their parents.	The CAF has a mean alpha of .95 and the Cam .94, indicating excellent internal consistency. Both have excellent stability; .96 (CAF) and .95 (CAM).	Hudson, 1997
Conflict Tactics Scale (CTS)	This frequently used scale measures psychological maltreatment, neglect, and physical and sexual abuse.	The CTS has support for internal consistency (alphas = .42–.88); and extensive support for validity, including correlations between CTS scores and risk factors of family violence, antisocial behaviors by child victims, and so forth.	Straus et al., 1998

* In Corcoran and Fischer, 2000. *Measures for Clinical Practice*, 3rd edition. New York: Free Press.

telephone or in person at the home, the first contact needs to be directed to introducing the worker as a source of help rather than as critic or judge so that the family can function effectively for all its members. Substantial effort should be devoted to listening and reducing defensiveness and helping family members to sense that the worker is there for them.

Police have often been involved early in the case, and the legal system's role is important in determining parents' capacity and rights in relation to their children. In these instances, parents come to treatment involuntarily. Although they prefer voluntary clients, therapists have seen the usefulness of the pressure of the legal system in initial engagement of the family, until the family's own recognition of problems and desire for help comes into play (Cirillo & DiBlasio, 1992). In any event, it is important to acknowledge the involvement of the legal system early in the contact.

It is useful at the time of first contact to have the referring person present and to tell the family what the worker has been told about their situation so that the family begins to understand that the relationship to the worker will be characterized by openness and forthrightness. The worker emphasizes the goals of helping the family with what they see as their difficulties and to be more the family they would like to be. This usually includes avoiding removal of an endangered child or abusive adult from the home if possible. Kagan and Schlossberg (1989) are explicit in recognizing that the families may have difficulty in trusting the worker and in being open about what has happened. This is what is hoped for, and there may be consequences if such an environment does not occur.

Little things at the time of a home visit, such as waiting to be invited in and asking where the family would like the worker to sit, serve to convey respect and leave them in charge. Giving each person the opportunity to talk and be heard takes everyone seriously and individualizes each of them. Kinney, Haapala, and Booth (1991) note that it may be necessary to separate family members for parts of the session, take time-outs, or even threaten to call the police if the level of hostility or danger becomes too great. It may also be entirely appropriate for the worker to share her fears of what might happen, or the sense of being overwhelmed.

The initial focus is on the crisis that resulted in the present contact. What were the stressful events? How did the events affect the various members? How did each respond? Since many of the families are crisis prone and have had agency contacts before, it is important to understand what their prior experience has been and with whom, as well as their understanding of the present referral.

Interventions with Parents   When dealing with abusive parents, the worker needs first of all to convey that he is there to understand, care, and help rather than to threaten or criticize. A nonjudgmental attitude is essential. The worker responds to the parents' strong dependency needs and to their need for a parenting, caring person in their lives. Consistency in this accepting and caring position is important because the parents' own feelings of guilt and their previous life experience may lead them to find such an attitude unbelievable and perhaps even frightening. A wish to flee may result from these feelings. Most workers have found that concern about the parents' own needs and feelings should be emphasized with the parents, rather than concern about the child, and this concern should be for the needs of both parents. By this approach, the worker avoids arousing the same feelings of jealousy and neglect that have characterized the family's internal interactions. The applicable principle from conjoint family treatment is the worker's ability to identify with each member present and to avoid siding with one family member against another.

The worker's ability to identify with both parents not only is critical in conjoint sessions but is also necessary in separate individual sessions. For some workers this may be particularly difficult, at least initially, in relation to the overt perpetrator of the abuse. Individual sessions may be necessary, especially early in the case. Separate workers from the interdisciplinary treatment team appear in these instances to be particularly useful.

The giving, nurturing approach is manifest first of all through the workers' attitudinal orientation, but giving comes in more concrete forms also. In residential and daycare programs, parents are given relief from childcare and given the opportunity to observe how others care for children. Parent aides offer assistance to parents in their own homes, providing support and companionship in addition to assistance with childcare. In still other programs, children may be left for short periods with child-care staff so that the parent has relief from this responsibility. Services that meet family needs for income maintenance, housing, employment, and medical care are also provided. Some programs consider nurturance to the parents sufficient in itself, since it meets deep needs of the parents that have in the past been unmet and thereby enables them to be more giving to their children. No program can be effective without this base; other elements of treatment may not begin until parents experience an alliance with the worker. However, meeting the needs of the parents by itself is not sufficient. Specifically, parenting skills must be developed, the parents' denial and guilt need to be dealt with, and the social isolation of the family should be ended. Next we will review interventions in the areas mentioned in the assessment phase: isolation from family and friends; negative interactions within the family; inappropriate expectations of the children and the lack of parenting skills; and high rates of stress (Collins et al., 1999, pp. 232–233). We will follow these with more detailed intervention suggestions for parents.

Isolation from Family and Friends   Child abuse and neglect may stem from the family's lack of social supports and resources. The treatment recommended for social isolation is family preservation, through in-home services. Skills training is recommended as an adjunct to the in-home intervention to help parents learn stable and healthy social relationships, which research shows are lacking for these families.

Negative Interactions within the Family   Negative parent-child relationships are due in large part to parents' inconsistent parenting. Children do not behave well under this situation when parents don't appropriately reward or discipline them. Children do not mind and "this leaves the parents with little influence over their children's behavior, who then turn to harsher disciplinary measures" (Collins et al., 1999, p. 232). Parenting skills training is an appropriate option for treatment.

Inappropriate Expectations of the Children and Lack of Parenting Skills
Lack of knowledge of child development leads parents to have inappropriate expectations of their children. This in turn leads to poor parenting and possible harm to the child from a parent who does not have a realistic idea of what children should be doing. Lack of parenting skills also has been associated with stress and an absence of personal and social resources. A psychoeducational approach where child developmental materials are provided along with parenting skills training is called for in this case.

High Rates of Stress   Child abuse is correlated with high stress that involves both social isolation and life crises. When a crisis occurs, such as a parent losing a job, the family has no one to call upon for help and support. Low income can further complicate the situation as well as "unemployment, low educational achievement, substance abuse, depression, anxiety, and the child's temperament. . . . larger than average family sizes, and single or step parenting" (Collins et al., 1999, p. 233). The primary treatment for stress is agency support.

Teaching Parenting   Many activities fall under this broad rubric. The work just described in meeting the parents' needs for nurturance serves to strengthen them as individuals and puts them in a better position to function as members of the parental hierarchy. Their task for the family is to give leadership and structure to the organization. With the nurturance they have been offered, energies are freed for them to individualize each other, to be more assertive in setting expectations, to set rules and develop behavioral guidelines for the children, to communicate verbally more frequently and effectively, and to see and respond to each child as a separate person. The following interventions contribute in one way or another to these ends.

Providing parents with the opportunity to observe how others care for their children offers them the chance to learn new skills in childcare and to overcome the deficits in their own parental role models. Seeing how others approach a colicky, unresponsive, stubborn, insistent, or otherwise difficult child enables them to learn other, more useful responses. These can be substituted for their own aggressive responses in order to arouse a positive reaction in the child. These opportunities are provided in residential and daycare programs but also constitute an aspect of parent-aide activity. Opportunities of this nature may also be provided by social workers during parental visits with children who are temporarily separated from the family.

In addition to modeling parenting skills, some programs teach specific aspects of childcare and offer parents instruction about what can reasonably be expected of children of a given age. Their own experience and models have not provided this knowledge, which is particularly crucial. Instruction is sometimes given individually to parents, sometimes in classes. It may be given by social workers or by other members of a treatment team.

Skills in behavior modification are developed. Parents are taught to "catch the child being good," to identify the child's positive behaviors, and to provide rewards for good behavior by giving positive attention through verbal communication and spending time. Parents learn about adapting the house to the child and developing behavioral contracts with the child. For parents who have withdrawn from their child out of fear or their own anger, gradual steps in reengagement are rewarded. Spouses can be involved in such training as well as in providing rewards to their partners. By these means, mothers improved their techniques for controlling the children, using less physical punishment. In addition, by increasing the parents' sense of competence as parents and adults, consistent improvement was shown in other areas of family functioning (Tracy, Ballard, & Clark, 1975).

We emphasize the importance of conjoint work with the parent or parents and the child in several of the projects cited. While didactic instruction for parents has its uses, the conjoint effort provides immediate opportunity for the parent to try new behaviors suggested by the worker, and for the worker to observe the interactional process and to give further guidance to both parent and child in response to what she sees.

Modeling, teaching parenting skills, and providing knowledge about the expectable behaviors of children are all useful in giving parents models and skills they can use to alter parent-child interaction. The negative cycle can be changed to a cycle of interactions that is more rewarding to both. The effort to alter parents' responses to their children, however, can take place only in the context of a relationship in which the parents can clearly experience concern for themselves as persons, and not only as instruments to meet their children's needs. Thus, their learning occurs in the context of being given to and nurtured. The modeling of caregiving behavior has teaching value because it provides parental relief from childcare. Learning can occur when teaching is experienced not as a criticism but as a means of achieving a more rewarding relationship with a child.

Parent skills training serves to develop more realistic and consistent responses of parent to child and a clearer expression of parental expectations. This makes the child more clear about the rules and less likely to deviate from parental expectations so that less demand is placed on the parent for direction and supervision. It also makes the child feel more comfortable, positive, and responsive to the parent. A changed interaction pattern should follow. In giving attention to the dyadic interactive process, the worker needs to bear in mind the balance of relationships throughout the family. This avoids re-arousal of jealousy between parents and children and prevents its appearance between family members and the worker or workers on the treatment team.

Teaching Communication   Wells (1981) draws attention to deficits of verbal communication in abusive families. Noting the earlier work by Polansky,

Borgman, and DeSaix (1972) on "verbal inaccessibility" in neglect families, she says that abusive families manifest similar inaccessibility. Communication rates are lower. Behavior occurs as a substitute and elicits minimal comment. The need is for talk and verbal exchange of observations, thoughts, feelings, and reactions instead of nonverbal communication. The worker effort promotes conversation, no matter what the topic. Conversation between parent and child conveys interest and caring. The worker stops nonverbal interaction to label actions and talk about them. Explanations by the parent to the child, which are often lacking, are encouraged and serve to provide instruction and structure. Expressing feelings and being listened to offer relief and provide understanding. Since feelings of futility, depreciation, and powerlessness lie behind the noncommunicativeness, the opening of communication stimulates hope and frees energy. Increased conversation between spouses can have similar effects. Listening as well as talking may be difficult, and worker effort may be needed to enable other family members to be attentive, to take seriously what has been said, and to respond with relevant verbalization of their own. Clarity of messages can be facilitated by worker suggestions for rephrasing when needed or by proffering verbalizations when the individual is having difficulty finding appropriate words. These need to be confirmed by asking the individual whether the worker's words convey accurately what she intended to say.

Communication problems other than verbal inaccessibility may be present. Interruptions, simultaneous talking, irrelevant remarks, or a general escalation of noise require worker regulation of verbal behavior so that family members listen to each other and convey respect and affirmation through their listening behavior. When noise levels are high, it may also be necessary to be clear about who is talking to whom and to require members to talk to each other rather than about each other.

We have placed this discussion of communications in the context of parent-child relationship treatment where it is clearly needed and useful. Regulation of communication may also be necessary with other family pairs and, in some aspects, more applicable when more family members are in conjoint sessions.

Encouraging Parental Acceptance of Responsibility   Parents also can be helped to move from a defensive denial of responsibility for the child's injury to ownership of responsibility, to concern for the child's welfare and recognition of their own wish to be better parents. In the context of a giving and nonjudgmental relationship, it becomes possible for them to do so. They are often relieved to reveal the assault and to talk about their emotions at the time and how they felt afterward. These sessions, timed rightly, can be individual with one parent or conjoint with both. Ounsted, Oppenheimer, and Lindsay (1974) found that parents can set for themselves the task of breaking the cycle of violence that has been characteristic of their families for generations. The worker's questions about the parents' own childhood family experiences help them become aware of this cycle and make it more possible for them to break the hostile identification with their own parents. Increasing the individuation of the parents and their own separateness from their own parents helps to establish a separate identity and increases confidence and competence. In instances in which the child is scapegoated because in a parent's eyes he is representative of some other hated person in the life of the parent, the displacement has to be recognized and the original feelings about those persons need to be resolved.

These interventions, which are of a psychotherapeutic nature, may occur in individual or conjoint sessions with parents. Group treatment has also been found to serve this purpose productively. But they may also occur when time is allowed in visits to daycare centers, in sessions in which plans are made for visiting a child who is separated from the home, or interspersed in parent skills training sessions.

The mix of the various interventions, with parent nurturance, parent skills training, and psychotherapy, will be different for different parents. The readiness of the parents to engage in parent training or emotional abreaction will come at various stages of contact, depending on their ability to trust the worker's acceptance and caring for them. The mix of interventions depends also on the family's material status and needs and the agency's ability to provide services such as daycare, parent aides, and other needed services in support of the parents and their parenting efforts. Worker assessment and reassessment of needs and readiness must be continuous.

Treatment of the Abused Child   We have described the great amount of effort devoted to nurturing abusive parents as family leaders, which enables them to fulfill themselves and their functions as parents. The children also need help, of course, and for some of the same reasons as the parents. Beyond immediate physical care, their emotional needs must be met, and their interaction with their parents needs to be changed.

The child's need to be given to and attended to can take many forms. At a minimum, physical injuries and health problems must be cared for. When the child feels physically well, the demands on parents for care are reduced, and child and parents can feel more friendly to one another. Caring attention can release the child from "frozen watchfulness," unresponsiveness, or withdrawal, and from the opposite behaviors of hyperactivity and unregulated or hostile responses. New behaviors appear first with substitute caretakers while the child is receiving residential or daycare, and only tentatively in contacts with the child's own parents. But as parents learn to respond to the child's changed responsiveness, the child's responsiveness to parents continues to improve. The changed interaction between parents and child is made possible initially through meeting each party's individual needs, and then through the more reasonable and explicit structure provided by the parents. Jeffrey's (1976) effort to teach children how to respond shows promise of promoting positive interactions between parent and child.

Beyond these efforts, play therapy or psychotherapy may enable abused children to cope with their feelings about injuries and illnesses, and about their parents and siblings. The hurts and rejection they have experienced will no doubt be alleviated by the changed behavior of the parents and the new interaction pattern that will result. But play therapy or psychotherapy can remove further blocks to children's growth and development and make it possible for them to behave in relationship-seeking ways that are rewarding to them and to the parents.

In extreme cases, when the child's life or health is in danger, practitioners need to consult with Child Protective Services (CPS). If the child needs protection from the abusive parents, CPS may remove the child if in-home services are not appropriate or do not help the situation. Options are foster care or adoption; sometimes relatives provide a home for the child (kinship care). Practitioners have a legal duty to report child abuse and neglect to CPS.

Marital Treatment　The treatment of the parents and the abused child described thus far is designed to help them as individuals and to change their interactions. However, the dyadic interaction between parent and child occurs in the context of other relationships, some of which do not involve the child's participation but which nevertheless result in child abuse. These relationships also need correction and alteration.

While we agree that a focus on marital problems in general may be out of place in the early stages of treatment, marital relationships as they affect behavior toward the child can be considered early in the contact. Once the parents have acknowledged their violence to the child, the relationship between spouses may be considered as a situational element in the specific act of abuse, what was going on at the time, how the spouse behaved, and how the abuser felt about these events. The parents can be encouraged to express not only feelings of anger and rejection but also their views of what was wanted from spouses and others and what would have been helpful. These feelings and the responses of the spouse to the abusing parent can be elicited in conjoint sessions. The worker is in a position to acknowledge the needs of each, to note the expectancies of the other that give rise to disappointment, jealousy, and scapegoating behavior. The spouse's ability or inability to respond, his or her wish or unwillingness to do so can be made explicit and can then be taken into account in the further development of the child-care plan and of the marital relationship.

The problem to be solved at this stage of treatment is the occurrence or avoidance of further abuse. The task of the family adults is to find a way, if they can, of helping each other to achieve avoidance of further abuse. At this stage of the treatment, the parents can learn what each needs from the other to achieve this goal.

These efforts may move them, over time, to deal with many aspects of their relationship so that in the long run they can depend on each other rather than on their child for positive responsiveness and affirmation. Alternatively, they may have to accept the knowledge that the dependability they seek will not be forthcoming, and they can learn to avoid further disappointment by looking to their own strengths or elsewhere for the support they need.

In addition to the clarification of roles and expectations, couples can benefit from help in learning how to communicate in ways that promote positive relationships. Communications that are vague or ambiguous, and sequences of communications that do not result in clarity, can be corrected by means we have suggested elsewhere. (See especially Chapter 6 on income loss and poverty.) Work on communications not only facilitates the clarification of roles and expectations but can also help to resolve differences and disagreements so that they do not build into reservoirs of ill will that might eventually spill onto spouse or child.

Our underlying assumption is that solid relationships between the parents or between a single parent and other supportive adults or agencies reduce parental dependence on positive responses from the child as a means for affirming parental identity and self-worth. These adult relationships, therefore, ought to be fostered and enhanced. The relationships of one or both adults to external systems may also need to be encouraged, changed, or enlarged so that these systems can be supportive of the nuclear family group.

We commented earlier that the mothers of abused children may themselves concurrently be battered, in which event it may be necessary, in addition to the work with the parent figures just described, to work on ending the abuse of the mother. Douglas (1991) offers a framework for understanding and assessing the parent interaction and the cycle of violence that occurs between them, providing a basis for work on the battering behavior. We cannot do more here than offer a brief outline of an approach to treatment of that aspect of family violence.

A dominant view is that the basic approach to the couple should be in separate groups for the battered women and their battering partners. Conjoint sessions tend to get stuck on the airing of complaints and accusations, which leave the abused woman in a more vulnerable state and thus not free to make maximum use of such sessions. Initial conjoint sessions may be used for establishing each partner's willingness to participate, to contract an agreement not to resort to violence, for defining what the wife should do, and for stating the consequences for treatment if violence occurs. Conjoint sessions may be useful later after group sessions have induced some change and some assurance that there will not be further resorting to violence.

Leeder (1994) takes a contrary position, insisting that conjoint work is preferable and that the therapist can, being aware of such risks, move to forestall the danger. One way to do this is to ask, at the end of each session, given the revelations and attributions of blame of the session, what the partners expect to happen on their way or at home; then, to work out a constructive plan for handling of feelings. Leeder is also of the opinion that the same therapist can work effectively with both spouses.

Treatment groups for the men work on developing a greater awareness of their own emotional processes; on restructuring the way they see women, women's roles and their own role; and on managing their anger by thinking before acting, by time-outs, and through the development of communicational skills (Gondolf, 1988).

Shelters are a much-needed resource for women and their children, whether they choose to use them or to return to their partners. Women work on their sense of entrapment and their "learned helplessness," on the costs and benefits of staying in or leaving the relationship, and on developing the skills and resources needed if they decide not to stay.

Treatment for the Family, Including Siblings   The net result of all the previously described aspects of treatment should be improved family relationships and functioning. While work on any part of the system can and should help the family as a whole, work with the whole system is still important and offers added advantages.

Extended and more intensive contact with the entire family around a variety of activities and circumstances allows workers to observe interactions between all family members, including siblings of the abused child, and to focus attention on interactive processes as they occur. In residential and all-day programs, multiple-family participation promotes interaction around work, food, and play as well as talk, and work in split groupings of children, couples, mothers, and fathers as well as whole-family meetings. In these situations, action is live and attention can be directed to changing interpersonal transactions, using many of the procedures just described for changing parent-child or spousal relationships, such as learning to respond to good behavior, improving communications, and sharing feelings.

Cohesiveness can be fostered by whole-family participation. Family structure can become more firm and clear. Individual isolation and blame are minimized. Children and their parents may be helped to negotiate behavior changes and the rewards that follow. Boundaries between parental and child generations may be strengthened through worker support of the parental subsystem. Multiple-family groups in all-day, residential, or outpatient programs allow families to see how other families work and to learn from each other.

External Family Systems Interventions

Work with the Extended Family   The need may exist for both parents to achieve greater separateness and detachment from their families of origin and to define an identity of their own. This work on differentiation of self is characteristic of the family therapy field. It may be accomplished by direct work on these relationships in contacts with members of the extended family or by asking individuals or couples to describe relationships in their families of origin. In these ways they may become aware of the origins of their expectations for current relationships, and this awareness can relieve them of the need to continue these relationships and enable them to negotiate new kinds of interaction.

In instances in which the parents' relationships with their own parents and with siblings are characterized less by hostility, ambivalence, and lack of differentiation and more by simple lack of contact, it may be possible for the worker to enable the extended family to be more of a resource for the parents.

This can provide the parents with avenues of social contact or, in some instances, emotional or tangible support.

Coping with Situational Stress   While relationships with spouses, paramours, and the extended family are one form of situational stress, other crises may also require intervention. These stress situations include pregnancy or birth of another child, loss of employment or other change in financial situation, illness of an adult or child, or loss of an immediate or extended family member. Any of these stresses can disrupt whatever balance has existed in the give-and-take of family relationships. They may overwhelm a child-caring parent or thrust the parent into an undesired role. New expectations can arise for all family members.

Workers should be available at such times to family members, either individually or as a group, to help them deal with feelings and find ways of coping. Tasks must be defined and agreement reached as to how they are to be accomplished and by whom. Where external resources are needed, the worker needs either to make arrangements for them, with family members' consent, or to serve in a broker or advocate role for the family. The worker's availability at times of crisis seems particularly important in this group of families, where the balance of relationships and personal and social resources is often precarious.

The social isolation of the family is another aspect of situational stress or, more specifically, a factor in the lack of relief from situational stress. Inputs from the extended family are, of course, one way of reducing the isolation. Initially, however, the treatment agency is the chief avenue for reducing social isolation. The agency provides the family with new feedback about its operations and supplies it with specific means of support and help. Treatment in groups, in residential settings, or even in weekend camps may open up new personal contacts for the family. These new experiences can provide them with the skills needed in interactions with individuals outside the immediate family group and offer them a bridge to relationships in the larger community. Referral to Parents Anonymous, a self-help group of abusive parents, can serve to reduce isolation and provide support.

A Note about the Organization of Services   The kind of connectedness of the agency to the family that we have described requires considerable outreach, substantial time in contact, and a variety of modes of helping and giving. These are not always available. Certainly, it is not enough to assign a single worker to a huge caseload of families. The literature refers repeatedly to the necessity for interdisciplinary teamwork for both diagnosis and treatment. This provides a variety of modes of helping and meets the need to work with all members of the family, not only with the person who has physically inflicted the abuse.

There is a great need to broaden and strengthen the range and availability of services to include all of these elements if families in which abuse has occurred are to be successfully helped. Treating agencies will increase their effectiveness to the degree that they are organized toward these ends.

McKay (1994) notes that agencies serving cases of conjugal violence and those providing child welfare services are not always alert to the abuse of other family members. Child welfare service providers should be alert to clues that suggest battering. Mothers with bruises, mothers who seem evasive about injuries and tend to attribute them to accidents, who seem sad or lethargic, who have somatic or emotional complaints, or who exhibit anxiety in the presence of their partners should arouse the worker's concern about possible abuse. Similarly, cues are offered whereby social workers with battered women may become aware of special situations of children. And both workers with battered women and with abused children need to be aware that the child welfare goal of protecting and perhaps rescuing the child may at times be at odds with the conjugal worker's goal of preserving the marriage, or that it may be hard to determine the mother's ability to care for children if she is being battered.

TREATMENT MANUAL

Jongsma and Dattilio (2000, pp. 242–251) provide a manualized treatment plan and intervention for physical/verbal/psychological abuse; the physical abuse component will be summarized here.

Behavioral Definitions

1. A family member injures others in the family intentionally.
2. A family member threatens to injure family members.
3. Family members fear a family member or feel intimidated.

Long-Term Goals

1. All types of abuse are discontinued by the family and replaced by other positive behaviors.
2. Victims are protected by nonabusive family members.
3. Alcohol and drugs are no longer used by family members.

Short-Term Objectives

1. Operationalize the abusive behavior.
2. Develop a protection plan for victims.
3. The abusive members sign a no-violence contract and commit to treatment.

Intervention

1. In response to the operationalized abusive behavior, identify appropriate family or individual treatment techniques.
2. Make a safety plan for the victim.
3. Use psychoeducational techniques to inform family members about abuse and its consequences, including legal consequences.

Table 9.2 | Research Studies

Family Treatment	Child Treatment	Parent Treatment
This meta-analysis of 25 controlled studies of interventions for parental anger and abuse toward their children revealed that social-learning, educational programs had greater effects than did psychodynamically oriented treatments (Videka-Sherman, 1989). Two reviews indicate that the benefits of Multiple Systemic Therapy (MST) versus other treatments are evidenced on parent and adolescent measures of parent and child psychopathology, family functioning and relationship, rearrest rates, severity of offenses, drug use, and reinstitutionalization. Additionally, MST is shown to be more cost effective than other efficacious treatments such as functional family therapy, special foster care, and parent problem solving (Burns et al., 2000; Henggeler, 1998).	This review of studies of child treatment for a variety of problems, including those likely experiencing trauma and associated symptoms of abuse, found cognitive and cognitive behavioral interventions (CBT) to be effective treatments for child problems, including: depression, anxiety, bulimia nervosa, and internalizing disorders. Externalizing disorders, the reviewer concluded, appear more helped by skills training approaches like PST, with the exception of ADHD, where a combination of medicine and behavior modification is more effective (Lambert, 2004). This study recommends the use of a combined intervention (experiential, educational, stress inoculation, and coping skills) with abused children experiencing post-traumatic stress disorder because of their abuse. While acknowledging that research on child interventions for PTSD are lagging behind, he draws on adult studies for the intervention (Reid, 2000).	In this meta-analysis of 50 studies of adults and children with anger problems, treatment group members showed 76 percent improvement over the control group in controlling anger (Beck & Fernandez, 1998). A review of outcomes studies shows that PMT has led to improved child behavior according to parent and teacher reports, and direct observation at home, at school, and in institutional records in children with conduct problems. PMT is the only well-established intervention for child conduct problems in RCTs (Brestan & Eyberg, 1998).

Table 9.3 | Treatment Manuals

Manual Reference	Author's Contact Information
Cognitive-Behavioral Treatment of Sex Offenders. Marshall, W. L., Fernandez, Y. M., Hudson, S. M., and Ward, T. (Eds.). 1998. *Sourcebook of Treatment Programs for Sexual Offenders.* New York: Plenum Press.	
Task Planner for Child Neglect, Couple or Family Conflict, and Child Abuse: Parental Anger and Stress Management. Reid, W. 2000. Task Planner. New York: Columbia University Press.	Columbia University Press 61 W. 62nd Street New York, NY 10023 Telephone: 212-459-0600 Fax: 212-459-3678 http://www.columbia.edu/cu/cup
Managing Marital Therapy: Helping Partners Change. Weiss and Halford. 1996. "Managing Marital Therapy: Helping Partners Change." In *Sourcebook of Psychological Treatment Manuals for Adult Disorders,* eds. V. Van Hasselt and M. Hersen. NewYork: Plenum.	Plenum Press New York, NY http://www.plenum.com

See the following case example demonstrating this intervention, Table 9.3 for a list of available treatment manuals for this population, and Box 9.2 for a list of Internet resources on family and child violence issues.

CASE EXAMPLE

The clients are Fay Montgomery, age 32 and recently divorced mother; Hal, her 11-year-old son; and Lilly, Hal's 14-year-old sister. The children's father, John, moved to another state and remarried within the past year, leaving Hal and Lilly with Fay. John has little contact with the boy, and Hal has been angry about this, blames the mother for his dad's leaving, and is acting out at home and at school. Lilly has been a second mother to Hal and has been the "perfect" daughter, according to Fay. Fay has disciplined Hal strictly, using a belt that left marks on his arms and legs and drew the attention of the school teachers and counselor. They referred the family to the local Child Welfare Department; the family was then referred for counseling to our clinic. Following is an excerpt of a session using the Jongsma and Dattilio (2000) model from the Treatment Manual example.

THERAPIST: Thank you three for agreeing to participate in family therapy to address the issue of family. This is our second session; last week we got to know each other and I learned something about your home and family. I'd like to continue with that. Last week you were telling me, Fay, about ways you discipline the children. Can you talk about that? (Step 1: Initiate family therapy to address the issues of the abuse.)

FAY: Well, I don't have to discipline Lilly much. She is so perfect. I don't know what I'd do without her. She cooks the meals and has dinner ready when I get home from working. I'm so tired I really appreciate that. She watches Hal, but he is so rebellious. He won't mind Lilly, and he won't mind me! I'm always getting reports from the teachers about how he got in a fight with this boy or that one. I've been so frustrated, I used the belt to try and get my point across that Hal has to mind. He has to mind me and he has to mind the teachers! I guess I went a little too far. I didn't realize that I left those bruises on Hal.

THERAPIST: Fay, have you tried other ways of disciplining Hal?

FAY: I've tried everything and nothing works! It takes a good wallop to get his attention. He doesn't pay attention to anyone. But I know that I've been spanking him too hard. I get so mad, I just don't realize it 'til things get out of hand.

THERAPIST: Hal, what's your view of the situation?

HAL: Things are different than when my daddy was here. Mom just can't take care of us the way dad did. I try to control myself at school, but I just get so mad sometimes. I lose it.

THERAPIST: Lilly, what's your view of the situation at home . . . with you and Hal?

LILLY: Well, Hal and Mom are a lot alike. They both "lose it," as Hal says, when they get stressed out or frustrated. It scares me when Mom loses it, too. I'm afraid she'll kill Hal, she gets so angry at him. I know she has a lot of stress since Daddy left us all alone. So I try to help as much as I can, so she won't have to do everything. But Hal just won't stay out of trouble.

THERAPIST: It sounds like the three of you understand the situation pretty well. Fay, I think we can come up with some ways of disciplining Hal that will work for you and for him. But first, let's make a safety plan so that Hal won't get hurt so badly again. (Step 2: Explore the dynamics that facilitate the abusive behavior; make a safety plan.)

FAY: That sounds good. (The children nod in agreement.)

THERAPIST: Where is a safe place Hal can go?

HAL: I could leave the house when Mom starts getting so mad. I could go down the street to my friend Matt's house. I sleep over there and he stays at my house some, too. His mother wouldn't mind. (Fay nods confirmation.)

LILLY: And the social worker and Children's Services gave me her phone number. I could call her to talk with Mom. (Step 3: Assist the family in developing a plan that ensures the safety of abused members.)

| BOX 9.2 | Internet Resources |

Due to the living nature of the Internet, website addresses often change and thus we have not printed the addresses in this text. Links to the following websites are posted at the Book Companion Site at www.wadsworth.com.

Child Abuse and Neglect
National Clearinghouse on Child Abuse and Neglect Information—a resource for professionals and others seeking information on child abuse and neglect, including reporting issues

National Data Archive on **Child Abuse and Neglect**—a national database on child abuse and neglect ISPCAN Home Page—report of European Regional Conference on child abuse and neglect **National Committee to Prevent Child Abuse**—child abuse and neglect statistics **Child Abuse Prevention Network**— provides resources for professionals, in child abuse, neglect, maltreatment, sex abuse, child sexual abuse, and family issues

Prevent Child Abuse America—works at the national, state and community levels to prevent child abuse in all its forms

MedlinePlus: Child Abuse—provides articles from *Child Abuse and Neglect* (American Academy of Pediatrics); JAMA Patient Page: Protecting Our Children from Child Abuse (American Medical Association), and so forth

National Clearinghouse on Family Violence—provides child abuse and neglect publications . . .

VCU.edu—provides a training module on recognizing and reporting child abuse and neglect

Childhelpusa.org—one of the largest and oldest national nonprofits dedicated to the treatment and prevention of child abuse and neglect

Modental.org—Prevent Abuse and Neglect through Dental Awareness (PANDA) coalition was started in Missouri in 1992 to address a lack of child abuse and neglect reporting by dentists

National Center on Child Abuse and Neglect—U.S. Department of Health and Human Services National Center provides information on child abuse and neglect

Child Abuse and Neglect Prevention Task Force—a nonprofit group organized solely for the purpose of education, prevention, and treatment in the child abuse and neglect fields

Kempecenter.org—aims to educate and increase awareness about child abuse and neglect; Welcome to Kempe

---

THERAPIST: Sounds good! Maybe you could write this plan down and post it somewhere, like the refrigerator, where everyone could see it. Now, I'd like to talk with you about some of the consequences of harsh punishment. Okay? (Step 4: Educate all family members about the emotional destructiveness and illegality of even the slightest incident.)

Caliber Associates—provides high-quality research and consulting services that help organizations develop and manage effective programs for the public good

Family Violence
Family Violence Prevention Fund—the nation's foremost expert on domestic violence, advocating to improve public policies
National Clearinghouse on Family Violence (NCFV)—Health Canada operates the National Clearinghouse on Family Violence (NCFV) on behalf of the government of Canada and its Family Violence Initiative (FVI)

Stop Family Violence Now—provides information and leads in social action techniques to stop family violence

The Family Violence & Sexual Assault Institute—provides information, training, and resources on family violence and sexual assault

Domestic Violence Hotline—1-800-799-SAFE (7233) or TTY 1-800-787-3224; join the Texas Council on Family Violence mailing list

BC Institute Against Family Violence—established in 1989 as a private, non-profit organization

National Council on Child Abuse & Family Violence—reports on its American Campaign for Prevention of Child Abuse and Family Violence

Kluwer Academic Publishers—Journal of Family Violence—articles on topics related to family violence

Australian Domestic and Family Violence Clearinghouse—archives information from Australia on issues related to domestic violence

Statcan.ca—a statistical profile of family violence in Canada

Facts about Family Violence—from the American Psychological Association

Texas Department of Human Services, Family Violence—managed by the Texas Council on Family Violence, this site reports on services for victims of family violence **Landwave.com**—reports on screening for family violence; includes a Guide to Clinical Preventive Services, Second Edition

The Tribal Court Clearinghouse—presents studies of tribal law in the United States, focuses on law developed by and for Indian Nations and Native people, and addresses the power of tribal courts and tribal legal systems on issues including child welfare and civil rights

National Council of Juvenile and Family Court Judges—dedicated to improving the way courts and law enforcement respond to family violence

Animal Abuse and Family Violence—reports on the link between animal abuse and family violence

SUMMARY

In this chapter we have taken a brief look at various forms of family violence and offered a frame of reference for analyzing and understanding it. Further, we have taken note of some specific characteristics of abusing parents and abused children and have observed how these characteristics give rise to negative patterns of interaction. We have noted that the interaction of abusive parent and abused child does not take place in isolation but is affected by other interactions in the family and events in the family's situation. The relationship between the parents is seen as particularly crucial, perhaps as crucial as the relationship between parent and child. There has been relative neglect in the field of the experiences of siblings of the abused child, and the family as a whole is seen as likely to be isolated from external supports, or in difficult relationships with extended family. Unlike other writing on child abuse, which focuses primarily on the abused child and the overt perpetrators of the abuse, we have emphasized the transactions between family members and with the larger family system.

We also find useful the techniques identified by Star (1983) in helping the abuser, supportive confrontation, enhancement of self-esteem, problem solving, providing structure and direction, honesty, modeling desirable behavior, role-playing (perhaps with an empty chair to represent an absent other), and the use of a buddy system.

The treatments described are designed to strengthen individual identity and competence, to improve interpersonal transactions, and to alter relationships within and beyond the immediate family. The efforts include nurturance of the parents, imparting skills and knowledge for parenting, help in dealing with feelings, and recognition of reactions to members' own behavior and that of others. These activities are useful in interrupting old patterns and initiating new behaviors, and thereby altering interactional patterns. Enabling the parents to alter their relationships so that they can support each other in child-caring and parenting activities is an important means of helping the child, as well as providing greater satisfaction for the parents themselves. Where other situational stresses affect the balance of family relationships, agency action is needed to provide relief and support.

The range of services encompassed requires comprehensive care that cannot be provided by a single worker assigned to a huge caseload. Thus, the interdisciplinary teams that are widely noted in the literature, and services to the entire family are valued and needed in effective programming for families in which abuse of the child occurs.

DISCUSSION QUESTIONS

1. Define and describe the various types of domestic violence.
2. Identify the appropriate assessment techniques for the categories discussed in this chapter. Practice their use in a role-play.
3. Pick a case example from your field placement that has a possible family violence component. Design an assessment and treatment plan for the family. Be sure the assessment and treatment are linked together.

References

Alexander, H., McQuiston, M., and Rode-heffer, M. 1976. "Residential Family Therapy." In *The Abused Child*, ed. H. P. Marten. Cambridge, MA: Ballinger Publishing Co.

Avis, J. 1992. "Where Are All the Family Therapists? Abuse and Violence within Families and Family Therapy's Response." *Journal of Marital and Family Therapy* 18(3):225–32.

Baldwin, J., and Oliver, J. 1975. "Epidemiology and Family Characteristics of Severely Abused Children." *British Journal of Preventive and Social Medicine* 29:205–21.

Beck, A., and Fernandez, E. 1998. "Cognitive-Behavioral Therapy in the Treatment of Anger: A Meta-Analysis." *Cognitive Therapy and Research* 22(1):63–74.

Beezley, P., Martin, H., and Alexander, H. 1976. "Comprehensive Family Oriented Therapy." In *Child Abuse and Neglect*, eds. R. Helfer and C. Kempe. Cambridge, MA: Ballinger Publishing Co.

Belsky, J. 1980. "Child Maltreatment: An Ecology Integration." *American Psychologist* 35(4):320–35.

Bennie, E. H., and Sclare, A. B. 1969. "The Battered Child Syndrome." *American Journal of Psychiatry* 125:975–79.

Bentovim, A. 1977. "Therapeutic Systems and Settings in the Treatment of Child Abuse." In *The Challenge of Child Abuse*, ed. A. W. Franklin. New York: Grune and Stratton.

Berry, M. 1999. "Family Preservation Practice." Chapter 9 in *Family Practice: Brief Systems Methods for Social Work* (pp. 199–224), eds. Franklin and Jordan. Belmont, CA: Brooks/Cole.

Blumberg, M. L. 1974. "Psychopathology of the Abusing Parent." *American Journal of Psychotherapy* 28:21–29.

Bograd, M. 1990. "Why We Need Gender to Understand Human Violence." *Journal of Interpersonal Violence* 5(1):1332–35.

Bolton, F., and Bolton, S. 1987. *Working with Violent Families*. Newbury Park, CA: Sage Publications.

Brestan, E., and Eyberg, S. 1998. "Effective Psychosocial Treatments of Conduct-Disordered Children and Adolescents: 29 Years, 82 Studies, and 5,272 Kids." *Journal of Clinical Child Psychology* 27(2):180–89.

Burns, B., Schoenwald, S., Burchard, J., Faw, L., and Santos, A. 2000. "Comprehensive Community-Based Interventions with Severe Emotional Disorders: Multisystemic Therapy and the Wraparound Process." *Journal of Child and Family Studies* 9:283–314.

Cautley, P. 1980. "Treating Dysfunctional Families at Home." *Social Work* 25(5): 380–86.

Cichetti, D., and Rizley, R. 1981. "Developmental Perspectives on the Etiology, Intergenerational Transmission and Sequellae of Child Maltreatment." In *New Directions for Child Development: Developmental Perspectives on Child Maltreatment*, eds. C. Cichetti and R. Rizley. San Francisco: Jossey-Bass.

Cirillo, S., and DiBlasio, P. 1992. *Families that Abuse*. New York: W. W. Norton & Co.

Collins, D., Jordan, C., and Coleman, H. 1999. *An Introduction to Family Social Work*. Chicago: Lyceum.

DeGenova, M. K., and Rice, F. P. (2005). *Intimate Relationships, Marriages, and Families*, 6th edition. Boston: McGraw-Hill.

Dobash, R. E., and Dobash, R. 1979. *Violence against Wives*. New York: Free Press.

Douglas, H. 1991. "Assessing Violent Couples." *Families in Society* 72: 525–33.

Erickson, Beth. 1992. "Feminist Fundamentalism: Reactions to Avis, Kaufman, and Bograd. *Journal of Marital and Family Therapy* 18(3):263–67.

Franklin, C., and Jordan, C. 1999. *Family Practice: Brief Systems Methods for Social Work*. Belmont, CA: Brooks/Cole.

Gaensbauer, T., and Sands, K. 1980. "Distorted Affective Communications in Abused/Neglected Infants and Their Potential Impact on Caretakers." *Journal of the American Academy of Child Psychiatry* 18:236–51.

Galdston, R. 1965. "Observation on Children Who Have Been Physically Abused and Their Parents." *American Journal of Psychiatry* 122:440–43.

Gondolf, E. 1988. "How Some Men Stop Their Abuse: An Exploratory Program Evaluation." In *Coping with Family Violence*, eds. G. Hotaling, D. Finkelhor, J. Kirkpatrick, and M. Straus. Newbury Park, CA: Sage Publications.

Goodwin, D. 1978. "Dwarfism: The Victim Child's Response to Abuse." *Baltimore Sun*, September 24.

Hampton, R. L. 1991. *Black Family Violence*. Lexington, MA: Lexington Books.

Henggeler, S., Schoenwald, S., Borduin, C., Rowland, M., and Cunningham, P. 1998. *Multisystemic Treatment of Antisocial Behavior in Children and Adolescents*. New York: Guilford.

Holland, C. 1973. "An Examination of Social Isolation and Availability to Treatment in the Phenomenon of Child Abuse." *Smith College Studies in Social Work* 44:74–75.

Jeffrey, M. 1976. "Practical Ways to Change Parent/Child Interaction in Families of Children at Risk." In *Child Abuse and Neglect*, eds. R. Helfer and C. Kempe. Cambridge, MA: Ballinger Publishing Co.

Johnson, B., and Morse, H. 1968. "Injured Children and Their Parents." *Children* 15:147–52.

Jongsma, A. E., Jr., and Dattilio, F. M. (2000). *The Family Therapy Treatment Planner*. New York: Wiley.

Jordan, C., and Franklin, C. 2003. *Clinical Assessment for Social Workers: Quantitative and Qualitative Methods*, 2nd edition. Chicago: Lyceum.

Kadushin, A., and Martin, J. 1981. *Child Abuse: An Interactional Event*. New York: Columbia University Press.

Kagan, R., and Schlossberg, S. 1989. *Families in Perpetual Crisis*. New York: W. W. Norton & Co.

Kinney, J., Haapala, D., and Booth, C. 1991. *Keeping Families Together*. New York: Aldyne-deGruyter.

Lambert, M. 2004. *Bergin and Garfield's Handbook of Psychotherapy and Behavior Change*, 5th edition. New York: Wiley.

Leeder, E. 1994. *Treating Abuse in Families: A Feminist and Community Approach*. New York: Springer Publishing Co.

Levinson, D. 1989. *Family Violence in Cross-Cultural Perspective*. Newbury Park, CA: Sage Publications.

Lynch, M. 1975. "Ill Health and Child Abuse." *Lancet* 2:317–19.

McKay, M. 1994. "The Link between Domestic Violence and Child Abuse: Assessment and Treatment Considerations." *Child Welfare* 73(1):29–39.

McNeil, J., and McBride, M. 1979. "Group Therapy with Abusive Parents." *Social Casework* 60(1):36–42.

National Institutes of Mental Health. 1977. *Child Abuse and Neglect Programs: Practice and Theory*. Washington, DC: NIMH.

Newberger, E. H. 1973. "The Myth of the Battered Child Syndrome." *Current Medical Dialogue* 40:327–34.

Oppenheimer, A. 1978. "Triumph over Trauma in the Treatment of Child Abuse." *Social Casework* 59:352–58.

Osnes, P., and Stokes, T. 1988. "Treatment of Child Abuse and Neglect: The Role of Functional Analyses of Observed

Behavior." *Journal of Child and Adolescent Psychology* 5(1):3–10.

Ounsted, C., Oppenheimer, R., and Lindsay, J. 1974. "Aspects of Bonding Failure: The Psychopathology and Psychotherapeutic Treatment of Families of Battered Children." *Developmental Medicine and Child Neurology* 16:447–56.

Pardeck, J. 1988. "Family Therapy as a Treatment Approach to Child Abuse." *Child Psychiatry Quarterly* 21(4):191–98.

Pecora, P., Wittaker, J., & Maluccio, T. 1992. *The Child Welfare Challenge*. New York: Aldine-deGruyter.

Polansky, N., Borgman, R., and DeSaix, C. 1972. *Roots of Futility*, San Francisco: Jossey-Bass.

Post, S. 1982. "Adolescent Parricide in Abusive Families." *Child Welfare* 61(7):445–55.

Reid, W. 2000. *The Task Planner*. New York: Columbia University Press.

Roy, M. 1988. *Children in the Crossfire*. Deerfield Beach, FL: Health Communications, Inc.

Russell, D. 1984. *Sexual Exploitation: Rape, Child Sexual Abuse, and Sexual Harassment*. Beverly Hills, CA: Sage Publications.

Sargent, D. 1962. "Children Who Kill." *Social Work* 7(1):35–42.

Segal, E., Gerdes, K. E., and Steiner, S. 2004. *Social Work: An Introduction to the Profession*. Belmont, CA: Brooks/Cole.

Smith, S. 1984. "Significant Research Findings in the Etiology of Child Abuse." *Social Casework* 65(6):337–46.

Smith, S., and Hanson, R. 1975. "Interpersonal Relationships and Child Rearing Practices in 214 Parents of Battered Children." *British Journal of Psychiatry* 127:513–25.

Stacey, W., and Shupe, A. 1983. *The Family Secret*. Boston: Beacon Press.

Stanley, J., and Goddard, C. 1993. "The Association between Child Abuse and Other Family Violence." *Australian Social Work* 46(2):3–8.

Star, B. 1983. *Helping the Abuser*. New York: Family Service Association of America.

Stark, E., and Flitcraft, A. 1988. "Women and Children at Risk: A Feminist Perspective on Child Abuse." *International Journal of Health Services* 18(1):97–118.

Steele, B., and Pollock, C. 1972. "A Psychiatric Study of Parents Who Abuse Infants and Small Children." In *Helping the Battered Child and His Family*, eds. C. Kempe and R. Helfer. Philadelphia: J. B. Lippincott Co.

Straus, M., Gelles, R., and Steinmetz, S. 1980. *Behind Closed Doors: Violence in American Families*. Garden City, NY: Doubleday.

Tracy, J., Ballard, C., and Clark, E. 1975. "Child Abuse Project: A Followup." *Social Work* 20:398–99.

Van Soest, D., and Bryant, S. 1995. "Violence Reconceptualized for Social Work: The Urban Dilemma." *Social Work* 40(4):549–57.

Videka-Sherman, L. 1989. "Therapeutic Issues for Physical and Emotional Child Abuse and Neglect: Implications for Longitudinal Research." Paper, Research Forum on Issues in the Longitudinal Study on Child Maltreatment. Toronto, Ontario, Canada, Oct. 15–18.

Vogel, E., and Bell, W. 1968. "The Emotionally Disturbed Child as the Family Scapegoat." In *A Modern Introduction to the Family*, eds. N. Bell and E. Vogel. New York: Free Press.

Watzlawick, P., Beavin, J., and Jackson, D. 1967. *Pragmatics of Human Communication*. New York: W. W. Norton & Co.

Wells, S. 1981. "A Model for Therapy with Abusive and Neglectful Families." *Social Work* 26(2):113–18.

Evidence-Based Family Treatment of Substance Abuse

CHAPTER 10

INTRODUCTION

Substance abuse in its many forms is a prevalent problem in the United States that affects not only the individual but the family and extended social system as well. In 2002, an estimated 19.5 million Americans, or 8.3 percent of the population aged 12 or older, were current illicit drug users. Current drug use means use of an illicit drug during the month prior to the survey interview. An estimated 120 million Americans aged 12 or older reported being current drinkers of alcohol in the 2002 survey (51 percent). About 54 million (22.9 percent) participated in binge drinking at least once in the 30 days prior to the survey, and 15.9 million (6.7 percent) were heavy drinkers. An estimated 71.5 million Americans (30.4 percent of the population aged 12 or older) reported current use (past month use) of a tobacco product in 2002. About 61.1 million (26 percent) smoked cigarettes, 12.8 million (5.4 percent) smoked cigars, 7.8 million (3.3 percent) used smokeless tobacco, and 1.8 million (0.8 percent) smoked tobacco in pipes (SAMHSA, 2002). Substance abuse is both a prevalent and a challenging issue that family therapists will face in their work with families. This chapter reviews the evidence-based family treatment of substance abuse. The chapter covers population and family dynamics such as codependency and enabling. The chapter focuses on effective family treatments for alcohol users and evidence-based family treatments for adolescent substance abusers. A case example is presented for one of the evidence-based treatments for adolescents. Information on treatment considerations for ethnic minority groups is also covered. Finally, because substance abuse is a complex disorder involving multiple systems, the chapter summarizes several individual and behavioral treatments that family therapists will need to be aware of in order to be effective with these clients and their family.

POPULATION DESCRIPTION AND DEFINITIONS

Families with alcoholic or substance-abusing members are increasingly involved in the treatment of alcoholics and abusers of other drugs. They come to agencies for help with or without the abuser. The help provided may do much for the family and may or may not resolve the drinking problem. Often times the family work may not resolve the drinking or drug use but may help the family function more productively. Spouses, children, and other relatives often need help in learning how to manage their lives, given the substance abuse of another family member.

Marital Relationships and Alcoholism

Several different views have been held about the spousal or partner relationships of alcoholics over the years. In early writings, the wife was seen as disturbed, struggling with strong feelings of inadequacy and dependency, which prompted her to relate to the alcoholic in a controlling and aggressive manner. Some research has supported the viewpoint that substance abuse is a family disease. Morris et al. (1992), for example, studied predictors of spousal psychopathology in 50 addicts and their spouses and found that the scores of both addicts and their spouses on a number of MMPI scales were elevated significantly higher than those of the general population. Alcohol and/or other drugs are used to manage anxiety and attachment difficulties and contribute to the multigenerational transmission of dysfunctional system dynamics. There is no doubt that chemical dependency affects marital relationship, family, and child functioning. The behavior and responses of family members may influence the impaired individuals as well. Social workers and family therapists must critically asks themselves, however, the same cause-and-effect questions posed in Chapter 7 on persistent mental disorders. Are families really to blame for the family disease or substance abuse problems or are their dysfunctional behavior patterns a response to coping with the substance abuse and associated problems themselves? This chapter addresses some of these issues and controversies.

A clearer understanding of family dynamics is emerging as we learn more about substance abuse disorders and the family issues that surround substance abuse. Codependency and enabling have become the focal characteristics of families dealing with substance abuse. Family members typically engage in different and often-changing means of coping with substance abusers. They report experiencing significant mental and physical strain as well. Clinicians have identified particular coping behaviors displayed by these family members of substance abusers that usually include specific types of care taking and attempts to stabilize situations caused or exacerbated by one member's sub-stance abuse. These behaviors are referred to as enabling but are often described as *codependent behaviors*. Female partner of male alcoholics have frequently been labeled as codependents, co-alcoholics, or enablers. Codependency and enabling are defined and described in greater detail in the next section.

Before launching into an in-depth discussion of these terms, it is impor-tant to keep in mind that in a study investigating codependency of Caucasian individuals, Prest, Benson, and Protinsky (1998) found little difference between alcoholic family members and their spouses with respect to dysfunc-tion in their families of origin or current families, or to their codependency levels. The etiology and function of codependency, however, were different in clinical and nonclinical families. In the clinical sample, the family of origin and current relationship characteristics were related to codependency in pat-terns consistent with previous theory and research. For the nonclinical sam-ple, however, the findings contradicted conventional codependency theory. In contrast to clinical populations, codependency in nonclinical populations has some links with favorable characteristics of family functioning. This study supports the viewpoint that codependency is not inherently dysfunctional but that it is the context of the addictive situation that makes it so. In the nonclin-ical sample, codependency was associated with greater intimacy, and in some relationships between partners, the behaviors that get labeled codependent may not be a problem but a strength.

Enabling and Codependency

Enabling refers to a wide gamut of actions that potentially reinforce contin-ued use of alcohol or other drugs. Themes of care taking, pleasing others, and association with a person with substance problems were found to be common conceptions of the term held by women married to alcoholics (Asher & Brissett, 1988). Family members of substance abusers are a part of a dysfunc-tional family system to which they often unwittingly contribute to the perpet-uation of the substance abuse behavior. It is useful to think of enabling as a learned set of behavioral responses enacted by significant others that have the potential to reinforce drinking or drugging responses, thus increasing the probability of such a response in the future.

Clinicians must exercise caution in indiscriminately labeling people as *codependent*. An informed assessment of both intergenerational relationship dynamics, the presence of addictions, and socialized gender roles must be made prior to assumptions about the "codependent" person. In any event, codependent-type behaviors and attitudes must be understood within the rela-tional context and not solely as a set of characteristics or attributes of the individual (Haaken, 1990). There is no current support for codependency becoming a diagnostic criterion, and many clinicians suggest eliminating the label in an effort to make the family members feel less pathological. Instead of label-ing the person, the focus should be on the enabling behaviors, externalizing the problem in the family. It is clinically more helpful, for example, to focus on how the helping behavior of a person is not making things better in that situation than to say someone is an enabler. The helping behavior can be given a label "making up for him," for example, and externalized as being something the person would like to decide to stop or to change as another way of being helpful.

A strengths orientation is also more consistent with current thinking in the field in that personality traits that cause these individuals to exhibit irrational enabling behaviors has been abandoned by some clinicians and researchers, and replaced with the view that enabling behaviors are normal reactions to the stress that is present in the alcoholic family. Ten components make up these behaviors: discord, avoidance, indulgence, competition, antidrink, assertion, sexual withdrawal, fearful withdrawal, taking special action, and marital breakdown. Correlations have been found connecting significant enabling behaviors of one spouse/partner with lower treatment of success of the other. It indicates that the increase in the coping behaviors exhibited in response to a worsening family situation coincide with poor treatment outcomes, causing the family situation to worsen more and the coping behaviors to increase—thus solidifying the substance abuse cycle.

Reaching the spouses/partners of alcoholics early in the process of the alcoholism is critical. In one study, there was a significant difference between the Spouse Situation Inventory (SSI) scores of an Al-Anon group and a non–Al-Anon group. The Al-Anon group showed higher scores, indicating higher coping skills (Rychtarik, Carstensen, Alford, Schlundt, & Scott, 1988).

Spouses of alcoholics could be trained to reduce their behaviors aimed at trying to control the drinking of their partners. Treatment intervention is designed to prepare the spouse to assume a more positive rehabilitative role and to carry out an active intervention intended to influence the abuser to reduce drinking, enter treatment, or both. The earlier a family comes into treatment, the more likely the enabling behavior can be changed to help influence the reduction of substance abuse (Yoshioka, Thomas, & Ager, 1996)

Thomas, Yoshioka, and Ager (1996) devised a successful disenabling program for the spouse and administered the Spouse Enabling Inventory (SEI). The spouses were educated about enabling and selected the behaviors to be targeted for change. Possible consequences of change with regard to such matters as marital distress, the abuser's employment, and the safety of the abuser and others should be always be considered when implementing partner intervention.

Another successful intervention, "Pressures to Change," uses principles of learning theory to train spouses of alcoholics in identifying behaviors and responses that both empower the partner and provide incentive for the drinker to change. Barber and Crisp (1995) defined change as seeking treatment, ceasing drinking, or reducing drinking to a level acceptable to the partner. Five levels of treatment are included: (1) feedback and education, (2) discussion of activities incompatible with drinking, (3) responding to the drinker, (4) contracting, and (5) confrontation. The authors suggest that working with spouses/partners of drinkers can indeed begin the process of change.

Fals-Stewart, O'Farrell, and Feehan (2000) found that husbands in behavioral couples therapy (BCT) showed higher levels of success in their treatment as well as in communication with their partners. The BCT sessions were used to (1) help husbands remain abstinent from drugs and alcohol by reviewing and reinforcing compliance with a verbal contract, negotiated by the partners during the first two BCT sessions, for the partners to discuss and positively support the husbands' sobriety on a daily basis; (2) teach more effective communication skills, such as active listening and expressing feelings directly; and (3) increase positive behavioral exchanges between partners by encouraging them to acknowledge pleasing behaviors and engage in shared recreational activities.

Scaturo, Hayes, Sagula, and Walter (2000) argue that the concept of codependency is theoretically linked to already well-established concepts in the field of family systems theory. These concepts include the notions of complementarity, interlocking pathology, the one-up versus one-down marital relationship, and the overadequate versus underadequate relationship. The popularized definition of codependency is contextualized as one of several relationship patterns designed to modulate fusion in an intimate relationship, examining also the characteristic patterns of inadequate conflict resolution and triangulation. This view is interactional and takes into consideration the whole family system but also may be misconstrued to a pathological view of family members.

Family therapists must always be aware of their viewpoints toward their clients and work to maintain an empathetic and strengths orientation to the family situation and context. When understood, the context of the situation in which people live and cope often explains irrational and pathological behavior.

Finally, several clinical considerations are given to the treatment of families with alcoholic members and the management of codependent family dynamics. These considerations include techniques for confronting codependent behavior, psychoeducational interventions surrounding what precisely constitutes codependency, and the distinction between self-labeling versus self-exploration in family therapy. Family therapists must be prepared, however, to respond to multiple problems that may exist in these families. Substance abuse, for example, often coexists with other family problems such as emotional or physical abuse and family violence. It may also be necessary to treat mental health disorders (e.g., depression, anxiety disorders or personality disorders) that may co-occur with substance abuse. See other chapters in this book for guidance on working with these issues.

The following is a list of statements characteristic of codependency:

- My good feelings about who I am stem from being liked by you.
- My good feelings about who I am stem from receiving approval from you.
- Your struggle affects my serenity. My mental attention focuses on solving your problems/relieving your pain.
- My mental attention is focused on you.

- My mental attention is focused on protecting you.
- My mental attention is focused on manipulating you to do it my way.
- My self-esteem is bolstered by solving your problems.
- My self-esteem is bolstered by relieving your pain.
- My own hobbies/interests are put to one side. My time is spent sharing your hobbies/interests.
- Your clothing and personal appearance are dictated by my desires, and I feel you are a reflection of me.
- Your behavior is dictated by my desires, and I feel you are a reflection of me.
- I am not aware of how I feel. I am aware of how you feel.
- I am not aware of what I want—I ask what you want. I am not aware— I assume.
- The dreams I have for my future are linked to you.
- My fear of rejection determines what I say or do.
- My fear of your anger determines what I say or do.
- I use giving as a way of feeling safe in our relationship.
- My social circle diminishes as I involve myself with you.
- I put my values aside in order to connect with you.
- I value your opinion and way of doing things more than my own.
- The quality of my life is in relation to the quality of yours. (http://divorcesupport.about.com)

Children of Substance Abusers

Children are affected by and may affect relationships in substance abusing families. Cork (1969) was the first of many who have documented a variety of effects on children over the years. Effects have been noted over the life span of children beginning prior to birth as manifest in prenatal alcohol syndrome (Young, Wallace, & Garcia, 1992). Goldman and Rossland (1992) note higher absenteeism and lowered achievement in school, the frequency with which such children become abusers of alcohol and other drugs, and the tendency to marry alcoholics. Different problems may occur at different ages, including stuttering, fears, bed-wetting, tantrums, and fighting. Similar problems have been noted in children of drug-abusing parents (DeCubas & Field, 1993). Incest is not uncommon in families where there is a substance abuser (Yama, Fogas, Teegarden, & Hastings, 1993). Problems continue into adulthood and have resulted in the formation of support groups for adult children of alcoholics (ACOA) (Sheridan & Green, 1993; Goglia, Jurkovic, Burt, & Burge-Callaway, 1992).

Children in families where there is an alcoholic member are often caught in triangular relations with their parents (Goglia et al., 1992). The mother may seek the child's support and understanding in her difficulties with her husband, forming an alliance against him. Or she may involve the child in her attempts to control the drinking. Likewise, the alcoholic may air his complaints to the child about being misunderstood and abused by his wife. The child, caught in the tug-of-war, is put in the position of having to decide between the parents or take the role of peacemaker. Taking sides loses the support of the other parent. All three get locked into their respective roles, and nothing happens to diminish either the conflict or the alcoholism. In addition to the emotional abuse and psychological suffering, the child may even be physically hurt in attempts to interfere when conflicts between the parents become physical. Efforts to mediate parental conflict require more maturity than the parents themselves possess and put the child in a parental role with them. In taking any of these roles in the family interaction, the child is not only experiencing the effects of parental behavior but unwittingly serving to perpetuate the problematic interaction as well.

Adult Children of Substance Abusers

Professionals providing therapy for adults have long known that the problems of children of alcoholics continue into adulthood (Sheridan & Green, 1993). There is now an expanding self-help movement within this population that is becoming more accessible with expansion in numbers of groups and that is providing an extremely useful service. Referral to such groups can supplement therapy.

ASSESSMENT ISSUES

A thorough functional analysis of the couple's interactions (the affective, behavioral, and cognitive contributions to the couple's distress) is necessary during the assessment phase of treatment. Behavior can be assessed through direct observation; the Spouse Observation Checklist (SOC) can be used to access behavioral performance in a natural setting (Weiss & Perry 1983). A cost-benefit analysis (CB) can be completed in which spouses rate the perceived benefit for each of the 400 behaviors if were they to receive it. In addition, they rate the perceived cost were they to perform each behavior to provide the therapist with a list of good therapy items and high-conflict items (Weiss & Perry, 1983). Inventory of Rewarding Activities (IRA) is an inventory of 100 recreational or pleasurable activities (Birchler & Weiss, in Weiss & Perry, 1983) and the Conflict Tactics Scale (CTS) assess the frequency of 18 conflict behaviors (Straus, 1979). These scales and tools will all help in developing a complete and accurate assessment.

Cognition can be assessed with the Relationship Beliefs Inventory (RBI), a 40-item measure that taps five dysfunctional beliefs (Eidelson & Epstein, 1982); the Marital Attitude Survey (MAS), a 74-item questionnaire that measures expectancies (efficacy and outcome) and attributions (causal attributions of spouse's malicious intent and lack of love) (Pretzer et al., 1992); as well as the Marital Agendas Protocol (MAP), 10 causes of conflict in marriage (Notarius & Vanzetti, 1983).

Adjustment and desired changes can be assessed with the Areas of Change Questionnaire (AOC), which rates the amount of change they desire on 34

Table 10.1 | Assessment Instruments

Instrument	Description	Reliability	Validity	Source
Addiction Severity Index	Assesses frequency and severity of substance abuse and severity of accompanying psychosocial problems	.89 Concurrent reliability and good test-retest reliability: .89 (McClellan et al., 1985)	Good concurrent validity (.55–.39)	Kosten, Rounsaville, & Kleber, 1983
Assertion Questionnaire in Drug Use (AQ-D)	A 40-item instrument designed to measure assertion in heavy drug users	7-day test-retest correlation of .86	Excellent concurrent validity	Fisher & Corcoran, 1994
Alcohol Beliefs Scale (ABS)	A 29-item scale to assess one's beliefs about the effects of alcohol. Subscales are useful in measuring changes, treatment planning, and cognitive restructuring.		Demonstrated known-groups validity	Fisher & Corcoran, 1994
Index of Alcohol Involvement (IAI)	A 25-item instrument to measure magnitude of problem with alcohol abuse	Excellent internal consistency (alpha .90)	Very good factorial and construct validity	Fisher & Corcoran, 1994
McMullin Addiction Thought Scale (MAT)	A 42-item instrument used to measure irrational thoughts in chemically dependent clients. Can be used for assessment and evaluation.		Good predictive validity. It is sensitive to changes due to treatment.	Fisher & Corcoran, 1994

Instrument	Description	Reliability	Validity	Source
Michigan Alcoholism Screening Test (MAST)	A 24-item scale to assess for alcoholism	Excellent internal consistency. Long form: .95; short form: .93.	Excellent known-groups validity	Fisher & Corcoran, 1994
Sensation Scale (SS)	A 26-item scale used to assess a person's sensitivity to physiological changes after alcohol consumption.		Good known-groups validity	Fisher & Corcoran, 1994
TCU Depression (TCU-D) and TCU Decision-Making (TCU-DM) Scales	Two parts of a 15-part scale used to measure depression and decision-making skills in IV drug users	Good internal consistency. Depression: .89; decision-making: .77.	Good concurrent validity, correlating with BDI .75	Fisher & Corcoran, 1994
Spouse Enabling Inventory (SEI)	A 46-item instrument for rapid assessment and monitoring or spouse enabling regarding alcohol abuse	Good to excellent internal consistency of .89	Content and construct validity are both indicated.	Fisher & Corcoran, 1994
Spouse Sobriety Influence Inventory (SSII)	A 52-item inventory to assess spousal efforts to control partner drinking and spousal efforts to increase nondrinking behavior	Excellent internal consistency .92	Content and construct validity are both supported.	Fisher & Corcoran, 1994
Beck Codependence Assessment Scale (BCAS)	A 35-item instrument designed to measure codependence	Good internal consistency, family conflict subscale .89	Excellent predictive and known-groups validity	Fisher & Corcoran, 1994
Co-Dependence Inventory (CODI)	A 29-item scale to assess codependence in family and friends	Fair internal consistency with overall alpha of .79. Subscales range from .45–.75.		Fisher & Corcoran, 1994

different behaviors (Weiss & Perry, 1979). Affect can be assessed with the Measures of Marital Adjustment (MAT) (Locke & Wallace, 1959), Marital Satisfaction Inventory (MSI) (Weiss & Cerreto, 1980), and Positive Feelings Questionnaire (O'Leary et al., 1983).

When Children and Adolescents are Substance Abusing

The family and the substance abuser may both resist involving the family in treatment. At this stage of the family life cycle, it is usual for them to be thinking about the child's emancipation, or movement out of the family. The adolescent tends to deny need for the family. The family, depending on how long or how difficult their endurance of the behaviors related to substance abuse has been, may feel guilty or that they have tried everything possible and are totally at a loss. Some may wish to bow out and be no longer bothered; others may be willing to keep trying.

The child with substance abuse problems may be the scapegoat and rebellious child in a family where alcohol abuse exists as described previously. Lee (1984) notes that the adolescent's drinking serves to distract attention from his parents' marital problems. In that sense, it is functional for the family, serving to contain and minimize anxiety. It also serves to diminish the adolescent's anxiety about the pain in the family, though it is destructive to him as well. Shifting alliances are observable in the family triangle. A parent may ally himself or herself with the drinking adolescent, thereby meeting a need of the parent and protecting the adolescent from the other parent's knowledge of his difficulty. Ultimately, parents may ally themselves against the adolescent, blaming him for all family problems. These shifts may be abetted by the alcoholism of one or the other or both parents.

An adolescent whose drinking creates problems for her in the community draws parental attention and engagement, leaving her more dependent and family-involved. The problems of separation and independence typical of adolescence are exacerbated and make it more difficult for both adolescent and parent to achieve a satisfactory degree of separateness. Substance abuse in adolescents is a growing problem with unique challenges for treatment. From assessment to treatment planning to intervention, adolescent development must be taken into account. The following is a list of concepts that must be taken into account during the assessment of an adolescent who is substance abusing (Wagner, Waldron & Feder, 2001):

- The substance use behavior itself
- The type and severity of psychiatric morbidity that may be present and whether it preceded or developed after the substance use disorder
- Cognition, with specific attention to neuropsychological functioning
- Family organization and interactional patterns
- Social skills
- Vocational adjustment
- Recreation and leisure activities

- Personality
- School adjustment
- Peer affiliation
- Legal status
- Physical health

The unique position of wanting independence and being dependent on family for an adolescent make family treatment for the adolescent substance abuser most effective. Many family therapies have been shown to most effectively treat adolescents. Addressing the family dynamics and the interactional patterns within the family seem to be key concepts in treating adolescents. Springer and Orsbon (2002) suggest the ideas for working with families who have a substance-abusing adolescent:

- Examine the family rules that maintain symptomatic behavior
- Work with the family to restructure the family's boundaries
- Consider the developmental life cycle of the family system (e.g., an adolescent's typical struggle for increased autonomy from the family system)
- Joining: building a relationship with each family member
- A family with a patriarchal hierarchy: address the father first to respect their family system, rules, structure, and culture
- Mimesis: Mirroring a family's mood, communication patterns, etc.
- Enactment: Allowing a family to act out its problems in front of the group
- Members provide direct feedback to the family based on their observation

EVIDENCE-BASED TREATMENTS/BEST PRACTICES

Functional Family Therapy

Functional family therapy has been shown as an effective treatment (Alexander & Parsons, 1973; Barton et al., 1985; Gordon et al., 1988; Alexander & Sexton, 2002). Problems of dysfunction in the system as a whole and relationships in the family become the focus of therapy. The focus of treatment is relational. Goals include changing family interactions and improving relationship functioning. Intervention attempts can lead to rapid change or resistance depending on how well the intervention strategy has been fitted to each family member's interpersonal function with each family member. The initial assessment is an important component in developing the family treatment plan for addressing adolescent substance abuse and should not be minimized.

During the initial assessment, the therapist should look beyond the apparent problem and focus on all relationships and the interpersonal impact of repetitive or problematic behavioral sequences (all behavior in terms of the interpersonal relatedness or interdependency). Identification of functions within each dyad in the family allows the therapist to develop a change plan that will target maladaptive behavior while preserving each family member's functions with others.

BOX 10.1 | Functional Family Therapy: Three Phases of Treatment

Phase I: Engagement and Motivation

- Aims: (1) Engage the family, (2) enhance motivation for change, and (3) assess the relevant aspects of individual and family functioning to be addressed in treatment
- Maximizing those factors that enhance the perception that positive change might occur and minimizing those factors that decrease that perception
- Develop respect for each family member (using relational skills—sensitive to personal and cultural issues and values, the ability to link behavior to affect and cognition, willingness to hear the pain of all family members without taking sides)
- Techniques: Reframing or Relabeling problem behavior (changes the meaning and value of a negative behavior by casting it in a more benign or even benevoldent, light) and related techniques to break the toxic negative cycle

Phase II: Behavior Change

- Develop intermediate and then long-term behavior change intervention plan that are culturally appropriate, context-sensitive, and individualized to the unique characteristics of each family member.
- Cognitive (e.g. coping strategies), interactive (e.g. competent parenting), and emotional components
- Cognitive-behavioral techniques used to effect change in risk and protective factors (e.g. parent and sibling drug use, ineffective supervision and discipline, negative parent/child relationships, family conflict)

Multidimensional Family Therapy (MDFT)

Multidimensional family therapy has been shown to effectively treat adolescent substance abusers in four clinical trials (Dennis et al., 2002; Liddle et al., 2001; Liddle et al., 2002; Rowe, Liddle, & Dakof, 2002). A prevention version of MDFT has also been shown to increase self-concept, family cohesion, and other protective factors. The U.S. Department of Health and Human Services (2002) listed MDFT as one of the most promising interventions for adolescent drug abuse. MDFT is a SAMHSA Model Program (http://model-programs.samhsa.gov), and an effective drug abuse treatment approach by NIDA's (n.d.) Behavioral Therapies Development Program. Assessment in MDFT is the basis for the therapeutic "map," directing therapists where to intervene in the multiple domains of the adolescent's life, primarily through a series of individual and family interviews and observations.

The following are the five core modules of assessment for MDFT:

1. *Intervention with the Adolescent*—This module addresses developmental issues, including identity formation, peer relations, and drug use consequences.

- Individualized and developmentally appropriate techniques (e.g. communication training, contingency management, negative mood regulation, developing family-specific tasks, basic parenting skills, conflict management)
- Therapist structuring skills is primary: the ability and willingness to plan
interventions that are individualized and respectful to all family members
and to match behavior change techniques to the interpersonal functions of
all family members.
- Pointing out the interactions between family members—aware of how they
affect each other
- Facilitating a relationship focus by questioning and identifying sequences
of behavior that focus on the relational impact of family behavior and
thoughts, and feelings
- Confronting family members by challenging them directly about their
behavior and their need to change (in a non-blaming tone)

Phase III: Generalization—Multisystemic Phase

- Expanding positive family change into other problem areas and different
(multi-system) situation
- To maintain change through relapse prevention and supports change
through linking individualized family functional needs with available community resources
- Therapist qualities: (1) Know the community (current list of
providers/agencies, know the school/legal/transportation systems)
(2) Develop contracts (have specific referral persons in agencies) (3) Remember ethical responsibilities (4) Refer to follow-up services consistent with
family members' relational needs, culture, and abilities

2. *Intervention with the Parent(s)*—This module enhances parenting skills in
monitoring and limit setting, as well as rebuilds bonds with the adolescent.
3. *Intervention to Change the Parent-Adolescent Interaction*—This module
encourages participation in the teen's life outside of family activities and
focuses on the interactive aspect of the parent-adolescent relationship.
4. *Interventions with Other Family Members*—This module focuses on
change in relationship patterns by helping families develop the motivation
and skills to interact in more positive ways.
5. *Interventions with Systems External to the Family*—This module works
to develop collaborative relationships among all other systems in which
the adolescent is involved, such as school or the juvenile justice system.

Assessment begins with a meeting that includes the entire family during which
the therapist can observe family dynamics and begin to identify the roles that
different individuals play in the adolescent's life and current circumstances.
Then, the therapist meets with each family member individually to highlight
the unique perspective of individual family members, understand their

different views of the presenting problems, assess family relationships, and learn what each member would like to see change in the family. Depending on the size of the family and the direness of the current situation, these interviews may happen over a period of days or weeks. The following are the three phases of treatment with MDFT.

First Phase (3–4 Weeks)   This phase begins with a comprehensive, multi-systemic assessment in which the therapist develops relationships with all of the people who will be involved in treatment. During this phase, the focus is on relationship formation, establishment of therapy expectations, discussion of motivation for treatment, and a renewal of the connection between parent(s) and adolescent.

The individual meeting with the adolescent is important. The therapist should learn about the adolescent's unique life story, the severity and nature of drug use, family history, peer relationships, school and legal problems, and important life events. In addition, information should be gathered about health and lifestyle issues and sexual behavior. The assessment should include an understanding of psychiatric conditions through review of previous records and reports, clinical interviews, and psychiatric evaluations if available.

Assessment of extrafamilial influences can be done by gathering information from all relevant sources and combining this information with the adolescent and family's reports to compile a complete picture of each individual's functioning in relation to external systems. Sources of information might include the adolescent's educational/vocational placement, legal charges and level of risk for future problems, and peer networks.

Second Phase (2 Months)   This phase uses a problem-solving approach with the adolescent and the parent(s). During individual sessions with the adolescent, focus is on decision making and mastery, communications skills, and problem-solving skills. Sessions with the parents focus on distinguishing influence from control over their adolescent and acceptance that not all aspects of the adolescent's behavior need to change to be developmentally on task. Family sessions focus on interactional patterns from a problem-solving perspective. The frequency and type of sessions depends on the assessment that is conducted and will vary from one case to the next, depending on the specifics of the family.

Alliance-building techniques (adolescent engagement interventions, AEIs) are used to define therapeutic goals, generate hope, and attend to the adolescent's experience. It is important to articulate the treatment's focal themes and help the adolescent learn how to (1) communicate effectively with parents and others, (2) effectively solve interpersonal problems, (3) manage anger and impulses, and (4) enhance social competence.

Reaching parents as adults with their own needs and issues, and as parents who may have lost motivation or faith in their ability to influence the adolescent, will positively affect the treatment outcomes. Parental reconnection interventions (PRIs) (Liddle et al., 1998) include enhancing feelings or parental love and commitment, validating parents' past efforts acknowledging difficult past and present circumstances, and generating hope. Once parental involvement with the adolescent has increased, therapists then foster parenting competency by teaching and coaching about consistent and age-appropriate limit setting, monitoring, and support functions.

With other family members, emphasizing the serious circumstances of the youth's life and establishing a connection between their involvement in treatment and the creation of behavioral and relational alternatives for the adolescent help achieve cooperation. Close collaboration with the school, legal, employment, mental health, and health systems influencing the adolescent's life is critical for long-lasting therapeutic change.

Third/Final Phase (Last Month)   The final phase is a transition away from therapy that focuses on the shift of learning skills in therapy to using them in everyday real-world situations.

The training manual can be purchased with a training program from Dr. Liddle. It has been found that clinicians can be taught to the use this treatment with a high degree of fidelity (Hogue, Liddle, & Rowel, 1996; Hogue et al., 1998). See the case example of substance abuse treatment using MDFT found later in the chapter.

Brief Strategic/Structural Family Therapy (BSFT)

BSFT, developed by Jose Szapocznik, has evolved from more than 25 years of research and practice at the Center for Family Studies. It is a family-based approach that targets children and adolescents between the ages of 8 and 17 who are displaying or are at risk for developing behavior problems, including substance abuse. BSFT has been implemented as a prevention, early intervention, and intervention strategy for delinquent and substance-abusing adolescents (Center for Family Studies, 2001). The goal of BSFT is to target problem behavior in youths by improving family relationships. The theoretical underpinnings rely on the concept that problematic family relations are directly related to problem behaviors, including substance abuse. BSFT has been found to be an efficacious treatment in randomized clinical trials (Szapocznik et al., 1989 Santisteban et al., 1997).

BSFT is a short-term problem-focused intervention averaging 12–15 sessions over about three months. The average number of sessions and length of treatment may be doubled for severe cases needing more time. Sessions may be conducted in the office but due to the family situation may need to be conducted in the home or other community setting. The treatment is most successful when as many family members as possible are brought into treatment. Efforts should be placed on bringing in family members who are reluctant to participate.

BSFT has been implemented with a variety of minority youth and has been found to be an efficacious treatment for minority youth. Research on Hispanic adolescent substance abuse does not show drastic differences from

BOX 10.2 | Three Important Components for Implementing BSFT

✓ **Joining:** Establishing a therapeutic system or a work team made up of the counselor and the family. The therapist needs the ability to respond to the unique characteristics of individuals as well as to quickly discern the family's governing processes and become part of them. The therapeutic alliance is critical to the success of BSFT and can be demonstrated to the family by respecting each member individually as well as the family as a whole.

Techniques:

Maintenance—supporting the family's structure by accepting its rules; supporting areas of family strengths

Tracking—adopting the content of family communications or using the nature of family interactions to join the family

Mimesis—attempts to match the tempo, mood, and style of family member interactions

✓ **Diagnosis:** Identifying those family interactional patterns (structure) that are allowing or encouraging the individuals' behavior problems

✓ **Restructuring:** The ultimate goal is to move the family from their current set of maladaptive interactions to a more effective and adaptive set of interactions. Therapists orchestrate opportunities for families to interact in new ways. The change strategy is strengths based while correcting problematic behavior, and the therapist remains direction-oriented and practical. The focus will always be from moving from maladaptive behaviors to appropriate useful behaviors with the family.

Techniques:

Working in the present—having the family behave differently within the session

Reframing—creating a different sense of reality

Working with boundaries and alliances—A common pattern with drug-using youth involves parent-youth alliances that cross generational lines and work against the effective functioning of the executive parental hierarchy (e.g., strong bond with the mother figure when the youth has problems with the fatherfigure).

Shifting boundaries—creating a more solid boundary around the parental subsystem so the parental figures make executive decisions together, and removing the inappropriate parent-child alliance

---

non-Hispanic adolescents, but issues specific to Hispanics make it necessary for treatment protocols to take ethnicity into account. Many studies have found a relationship between substance abuse in Hispanic adolescents and acculturation. Acculturation challenges may affect the adolescent on an individual, family, societal, or systemic level, making treatment more challenging. Specifically, acculturation challenges may present as less effective parenting styles that directly affect substance abuse rates among adolescents (Gil, Wagner, & Vega, 2000; Santisteban, Coatsworth, Briones, & Szapocznik, 2002).

Multisystemic Family Therapy (MST)

MST is a family- and community-based treatment that has been evolving and developing for the past couple decades. It has produced positive outcomes for adolescents involved in violent behavior or substance-abusing/dependence behavior. The primary goal of MST is to empower parents with the skills and resources needed to address the difficulties of raising teenagers and to empower youth to cope with pressures associated with family, peer, school, and neighborhood. Many clinical trials have been completed and support the use of MST with this population (Henggeler, Melton, & Smith, 1992; Henggeler, Melton, Smith, Foster, et al., 1993; Henggeler, Melton, Smith, Schoenwald, & Hanley, 1993). The 2001 Surgeon General's report cited MST as a promising adolescent substance abuse treatment (U.S. Department of Health and Human Services, 2001).

MST, consistent with social-ecological models, is a home-based intervention that focuses on the individual while also focusing on the links between the youth and family, peers, school, and community. MST aims to increase protective factors by building on strengths of the youth and the family. Emphasis is placed on empowering the parent to balance the social peer network for the youth. It has several unique features (Randall & Cunningham, 2003):

- Comprehensive yet individualized—addresses issues of family, school, peers, and community that are known to impact maladaptive behavior
- High ecological validity—implemented where the problems are occurring
- Ongoing, extensive quality assurance
- Integration of empirically based models with ecological framework

Family interventions in MST focus on the family, peers, and school. The therapist works to give the parents in the family the resources to develop structure and discipline needed for effective parenting while increasing family connectedness. The youth is encouraged and worked with toward the goal of reduced contact with drug-using and delinquent peers. Collaboration between the parents and school staff is encouraged, and academic efforts are encouraged in the youth. The following are the nine principles of MST (http://www.musc.edu/fsrc/overview/atreatmentmodel.htm#treatmentmodel. Used with permission.

Principle 1: The Primary Purpose of Assessment is to Understand the Fit Between the Identified Problems and Their Broader Systemic Context During assessment, the therapist gathers information from a variety of sources in the youth's life, including school, family, peers, community, and so on. The information will guide the therapist to an hypothesized understanding of the behavior of the youth.

Principle 2: Therapeutic Contacts Should Emphasize the Positive and Should Use Systemic Strengths as Levers for Change The therapist must focus on the strengths of a family to ensure a collaborative effort in treatment. Focusing on the strengths not only helps the family buy into the process but it also increases the family's feelings of being able to succeed.

Principle 3: Interventions Should Be Designed to Promote Responsible Behavior and Decrease Irresponsible Behavior among Family Members   The goals of promoting responsible behavior apply to all family members in MST. Parents should be encouraged to provide more structure and discipline while youths should be encouraged to participate in school.

Principle 4: Interventions Should Be Present-Focused and Action-Oriented, Targeting Specific and Well-Defined Problems   Being well defined is important for helping members of the family be aware of the direction of treatment as well as the ways in which progress will be measured.

Principle 5: Interventions Should Target Sequences of Behavior within and between Multiple Systems That Maintain Identified Problems   This principle promotes a change in interpersonal transactions. Similar to systems theory, MST focuses on the transactions within a youth's multisystem world.

Principle 6: Interventions Should Be Developmentally Appropriate and Fit the Developmental Needs of the Youth   The specifics of the intervention should take into account the youth's chronological and developmental age. For example, a 13-year-old with antisocial behaviors may have a different treatment focus than a 17-year-old.

Principle 7: Interventions Should Be Designed to Require Daily or Weekly Effort by Family Members   Increased frequency of effort will increase the likelihood of success. In addition, many families engaging in MST have a long history of maladaptive behavior, and intense efforts are needed to overcome that history.

Principle 8: Intervention Effectiveness is Evaluated Continuously from Multiple Perspectives, with Providers Assuming Accountability for Overcoming Barriers to Successful Outcomes   Ongoing evaluation and feedback are critical for understanding whether the intervention is being effective. When the intervention is not being effective, it is the responsibility of the therapist to provide that feedback and assess where the problem in the intervention is occurring.

Principle 9: Interventions Should Be Designed to Promote Treatment Generalization and Long-Term Maintenance of Therapeutic Change by Empowering Care Givers to Address Family Members' Needs across Multiple Systemic Contexts   The long-term goal is for families to be able to handle challenges on their own. Thus, therapists must avoid "doing" for the family but rather help the family learn the tools to successfully maintain long-term change.

Table 10.2 | Family Therapy Models

Model	Author	Affiliation	Contact Information
Functional Family Therapy	James F. Alexander	University of Utah, Department of Psychology	http://www.psych.utah.edu/alexander/alexander.html
Multidimensional Family Therapy	Howard A. Liddle	University of Miami; Center for Treatment Research on Adolescent Drug Abuse	http://www.miami.edu/ctrada/ http://www.strengthening-families.org/html/programs_1999/10_MDFT.html10_MDFT.html
Brief Strategic/ Structural Family Therapy	Jose Szapocznik	University of Miami, School of Medicine	http://www.cfs.med.miami.edu/
Multisystemic Therapy	Scott W. Henggeler	Medical University of South Carolina; Family Services Research Center	http://www.musc.edu/fsrc/

MST usually lasts for about four months with several therapist visits per week to the home, school, or other community location. Treatment plans are developed with the family and therefore reflect the needs and goals of the family rather than the therapist. The plan places considerable consideration on factors in the youth's life that are linked to the maladaptive behavior. The intensity of the treatment as well as the commitment to being in the community where the problems occur are foundations of MST that contribute to success with this population.

Other Drug Addiction Treatment Methods

Drug addiction is a treatable disorder. People in treatment for drug addictions learn behavioral changes and often take medications as part of their treatment regimen. Behavioral therapies can include counseling, psychotherapy, support groups, or family therapy. Treatment medications offer help in suppressing the withdrawal syndrome and drug cravings, and in blocking the effects of drugs.

There are several types of drug abuse treatment programs. Short-term methods last less than six months and include residential therapy, medication therapy, and drug-free outpatient therapy. Longer-term treatment may include, for example, methadone maintenance outpatient treatment for opiate addicts and residential therapeutic community treatment.

The four most common forms of drug abuse treatment are all effective in reducing drug use. That is the major finding from a NIDA-sponsored nationwide study of drug abuse treatment outcomes. The Drug Abuse Treatment Outcome Study (DATOS) tracked 10,010 drug abusers in nearly 100 treatment programs in 11 cities who entered treatment between 1991 and 1993 (Mueller & Wyman, 1997). Short-term inpatient treatment programs yielded significant declines in drug use, even though patients stayed in these programs no more than 30 days. The percentage of patients reporting illegal acts and thoughts of suicide also declined significantly after treatment in these programs. The researchers are exploring whether continuing involvement in outpatient services and mutual help groups may have contributed to these positive outcomes.

Investigators with DATOS studied patients in the four most common kinds of treatment programs: (1) Outpatient methadone programs administer the medication methadone to reduce cravings for heroin and block its effects. Counseling, vocational skills development, and case management to help patients access support services are used to gradually stabilize the patients' functioning. Some patients stay on methadone for long periods, while others move from methadone to abstinence. (2) Long-term residential programs offer around-the-clock, drug-free treatment in a residential community of counselors and fellow recovering addicts. Patients generally stay in these programs several months or up to a year or more. Some of these programs are referred to as therapeutic communities. (3) Outpatient drug-free programs use a wide range of approaches, including problem-solving groups, specialized therapies such as insight-oriented psychotherapy, cognitive-behavioral therapy, and 12-step programs. As with long-term residential treatment programs, patients may stay in these programs for months or longer. (4) Short-term inpatient programs keep patients up to 30 days. Most of these programs focus on medical stabilization, abstinence, and lifestyle changes. Staff members are primarily medical professionals and trained counselors. Once primarily for alcohol abuse treatment, these programs expanded into drug abuse treatment in the 1980s.

More than two decades of scientific research have yielded a set of fundamental principles that characterize effective drug abuse treatment. These 13 principles, which are detailed in NIDA's new research-based guide, *Principles of Drug Addiction Treatment: A Research-Based Guide* (NIDA, 1999) are as follows:

1. No single treatment is appropriate for all individuals. Matching treatment settings, interventions, and services to each patient's problems and needs is critical.
2. Treatment needs to be readily available. Treatment applicants can be lost if treatment is not immediately available or readily accessible.
3. Effective treatment attends to multiple needs of the individual, not just his or her drug use. Treatment must address the individual's drug use and associated medical, psychological, social, vocational, and legal problems.
4. Treatment needs to be flexible and to provide ongoing assessments of patient needs, which may change during the course of treatment.
5. Remaining in treatment for an adequate period of time is critical for treatment effectiveness. The time depends on an individual's needs. For most

patients, the threshold of significant improvement is reached at about three months in treatment. Additional treatment can produce further progress. Programs should include strategies to prevent patients from leaving treatment prematurely.

6. Individual and/or group counseling and other behavioral therapies are critical components of effective treatment for addiction. In therapy, patients address motivation, build skills to resist drug use, replace drug-using activities with constructive and rewarding non-drug-using activities, and improve problem-solving abilities. Behavioral therapy also facilitates interpersonal relationships.

7. Medications are an important element of treatment for many patients, especially when combined with counseling and other behavioral therapies. Methadone and levo-alpha-acetylmethadol (LAAM) help persons addicted to opiates stabilize their lives and reduce their drug use. Naltrexone is effective for some opiate addicts and some patients with co-occurring alcohol dependence. Nicotine patches or gum, or an oral medication such as Bupropion, can help persons addicted to nicotine.

8. Addicted or drug-abusing individuals with coexisting mental disorders should have both disorders treated in an integrated way. Because these disorders often occur in the same individual, patients presenting for one condition should be assessed and treated for the other.

9. Medical detoxification is only the first stage of addiction treatment and by itself does little to change long-term drug use. Medical detoxification manages the acute physical symptoms of withdrawal. For some individuals, it is a precursor to effective drug addiction treatment.

10. Treatment does not need to be voluntary to be effective. Sanctions or enticements in the family, employment setting, or criminal justice system can significantly increase treatment entry, retention, and success.

11. Possible drug use during treatment must be monitored continuously. Monitoring a patient's drug and alcohol use during treatment, such as through urinalysis, can help the patient withstand urges to use drugs. Such monitoring also can provide early evidence of drug use so that treatment can be adjusted.

12. Treatment programs should provide assessment for HIV/AIDS, hepatitis B and C, tuberculosis and other infectious diseases, and counseling to help patients modify or change behaviors that place them or others at risk of infection. Counseling can help patients avoid high-risk behavior and help people who are already infected manage their illness.

13. Recovery from drug addiction can be a long-term process and frequently requires multiple episodes of treatment. As with other chronic illnesses, relapses to drug use can occur during or after successful treatment episodes. Participation in self-help support programs during and following treatment often helps maintain abstinence.

Alcoholics Anonymous (AA) is one of the most well-known alcohol treatment programs in the United States. This original 12-step organization was founded in 1935 to aid recovery from alcoholism (Brigham, 2003). The 12-step program has been adapted for drug use and overeating, as well as many other addictions. The following are the 12 steps in the order that they should be completed (Alcoholics Anonymous, 2003).

1. We admitted we were powerless over alcohol—that our lives had become unmanageable.
2. Came to believe that a Power greater than ourselves could restore us to sanity.
3. Made a decision to turn our will and our lives over to the care of God, as we understand Him.
4. Made a searching and fearless moral inventory of ourselves.
5. Admitted to God, to ourselves and to another human being the exact nature of our wrongs.
6. Were entirely ready to have God remove all these defects of character.
7. Humbly asked Him to remove these shortcomings.
8. Made a list of all the persons we had harmed, and became willing to make amends to them all.
9. Made direct amends to such people wherever possible, except when to do so would injure them or others.
10. Continued to take personal inventory and when we were wrong promptly admitted it.
11. Sought through prayer and meditation to improve our conscious contact with God as we understand Him, praying only for knowledge of His will for us and the power to carry that out.
12. Having had a spiritual awakening as a result of these Steps, we tried to carry this message to others, and to practice these principles in all our affairs.*

Historically, the principles of AA and other 12-step self-help organizations (e.g., Narcotics Anonymous [NA], Cocaine Anonymous) have been an integral part of the development of drug abuse treatment. The acceptance of open discussion of drug abuse in AA meetings has grown but still varies greatly from group to group. NA is an alternative 12-step organization for people addicted to drugs other than alcohol.

Substance abuse treatments utilizing a 12-step approach evolved to meet the needs of patients who are not successful at establishing recovery solely through 12-step organization. Maryhaven, a comprehensive, community-based drug abuse treatment facility, combines a core commitment to 12-step principles and practices with the use of scientifically derived treatment interventions. Over the years, Maryhaven has enhanced and modified its approach

---

* The Twelve Steps are reprinted with permission of Alcoholics Anonymous World Services, Inc. (A.A.W.S.). Permission to reprint the Twelve Steps does not mean that A.A.W.S. has reviewed or approved the contents of this publication, or that A.A.W.S. necessarily agrees with the views expressed herein. A.A. is a program of recovery from alcoholism only—use of the Twelve Steps in connection with programs and activities which are patterned after A.A., but which address other problems, or in any other non-A.A. context, does not imply otherwise.

so that today the range of services and resources resembles the description of "Components of Comprehensive Drug Abuse Treatment" in NIDA's booklet *Principles of Drug Addiction Treatment* (National Institute on Drug Abuse, 1999). Trained Maryhaven staff members can provide patients with motivational interviewing, motivational incentives, cognitive behavioral therapy, and use of medication in detoxification.

Treatment of Minority Substance Abusers

Substance abuse treatment with an individual or family from a minority group must take into account ethnic identity as well as their worldview, in addition to factors already discussed. A client's ethnic identity may have a strong impact on whether or not treatment becomes successful. Feelings of resistance and dissonant expectation may negatively influence the clients' ability to establish a trusting therapeutic relationship with a clinician from the majority group. Clients may bring issues regarding their ethnicity to treatment and may or may not be aware of this. It is important for the clinician to be aware of this possibility and make adjustments to allow the client to have an environment in which she feels safe and respected.

Clients who believe in external control and external responsibility may feel a sense of helplessness or hopelessness about the difficulties and stressors they are experiencing with regard to their minority status and may respond by giving up. In an effort to help these clients effectively address their problem, it may be necessary to acknowledge their experience as a member of a minority group and to help identify ways of coping in a more adaptive manner.

Native Americans   Spirituality is central to the many different Native American nations in this country (Coyhis, 2000). The commonalities of over 100 federally recognized tribes include a desire for harmony, a belief in the unseen world, and a belief in the interconnectedness of all life (Fleming & Manson, 1990). The 12-step program that is based in spirituality may often be appropriate for Native Americans in substance abuse treatment. Wording of the steps can be altered to fit their beliefs, as in this alternate wording of the 12 steps and 12 principles (Coyhis, 2000):

Step 1 (Honesty): ability to admit powerlesness

Step 2 (Hope): belief in a power greater than self

Step 3 (Faith): asking for help from a Higher Power and others

Step 4 (Courage): thoughtfulness about personal strengths and weaknesses

Step 5 (Integrity): admission to the Great Spirit, to ourselves, and to another person about personal flaws

Step 6 (Willingness): ready for change with help from a Higher Power

Step 7 (Humility): willingness to ask a Higher Power and friends for help to change

Step 8 (Forgiveness): willingness to apologize to those hurt by one's actions

Step 9 (Justice): making up for wrongs to those people who have been hurt when possible

Step 10 (Perseverance): continued thoughtfulness about self and ongoing admission of faults

Step 11 (Spiritual awareness): ongoing prayer for strength to do what is right

Step 12 (Service): attempts to help others in day to day practice of principals

African Americans   African Americans are overrepresented among those who abuse substances, and yet they have a lower rate of recovery than their counterparts (Recovery Publications, 1988). African Americans are more likely to view addiction as a spiritual possession or curse because of spiritual beliefs. In addition, this culture ritualizes the use of music and dance, and for some this ritualization may be associated with the substance abuse (Recovery Publications, 1988). If these issues are not understood and acknowledged by the clinician, the likelihood of treatment being successful declines dramatically.

Spirituality and religion are central to African Americans. Blacks and Hispanics are more likely to think that alcoholism results from a violation of spiritual values and that addiction represents moral weakness. A spiritually responsive presentation of the 12 steps was developed by Recovery Publications (1988) and divides the 12 steps in four categories: Peace with God includes steps 1–3, Peace with Ourselves includes steps 4–7, Peace with Others includes steps 8–10, and Keeping the Peace includes steps 11–12.

It is important for clinicians to be aware of gender issues. In the African American community, the role of the black woman has traditionally been that of head of household. This may make accepting that she has an addiction very difficult (Schmidt, 1996). Acknowledgement and incorporation of this is imperative for treatment planning.

Hispanics   Hispanic culture values those inner qualities that constitute the uniqueness of the person and his goodness in himself (Baron, 2000). To the Hispanic, family is more important than the individual. It is important to first assess level of acculturation, ethnic identity development, and worldview. For a Mexican American with a more traditional degree of acculturation, the need to seek help for a substance abuse problem may feel incongruent and undesirable. One often finds among Mexican Americans an attitude of permissiveness that encourages the use of alcohol among men. Drinking tends to be associated with socializing and celebrating. Male clients' resistance to treatment may be rooted in an unwillingness to admit a lack of control and weakness (machismo). The process of "motivational interviewing" (emphasis on a directive, client-centered style; exposing a discrepancy between future goals and current behavior) would be effective. The desirable meanings of machismo can be utilized (a bridge rather than an obstacle). Women are traditionally restricted from drinking. A traditionally acculturated Mexican American woman will expect to be subjected to a double standard and may be judged more harshly than males.

In the Hispanic culture, there is a strong emphasis on family with a clear hierarchy, in which men are usually the undisputed figures of authority. Family members are expected to achieve smooth and pleasant relationships that avoid confrontation and conflict. The use of indirect, implicit, or covert communication is consistent with Mexican American families' emphasis on harmony (Sue & Sue, 1990). The behavior of the chemically dependent person shapes the compensatory and defensive behaviors and patterns of interaction of the rest of the family. Family members may not be able to address openly or confront the substance abuse problem directly. It would be culturally congruent for family members to placate the alcoholic if the head of the household exhibits it. These dynamics may be labeled by a clinician as codependency and enabling. Considering these family dynamics, family therapy is congruent with the value system of the Mexican American culture. Motivational interviewing techniques may be helpful in increasing the individual and family's readiness for change. Knowledge of culturally based values also is helpful. Considering the intergenerational dyad of the Mexican family structure, it may be frequently useful to consider the incorporation of extended family members in family treatment when such intervention may be useful and appropriate.

Asian Americans   It is essential to begin with both a standard diagnostic workup of the type of severity of the addiction as well as an assessment of the individual's degree of acculturation (Chang, 2000). Address the multiple issues that involve the family of the addicted individual within the context in which treatment is to occur. A few unique treatment programs now exist in the United States that are specifically designed for Asian and Pacific Islander addicts (e.g., Asian American Recovery Services in San Francisco, the Asian American Drug Abuse Program in Los Angeles, and the National Asian/Pacific American Families Against Substance Abuse).

Most treatment of Asian clients still occurs within the general outpatient mental health system of this country. Most clients in a public mental health setting will likely not return for more than a handful of treatment sessions. Focusing just on the addicted individual is rarely successful. With the centrality of the family for Asians, it is imperative that treatment planning begin as early as possible with active consideration of the family's role in the person's addiction, as well as treatment and recovery.

Asian families can be especially compliant with treatment, given their cultural values regarding authority and conformity. Care must be exercised that the therapist not violate gender roles or cross-generational boundaries in communication, engaging the family by requesting their help with one's therapeutic role. A straightforward problem-solving approach is often most effective. Asian clients respond best to therapists who are expert and credible and can offer concrete suggestions or advice about their distress.

For Asians, disclosing about one's self, especially one's private emotions or feelings, is often neither a familiar nor an acceptable practice. Some clients are unfamiliar with the Western model of treatment. Clinicians need to give a thorough explanation about the therapist's plan of approach. Engaging the family in the addict's ongoing treatment is an important step in countering the enormous sense of shame and isolation. The tendency of family members is to protect the parents or elders from any sense of discomfort or shame. The clinician should not rush in too quickly to address areas of vulnerability but should join at the broad experiential level (sharing pain, grief, or any other aspect of salient traumatic experience) without pushing for details initially.

The therapist should focus on more tangible and behavioral matters, identify triggers for the addictive cycle, and track the cycle components for the client and the family. Given the common orientation among Asians to somatic experiences rather than emotional ones, this approach will assist in learning about their inner subjective world and understanding their personal feelings, emotions, needs, and desires. When family issues are clearly identified (e.g., a parent's unresolved trauma or loss), these attendant issues must then be incorporated into the treatment plan along with a further assessment of family members' accessibility for continued exploration of such issues.

The cultural norms regarding hierarchy and obligation often result in Asian addicts' inability to affect their concerns (overwhelmed by the family's problem and needs). The experience of futility and psychological numbness that ensues is often accompanied by a deep sense of anger and bitterness that further amplifies the emotional separation and isolation of the addict within the family.

The effects of Eastern and Western spiritual practices in promoting physical and emotional healing are increasingly being identified by professionals (Kissman & Maurer, 2002). During recovery from addiction, some methods for bridging the body/mind/spirit cleavage include connectedness with self and others, present-moment awareness, sharing and listening to stories to correct distortions of extreme opposites, prayer, and meditation. Buddhism, Hinduism and other Eastern spiritual beliefs and practices have much to contribute to Western ways of understanding the spiritual elements of holistic healing.

CASE EXAMPLE: MDFT

A social worker in a community treatment center conducts an intake assessment for a 14-year-old African American male and his mother. The mother brought her son into the center after a juvenile court ordered the family into therapy as part of the son's probation. The probation occurred after the adolescent was picked up for the second time on a possession-of-cocaine charge, this time with an accompanying distribution charge. The mother indicates that she is worried about her son but has no control over what he does anymore. She reports that her husband works two jobs and was too busy to come to therapy. Her two younger children (ages 2 and 4) came to the intake session.

The social worker begins by asking the adolescent why he is there and what is going on in his life. He is nonresponsive and only replies that the judge made him come so he didn't have to go to jail. When the social worker asks about his father, the adolescent simply says he's never around. The mother looks upset and reminds her son that he is working so they can have a better life, to which her son says that he makes more money than his father does. The mother is visibly distraught and looks helplessly toward the social worker.

During the initial assessment, it is determined that MDFT will be the treatment approach. The family has become distant from each other, and the parents seem to no longer have an effective parenting style with their son. The social worker discusses the importance of family members participating in the treatment and asks if the father would be able to come in. In addition, the social worker asks about other family members who are in the area. By the end of the session, the mother agrees to convince her husband to come and says she will discuss the treatment with two of her brothers who live nearby—she feels certain that they will come in as they have been very concerned about her son as well. In bringing in the husband and extended family, the social worker is laying the groundwork for working with the parents and other family members—two key components of MDFT.

The next part of the assessment focuses on the adolescent. The social worker asks about activities, peers, school, and other aspects of the adolescent's life. The adolescent begins to answer some questions and a rapport begins to develop. The social worker lays the groundwork for addressing issues of identity formation, peer relationships, and the consequences of drug use. Key adults and professionals in the school, as well as the juvenile justice system, are identified as people who will need to be involved in the process in a collaborative manner. During the assessment, the social worker is beginning to set the expectations and direction that therapy will take.

During the first few weeks of treatment, the assessment phase continues until a thoroughly comprehensive assessment is done, including parents, family, and external systems that impact this adolescent and his family. Due to the severity of the drug charges, it was determined that sessions would begin twice weekly.

Goals of the second phase of treatment will be to assist the parents in learning new parenting skills that help them set boundaries. A problem-solving approach is used to adjust to this new parenting and the challenges of their son. The parents work on learning how to influence their son rather than control him, and they learn to differentiate which behaviors need to be changed and which are developmentally appropriate. Individual work with the adolescent focuses on decision making and mastery, communications skills and problem-solving skills. The family focus is on interaction style and is practiced in the sessions. Parents and extended family are encouraged to get involved in aspects of the adolescent's life other than what occurs in the home. For example, this adolescent reported that he liked playing soccer before he got kicked off the team for his drug use—he also reported that his parents never came to watch him. The social worker collaborated with the family and the school to let him back on the team under a series of conditions, and the family agreed to make efforts to watch him play.

The second phase of treatment will last approximately two months and then the family will spend one month working with the therapist to become more independent in their problem-solving skills and less reliant on the therapy. Skills to help maintain newly learned behaviors would be worked on to ensure continued success for the family.

SUMMARY

Substance abuse in its many forms is an ever-complicated disorder to treat. The family therapy models presented in this chapter all focus on the family, as well as other social systems that impact both the substance abuser and the family unit as a whole. In addition to the multiple systems that affect an individual, ethnicity plays a part in the type of treatment chosen, as well as treatment adherence and effectiveness. Family therapists must be aware of the other types of treatment available to substance abusers, such as medication, inpatient treatment, and programs such as AA and NA. Families may be participating in these treatments in addition to family therapy or may have had unsuccessful experiences prior to family therapy. Individuals and families dealing with substance abuse have such a variety of needs and goals that it is critical for therapists to be as educated on treatments as possible so as to make appropriate and effective recommendations for their clients.

DISCUSSION QUESTIONS

1. How are ethnicity and culture taken into account when working with substance abusers and their families? Does ethnicity play a part in a therapist's decision about a treatment protocol for a particular person or family?
2. What key issues are incorporated into substance abuse treatment for families with substance-abusing adolescents?
3. Why is it that family therapies are effective in treating substance abuse?

References

Alcoholics Anonymous. 2003. *The Recovery Program*. Retrieved October 16, 2003, from http://www.alcoholics-anonymous.org/default/en_about_aa_sub.cfm?subpageid = 17&pageid = 24

Alexander, J. F., and Parsons, B. V. 1973. "Short-Term Family Intervention: A Therapy Outcome Study." *Journal of Consulting and Clinical Psychology* 2:195–201.

Alexander, J. F., and Sexton, T. L. 2002. "Functional Family Therapy: A Model for Treating High-Risk, Acting-Out Youth." In *Comprehensive Handbook of Psychotherapy* (Vol. 4, pp. 111–61), ed. J. Lebow. New York: John Wiley & Sons.

Asher, R., and Brissett, D. 1988. "Codependency: A View from Women Married to Alcoholics." *The International Journal of the Addictions* 23:331–50.

Barber, J. G., and Crisp, B. R. 1995. "The 'Pressures to Change' Approach to Working with the Partners of Heavy Drinkers." *Addiction* 90:269–76.

Baron, M. 2000. "Addiction Treatment for Mexican American Families." In *Bridges to Recovery: Addiction, Family Therapy, and Multicultural Treatment* (pp. 77–114), ed. J. A. Krestan. New York: The Free Press.

Barton, C., Alexander, J. F., Waldron, H., Turner, C. W., and Warburton, J. 1985. "Generalizing Treatment Effects of Family Therapy: Three Replications." *American Journal of Family Therapy* 13:16–26.

Berg, I. K. and Miller, S. 1992. *Working with the Problem Drinker: A Solution Focused Approach*. New York: W. W. Norton & Co.

Brigham, G. S. 2003. "12-Step Participation as a Pathway to Recovery: The Maryhaven Experience and Implications for Treatment and Research." *NIDA Science & Practice Perspectives* 2(1). Retrieved October 15, 2003, from http://www.nida.nih.gov/perspectives/vol2no1.html

Center for Family Studies. 2001. *Brief Strategic Family Therapy*. Retrieved October 14, 2004, from http://www.cfs.med.miami.edu/Docs/ClinicalApproach.htm

Chang, P. 2000. "Treating Asian/Pacific American Addicts and Their Families." In *Bridges to Recovery: Addiction, Family Therapy, and Multicultural Treatment* (pp. 192–218), ed. J. A. Krestan. New York: The Free Press.

Cork, M. 1969. *The Forgotten Children*. Toronto: Addiction Research Foundation.

Cowen, G., and Warren, W. 1994. "Codependency and Gender-Stereotyped Traits." *Sex Roles* 30:631–45.

Coyhis, D. 2000. "Culturally Specific Addiction Recovery for Native Americans." In *Bridges to Recovery: Addiction, Family Therapy, and Multicultural Treatment* (pp. 77–114), ed. J. A. Krestan. New York: The Free Press.

DeCubas, M. M., and Field, T. 1993. "Children of Methadone-Dependent Women: Development Outcomes." *American Journal of Orthopsychiatry* 63(2): 266–76.

Dennis, M., Titus, J. C., Diamond, G., Donaldson, J., Godley, S. H., Tims, F. M., et al. 2002. "The Cannabis Youth Treatment (CYT) Experiment: Rationale, Study Design and Analysis Plans." *Addiction* Suppl. 1:16–34.

Eidelson, R. J., and Epstein, N. 1982. "Cognition and Relationship Maladjustment: Development of a Measure of Dysfunctional Relationship Beliefs." *Journal of Consulting and Clinical Psychology* 50(5):715–20.

Fals-Stewart, W., O'Farrell, T. J., and Feehan, M. 2000. "Behavioral Couples Therapy Versus Individual-Based Treatment for Male Substance-Abusing Patients: An Evaluation of Significant Individual Change and Comparison of Improvement Rates." *Journal of Substance Abuse Treatment* 18(3):249–54.

Fischer, J., and Corcoran, K. (Eds). 1994. *Measures for Clinical Practice: Volume 2: Adults*, 2nd edition. New York: The Free Press.

Fleming, C. M., and Manson, S. M. 1990. "Indian Women and Alcohol." In *Women, Alcohol, and Other Drugs* (pp. 143–48), ed. R. C. Engs. Dubuque, IA: Kendall/Hunt Publishing Co.

Gil, A. G., Wagner, E. F., and Vega, W. A. 2000. "Acculturation, Familism, and Alcohol Use among Latino Adolescent Males: Longitudinal Relations." *Journal of Community Psychology* 28:443–58.

Goglia, L. R., Jurkovic, G. J., Burt, A. M., and Burge-Callaway, K. G. 1992. "Generational Boundary Distortions by Adult Children of Alcoholics: Child-as-Parent and Child-as-Mate." *American Journal of Family Therapy* 20(4):291–99.

Goldman, B. M., and Rossland, S. 1992. "Young Children of Alcoholics: A Group

Treatment Model." *Social Work in Health Care* 16(3):53–65.

Gordon, D. A., Arbuthnot, J., Gustafson, K. E., and McGreen, P. 1988. "Home-Based Behavioral-Systems Family Therapy with Disadvantaged Juvenile Delinquents." *The American Journal of Family Therapy* 16(3):243–55.

Haaken, J. 1990. "A Critical Analysis of the Codependence Construct. *Psychiatry* 53:396–406.

Henggeler, S. W., Melton, G. B., and Smith, L. A. 1992. "Family Preservation Using Multisystemic Therapy: An Effective Alternative to Incarcerating Serious Juvenile Offenders." *Journal of Consulting and Clinical Psychology* 60:953–61.

Henggeler, S. W., Melton, G. B., Smith, L. A., Foster, S. L., Hanley, J. H., and Hutchinson, C. M. 1993. "Assessing Violent Offending in Serious Juvenile Offenders." *Journal of Abnormal Child Psychology* 21:233–43.

Henggeler, S. W., Melton, G. B., Smith, L. A., Schoenwald, S. K., and Hanley, J. H. 1993. "Family Preservation Using Multisystemic Treatment: Long-Term Follow-Up to a Clinical Trial with Serious Juvenile Offenders." *Journal of Child and Family Studies* 2:283–93.

Hogue, A., Liddle, H. A., and Rowe, C. 1996. "Treatment Adherence Process Research in Family Therapy: A Rationale and Some Practical Guidelines." *Psychotherapy: Theory, Research, Practice, & Training* 33(2):332–345.

Hogue, A., Liddle, H. A., Rowe, C., Turner, R. M., Dakof, G. A., and LaPann, K. 1998. "Treatment Adherence and Differentiation in Individual Versus Family Therapy." *Journal of Counseling Psychology* 45(1):104–14.

Kissman, K., and Maurer, L. 2002. "East Meets West: Therapeutic Aspects of Spirituality in Health, Mental Health and Addiction Recovery." *International Social Work* 45(1):35–43.

Kosten, T. R., Rounsaville, B. J., and Kleber, H. D. 1983. "Concurrent Validity of the Addiction Severity Scale Index." *Journal of Nervous Mental Disorders* 171(10): 606–10.

Lee, J. 1984. "Adolescent Alcohol Abuse." *Focus on Family and Chemical Dependency* 7(3):22–25.

Liddle, H. A., Dakof, G. A., Parker, K., Diamond, G. S., Barrett, K., and Tejeda, M. 2001. "Multidimensional Family Therapy for Adolescent Drug Abuse: Results of a Randomized Clinical Trial." *American Journal of Drug and Alcohol Abuse* 27(4):651–88.

Liddle, H.A., Rowe, C. L., Dakof, G. A., and Lyke, J. 1998. "Translating Parenting Research into Clinical Interventions." *Clinical Child Psychology and Psychiatry* 3 (Special Issue: Parenting interventions):419–42.

Liddle, H. A., Rowe, C. L., Quille, T., Dakof, G., Sakran, E., and Biaggi, H. 2002. "Transporting a Research-Developed Adolescent Drug Abuse Treatment into Practice." *Journal of Substance Abuse Treatment* 22(Special Edition on Transferring Research to Practice): 231–43.

Locke, H. J., and Wallace, K. M. 1959. "Locke-Wallace Marital Adjustment Scale and Prediction Test: Their Reliability and Validity." *Marriage and Family Living* 21:251–55.

McLellan, A. T., Luborsky, L., Cacciola, J., Griffith, J., Evans, F., Barr, H.L., et al. 1985. "New Data from the Addiction Severity Index: Reliability and Validity in Three Centers." *Journal of Nervous and Mental Disease* 173(7):412–23.

Morris, J. A., Wise, R. P., Comensky, M. H., and Loney, T. E. 1992. "Bowenian Predictors of Spousal Psychopathology." Paper presented at a meeting of the American Association for Marriage and Family Therapy, Dallas, TX.

Mueller, M. D., and Wyman, J. R. 1997. "Study Sheds New Light on the State of Drug Abuse Treatment Nationwide." *NIDA Notes: Treatment Research* 12(5). Retrieved October 15, 2003, from http://www.drugabuse.gov/NIDA_Notes/NNVol12N5/Study.html

National Institute on Drug Abuse. n.d. *Behavioral Therapies Development Program.* Retrieved October 15, 2004, from http://www.nida.nih.gov/BTDP/Effective

———. 1999. "Thirteen Principles of Effective Drug Addiction Treatment." *NIDA Notes: Treatment Research* 14(5). Retrieved October 15, 2004, from http://www.drugabuse.gov/NIDA_Notes/NNVol14N5/tearoff.html

Notarius, C. I., and Vanzetti, N. A. 1983. "The Marital Agendas Protocol." In *Marriage and Family Assessment: A Sourcebook for Family Therapy* (pp. 209–27), ed. E. E. Filsinger. Beverly Hills, CA: Sage.

O'Leary, K. D., Fincham, F., and Turkewitz, H. 1983. "Positive Feelings toward Spouses." *Journal of Consulting and Clinical Psychology* 51:949–51.

Prest, L. A., Benson, M. J., and Protinsky, H. O. 1998. "Family of Origin and Current Relationship Influences on Codependency." *Family Process* 37(4): 513–28.

Pretzer, D., Schulteis, B., Vander, V. D. G., Smith, C. D., Mitchell, J. W., and Manning, M. C. 1992. "Effect of Zinc Binding on the Structure and Stability of Fibrolase, a Fibrinolytic Protein from Snake Venom." *Pharmaceutical Research* 9:870–77.

Quinn, W., Kuehl, B., Thomas, F., Joanning, H., and Newfield, N. 1989. "Family Treatment of Adolescent Substance Abuse: Transitions and Maintenance of Drug-Free Behavior." *American Journal of Family Therapy* 17(3):229–43.

Randall, J., and Cunningham, P. B. 2003. "Multisystemic Therapy: A Treatment for Violent Substance-Abusing and Substance-Dependent Juvenile Offenders." *Addictive Behaviors* 28:1731–39.

Recovery Publications. 1988. *The Twelve Steps: A Spiritual Journey.* San Diego: RPI Publishing.

Rotunda, R. J., and Doman, K. 2001. "Title Partner Enabling of Substance Use Disorders: Critical Review and Future Directions." *The American Journal of Family Therapy* 29(4):257–70

Rowe, C., Liddle, H. A., and Dakof, G. A. 2002. "Integrative Treatment Development: Multidimensional Family Therapy for Adolescent Substance Abuse." In *Comprehensive Handbook of Psychotherapy: Integrative/Eclectic* (Vol. 4, pp. 133–61), eds. F. W. Kaslow and J. Lebow. New York: John Wiley & Sons.

Rychtarik, R. G., Carstensen, L. L., Alford, G. S., Schlundt, D. G., and Scott, W. O. 1988. "Situational Assessment of Alcohol-Related Coping Skills in Wives of Alcoholics." *Psychology of Addictive Behavior* 2:66–73.

SAMHSA: Substance Abuse and Mental Health Services Administration—Department of Health and Human Services. 2002. *Results from the 2002 National Survey on Drug Use and Health: National Findings.* Retrieved October 15, 2004, from http://www.samhsa.gov/oas/oasftp.htm

Santisteban, D. A., Coatsworth, J. D., Briones, E. and Szapocznik, J. 2002. *Investigating the Role of Acculturation, Familism and Parenting Practices in Hispanic Youth Behavior Problems.* Manuscript submitted for publication.

Santisteban, D. A., Coatsworth, J. D., Perez-Vidal, A., Mitrani, V., Jean-Gilles, M., and Szapocznik, J. 1997. "Brief Structural Strategic Family Therapy with African American and Hispanic High Risk Youth: A Report of Outcome." *Journal of Community Psychology* 25(5):453–71.

Sayers, S. L., and Heyman, R. E. 2003. "Behavioral Couples Therapy." In

Textbook of Family and Couple Therapy (pp. 461–500), eds. G. P. Sholevar and L. D. Schwoeri. Washington, DC: American Psychiatric Publishing.

Scaturo, D. J., Hayes, T., Sagula, D., and Walter, T. 2000. "The Concept of Codependency and Its Context within Family Systems Theory." *Family Therapy* 27(2):63–70.

Schmidt, L. 1996. "Addressing Culture Issues in Treatment." *Addiction Letter* 12(5):3–5.

Sheridan, M. J., and Green, R. G. 1993. "Family Dynamics and Individual Characteristics of Adult Children of Alcoholics." *Journal of Social Service Research* 17(1/2):73–97.

Springer, D. W., and Orsbon, S. H. 2002. "Families Helping Families: Implementing a Multifamily Therapy Group with Substance-Abusing Adolescents." *Health & Social Work* 27(3):204–07.

Straus, M. A. 1979. "Measuring Intrafamily Conflict and Violence: The Conflict Tactics (CT) Scale. *Journal of Marriage and Family* 41:75–88.

Sue, D. W., and Sue, D. 1990. *Counseling the Culturally Different: Theory and Practice,* 2nd edition. New York: John Wiley & Sons, Inc.

Szapocznik, J., Rio, A., Murray, E., Cohen, R., Scopetta, M. A., Rivas-Vasquez, A., et al. 1989. "Structural Family Versus Psychodynamic Child Therapy for Problematic Hispanic Boys." *Journal of Consulting & Clinical Psychology* 57(5):571–78.

Szapocznik, J., Robbins, M. S., Mitrani, V. B., Santisteban, D. A., Hervis, O., and Williams, R. A. 2002. "Brief Strategic Family Therapy." In *Comprehensive Handbook of Psychotherapy* (Vol. 4), ed. J. Lebow. New York: John Wiley & Sons.

Thomas, E. J., Yoshioka, M. R., and Ager, R. D. 1996. "Spouse Enabling of Alcohol Abuse: Conception, Assessment and Modification." *Journal of Substance Abuse* 8:61–80.

U.S. Department of Health and Human Services. 2001. *Youth Violence: A Report to the U.S. Surgeon General.* Rockville, MD: U.S. Department of Health and Human Services, Substance Abuse and Mental Health Services Administration, Center for Mental Health, National Institutes of Health, National Institute of Mental Health.

U.S. Department of Health and Human Services Best Practice Initiative. 2002. *Multidimensional Family Therapy for Adolescent Substance Abuse.* Retrieved October 15, 2004, from http://phs.os. dhhs.gov/ophs/BestPractice/mdft_ miami.htm

U.S. Department of Health and Human Services Best Practice Initiative Substance Abuse and Mental Health Services Administration. n.d.. *SAMHSA Model Programs.* Retrieved October 15, 2004, from http://modelprograms.samhsa.gov/template.cfm?CFID = 15247&CFTOKEN = 81035307

Wagner, E. F., Waldron, H. B., and Feder, A. B. 2001. "Alcohol and Drug Abuse." In *Handbook of Conceptualization and Treatment of Child Psychopathology* (pp. 329–52), eds. H. Orvaschel, J. Faust, and M. Hersen. New York: Pergamon.

Weiss, R. L., and Cerreto, M. C. 1980. "The Marital Status Inventory: Development of a Measure of Dissolution Potential." *The American Journal of Family Therapy* 8:80–86.

Weiss, R. L., and Perry, B. A. 1983. "The Spouse Observation Checklist," In *A Sourcebook of Marriage and Family Assessment,* ed. E. E. Filsinger. Beverly Hills, CA: Sage.

Wynne, M. 1984. "Teenage Chemical Dependency Treatment." *Focus on Family and Chemical Dependency* 7(3):20–21.

Yama, M. F., Fogas, B. S., Teegarden, L. A., and Hastings, B. 1993. "Childhood Sexual Abuse and Parental Alcoholism: Interactive Effects in Adult Women." *American Journal of Orthopsychiatry* 63:300–305.

Yoshioka, M. R., Thomas, E. J., and Ager, R. D. 1992. "Nagging and Other Drinking Control Efforts of Spouses of Uncooperative Alcohol Abusers: Assessment and Modification." *Journal of Substance Abuse* 4:309–18.

Young, N. K., Wallace, V. R., and Garcia, T. 1992. "Developmental Status of Three- to Five-Year-Old Children Who Were Prenatally Exposed to Alcohol and Other Drugs." *School Social Work Journal* 16(2):1–15.

Evidence-Based Treatment during Separation and Divorce

CHAPTER 11

INTRODUCTION

Marital separation and the consequent disruption of family life are stressful and painful, even when the family's life together may have been painful and the separation had been earnestly sought. Both partners suffer, as do the children. Although there may be relief for the partners, and in some instances for the children, breakdown of family relations to the point of separation of family members is still seen and experienced as deviant because of the pain, loss, increased difficulty in relationships, and the new and unknown complexity of the ensuing years. Yet, because of its frequency and the fact that so many lives are affected, it is a family life experience that needs to be understood so that it can be normalized, perhaps even ritualized, in order to give people the means to cope when they come face to face with such a major transition in their lives. A massive amount of experience, research, and publication has been devoted to understanding the formation of families, giving guidance for that life transition. By comparison, relatively little guidance, and consequently little support, has been available for the transition out of the nuclear family group. People have been left to suffer and cope alone and on their own as best they could. Professionals have similarly been at a loss for knowledge and the best ways to help.

This chapter will be devoted only to the family during separation and divorce. This phase is a transitional crisis for the family in which psychological and social stresses place severe demands on individual adjustment and interpersonal relationships, and during which personal and social resources may be lacking. Within the dissolution phase, there are smaller identifiable phases, which we will describe in terms of their impact on family members. We will also suggest goals for treatment. Without doubt, research on what helps most, for what kinds of situations, and for which phase or dissolving family type is still in short supply.

Our overall objectives in working with dissolving family units are to help the couple achieve a successful psychic separation (emotional divorce) and to enable them to continue a positive parental role and relationship with their children. Achieving an understanding of how the relationship failed and defining the kind of relationship that had been dissatisfying to the partners can facilitate the detachment and also forestall the possibility that the ex-spouses will repeat a bad relationship with a new partner. In initial stages of treatment, reasons for breakup are put forth to justify it and put it in perspective.

Our emphasis is on situations in which the spouses decide for reasons of their own not to continue the marriage. Other circumstances prompting family breakup will not be part of our discussion, such as instances of physical or sexual abuse, which often result in the removal of the abuser or the victim of the abuse from the family.

POPULATION DESCRIPTION AND DEFINITIONS

Disruption of marital relationships, as well as separation of the partners and children to different residences, are increasingly facts of everyday life. Census data suggest that almost one-half of all first marriages end in divorce (U.S. Bureau of the Census, 2000). Four out of ten marriages are remarriages for one or both partners. Data also indicate that 20 percent of men and 22 percent of women are divorced. Family finances seem to play a large role in this: Two-parent families were more likely to break up if the father was unemployed, if both parents worked full time, or if the family was poor rather than nonpoor (U.S. Bureau of the Census, 2000). Divorce also has a negative impact on family economic well-being. Two-parent families typically have more economic resources than single-parent families because both parents are likely to work and contribute to the family income. In addition to affecting economic well-being, divorce also has negative effects on psychological, social, and physical well-being (Heatherington & Kelly, 2002). Marital discord is associated with a range of other problems, such as depression and alcohol abuse among parents, as well as conduct disorders and depression among children (Christensen & Heavey, 1999).

Causes of difficulty in marriage are many, but they do not always lead to complete breakdown of marital relationships and divorce. The combination of factors leading to a decision on the part of one or both partners to separate is not clear for marriages in general or often even for a particular marriage. The decision may be seen as the product of a formula that on one side of the equation includes the sum of dissatisfactions to be endured if one remained in the relationship minus the remaining satisfactions in the relationship. On the other side of the equation are the satisfactions to be gained by leaving minus the additional stresses that would come into play if one left the relationship. Some of the specific reasons for seeking divorce have been identified in various studies.

Subjects in a study by Kincaid and Caldwell (1995) cited emotional abuse, communication difficulties, and excessive demands most frequently as reasons for separation. Somewhat surprisingly, initiators of divorce did not have a larger support network for assistance in coping during this stressful phase, and non-initiators did not have more emotional support available to them than initiators.

Decisions to leave or stay in a relationship will also be affected by the cultural context of the couple or family. Broad social forces such as the changing place of women in society are factors in marital dissolution. Their entry into the work force, whether for reasons of financial necessity or personal gratification, as a factor draws attention to this larger picture. The position of women, their prerogatives and their power in the culture of which the spouses are a part, and the degree to which they are embedded in it will be factors in the decision process. In studies examining the reasons for divorce, men and women often differ in their reports (Amato & Previti, 2003). Kitson, Moir, and Mason (1992) found that women were more likely to initiate divorce and to report relational or emotional issues as the reason for divorce. Women are also more likely than men to report their spouse's negative behaviors, such as physical abuse, emotional abuse, neglect, and substance use, as reasons for divorce (Amato & Previti, 2003). Men are more likely to cite external factors, such as problems at work or difficulty with in-laws as a reason for divorce (Amato & Previti, 2003).

We do not suppose that in the foregoing material we have exhausted the discussion of reasons for divorce. The specific impact of each differing cause on the way the divorce proceeds remains to be understood for each situation. However, awareness of at least some of the reasons can give the social worker an idea of the issues the partners will bring to the help-seeking effort. Conceptually framing the specifics as role-image disparities and as a balancing of bonds of cohesiveness and bars to dissolution also provides the worker with a way of looking at the specifics. In some instances, the specific reasons will also influence the ease or difficulty with which the divorcing process flows.

ASSESSMENT ISSUES

Since many divorces occur within the first four years of marriage, several studies have focused on assessing a newly married couple's risk of divorce. These studies follow couples for several years after marriage to determine whether there were signs of future trouble at the beginning. In a longitudinal study of 128 couples, Gottman and associates (1998) found that the frequency of positive affect (humor, affection, interest, positive words) expressed by a newly married couple during 15 minutes of discussion about a problem in the marriage was the best predictor of marital satisfaction and stability. In a similar study observing 60 newly married couples, Rogge and Bradbury (1999) found that negative affect (e.g., criticism, complaining, contempt, and stonewalling) displayed during a brief interaction predicted unhappiness in the marriage four years later, and physical aggression predicted marital instability.

Huston and associates (2001) interviewed couples at the beginning of their marriages and followed up with the couples two years later. They found that couples who expressed less love for each other, more ambivalence, and less responsiveness were more likely to divorce early in the marriage. In a study of 127 couples, Kurdek (2002) found that newly married couples who expressed lower levels of liking and trusting a partner predicted quick separation, and decreases in levels of liking, loving, and trusting partners during the first four years of marriage predicted quick separations. Psychological distress at the beginning of the marriage or during the first four years of marriage also predicted quick separations. These studies indicate that therapists may be able to assess a newly married couple's risk for future relationship problems and separation.

Phases of Separation and Divorce

Couples experience various stages in the decision-making process that may ultimately lead to separation. In order to conduct a thorough assessment of a couple who is considering divorce, it is important to understand these phases a couple often experiences in making the decision to separate or divorce. The goals of treatment will be determined to some extent by the phase the couple is currently experiencing. Clinicians will need to know, for example, whether the couple has decided definitively to separate or divorce or whether they are still in the process of making that decision. Each phase may bring different emotions and stressors that require different treatment approaches. The stages described here are the predivorce phase, negotiating and restructuring, and the reestablishing phase.

Predivorce Phase   For most couples, the decision to divorce is difficult for many reasons, including cultural and religious views and family belief systems that discourage divorce. Couples often have mixed emotions about separating or divorcing each other because they may still be happy with some aspects of the relationship (Walsh, Jacob, & Simons, 1995). However intense the struggle for individuality has been, attachment to the spouse continues to affect the decision to separate and divorce. The remaining attachment can make separation difficult. Furthermore, one is never left unchanged by a relationship. Divorce is leaving part of the self behind, and that adds to the difficulty and stress of separation and divorce. Todorski (1995) attests to the importance of this in the helping process.

If the couple is in this phase, the clinician will need to assess the couple's commitment to the marriage to determine whether the goal of treatment will be to preserve the marriage or achieve separation. One or both partners in this phase may deny problems that exist in the marriage. They may also be engaged in compensatory activities to distract attention from marital problems. These activities could include spending excessive time on career activities or beginning an extramarital affair. Relationship alienation occurs when partners are no longer invested in the marriage and distance themselves from their partner. Partners may have great difficulty taking responsibility for the problems in the marriage and blame their spouse for the difficulties (Hackney & Bernard, 1990).

By the time some couples enter therapy, one of the partners may have already decided that divorce is the best option. Divorce is most often initiated by one of the partners rather than by mutual agreement. The individual may no longer be putting any effort into the relationship and may provoke their partner to end the relationship. A therapist needs to help couples avoid making abrupt decisions even though they may want to quickly put the task of separation or divorce behind them. One partner may expect the therapist to help them resolve their differences to save the marriage while the other partner wants to facilitate a separation. The therapist helps to clarify these expectations and collaborates with the couple to consider how to proceed through the separation and divorce process (Walsh et al., 1995).

Actual consideration of divorce is devastating for both partners. Intensity and difficulty vary. The initiator of the divorce may have handled many feelings and developed a fairly clear picture of what it was all going to be like before announcing intent, but for the abandoned spouse the announcement comes as a shock. "I am being rejected. I am a failure. You are being unfair. I am hurt. I am angry. You can't, you shouldn't do this to me. What have I done? What do you want me to do? Please stay! I'll do anything. Don't leave me alone." In any event, ambivalence runs high. Fighting alternates with clinging when the anxiety level engendered by the prospects of the future is raised or when self-confidence flags and doubts occur about whether this is really the best course to take. Grief is strong. Loss of the love relationship is no doubt central. An important someone no longer cares. Separation also means loss of familiar routines, familiar environment, and familiar associations outside the family with friends and kin. The experience is emptiness, with no prospect of filling it or the confidence that one would even know how to go about it, and loss of prospects, disruption of hopes and plans. It is losing an investment in the relationship and leaving a part of one's self. It is loss of an image of what might have been and of what one had waited for, the end of hope that what was desired will ever be attained.

Each spouse also begins at this stage to deal with feelings of badness and failure, with their sense of loss and with what lies ahead. They also begin to develop ways to present themselves to the outside world and to anticipate how friends and kin will respond to them. They begin to hear how the other is thinking about who will move, who will have the children, what their financial situation will be. All of these considerations enter the basic decision to be made at this stage about whether to stay together or to part.

There is also the loss of outside relationships for both spouses. Friends have often been friends of the couple, rather than of one or the other, and are uncertain how to relate, whether with sympathy or congratulations. They too feel a loss and tend to withdraw. Further, they are unwilling to be caught in taking sides. The latter may be less true for kin than for friends. It is not unknown for kin to side with their in-law rather than with blood relatives. All these losses serve to leave the parting couple with minimal sources of support at a time when support is most needed and could be most helpful.

One issue that arises during this decision-making stage is posed by the partner who has edged into another relationship and is ambivalent about giving up either the marriage or the extramarital affair. Continuation of the affair generates strong reaction in the spouse and needs to be dealt with by both. We have come to the conclusion that that is not a workable arrangement for therapy and that what is likely to be more productive in resolving the ambivalence and/or improving the marriage is for the partner to make a decision to work on the marriage and give up the other relationship. This may still lead to a resolution to terminate the marriage, but at least the effort will have been made. It also forestalls the feeling that not all alternatives have been tested. Suggestions that the third person be brought into the treatment are generally opposed.

When therapy has included individual sessions along with the conjoint ones, extramarital affairs, current or past, are sometimes revealed to the therapist but are unknown to the other spouse. Such secrets create a dilemma for therapists. How they are handled depends on what has been said about confidentiality and on the goals of the partners at the time the secret is revealed.

Negotiating and Restructuring   This phase begins when a couple has made the decision to divorce. In order to facilitate a healthy divorce process, couples must be able to communicate effectively and collaborate to make decisions about practical and financial issues associated with divorce, as well as a custody arrangement for children. The therapist must assess the couple's needs related to communication and problem solving in order to intervene appropriately. Work on emotional issues will have begun in the initial phase. The couple's efforts to arrive at a decision about dissolution of the marriage expose feelings of rejection, pain of loss, anxiety about the future, guilt over past behavior, feelings of inadequacy, and the hostility and anger directed at the other for being incompetent, irresponsible, or unfair.

Reestablishing Phase   By this time in the course of events the active steps of dissolution of the marriage have occurred. New households have been established, and the financial picture is fairly clear. The families are settling into a new life and continuing the task of recovery. Reports vary about the length of time involved, but periods of one to five years are mentioned. The first year following divorce can bring many emotional challenges because individuals are struggling with changes in their self-concept. Their marriage may have largely defined their sense of identity. They may experience mood swings of intense emotions, depression, rage, relief, and joy. The partner who initiated the divorce may have lingering feelings of guilt while their former partner harbors feelings of abandonment and betrayal. Many continue to feel attached to their former spouse and nostalgic about the relationship (Walsh et al., 1995).

Questions continue to arise about relationships with the ex-spouse and with one's own and the ex-spouse's family. Management of the children and the effects of the divorce on them are of ongoing concern. Movement to enter new relationships begins and with it new fears and doubts that the new relationship will repeat the old, that rejection may be experienced anew, that unwanted demands may be made. People often feel as if they are adolescents again when it comes to forming new relationships. They have questions about their identity, handling themselves socially, the rules of the dating game, and handling sexual matters.

Development of skills in management of everything that one now has to do is another aspect of the overall adjustment task. Depending on the person and who did what in the marriage, the individual may lack skills in such things as food preparation, caring for the car, or making minor repairs on the house. It is not only a matter of learning to get all these things accomplished but also a matter of not being overwhelmed by them.

Mitchell-Flynn and Hutchinson (1993) found that, for men, different problems took priority over the space of a year. At first, finances, social relationships, and loneliness were primary concerns. A year after the separation, there was a significant decrease in concern about loneliness and about the reactions of friends and relatives. Garvin, Kalter, and Hansell (1993) found that divorced women experienced more stressful events than a normative comparison sample and had more psychiatric symptoms and poorer social adjustment. The strongest mediating factor in their difficulties was their social support system.

Children in the Divorce Process

As divorce is difficult for the spouses, it is also hard on the children. Their short-term and long-term adjustment are affected by the level of stress and by how their parents handle their relationship to each other and to the children. We have noted earlier that, though the marriage ends, the family does not. The parenting relationship continues, and if both parents wish to continue a relationship with the children, they must learn to work together in doing so. To the extent that they can do so, the children's adjustment will be bettered.

Stress and tensions for children in divorcing families manifest themselves in anxiety, depression, and conduct disturbances. Many factors affect children's adjustment to the situation. A study by Lengua, Wolchick, and Braver (1995) identifies three groups of factors and looks at the contribution of each group on children's adjustment. The first set of factors, which they call the ontogenic system, are child variables: their age, sex, internal locus of control, and misconceptions about divorce. "Did I cause it? The family will get together again. It is mom's fault." Group two factors are microsystem variables: quality of parent-child relationship, parental conflict, social support from nonparent adults, and so forth. Group three variables (exosystem) are place of residence, change in residence and school, financial hardship, and the residential parent's own adjustment. The three sets altogether and sets two and three separately accounted for significant amounts of variance in the child's self-report of adjustment but not in the parents' report of child adjustment.

Many reports of child adjustment have been of white, middle-class children. Wolchick et al. (1993), using a similar set of variables, studied the reaction of poor inner-city children to divorce. Their sample was 51 percent Hispanic, 17 percent African American, 25 percent Caucasian, and 5.7 percent Native American. There were no significant differences between different ethnic groups. Children's adjustment was positively related to negative divorce events, for example, parents acting worried, missing visits, saying bad things about each other, hurting each other. One factor, fear of abandonment, also positively related to child adjustment. Beliefs involving maternal blame were marginally related. Not related were hope for reunification and paternal blame. Findings about divorce-related events, resident parent acting worried, nonresident parent missing a visit, parents arguing, parents saying bad things about each other, and beliefs about divorce replicate findings of previous studies of white, middle-class children.

Good father-child relationships following divorce are associated with good cognitive skills, fewer externalizing behaviors, and fewer internalizing symptoms. The amount of time a father spends with his child is predicted by the father's level of involvement with the child prior to separation. If the mother and father have a hostile relationship with each other, the father is less likely to be involved with his child after separation. Parents will need to constructively work through conflicts rather than expressing a great deal of hostility in order to improve their children's adjustment after separation or divorce. Having a good relationship with both the mother and father was associated with fewer internalizing symptoms, better social skills, and better cognitive competence (Whiteside & Becker, 2000).

Gardner (2002) discusses what he calls *parental alienation syndrome*, where the custodial parent uses psychological and verbal tactics like ongoing criticism and hostility to brainwash children and turn them against their noncustodial parent. The child then forms a coalition with the custodial parent against the noncustodial parent, and this creates dysfunction in the parent-child relationship system. He differentiates this problem from simple parental alienation, where a custodial parent may act as if he or she wants the noncustodial parent involved but continually undermines the relationship between the child and the noncustodial parent. In the latter case, the custodial parent may limit access, register false complaints, and even feign abuse of children. Such hostility from one parent toward another creates problems for children in divorcing families. Parental alienation is sometimes observed during custody negotiations or during court proceedings. It is important for social workers to hear both sides of any allegations made against a parent by another parent or a child, and to do a careful assessment using multiple sources of information to corroborate information. Be wary of being drawn into taking sides with one parent against another. Remember the old adages, "There are two sides to every story" and "It takes two to tangle." A parent can be very convincing about their side of the story, for example, because there are a lot of hurt and angry emotions involved in their own perceptions of what happened. It is important to be thoroughly trained in custody and court situations when working with divorcing families. See Chapter 12 on working with reconstituted families for more helpful information.

The context of the parent-child relationships is further important to consider when determining the effects of parental separation on the children. For example, the potential benefits of having the father spend a lot of time with his child after a separation is affected by the quality of their relationship. Children's adjustment is best when the father has frequent visits with the child and has a strong, positive relationship. In addition, the level of hostility between the parents affects child outcomes because it affects the amount of time the father is likely to spend with his child as well as the mother's parenting style (Whiteside & Becker, 2000).

Assessment instruments, such as the Dyadic Adjustment Scale and the Marital Satisfaction Inventory, can be helpful in assessing whether a couple is committed to staying together or wants to end the relationship. The Minnesota Multiphasic Personality Inventory is useful in assessing the personality profiles of the couple and can provide insight into why the couple is experiencing communication problems. Because individuals often experience depression during the separation and divorce process, depression measures, such as the Beck Depression Inventory and the Hamilton Rating Scale for Depression, can help clinicians assess the severity of depressive symptoms. When the couple has children, the clinician can assess whether the children's functioning and adjustment are affected by the marital difficulties using tools such as the Child Behavior Checklist. Information about these instruments is presented in Table 11.1.

EVIDENCE-BASED TREATMENT/BEST PRACTICES

After the clinician conducts a thorough assessment of the family, it should become clear which phase the couple is currently experiencing in the divorce process. The phase will help the clinician decide which interventions are most appropriate. The following section describes practices that can be used at each of the three phases described in the last section.

Predivorce Phase

As couples make the decision to divorce, they may express more negative feelings about the relationship. The therapist may need to help the couple discuss positive things about each other and the relationship. The therapist may ask, for example, about the strengths that they see in each other that will help them through this difficult time and about the ways they have been able to work together even though they would like to separate. It is helpful to ask the couple which aspects of the relationship will help them move forward and what they have learned from the experience (Walsh et al., 1995).

Table 11.1 | Assessment Instruments

Measure	Description	Reliability	Validity	Source
Dyadic Adjustment Scale	A 32-item questionnaire designed to measure the quality of a relationship.	Internal consistency reliability ranges from .75–.80 (Hunsley et al., 2001)	Content and concurrent validity (Hunsley et al., 2001)	Hunsley, Best, Lefebvre, & Vito, 2001
Marital Satisfaction Inventory	A 280-item questionnaire designed to measure distress, communication, problem solving, satisfaction with each other and children, and conflict over children.	Internal consistency reliability ranges from .97–.98 (Roach et al., 1981)	Concurrent and discriminant validity (Roach et al., 1981)	Snyder, 1981
Minnesota Multiphasic Personality Inventory-2 (MMPI-2)	Self-report measure of adult personality and psychopathology; can be administered to persons age 16 and older and requires an 8th-grade reading level.	Test-retest reliabilities range from .58–.92 (Butcher et al., 1989)	Evidence supports predictive validity (Grove et al., 2000)	Lubin, Larsen, & Matarazzo, 1984
The Beck Depression Inventory (BDI)	A 21-item self-administered questionnaire designed to measure depressive symptoms; age range: 13–80; time required: 5–10 minutes.	Test-retest reliability ranges from .48–.86	Content, discriminant, and convergent validity	Beck, Steer, & Brown, 1996
The Hamilton Rating Scale for Depression (HAMD)	A 17-item scale designed to measure the severity of depression symptoms.	Test-retest reliability ranges from .65–.96 (Kobac et al., 1990)	Concurrent and discriminant validity (Maier et al., 1988)	Hamilton, 1986
Child Behavior Checklist	A parent report form designed to measure strengths and problems in children between the ages of 4 and 18.	Internal consistency reliability ranges from .89–.96 (Joint Committee on Standards for Educational and Psychological Testing, 1999)	Evidence supports construct validity (Achenbach, 1981)	Achenbach, 1991

Once the decision to divorce has been made, the couple may face emotional turmoil because divorce causes them to re-examine and challenge their beliefs about themselves. The therapist can help couples explore and articulate the complex feelings about the relationship. They begin the process of seeing themselves as individuals rather than defining themselves in relation to their partner. During this stage of the divorce process, it is helpful for therapists to ask if the couple has ever faced a similar loss and discuss what they have learned from other losses they have experienced (Walsh et al., 1995).

Goals of treatment in the decision-making phase are to help the partners become clear about the nature of their relationship and whether there is any possibility that either partner could or would make the changes needed for the relationship to become satisfying. If one of the spouses has already decided to separate, the contact can demonstrate whether the decision can be reversed and/or help the other spouse to make a case for reversal or to accept the inevitable. Communication can be promoted in conjoint sessions that identify the issues and the capacity of the partners to respond to them. Each can evaluate the importance of the issues and the possibilities of change. Clients differ in their wishes for the conduct of the treatment sessions. Some simply want to hear what their spouses have to say or to have their spouses listen to what they have to say. Others seek more active help in resolving as well as in clarifying issues.

A general goal for all the succeeding phases of treatment is for a quality of emotional detachment that frees the partners from a need to continue to fight or blame or pressure each other to change, which eliminates their using the children as pawns or allies and which leaves them clear about their own contribution to the difficulties. Aside from the increase in individual well-being, the outcome should enable each partner to have a fairly clear understanding of the relationship and why it didn't work, thus reducing the likelihood of moving into another identical relationship, an oft-observed occurrence in our experience. Marek (1989) identifies similar goals such as increased self-understanding, a mourning of the now-disrupted relationship, a balanced view of the marriage, the ability of the partners to work together regarding the children, and a satisfactory resolution of terms of legal settlement.

Negotiating and Restructuring

Once the decision to separate and divorce has been made, the central task is to restructure the family. This means achieving an end to the marriage that is as constructive as possible and at the same time recognizing that a family continues to exist if children are involved, and making workable plans for that family. For constructive resolution for the children, and for themselves as well, the former spouses must achieve an ability to cooperate in responsible care for the children and in continuing their own separate relationships to them. Housing, financial support, property settlement, child custody, and visiting arrangements must all be negotiated.

Restructuring has an emotional and a rational, practical component. For the crisis of divorce to be resolved successfully, both components must be addressed. Rational planning and handling of reality matters cannot be completed if the emotional issues are unresolved. And unless reasonable plans are made, emotional tension will remain at a high level. Skill for assisting the couple with both aspects should be part of the social worker's repertoire, although, as we suggest later, referrals to mediators for financial and custody mediation may be useful.

Emotional Issues   Tension and anger levels may still be high. In some instances attacks, retaliatory behavior, and even suicide threats are made in efforts to keep the other bound to the relationship. These may be based on a concept of self as unlovable and unworthwhile, and a conviction that "no one else will ever want me." Limits on such behavior need to be set. Drawing attention to the incendiary results of threatening and get-even behavior may help. Interventions need to be designed to build confidence in self and one's ability to survive. By expressing interest and caring, praise for small achievements, and reassurance that the client is worthwhile, the worker helps to build such confidence. Teaching practical skills needed for survival, such as cooking, banking, or organizing, will not only aid survival but build confidence and hope as well.

Separate individual as well as conjoint sessions are useful to enable each spouse to express feelings and to be listened to and understood. Even though there may be cognitive recognition that the marriage is over, opportunity to mourn the loss, to consider one's own and the other's contributions to the breakdown of the marriage, and to let go of the relationship are provided in the treatment process. In this connection, it may be useful to wonder why the reluctant spouse is not more dissatisfied. Achieving an understanding of one's own behavior in the marriage and of the responses of the spouse should lead to an acceptance of self and a reasonable degree of toleration of the spouse, enough at least so that they do not continue efforts to fight and destroy each other and so that they do achieve the ability to cooperate on behalf of the children. Both partners should also gain a sense of their strengths and individual rights to enable them to put their feelings of inadequacy and guilt in some perspective. Hopefully each spouse will be able to acquire a greater sense of separateness and wholeness as a person as a result of these crisis resolution efforts and achievements. When couples have decided on a divorce, it is important that the therapist help couples take responsibility for the decision to divorce (Walsh et al., 1995).

Practical Matters   Resolving practical issues becomes easier as the treatment succeeds in diminishing anger, building self-respect, and achieving mutuality of conviction about the inevitability and advisability of divorce. The spouses, if at this phase one can still call them that, can begin to cooperate better in deciding who is to move and who is to stay, how to divide possessions, what degree of financial self-sufficiency is possible for each, and who will need the support of the other. Once a couple with children has decided to separate or divorce, it is important for the therapist to help the couple separate from each other and begin to live their lives as individuals but planning to maintain a relationship as parents (Hackney & Bernard, 1990). Good communication will make decisions about custody of the children and visiting rights easier.

When couples on their own are unable to resolve these issues and seek help for them, the worker's primary task is to elicit facts about what has been, what resources there are, and what the persons involved want to have happen. The information provided can suggest what the range of possibilities might be. While the acquisition of information may be difficult due to enduring anger and reluctance, an even greater difficulty lies in achieving agreements about all of these matters that are fair to all concerned. Workers need to be as attentive to the possibility that one or the other of the participants has been insufficiently assertive in stating expectations or making demands as to the possibility that the other has been overly demanding.

Reestablishing Phase

During this phase, the ex-spouses have the individual tasks of developing new lives for themselves and the joint task of coparenting. We will address the first of these tasks here and defer discussion of the coparenting tasks to the subsequent section on children.

The absence of rituals of induction into the divorced status has been frequently noted. Ceremonies to solemnize entry to marriage are deemed useful in assuring newlyweds of community consent and support. Such consent and support are markedly lacking for divorcing family members. Some couples, when both are convinced that divorce should occur, have made public announcement of the event in newspapers and even sponsored receptions to honor it. Lewis (1983) reports a variety of rituals that have been used, including religious ones to pronounce the end of a relationship and the commencement of a new life. While rituals may not be necessary or may not do the job, what does seem necessary in this day of dissolving marriages is the gaining of acceptance, support, encouragement, and direction for the new life ahead.

The emotional issues of the previous stages are still alive, though possibly less intense. Working through positive and negative feelings continues. Self-doubt and guilt, and feelings of loss and rejection continue to surface but are put into perspective by increasing acceptance of self and more or less successful adaptation. Emotional release and cognitive restructuring facilitate this process. Coping with loneliness and the absence of another adult are added to the stress of this period.

One of the first issues the parents must resolve is custody and domicile for the children. Unfortunately, in early stages of the dissolution, children can become objects for barter. "If you leave, I'll keep the children and you won't get to see them." Or, when anger is strong, "You are not a fit parent, and I will see that you don't get them." Children can get drawn into taking sides.

They can also come to feel that they are the cause of their parents' problems with each other and that they are not really wanted.

In the past, custody of the children was usually acquired or assigned to one parent or the other. Most generally in recent times, this has been the mother, though fathers are increasingly seeking it. Legal custody means that the parent to whom custody is assigned has all rights and responsibilities for the child (Bernstein, 1982) and that the noncustodial parent has none, except for the privilege of visitation and the responsibility of support or whatever else is granted by a custody agreement or court decree. Joint custody means that responsibility is shared and that contact between the parents over many issues will need to be frequent. Though it does not differ greatly in outward appearance from single-parent custody with extensive visitation rights for the other parent, it is increasingly sought and agreed to by both parents.

Divorce and custody issues can have a profound effect on children's relationships with their parents. Research indicates that children's relationships with the nonresidential parent are less close after marital dissolution. Children experience significant declines in affective ties and involvement with the non-residential parent as well as declines in parental supervision (Videon, 2002).

Research often favors joint custody over sole custody because the child benefits from an ongoing relationship with both parents. However, an ongoing conflictual relationship between parents can harm children. In these cases, researchers favor sole custody arrangements. Several factors can affect children's adjustment, including the loss of a parent, conflict between parents, and diminished parenting quality from the custodial parent (Buchanan, Maccoby, & Dornbush, 1996). In cases in which the mother has sole custody, the reduced supervision, financial resources, and a smaller social network all can have a negative effect on children's adjustment. Amato and Gilbreth (1999) conducted a meta-analysis of studies examining the father's role in children's well-being after divorce and found that an authoritative parenting style and a close father-child relationship predicted better well-being in children (Bauserman, 2002). In Bauserman's (2002) meta-analysis of custody and its effect on children's adjustment, children in joint custody were better adjusted than those in sole-custody arrangements. A commonly held belief is that mothers may experience joint custody as a loss of control and may report that children benefit more from sole custody. However, Bauserman (2002) found that mothers, as well as fathers, reported that children were better adjusted when both parents had custody.

Farmer and Galaris (1993) report that support groups for children serve an important function in lessening the negative effects of the divorce process on them. These treatment groups can help children to acknowledge the reality of the marital rupture; to disengage from the parental conflict; to resume normal pursuits; to resolve their loss, anger, and self-blame; to accept the permanency of the divorce; and to achieve a realistic hope regarding future relationships and to become willing to take a chance on loving and closeness.

Clinicians can be helpful to divorced individuals who remarry by facilitating resolution of emotional attachment to the former spouse. They can help families form flexible boundaries so that children from the previous marriage can maintain a relationship with both parents. Parental roles may be different in the new marriage because the partners may each have to take primary responsibility for children from their previous marriage, and financial responsibilities may be more equally shared. Emotional issues can make it difficult to maintain permeable boundaries for children because a parent may feel threatened when a child forms a relationship with a stepparent. Children may experience confusion and worries that they will hurt a parent by spending time with a stepparent as well. When working with remarried families on issues that concern the children, it is often important to invite both parents as well as the stepparent. Remarried families face many challenges in defining family roles and determining when and where children spend their time. The remarriage may also trigger painful emotions that were never resolved from the previous divorce. Individuals may have difficulty forming a strong attachment to a new partner (Walsh et al., 1996).

Little research has examined effective treatment approaches for separating and divorcing couples. Much more research has examined therapies that effectively help couples at the predivorce stage communicate more effectively and problem solve. Since effective communication and low hostility are important during divorce as well as in marriage, some of these approaches can be helpful as well for couples who are separated or divorced. Cooperation between parents not only benefits the children but the parents as well, because it ameliorates negative feelings about the spouse during the divorce process and can, therefore, result in better adjustment after the divorce (Ehrenberg, Hunter, & Elterman, 1996).

Three treatment approaches that have growing empirical support include emotionally focused therapy, cognitive behavioral couple therapy, and behavioral marital therapy. Some of these treatments may be more effective than others during different phases of separation and divorce (Bertoli, 2002). Emotionally focused couple therapy, developed by Greenberg and Johnson (1988), is based on attachment theory. Problems in the relationship are defined as a failure to provide a secure attachment base for one or both of the partners. This disruption in attachment results in the couple expressing strong emotional reactions to each other's behavior. The therapist works to process the emotional experience of each partner and restructure patterns of interaction. They expose the emotional reactions the couple experiences and helps them develop new ways of interacting that result in stronger attachment. A few studies suggest that this approach improves relationship quality (Dunn & Schwebel, 1995).

Emotionally Focused Therapy

Emotionally focused therapy (EFT) assumes that negative interaction cycles result from feelings of fear of losing their primary attachment object. Because of this fear, couples often become entangled in destructive ways of communicating, like withdrawing or attacking, being overly rational, discounting the partner's concerns, or criticizing. EFT leads couples through a process of (1) identifying their own core emotions, (2) communicating those emotions (thereby letting go of the less destructive ways of communicating), (3) understanding and taking responsibility for how their communication evokes responses in their partners, such as anger or withdrawal, and (4) restructuring their interactions to be more genuine and vulnerable because of the renewed safety of the relationship (Greenberg & Johnson, 1988).

Johnson and Greenberg (1995) do not recommend this therapy for separating couples because it aims to make the primary attachment more secure. It is more appropriate for people who seek to maintain or reestablish primary attachment with each other. The therapist typically begins by working with each adult separately for approximately three sessions. The therapist helps the client identify underlying emotions, see interactional patterns, and take responsibility for each person's part in the pattern and the emotions she or he evokes in the other person. The therapist then works with the couple together for four to six sessions at two-week intervals. The children are included in two to three sessions, during which parents allow the children to experience their new way of interacting. Children express their feelings and concerns to their parents (Johnson & Greenberg, 1995).

Cognitive Behavior Couple Therapy

Cognitive behavior couple therapy is another approach that has been evaluated in many studies. Cognitive restructuring is used to change harmful cognitions. Clients may be taught to logically analyze their communication patterns, and the therapist will often ask for concrete evidence supporting partners' complaints about each other to challenge their perceptions. Clinicians help spouses to consider alternative reasons for their partner's behavior. The couple may also be asked to reevaluate their standards for marriage. These cognitive strategies are often used in conjunction with behavioral marital therapy techniques described next (Baucom et al., 1998).

Behavioral Marital Therapy

Behavioral marital therapy (BMT) is another treatment approach that is helpful during marital dissolution. BMT assumes that marital satisfaction and distress can be reinforced behaviorally and that couples are satisfied in a relationship if the reinforcement they receive in a relationship is greater than the amount of perceived punishment. BMT attempts to increase the reinforcement and minimize punishment couples receive from each other by teaching new communication and problem-solving skills. Communication skills training emphasizes the importance of expressing emotion without blaming or accusing the partner. Couples also learn how to clearly and explicitly define problems.

BMT assumes there is a discrepancy between intention and impact. A dysfunctional exchange may take place between spouses when a verbal message or behavior is received and given a different meaning than was intended.

Distress may result from a client's perception of the problem or attribution of blame that results in cognitive distortion, such as overgeneralizations or assumptions of malevolent intent. Spouses' expectations regarding their ability to bring about a particular outcome are considered to have a great bearing on attributional conclusions reached and subsequent actions taken to minimize conflict. Expectations are considered to be significant active ingredients in cognitive processing, leading to effective marital problem solving and change. Marital partners make assumptions regarding human functioning. The cognitive restructuring of ill-founded assumptions may be indicated to reduce marital conflict.

BMT employs explicitly stated goals for the couple and fosters collaboration in forming a treatment plan and acceptance by each partner that the marital problems are interactional. This acceptance is necessary for effective engagement in couple treatment. The therapist also promotes positive expectancies and creates homework assignments for the couple. The therapy consists of behavioral and cognitive restructuring components. The behavioral treatment engages the clients in positive tracking and control of behavior, training in communication and problem solving, and contingency contracting. Cognitive restructuring involves modifying information processing errors and other cognitive distortions, such as absolutistic and dichotomous thinking, selective abstraction, arbitrary inference (mind reading, negative prediction), magnification and minimization, personalization, and faulty interpretation (Granvold & Jordan, 1994). This approach has been evaluated in more that two dozen clinical trials, which support its effectiveness in helping couples resolve conflict. Positive outcomes obtained in these trials typically lasted for over one year following participation in the intervention (Christensen & Heavey, 1999).

The meta-analyses that have been conducted on couples treatment show that all of these approaches result in improvements in the relationship. However, the analyses do not demonstrate that any one of the approaches is significantly better than the other (Christensen & Heavey, 1999). Table 11.2 displays a list of studies evaluating these approaches along with relevant meta-analyses.

TREATMENT MANUAL

Jacobson and Holtzworth-Monroe (1986) present the following treatment protocol for practicing behavior marital therapy. See Table 11.3 for examples of evidence-based treatment manuals that can be helpful in work with couples.

Assessment

The therapist conducts a comprehensive assessment that emphasizes communication and problem solving. The assessment process includes using assessment tools, such as those described earlier in the chapter. The therapist asks questions designed to assess the couple's strengths and problem areas. Questions

Table 11.2 | Research Studies

Behavioral Marital Couple Therapy	Cognitive Behavioral Couple Therapy	Emotionally Focused Couple Therapy	Meta-Analyses
Baucom and Lester (1986) evaluated cognitive strategies combined with behavioral marital therapy and found that participating couples experienced improvements in communication, adjustment, and presenting problems when compared to those who received no treatment.	Baucom and Lester (1986). See description in previous column.	Goldman and Greenberg (1992) compared emotionally focused therapy and behavioral marital therapy and found that they were equally effective in improving couples' adjustment.	Dunn and Schwebel (1995) conducted a meta-analysis of couples therapy that found cognitive behavioral and behavioral couple therapy approaches to be effective.
Baucom, Sayers, and Sher (1990) compared behavioral marital therapy and cognitive restructuring and found that both treatment conditions resulted in improvements in communication and adjustment when compared with those receiving no treatment.	Baucom et al. (1990). See description in previous column.	James (1991) found that couples receiving emotionally focused therapy improved marital adjustment.	Hahlweg and Markman (1988) conducted a meta-analysis of 17 studies of behavioral couple therapy and found the approach to be effective.
Bennun (1985) compared conjoint, group, and individual behavioral marital therapy conditions and found that all conditions were effective in reducing marital distress.	Emmelkamp et al. (1988). See description in previous column.	Johnson and Greenberg (1985) found that emotionally focused therapy was superior to behavioral marital therapy in reducing couples' distress.	Shadish et al. (1993) conducted a meta-analysis of 163 clinical trial studies of family and marital psychotherapies and compared the effectiveness of many different approaches in addressing a wide range of problems.

Emmelkamp, et al. (1988) found that both behavioral marital therapy and cognitve therapy improved couples' adjustment.

Snyder and Willis (1989) found that behavioral marital therapy and insight-oriented therapy were both effective in reducing distress for couples. Wilson, Bornstein, and Wilson (1988) found that both conjoint and group behavioral marital therapy conditions resulted in decreased distress for couples.

Halford, Sanders, and Behrens (1993) compared behavioral marital therapy with cognitive restructuring and found that both improved couple's adjustment when compared with those receiving no treatment.

Walker et al. (1996) found that couples caring for a chronically ill child who received emotionally focused therapy experienced less distress than couples who received no treatment.

Table 11.3 | Treatment Manuals

Manual Reference	Author's Contact Information
Jacobson, N. S., and Margolin, G. 1979. *Marital Therapy: Strategies Based on Social Learning and Behavior Exchange Principles.* New York: Brunner/Mazel.	unavailable
Jacobson, N. S., and Christensen, A. 1996. *Acceptance and Change in Couple Therapy: A Therapist's Guide to Transforming Relationships.* New York: W. W. Norton & Co.	http://www.psych.ucla.edu/Faculty/Christensen/
Baucom, D. H., and Epstein, N. 1990. *Cognitive-Behavioral Marital Therapy.* New York: Brunner/Mazel.	http://www.unc.edu/depts/clinpsy/fachp/baucom. html
Gottman, J. M. 1995. *The Marital Clinic.* New York: W. W. Norton & Co.	http://www.gottman.com/
Johnson, S. M. 1996. *The Practice of Emotionally Focused Marital Therapy: Creating Connection.* New York: Brunner-Mazel.	http://www.sciencessociales.uottawa.ca/psy/eng/profdetails.asp?login = sjohnson
Halford, W. K., and Markman, H. J. 1997. *Clinical Handbook of Marriage and Couples Interventions.* Chichester, UK: John Wiley & Sons, Inc.	http://www.gu.edu.au/school/psy/

often encourage the partners to discuss the positive aspects of the relationship. Thus, the assessment process itself can have therapeutic benefits for the couple.

Roundtable Discussion

Following assessment, the therapist presents a description of the problems the couple is facing, the couple's strengths, and a treatment plan. The therapist and couple agree on specific treatment goals. The session is highly structured and the therapist takes a directive role in the process. The therapist interrupts, for example, when couples deviate from discussing the behaviors that are consistent with the goal of the session.

Instigation of Increases in Positive Behavior

The therapist directs the couple to make immediate changes designed to increase the amount of positive behavior exchanges. The therapist instigates change by inducing a collaborative discussion and encouraging compliance with homework assignments. In order to induce the couple's collaboration, the therapist asks the couple to commit to proceeding with the assumption that the therapist's model of therapy is correct, and they commit to collaboration, compromise, and change.

The therapist induces the couple to comply with homework assignments by choosing appropriate assignments, provide clear rationales for tasks, and asking partners to commit to completing tasks in the homework assignments. When couples do not comply with homework assignments, the therapist typically tells the couple that they cannot proceed with the planned agenda for the therapy session because the homework has not been completed. Instead, the discussion is focused on the noncompliance and how they can work to resolve problems associated with completing the assignment.

Skill Acquisition

Most of the time spent in BMT sessions is devoted to learning new communication and problem-solving skills. It is important that the therapist begin teaching skills using neutral topics so that couples can focus on the new techniques rather than becoming too emotionally involved in the topic of discussion. The therapist teaches communication and problem-solving skills, and the couple rehearses the new skills with each other. In teaching new skills, the therapist takes a directive role and uses psychoeducation in structured sessions to teach the new skills, always providing specific examples and repeating important ideas frequently. The therapist also provides feedback when couples practice behaviors. The couple may also be asked to summarize the content of the therapy session and state the important principals they have learned. Listening and expressing feelings are important communication skills included in this phase of treatment. The therapist teaches clients to share feelings in a supportive, understanding way. In learning listening skills, clients practice paraphrasing, reflecting, and validating each other's feelings. The therapist also teaches clients nonverbal communication skills, such as expressing interest with facial expressions and using eye contact.

Couples also learn to adopt discrete roles of either listener or speaker. The listeners quietly listen, expressing interest, and do not interrupt the speaker. After the couple learns listening skills, the therapist teaches expressive skills. Expressive skills include using "I" statements, such as statements that begin with "The way I see it," or "I feel that . . ." These statements communicate that each person's views are subjective and can differ from another's views.

Another commonly used communication technique is being specific and positive when asking the partner to change a behavior. One partner could say, for example, "If you were to pick up the kids from school tomorrow, I would feel supported." Couples also need to learn how to say no in a positive way when they are unable to meet their partner's request. The therapist teaches couples these skills and models them. Clients are then asked to rehearse these behaviors, and the therapist assigns homework assignments so the couple can practice newly learned behaviors at home.

Problem-solving and conflict resolution training are typically taught after the couple has practiced the communication skills just described. The couple is taught that they should express appreciation for their partner before discussing a problem. For example, one partner may say to the other, "I really appreciate that you helped with the laundry yesterday, although I did become frustrated that you did not put your clothes away."

Problems are identified in specific behavioral terms without using labels. For example, instead of saying, "You are so inconsiderate to come home late without calling to let me know," the couple would learn to say, "When you work late, you often forget to call and let me know." Couples are also taught to use expressions of feeling when discussing problems. They may rehearse using expressions such as, "I feel angry and anxious when you come home late without calling."

After defining the problem using these techniques, the couple collaborates to define a solution to the problem. One technique involves brainstorming about possible solutions. The couple verbalizes all ideas that come to mind without evaluating or censoring them. They then create a list of solutions that is used to create a behavioral contract. The couple goes through the list and eliminates those that seem completely unreasonable, and then discuss all remaining ideas on the list. They think about whether each idea would help solve the problem, as well as the benefits and costs to each spouse. At the end of this process, the couple should be left with the most feasible ideas for solving the problem and can form a written contract that outlines specific behavioral goals. Each partner signs the contract and agrees to reassess the contract at a future date and time.

Generalization and Maintenance

During this phase of treatment, the therapist becomes less directive in an effort to encourage the couple to use the newly acquired skills independently. The therapist encourages ongoing maintenance of newly learned behaviors by gradually increasing the length of time between therapy sessions and holding booster sessions to practice skills after treatment is completed.

CASE EXAMPLE

The following case depicts a session of behavioral marital therapy dedicated to teaching communication skills to a couple that has made the decision to separate.

SOCIAL WORKER: As you know, we have identified some problems in communication that we would like to work on together in this session. In the last session, Carla, you told me that you were upset because you did not feel that Jim was helping enough with caring for the children. You said you were worried that with the separation, the problem could become worse.

CARLA: Yes, and you know we had a problem this week that is a perfect example. Jim was supposed to pick up the kids from school, and he called me at the last minute to tell me about a lunch meeting that went really late and that he would not be able to pick up the kids. I had to leave my job early to pick them up. It was so inconsiderate and unthoughtful.

JIM: You know I can't control whether my meeting went late. My boss was there along with a lot of other important people, and I just couldn't walk out. It would have looked really bad.

CARLA: Well, it's clear that the people you work with are more important to you than your own children.

SOCIAL WORKER: I'm going to stop you both now. Carla, do you know why I interrupted you?

CARLA: Because I'm getting very upset.

SOCIAL WORKER: I want you to talk about the problem and how it made you feel. When we include negative adjectives and labels, it makes it hard for others to hear what we are saying because it stirs up a lot of emotion. Why don't you try telling Jim about this same situation, but don't use any adjectives to describe him or the problem. I don't want you to say "inconsiderate" or "unthoughtful" this time. Instead, just give me the facts. What happened, and how did it make you feel?

CARLA: Jim, you called at the last minute to tell me that you could not pick up the kids from school. This made me feel that the kids and I are not important to you.

SOCIAL WORKER: Jim, would you like to respond to what Carla is saying?

JIM: I understand why she is upset.

SOCIAL WORKER: I'm just going to interrupt to ask you to address yourself to Carla instead of me.

JIM: Carla, I understand why you are upset. I am sorry that I called you at the last minute. That is the first time I have called because a meeting went late, and I will try to make sure it doesn't happen again.

SOCIAL WORKER: You are both doing a great job of talking about the problem without using negative labels. Carla, you have communicated exactly the behavior that you see as a problem and explained that it made you feel unimportant. Jim, you also did a good job of responding to those feelings.

JIM: It still worries me because I need to feel that it is okay to call Carla to step in if I'm in a difficult situation and not have her become so upset.

CARLA: Well, the problem is that you do things like that a lot. I know this is the first time that you called because a lunch meeting went over, but you will often be late when you say you'll be coming to pick up the kids and take them out. I need to know that I can count on you.

JIM: Now you're exaggerating a bit, don't you think? When was the last time I was late?

CARLA: Just last Saturday, you were supposed to take the kids to a movie and you ended up coming too late for the movie. You just took them out to eat. That was very hurtful.

SOCIAL WORKER: Carla, I'm going to interrupt you. Do you know why?

CARLA: Because I said he was hurtful. I know that's a label, but that's really how I feel.

SOCIAL WORKER: I mentioned the "I" statements in our last session. Instead of using a negative label for Jim's behavior, you can use an "I" statement to communicate how the situation made you feel. That can make it easier for Jim to hear what you're saying and understand the effect of his behavior rather than feeling that he has to defend himself. "I" statements begin with "I feel . . . ," something like that.

CARLA: I feel very hurt when Jim lets the kids down.

SOCIAL WORKER: Can you tell Jim exactly the behavior that makes you feel that way?

CARLA: Yes, I feel hurt when Jim comes to see the kids later than he said he would. I think it disappoints the kids, even though they are really excited to see him.

SOCIAL WORKER: You did that very well, Carla. You explained exactly the behavior that upsets you and how it makes you feel. Sometimes it can help to say something positive about Jim before telling him about the problem. For example, saying something like, "I really appreciate the time you spend with the kids, although it hurts me when you come late," can help Jim hear what you're saying. Can you think of something positive you can add to your statement?

CARLA: Yes, I do really appreciate that you are so good with the kids, Jim.

SOCIAL WORKER: Can you be more specific?

CARLA: I really appreciate how you give your undivided attention to the kids when you come to visit. You usually stay a little longer than you say you will, and I notice that you won't answer your cell phone when you're with the kids. I really appreciate that even though it does hurt me when you arrive later than you promised you would be there.

SOCIAL WORKER: Carla, you did a wonderful job of explaining what you appreciate along with the problem as you see it. Jim, could you summarize what you heard Carla say? This willl help her know that you are listening to her.

JIM: Carla, I understand that you feel hurt when I arrive late for my visits with the kids. I apologize for being late, but I really think you are being unreasonable. Sometimes things come up. I may be a little late sometimes.

SOCIAL WORKER: Jim, when you call Carla unreasonable, that might make it difficult for her to listen to the important things that you say after that. Can you use an "I" statement to rephrase what you just said?

JIM: I feel anxious and frustrated about Carla's expectation that I always be on time, especially when things are not always in my control.

SOCIAL WORKER: Could you be more specific?

JIM: Well, I feel frustrated that Carla would be upset when I am late because an important meeting lasted longer than I expected.

SOCIAL WORKER: Jim, you did a good job of showing Carla that you heard what she said by reflecting her words back to her. You also were able to express your feelings without using negative labels, and you explained exactly the type of situation that makes you feel that way. You have both shown a lot of progress in your communication skills. In the next session, we will explore some solutions to the problem we have been discussing. In the meantime, I would like to give you a homework assignment. Every time you talk about this issue during the next week, I want you to use an "I" statement. Also, write down any negative labels that you hear each other say and, next to it, write an "I" statement that could replace it. I would like for you to bring this list of labels and "I" statements to our next meeting.

SUMMARY

Family dissolution is an increasingly common phenomenon. Because it has been considered a deviant form in the family life cycle, there are no firm pathways for the participants to follow to guide and support them through it. But because it is so common, it is important to understand what happens and what is needed for all family members to survive the process and make post-dissolution adjustment as successful as possible.

The time span between marital dissatisfaction and post-divorce adjustment may be seen in three phases. The predivorce phase focuses on the decision to continue or end the marriage. Treatment may begin with an effort to rescue the marriage and end in this phase with a decision to separate and divorce. A restructuring phase centers on the planning needed to reorganize the family, who is to move or to stay, where the children will go, what the financial situation will be, and what each parent's relationship to the children will be like. A resettlement phase completes the work of resolving all the issues raised in the dissolution and the work of developing an ongoing lifestyle.

Divorce is a crisis for family members and engenders great emotional pain for them. Coping with the crisis is facilitated by enabling family members to handle their emotions and to achieve a cognitive grasp on what is needed to reorganize their lives. Personal and interpersonal issues must be dealt with through all phases of the crisis. Individual goals for the adults are to achieve a constructive dissolution of the marriage in as humane a way as possible and to enable them to regain their self-respect and confidence so that they can build their future lives as stronger and more capable persons. While ending the marriage constructively is necessary, it is also necessary, if there are children, to enable the ex-spouses to develop and continue a constructive coparenting relationship because the family of parents and children continues to exist. Success in achieving a constructive divorce is crucial for the subsequent adjustment of the ex-spouses. Their ability to be constructive also enables better adjustment of the children.

Substantial numbers of divorcing spouses do seek treatment at some point during the divorce process. Children are brought to treatment less frequently during the divorce process, but from knowledge gained about children from divorcing families who have been brought to treatment, it is clear that the divorce has not been adequately handled in their adjustment. Individual treatment has in the past been seen as the treatment method of choice for the divorce process. We have taken the position that in the predivorce decision-making phase and in the restructuring phase, conjoint family sessions can be very useful. In addition, particularly during the restructuring and resettlement phases, support groups for the adults and for the children have been shown to be helpful in facilitating change.

References

Achenbach, T. M. 1999. *Manual for the Child Behavior Checklist/4-18 and 1991 Profile*. Burlington, VA: University of Vermont Department of Psychiatry.

Amato, P. R., and Gilbreth, J. G. 1999. "Non-Resident Fathers and Children's Wellbeing: A Meta-Analysis." *Journal of Marriage and the Family* 61:557–73.

Amato, P. R., and Previti, D. 2003. "People's Reasons for Divorcing: Gender, Social Class, the Life Course, and Adjustment." *Journal of Family Issues* 24:602–26.

Baucom, D. H., and Lester, G. W. 1986. "The Usefulness of Cognitive Restructuring as an Adjunct to Behavioral Marital Therapy." *Behavior Therapy* 17:385–403.

Baucom, D. H., Sayers, S. L., and Sher, T. G. 1990. "Supplementing Behavioral Marital Therapy with Cognitive Restructuring with Emotional Expressiveness Training." *Journal of Consulting and Clinical Psychology* 58:636–45.

Baucom, D. H., Shoham, V., Mueser, K. T., Dajuto, A. D., and Stickle, T. R. 1998. "Empirically Supported Couple and Family Interventions for Marital Distress and Adult Mental Health Problems." *Journal of Consulting and Clinical Psychology* 66(1):53–88.

Bauserman, R. 2002. "Child Adjustment in Joint-Custody Versus Sole-Custody Arrangements: A Meta-Analytic Review." *Journal of Family Psychology* 16(1): 91–102.

Beck, A. T., Steer, R. A., and Brown, G. K. 1996. *Manual for the Beck Depression Inventory*. 2nd edition. San Antonio, TX: The Psychological Corporation.

Bennun, I. 1985. "Behavioral Marital Therapy: An Outcome Evaluation of Conjoint, Group, and One Spouse Treatment." *Scandinavian Journal of Behavior Therapy* 14:157–68.

Bernstein, B. 1982. "Understanding Joint Custody Issues." *Social Casework* 63(3):179–81.

Bertoli, J. M. 2002. "The Use of Neuro-Linguistic Programming and Emotionally Focused Therapy with Divorcing Couples in Crisis." In *Brief Treatments for the Traumatized: A Project of the Green Cross Foundation: Contributions in Psychology,* ed. C. R. Figley. Westport, CT: Greenwood Press/Greenwood Publishing Group, Inc.

Buchanan, C. M., Maccoby, E. E., and Dornbush, S. M. 1996. *Adolescents after Divorce*. Cambridge, MA: Harvard University Press.

Butcher, J. N., Dahlstrom, W. G., Graham, J. R., Tellegen, A., and Kraemmer, B. 1989. *Minnesota Multiphasic Personality Inventory-2 (MMPI-2): Manual for Administration and Scoring*. Minneapolis: University of Minnesota Press.

Christensen, A., and Heavey, C. L. 1999. "Interventions for Couples." *Annual Review of Psychology* 50:165–90.

Dandeneau, R. J., and Johnson, S. M. 1994. "Facilitating Intimacy: Interventions and Effects." *Journal of Marital and Family Therapy* 20:17–33.

Dunn, R. L., and Schwebel, A. I. 1995. "Meta-Analytic Review of Marital Therapy Outcome Research." *Journal of Family Psychology* 9:58–68.

Ehrenberg, M. F., Hunter, M. A., and Elterman, M. F. 1996. "Shared Parenting Arrangements after Marital Separation: The Roles of Empathy and Narcissism." *Journal of Consulting and Clinical Psychology* 64(4):808–18.

Emmelkamp, P. M. G., van Linden den Heivell, C., Ruphan, M., Sanderman, R., Scholing, A., and Stroink, F. 1988. "Cognitive and Behavioral Interventions: A Comparative Evaluation with Clinically Distressed Couples." *Journal of Family Psychology* 1:365–77.

Farmer, S., and Galaris, D. 1993. "Support Groups for Children of Divorce." *American Journal of Family Therapy* 21:40–50.

Gardner, R. A. 2002. "Parental Alienation Syndrome Versus Parental Alienation: Which Diagnosis Should Evaluators Use in Child Custody Disputes?" *The American Journal of Family Therapy* 30:93–115.

Garvin, V., Kalter, N., and Hansell, J. 1993. "Divorced Women: Individual Differences in Stressors, Mediating Factors, and Adjustment Outcome." *American Journal of Orthopyschiatry* 63(2):232–40.

Goldman, A., and Greenberg, L. 1992. "Comparison of Integrated Systemic and Emotionally Focused Approaches to Couples Therapy." *Journal of Consulting and Clinical Psychology* 60:962–69.

Goldman, J., and Coane, J. 1983. "Separation and Divorce." In *Helping Families with Special Problems,* ed. M. Textor. New York: Jason Aronson.

Gottman, J. M., Coan, C., Carrère, S., and Swanson, C. 1998. "Predicting Marital Happiness and Stability from Newly-wed Interactions." *Journal of Marriage and the Family* 60:5–22.

Granvold, D., and Welch, G. 1977. "Intervention in Post Divorce Adjust-ment Problems: The Treatment Seminar." *Journal of Divorce* 1(1):81–92.

Granvold, D. K., and Jordan, C. 1994. *The Cognitive-Behavioral Treatment of Marital Distress: Cognitive and Behavioral Treatment.* Belmont, CA: Brooks/Cole Publishing Co.

Greenberg, L., and Johnson, S. 1988. *Emotionally Focused Therapy for Couples.* New York: Guilford Press.

Grove, W. M., Zald, D. H., Lebow, B. S., Snitz, B. E., and Nelson, C. 2000. "Clinical Versus Mechanical Prediction: A Meta-Analysis." *Psychological Assessment* 12:19–30.

Hackney, H., and Bernard, J. M. 1990. "Dyadic Divorce Adjustment Processes Model." *Journal of Counseling and Development* 69(2):134–43.

Hahlweg, K., and Markman, H. 1988. "The Effectiveness of Behavioral Marital Therapy: Empirical Status of Behavioral Techniques in Preventing and Alleviating Marital Distress." *Journal of Consulting and Clinical Psychology* 56:440–47.

Halford, K. W., Sanders, M. R., and Behrens, B. C. 1993. "A Comparison of the Generalization of Behavioral Marital Therapy and Enhanced Behavioral Marital Therapy." *Journal of Consulting and Clinical Psychology* 61:51–60.

Hamilton, M. 1986. "The Hamilton Rating Scale for Depression." In *Assessment of Depression* (pp. 143–152), eds. N. Sartorius and T. A. Ban. Berlin: Springer-Verlag.

Heatherington, M. E., and Kelly, J. 2002. *For Better or For Worse—Divorce Reconsidered.* New York: W. W. Norton & Co.

Hunsley, J., Best, M., Lefebvre, M., and Vito, D. 2001. "The Seven-Item Short Form of the Dyadic Adjustment Scale: Further Evidence for Construct Validity." *American Journal of Family Therapy* 29(4):325–35.

Huston, T. L., Caughlin, J. P., Hours, R. M., Smith, S. E., and George, L. J. 2001. "The Connubial Crucible: Newlywed

Years as Predictors of Marital Delight, Distress, and Divorce." *Journal of Personality and Social Psychology* 80:237–252.

Jacobson, N. S., and Holtzworth-Monroe, A. 1986. "Marital Therapy: A Social-Learning Cognitive Perspective." In *Clinical Handbook of Marital Therapy* (pp. 29–70), eds. N. S. Jacobson and A. S. Gurman. New York: Guilford Press.

James, P. S. 1991. "Effects of a Communication Training Component Added to an Emotionally Focused Couples Therapy." *Journal of Marital and Family Therapy* 17:263–75.

Johnson, S., and Greenberg, L. 1985. "Differential Aspects of Experiential and Problem-Solving Interventions in Resolving Marital Conflict." *Journal of Consulting and Clinical Psychology* 53(2):175–84.

———. 1995. "The Emotionally Focused Therapy: Restructuring Attachment." In *Clinical Handbook of Couples Therapy* (pp. 121–41), eds. N. Jacobson and A. Gurman. New York: Guilford Press.

Joint Committee on Standards for Educational and Psychological Testing. 1999. *Standards for Educational and Psychological Testing.* Washington, DC: American Educational Research Association.

Kincaid, S., and Caldwell, R. 1995. "Marital Separation: Causes, Coping, and Consequences." *Journal of Divorce and Remarriage* 22(3):109–28.

Kitson, G., Moir, R., and Mason, P. 1992. "Family Social Support in Crisis: The Special Case of Divorce." *American Journal of Orthopsychiatry* 52(1):161–65.

Kobak, K. A., Reynolds, W. R., Rosenfeld, R., and Greist, J. H. 1990. "Development and Validation of a Computer Administered Hamilton Depression Rating Scale." *Psychological Assessment* 2:56–63.

Kurdek, L. A. 2002. "Predicting the Timing of Separation and Marital Satisfaction:

An Eight-Year Prospective Longitudinal Study." *Journal of Marriage & The Family* 64(1):163–169.

Lengua, L., Wolchik, S., and Braver, S. 1995. "Understanding Children's Divorce Adjustment from an Ecological Perspective." *Journal of Divorce and Remarriage* 22(3/4):25–47.

Lewis, P. N. 1983. "Innovative Divorce Rituals: Their Psychosocial Function." *Journal of Divorce* 6(3):71–82.

Lubin, B., Larsen, R., and Matarazzo, J. D. 1984. "Patterns of Psychological Test Usage in the United States: 1933–1982." *American Psychologist* 39:451–54.

Maier, W., Phillipp, M., Heuser, I., Schlegel, S., Buller, R., and Wetsel, H. 1988. "Improving Depression Severity Assessment—I. Reliability, Internal Validity, and Sensitivity to Change of Three Observer Depression Scales." *Journal of Psychiatric Research* 22:3–12.

Marek, Terry. 1989. "Separation and Divorce Therapy: A Struggle to Grow for Clients and Therapists." In *Treating Couples,* ed. Gerald R. Weeks. New York: Brunner/Mazel Publishers.

Mitchell-Flynn, C., and Hutchinson, R. L. 1993. "A Longitudinal Study of the Problems and Concerns of Divorced Men." *Journal of Divorce and Remarriage* 19(2):161–82.

Roach, A. J., Frazier, L. P., and Bowden, S. R. 1981. "The Marital Satisfaction Scale: Development of a Measure for Intervention Research." *Journal of Marriage & Family* 43(3):537–44.

Rogge, R. D., and Bradbury, T. N. 1999. "Till Violence Does Us Part: The Differing Roles of Communication and Aggression in Predicting Adverse Marital Outcomes." *Journal of Consulting and Clinical Psychology* 67:340–51.

Shadish, W. R., Montgomery, L. M., Wilson, P., Wilson, M. R., Bright, I., and Okwumabua, T. 1993. "Effects of Family and Marital Psychotherapies:

A Meta-Analysis." *Journal of Consulting and Clinical Psychology* 61:992–1002.

Snyder, D. K. 1981. *Marital Satisfaction Inventory (MSI) Manual.* Los Angeles: Western Psychological Services.

Snyder, D. K., and Willis, R. M. 1989. "Behavioral Versus Insight-Oriented Marital Therapy: Effects on Individual and Interpersonal Functioning." *Journal of Consulting and Clinical Psychology* 57:39–46.

Spanier, G., and Thompson, L. 1984. *Parting: The Aftermath of Separation and Divorce.* Beverly Hills, CA: Sage Publications.

Todorski, J. 1995. "Attachment and Divorce: A Therapeutic View." *Journal of Divorce and Remarriage* 22(3):189–204.

U.S. Bureau of the Census. 1993. *Current Population Reports.* Population Profile of the United States.

———. 2000. *Current Population Reports.* Population Profile of the United States.

Videon, T. M. 2002. "The Effects of Parent-Adolescent Relationships and Parental Separation on Adolescent Well-Being." *Journal of Marriage and Family* 64:489–503.

Walker, J. G., Johnson, S., Manion, I., and Clotier, P. 1996. "Emotionally-Focused Marital Intervention for Couples with Chronically Ill Children." *Journal of Consulting and Clinical Psychology* 64:1029–36.

Wallerstein, J. 1983. "Children of Divorce: The Psychological Tasks of the Child." *American Journal of Orthopsychiatry* 53(2):230–43.

Walsh, F., Jacob, L., and Simons, V. 1995. "Facilitating Healthy Divorce Processes: Therapy and Mediation Approaches." In *Clinical Handbook of Couple Therapy* (pp. 340–68), eds. N. S. Jacobson and A. S. Gurman. New York: The Guilford Press.

Whitaker, C., and Keith, D. 1984. "Counseling the Dissolving Marriage." In *Counseling in Marital and Sexual Problems,* eds. R. Stahmann and W. Hiebert. Lexington, MA: Lexington Books.

Whiteside, M. F., and Becker, B. J. 2000. "Parental Factors and the Young Child's Postdivorce Adjustment: A Meta-Analysis with Implications for Parenting Arrangements." *Journal of Family Psychology* 14(1):5–26.

Wilson, G. L., Bornstein, P. H., and Wilson, L. J. 1988. "Treatment of Relationship Dysfunction: An Empirical Evaluation of Group and Conjoint Behavioral Marital Therapy." *Journal of Consulting and Clinical Psychology* 56:929–31.

Wolchick, S. A., Ramirez, R., Bandler, J. N., Fisher, J. J., Organista, P. B., and Brown, C. 1993. "Inner-City Poor Children of Divorce: Negative Divorce-Related Events, Problematic Beliefs and Adjustment Problems." *Journal of Divorce and Remarriage* 19(2):1–20.

Evidence-Based Treatment of the Reconstituted Family

CHAPTER 12

INTRODUCTION

A second marriage is structurally and psychologically different from the intact nuclear family that normally results from a first union. This necessitates viewing the structure and functioning of this unit in a different way than we view the family generated by the initial union. This "second" family has a beginning that is different from the nuclear family of the first union; thus it presents a different set of problems. Understanding the structure of this new family, as well as its development, functioning, and struggles to reach a cohesive existence, is the therapeutic task (Smith, 1991). We assume that all families, regardless of how they are constituted, operate as a system, and the best understanding of the structure and functioning of reconstituted families is reached by the application of a family systems approach when considering the adjustment problems of this group.

In keeping with this position, the remainder of the chapter presents the reconstituted family from a family systems perspective, with consideration given to descriptions of various family patterns, assessment issues, and the interventions necessary to facilitate appropriate family functioning.

POPULATION DESCRIPTION AND DEFINITIONS

When considering the family created by the coming together of two people, one or both of whom have experienced a previous marriage or cohabitation with a partner, the first concern is what to call the new family. Since these families are made up of individuals from various lifestyles and experiences, we have chosen a definition with sufficient breadth to include people from all walks of life. We believe *the reconstituted family* is an appropriate definition for families formed under these conditions. Therefore, throughout our discussion we shall refer to this union of individuals as the reconstituted family. We also realize there are other labels and definitions applicable to this group—for example, blended family, stepfamily, remarried family, and recoupled family—and our choice in no way denies the appropriateness of different definitions used by other authors. While our discussion may not always reference all the different types of reconstituted families specifically, we wish to point up the fact that the skills, techniques, and processes we discuss are generally applicable to a wide range of different families, including the nontraditional family constellation consisting of a union of two adults of the same sex. This family composition is becoming more prevalent in contemporary society, yet it continues to struggle for acceptance of the right to serve as parents. We believe the suffering of all families deserves the full attention of professional helpers, and this will be reflected in our discussions. We will also refer to all relationships involving cohabitation by adults as *unions* instead of identifying their existence by legal definition.

ASSESSMENT ISSUES

The complexity of the reconstituted family is reflected in the many different compositions resulting from the joining of individuals who bring to the new family various pre-established and continuing nuclear and extended family relationships. We will describe these and the issues surrounding each, followed by a discussion of the tasks reconstituted families must complete to successfully integrate.

Issues of Family Composition

To consider a few patterns of the reconstituted family organization, there are divorced men and women who have children from previous marriages, all of whom live together in a single household; divorced men without children married to women with children; women without children or previous marriage married to men with children; men without previous marriages and divorced women with children from the previous marriage; reconstituted families composed of widows and widowers, both with children, who live together part or all of the time; same-sex couples who have experienced previous unions; and, finally, divorced parents with children from previous marriages and children from the present marriage.

While all reconstituted families go through varying periods of adjustment, a number of situations can be anticipated (Jongsma, Peterson, & McCinnis, 2000). For example, the household with children from previous unions will most likely have to struggle with sibling jealousies centering on attention from the biological parent, resistance to the authority of the new parent, and turf battles over sharing space and possessions. In the case of the woman without children or a previous union who joins with a divorced man with children, the lack of experience in being a mother may well be a handicap, as she does not know what to expect from children, who are likely to react in a hostile manner to what is perceived as her intrusion into their lives. The opposite may be true as well, with an inexperienced new stepfather. Children who spend time with both a stepparent and a divorced biological parent might experience some difficulty with a perception of divided loyalty or, in most cases, might struggle with feelings of resentment toward the stepparent, especially in the early phase of reconstituted family development.

Impact of Past Experiences   Reconstituted families are created out of a past union experience. Many of these experiences have been unhappy due to incompatibilities between partners, which have ended in dissolution of the partnerships, and other unhappy experiences have come as the result of losing a mate by death. In any case, a reconstituted family begins under the weight of what might be described as a long cast of characters. This is to say that a number of people are likely to be involved. Both partners may bring positive or negative relationships from a previous union as well as friendships developed in different contexts over time. Children from previous unions bring to the new family current relationships with grandparents, aunts, uncles, cousins, and other acquaintances (Hobart, 1990). Stuart and Jacobson (1985) refer to beginning a reconstituted family under these conditions as not joining just a mate but joining a family, and this can put a strain on new relationships. This is especially so as there are new sets of grandparents, in-laws, and other relatives with whom to interact, which increases the possibility of conflict around divided loyalties, jealousies, and inappropriate expectations. For example, the biological grandparents may think they have first call on the grandchildren's attention and behave in such a way as to discourage the development of an amicable relationship with the stepparent or stepgrandparents. On the other hand, the new "steprelatives" may embrace the new family and expect its members to become a part of their network. This places the children in the uncomfortable position of being expected to maintain loyalty to established relationships while at the same time entering freely into new relationships with "steprelatives."

Children are not the only ones affected by previously established relationships. In cases where members of the family of origin enjoyed good relationships with the former spouse, the new spouse may find acceptance difficult. Instead of being accepted by reason of position in the family, by becoming the partner of a family member, new partners may be required to earn their way into the family, and comparison with the former partner is likely to make this a very difficult process. Past experiences may also contribute to the reconstituted family in positive ways. If both partners have parenting experience, they will enter this new situation with knowledge of what it is like to be a parent as well as some understanding of the behavior of children and the strategies they use to gain attention and protect themselves against the hurt of rejection. This should be useful in negotiating some of the conflicts they are likely to encounter.

Myths and Other Expectations   Perhaps the most prevalent myth associated with the reconstituted family is the "wicked stepmother." The belief that stepmothers do not function in the best interest of stepchildren is exemplified in the case of the biological parent who always manages to find a way to interrupt all efforts on the part of the stepmother to discipline the children or have sustained meaningful interaction with them. In this case, the belief regarding the "wicked stepmother" has been internalized and will likely remain as part of the couple's interaction until change in the biological parent's belief system is effected. However, it should be noted that most stepmothers do not fit the "wicked and cruel" model that has been perpetuated nor do they experience serious problems in relating to stepchildren.

Another common myth about reconstituted families is that of instant love (Bray & Berger, in DeGenova & Rice, 2005). The assumption is based on the belief that stepparents are the same as natural parents and, therefore, feel no differently toward stepchildren than they do toward their own natural children. In other words, when new partners take on the role of stepparent, they are expected to feel instant love for children with whom there is no shared history or bonding experience, and, in return, these children will show love and admiration for the new stepparent. This is certainly a myth because it implies an instant relationship between people who are for the most part strangers. Relationships between them will require time to build and grow. To expect anything different from people who suddenly find themselves living together as the result of a union by two adults is to invite feelings of insecurity, disappointment, and anger. Cherlin and Furstenberg (in DeGenova & Rice, 2005) estimate that restabilization in stepfamilies takes from five to seven years. It is well to remember that building new relationships between stepchildren and stepparents will involve adjusting to new rules and new roles as well as adjusting to each other over time. And this process is usually made easier if the stepparents can refrain from forcing themselves on the children. Stepchildren must be given the opportunity and time to test out the new situation and move closer to the stepparent at their own pace.

In contrast to the myth of instant love, some stepchildren hold a belief that "step is less" (Wald, 1981). This means that the stepchildren cannot be loved in the same way as natural children can and that the children cannot love the stepparent as they love the natural parent. However, more recently, Amato and colleagues (in DeGenova & Rice, 2005) found that level of conflict in the family of origin prior to the divorce influenced children's behavior problems after the divorce, with children whose parents had a conflictual relationship faring worse. As in the case of all these myths, these allegations about the reconstituted family are unverifiable and should not be taken as a logical starting point from which to view this new family. In addition to the unverifiability of myths, holding on to these beliefs denies the presence of individual strengths and the fact that positive relationships can be developed within the structure of the reconstituted family.

Reconstituted Family Structure   The organization of the reconstituted family can be best understood when viewed as a social system in the same manner as the nuclear family. It operates from a set of functional demands that determine and guide the interaction of its members. It adheres to a power hierarchy that gives different levels of authority to parents and children. It is composed of subsystems and protected by boundaries, and it passes through stages of development, all of which is common to the nuclear family formed by the initial joining of two adults for the purpose of creating a family. However, the reconstituted family frequently encounters difficulty in its development because of a number of circumstances peculiar to its origin. Among the things that interfere with the various developmental tasks is the composition or makeup of the family, which brings together individuals with different lifestyles, different values, and different worldviews (Hobart, 1989). In spite of the prevalence of reconstituted families in society, we have not established a clear set of guidelines that can be applied to this family. This handicaps not only family members but also practitioners who seek to help this group negotiate developmental tasks. If we are to be successful in this undertaking, we must be informed of the makeup of the subsystems and something of the history of those who participate in them.

Couple Subsystem   As architects of the reconstituted family, the couple subsystem carries major responsibility for family development. As mentioned earlier, these two people may come together from a variety of statuses to form the new family. For example, the union may bring together two people who are divorced from previous marriages; one divorced and the other single; one widowed and one divorced; both widowed; one widowed and the other single; or a couple of the same sex who have ended their previous relationships. This is important information for practitioners, as it provides a history and some notion of where knowledge and common experiences may or may not exist.

To these unions, each partner may bring children, only one partner may bring children, or neither may bring children. In some cases, children may become permanent members of the stepfamily or divide time between the stepfamily and the natural parent. This is also useful information for practitioners, as both partners must accommodate each other and differentiate the couple subsystem by developing clear boundaries. These tasks may become more difficult when children from previous unions are brought into the family. The presence of these children may stress the functioning of the couple subsystem, which exists primarily as a workplace for the couple in negotiating a complementary relationship. Under normal conditions of beginning a nuclear family, children would not be present, and the boundary of the couple subsystem would allow the couple an opportunity to focus on their own interest as it pertains to sharing space, developing mutuality, and establishing individuality within this new relationship. The presence of children from the beginning limits the time the couple can spend together in defining what their relationship will be, as some time must be spent involving the children within the context of the parent-child subsystem. Further complication is likely in the relations of the stepchild and stepparent around a number of experiences. For example, if both parents bring children from previous unions, there is the potential for a "we/they" complex, with children vying for the attention of their biological parent to the exclusion of the stepparent and her children. There is also the problem of how much and in what ways the demands of children affect the perception both parents have of each other. If one parent perceives the other as caring more for her natural children at the expense of neglecting the stepchildren, this will create tension within the couple subsystem, which will interfere with the normal processes of this subsystem. As a result, each parent may not only be drawn closer to her natural children but see the other parent as disliking the stepchildren. And, out of a need to protect her own, a parent will allow the children to invade freely the boundaries of the couple subsystem, thereby preventing the development of an appropriate (permeable) boundary that controls the children's access to this subsystem.

In cases where only one parent brings children to the reconstituted family, a satisfactory adjustment may well depend on the experience of the other parent in child-rearing and the expectations these parents have of each other and the children. This understanding can be quite helpful in negotiating with the child in relation to developing trust and gradually giving up some of the closeness to the natural parent and moving into a relationship with the stepparent. This is not to say parents with child-rearing experience are always successful in effecting an adjustment in a reconstituted family situation with children. If the experience causes the parent to assume expert status in dealing with children, leaving no room for error, the stepparent will likely behave in such a way as to demand too much from himself and in turn expect too much from the child. In this case, the stepparent must be helped to reassess his role and allow the child to remain closer to the natural parent while gradually developing trust and comfort in relating to the stepparent.

The stepparent who has no experience in parenting may find the stepparent role very frustrating. The lack of knowledge of how to proceed in fulfilling a role already established with the child, who is likely to resent an outsider attempting to take the place of the natural parent, can reinforce feelings of inadequacy and cause the stepparent to withdraw or, in some cases, react negatively toward the child. Such experiences often create tension within the couple subsystem. The natural parent is not likely to understand or accept the stepparent's negative reaction, while failure in relating to the child causes the stepparent to feel inadequate and in need of support from her partner. However, to ask the natural parent for help would further damage the stepparent's self-esteem, and if support is not volunteered, she usually chooses to remain silent and resentful of the other's failure to come to the rescue. In this situation, priority should be given to work on improving communication between the parents and helping the stepparent to a better understanding of the parenting role.

Parental Subsystem   This subsystem is composed of the same two people as the couple subsystem. However, it is child-focused and requires the parent to reach a delicate balance between exercising control and promoting independence among family members. When compared to the parental subsystem of the nuclear family, this subsystem in the reconstituted family clearly deals with some of the same problems but also deals with a set of problems quite different from those experienced in the initial family. In the first place, the parents in this new family do not have the opportunity to experience the couple subsystem role and effect a beginning adjustment to each other. Instead, they are faced with the necessity of moving into the couple and parental subsystem roles at the same time. This is to say that at the same time the couple is undertaking an initial adjustment to each other, they must also be concerned with responding to the demands of a sibling subsystem composed of individuals without kinship ties or shared experiences. As a result, the parental subsystem is likely to be stressed in carrying out executive responsibility for the reconstituted family.

Among the areas of stress are likely violations of boundary structures. For example, children should experience freedom in moving back and forth across the boundaries of a parental subsystem to receive guidance in self-development and assimilation into the wider society. However, in the case of reconstituted families, care must be taken to prevent children from seeking and receiving unilateral guidance from the natural parent (except perhaps in cases where unalterable dislike exists between stepparent and stepchildren). In any case, unilateral guidance by the natural parent tends to divide family authority and create tension within the parental subsystem. And with increased tension, boundaries between natural parent and child may become blurred and lead to involvement of the child not only in the functioning of the parental subsystem but in problems of the couple subsystem as well. Such involvement may seriously interfere with the carrying out of appropriate parental subsystem tasks.

Adolescence is a time at which balancing control and promoting autonomy is perhaps most difficult for parents of the reconstituted family. This is the point at which parents' demands are likely to be in conflict with the children's desire for age-appropriate autonomy (Minuchin, 1974). Parental demands in the reconstituted family are not always the result of consensus between the parents. In many cases, the marital pair have not discussed their similarity or difference with regard to what represents appropriate behavior or responsibility for the children. Nevertheless, failure to communicate does not mean an absence of firm conviction on the part of each parent about how children should behave and how much autonomy they should be given. In the absence of agreement about what will be expected of the children, different messages are likely to be given that will reflect the past experiences of each parent. For example, a parent from a family that tended toward enmeshment would likely be reluctant to allow children to move freely outside family boundaries, which would increase opportunities for developing autonomy. In contrast, the parent from a family that tends to be disengaged would not be comfortable with close family ties but would be interested in the development of independence. These opposite views signal the need for increased communication within the parental subsystem, and change efforts should be directed toward open discussion of parenting issues and mutual accommodation between parents on the matters of child-rearing, and between parents and children with regard to effecting a healthy balance between autonomy and control. Hetherington (in DeGenova & Rice, 2005) reported that even in long-term stepfamilies, bonding is difficult between stepparents and stepchildren, and warm, close relationships usually do not develop as they do between biological parents and their children.

Sibling Subsystem   In this subsystem within the natural family, children are customarily afforded their own turf and the opportunity to develop and experiment with behaviors in learning to relate to peers and adults in the larger contexts of the family and society. This subgroup is normally composed of individuals with kinship ties who share common parentage, rules, and values. The sibling subsystem in the reconstituted family may exist in many forms. Children from one union may be joined by children from another union, only the children of one parent may be included in the subsystem, or the children from the new marriage may be born into the family and join children from previous unions of one or both parents. In each case, a complex group is brought into existence, and a crisis may be precipitated by the failure of old roles and old boundaries defined within the context of a previous family structure.

If the reconstituted family assumes residence in the home of a parent with children from a previous union, these children may perceive the children of the other parent as intruders into their territory and react by attempting to exclude these new members. From a systems perspective, rejecting the new members is their way of safeguarding the boundaries of the old subsystem by closure, which will control the input of new energy from the new group. If this new energy is allowed to enter the system, it may threaten the existence of the old subsystem in which the previous occupants have found comfort and that they wish to preserve.

Sibling rivalry, common to all sibling subsystems, is likely to be more stressful in the reconstituted family as members seek changes in coalitions and alliances generated by losses experienced in the breakup of the nuclear family. Jealousies may be acted out in rather destructive ways as children attempt to hold on to natural parents and reject stepparents and siblings. For example, children with a natural parent living elsewhere may attempt to move back and forth between this parent and the reconstituted family whenever they choose not to abide by the rules established in either household.

The development of the sibling subsystem in the reconstituted family is not always characterized by continuing conflict. If the parents of this family have sufficiently resolved their own adjustment problems and are able to pursue relaxed relationships with the children, their behavior will serve as a role model for the children and help them develop a sibling subsystem that will promote the growth and development of its members. However, when intervention is necessary, attention must be given to what the children bring to this new subgroup experience from past associations. Losses and expectations should be dealt with and assurance offered, where possible, that further losses are not likely to occur as a result of developing new relationships with stepsiblings, and that old relationships that are important to children need not be abandoned.

Parent-Child Subsystem   This subsystem is characterized by interaction between parents and children. Clarity of boundaries and lines of authority are important factors in the successful functioning of this subsystem. In the nuclear family, the parents have shared with each other in a relationship before children are born or adopted into the family. And all children in this case belong to the couple, forming a nuclear family that customarily lives together until the children reach the appropriate age for separation. This is not the case with the reconstituted family. At least one parent has shared a relationship with the children, who are now a part of the new family, before joining the other partner in this union. In many instances, both parents have experienced ties with some of the children but not with others prior to joining and forming the new family.

For these reasons, the stepparent begins at a different point than the natural parent in interacting with children. The parent who brings children to the reconstituted family has close ties with this part of the sibling subsystem but must begin to establish new relationships with everyone else. Such an entry into the family system may cause an imbalance in relationships. One of the difficulties in building relationships is that stepparents are often cautious in attempting to establish a relationship with stepchildren out of concern for how they are perceived in this role by these children as well as by other members of the family. At the same time, the parent-child relationship from the previous union is in place, and the interaction within this relationship is likely to be viewed by others as closing the boundary around this part of the subsystem and denying entry to others. As a result, tension increases and family homeostasis may be disrupted until an understanding is reached regarding new roles and new ways of relating among family members.

The perception of the parenting role by stepparents and stepchildren is an important factor in determining how they will interact in forming a viable family relationship. Some adults who enter into a new union after the breakup of a previous one expect too much of themselves and other family members. For example, many stepparents try too hard to be exceptionally good parents in order to please their mates and expect in return to gain love and respect from the children. Yet, stepchildren are likely to be hesitant in responding to the overzealous efforts of these "superparents" who want to receive instant love from them and immediately enjoy a happy family. Stepparents must learn to relax and allow positive interaction with stepchildren to occur gradually. Immediate acceptance of a stepparent is difficult for stepchildren, who are likely to be grieving the loss of the natural parent. In most cases of children of divorced parents, accepting a stepparent is further complicated by the fact that there is an ongoing relationship with the natural divorced parent. And the thought of replacing this parent with another creates feelings of guilt and disloyalty. In the case of deceased parents, many children experience similar feelings, especially in the early stages of the stepparent relationship, as interacting with the stepparent is likely to rekindle painful feelings of this previous loss.

Another problem in the parent-child relationship in reconstituted families may be brought on by the stepparent's immediately attempting to assume the authority formerly held by the absent natural parent relative to family rules and discipline. In most cases, this not only causes anger and rebellion among the children but also creates tension between the parents. If the stepparent continues to carry the instant authority role, the natural parent and her children will likely be drawn together against the stepparent, and professional help is usually needed if the family is to become a viable unit. Change efforts should be directed toward the natural parent's taking a more active role in setting rules, disciplining the children, and sharing her thoughts and wishes about parenting with the stepparent. At the same time, the stepparent should be helped to accept a lesser role in parenting until appropriate rules governing family conduct are established and the role of the hierarchical structure is agreed upon.

Tasks and Issues in Reconstituted Family Development

The tasks and issues facing the reconstituted family are slightly different from those faced by the natural family as it proceeds toward realization of basic goals. Thompson and Rudolph (1992) and Visher and Visher (1982, p. 343) point to the need for the new family to address previous losses, develop new traditions, preserve important old alliances and form new ones, achieve integration within the current family unit, and deal with such issues as financial power and sexual boundaries.

Recognizing Losses   Members of a reconstituted family have experienced a number of losses that may prove devastating in establishing the new family if they are not recognized and dealt with by each individual. The partner who has experienced a previous union and has lost a mate experiences a sense of loss. In the case of divorce, regardless of how unsatisfactory the relationship may have been, there is a sense of loss over failure to have made the marriage the success that was envisioned at the beginning, and the personal investment in trying to make it succeed cannot be recovered. There are always feelings of sadness and loss associated with the death of a mate; the good times spent together and many old friends that were a part of that experience will not continue to be a part of the new life being fashioned. As for the children, the death of a parent is one of the most painful losses possible. And disruption of the parent-child relationship by divorce is also a serious loss, together with the disappearance of familiar surroundings such as friends and extended family members who may no longer be readily available due to relocation of the reconstituted family.

These losses contribute to feelings of sadness and anger that may be displaced in the reconstituted family relationships. In this case, help is usually needed to assist family members in sorting out feelings, identifying sources of sadness and anger, and looking at the new family as an opportunity to develop and share meaningful relationships without being disloyal to friends and relatives or desecrating pleasant memories from previous experiences.

Establishing New Traditions   Reconstituted families may come together from very different places, bringing values, goals, and traditions established through previous experiences. Although reconstituted family members may have been served well by these structures in the past, it is highly unlikely that they will work effectively to bind the new family together. It is well to remember that family relationships are built around shared experiences, and reconstituted families have usually had few, if any, shared experiences. Therefore, it is necessary for family members to establish new goals and traditions through engaging in activities of interest to the new family and deciding together what the family likes and values and how it will go about realizing desired objectives.

Forming Alliances   We agree with those who suggest a relaxed and gradual formation of alliances in the reconstituted family. Forming a new family from members who bring experience and traditions from a previous nuclear family always reactivates old memories and often introduces conflict. Efforts to expedite this process by exerting pressure on family members, including showing excessive amounts of affection or increasing interaction within the family at the expense of eliminating contacts with friends and relatives outside of the new family, will most likely fail. It is appropriate for the parents to spend time together without interference from real or imagined demands of the family. Stepparents also need to spend some time with stepchildren. This should be done without the natural parent being present; however, care must be taken to keep this time between stepmembers of the family casual and of short duration in the early stage of family development (Visher & Visher, 1982). A useful strategy might begin by complimenting the child on something he likes to do, such as coloring pictures or working with building blocks, and later participating briefly in this activity with the child whenever the opportunity is presented.

It is very important while developing new alliances to allow reconstituted family members to continue important old alliances established through previous associations. For example, children should be expected to continue communication with grandparents with whom they share close relationships and with friends whose company they enjoy. Stepparents should also continue to be in touch with relatives and friends whose associations they value. By continuing important old alliances, the pressure to become totally engaged in the immediate development of a new family is lessened. And with this lessening of pressure to become completely involved in the processes of the reconstituted family, both stepparents and stepchildren can gradually move toward getting to know each other, which sets the stage for development of a viable reconstituted family. When there is total commitment to instant success in becoming a new family, the members experience tremendous pressure to interact positively, and this often leads to anger, frustration, and failure.

Integration   Integration within the reconstituted family is an important task that is facilitated by knowing what to expect. The primary responsibility for achieving integration rests with the parents, who must create conditions conducive to family organization. Since the parents are the architects of the family, they must clarify what is expected and reach consensus on important rules before attempting to involve the children in forming a new family. The relationship of the new couple will need to be strengthened, and new relationships must be developed between parents and children. This will enhance the development of a sense of membership in the new family (Visher & Visher, 1990). This is supported as well by Duncan and Brown (1992), who also posit a necessary family connection with supportive institutions in the community. This agreement between the parents should help with involvement of the children and provide some support for the stepparent in dealing with them around the issues of roles and expectations.

In addition to arriving at an understanding between the parents, integrating the reconstituted family requires nurturing children and setting limits that will allow them to continue appropriate development while the parents remain in control. This is not an easy task for the natural family and a very difficult one for a new family. Stepparents inherit a family already in existence, where controls are needed, without having carried out the nurturing elements of child-rearing of the stepchildren. As a result, these children are without the experience of having received, at an earlier age, the giving aspects of a relationship with the stepparent but are now faced with accepting the limits this stepparent imposes. This is tantamount to having missed the initial phase of the parent-child relationship in which a basis is established for the child's wish to please the parent. Therefore, stepchildren are likely to resent limits imposed by the stepparent, and this will complicate integration of the family.

Time is also a factor in achieving integration, as members of the reconstituted family must get to know each other before the trusting and sharing needed for the family to function as a cohesive unit can develop. A time period of from two to five or more years is required before a satisfactory state of integration is reached. And stepparents should not become discouraged by the gradual pace at which relationships are developed.

Complex Issues   The development of the reconstituted family involves a number of roles, tasks, and issues related to family relationships that preceded the start of this new family. It begins with the coming together of the couple, at least one of whom has experienced this process before. In many cases, both have experienced it previously. One of the most important considerations for those repeating the process is how well they have resolved issues relating to their experience in the previous family. It is not uncommon for individuals to enter a reconstituted family with very strong positive or negative feelings about their former mate, which may be reflected in a number of ways. Feelings of guilt over the breakup of a relationship may interfere with the sharing of one's self with the other or cause one to invest too much in trying to make up for past mistakes by becoming the perfect partner. In some situations, unresolved positive feelings may surface as divided loyalty between past and present mates. On the other hand, unresolved negative feelings may contribute to distrust in relating to the new mate or an overinvestment in trying to make life difficult for the former partner.

Visher and Visher (1982) speak of the exaggeration of power issues in reconstituted families. For example, if the wife is divorced and successfully carried family responsibility as a single parent prior to joining the family, she may enter the new family with confidence in her capability to provide for herself and her children. This self-sufficiency represents power and control of her own life, and sharing these through a union with someone new may threaten a return to an unsatisfying pattern of dependency. Divorced men who remarry after experiencing difficult financial settlements with previous mates may feel they have unjustly lost their power and control and become vulnerable to future attacks on their finances, ergo their power. In such cases, they may be unwilling to share information about finances with the new mate or may live in a miserly fashion in order to prevent further erosion of their power and control.

Sager and associates (1983) suggest that in-laws and former in-laws sometimes have a strong influence on the reconstituted family system. If in-laws have played a major role in the life of a partner, especially between the breakup of the previous relationship and uniting with a new partner, during which time the support and assistance they gave was crucial, they may find themselves seeking a decision-making role in helping to establish the new family. This is likely to prove disruptive to forming appropriate relationships in the new family system. Former in-laws who enjoy good relationships with their grandchildren may have difficulty accepting the replacement of their son or daughter by someone else who will assume the role of parent.

When children from previous families are brought into the reconstituted family, there is a parent-child relationship that precedes the relationship of the new parents. This prior parent-child attachment is likely to create an emotional imbalance in family relationships, with the child favoring the natural parent while having only minimal contact with the stepparent (Goldenberg & Goldenberg, 2004). Unlike the family situation where the couple has time to accommodate to each other before turning their attention to the needs of children, the presence of children in the reconstituted family makes it necessary for the parents to assume both couple and parental roles simultaneously. This makes it more difficult to accomplish marital tasks, as it limits the time, privacy, and energy available to stepparents.

In all families, boundaries play a significant role in family development and family homeostasis. In reconstituted families, issues around boundaries take on a special significance due to the unique structure of these families. Boundary violations may occur at many levels, as indicated earlier in our discussion of subsystems. Children may violate the boundary around the couple subsystem as a result of the previous close association with the natural parent and the lack of experience in relating to the stepparent. This makes it easy for children to turn to natural parents for support and guidance in the same manner as before the new family was established. If the natural parent is ambivalent about the stepparent's relations with his children, a closer relationship is likely to be encouraged by the natural parent's own reactions to this situation. Repeated transactions between these principals while excluding the stepparent will interfere with the performance of normal couple tasks and represent a violation of the boundary that should limit the children's access to the private domain of the parents.

A blurring of boundaries may also occur when children share the homes of both the reconstituted family and the other natural parent. This often centers on arrangements for the children visiting and spending time in both households. Each household must recognize and respect the boundary of the other, thus allowing for a clear separation of the households, with each unit free to exercise control over what takes place within its domain (Visher & Visher, 1982). In this way, boundaries remain clear and children are able to function within the boundaries established by each household.

Another problem facing practitioners who work with reconstituted families is the issue of sexual boundaries. Sager and associates (1983) describe a loosening of sexual boundaries in the new family that is related to "the heightened affectionate and sexual atmosphere in the home during the new couple's early romantic bonding period" (p. 293). The inclusion of teenagers of the opposite sex in the new family tends to intensify the sexual climate. This, together with the fact that members of reconstituted families have not shared close emotional ties and are without biological ties, makes possible a complete breakdown of sexual boundaries. The extremes of a breakdown of sexual boundaries may be reflected in sexual relations between stepsiblings and sexual abuse, usually between stepfathers and stepdaughters.

One of the mistakes frequently made is to assume there is no difference in family functioning between the reconstituted family and the natural family. This occurs largely out of a lack of knowledge about the complexity of this family, its structure, and its functions in carrying out various tasks. The confusion begins with the variety of names used to identify this family unit, which we have chosen to refer to as the reconstituted family. Neither society, by tradition, nor research efforts have as yet developed a widely accepted set of norms for this family. Many myths, some of which we discussed earlier in this chapter, still exist relative to what should be expected from the members of a family that begins without biological ties. Nevertheless, research and experience in working with this type of family have provided some information regarding the processes in which it engages that should be recognized by family members and social workers engaged in helping with family adjustments.

The couple who joins to establish a reconstituted family should realize that adjustment among all family members will not automatically occur as a result of bringing family members together. Adolescent children are likely to be resentful of the stepparent and openly demonstrate preference for the natural parent. Efforts to force the development of relationships between stepmembers of the family will result in frustrations and defeat. In most situations, children will be relating to at least the biological parent outside of the reconstituted family and, in many cases, extended natural family members as well. This does not mean a problem will develop; however, the potential for family boundary disputes and conflicting loyalties is always present in these interactional processes.

When both parents bring children into the reconstituted family, they should be aware that a difference in feeling toward biological children and stepchildren may exist and that a display of this difference in affection might create tension throughout the family. Disciplining children is another potential area of tension, and unless there has been prior discussion and agreement on how authority will be used in this respect, problems are likely to develop.

Disagreement over the use of money is not uncommon in the reconstituted family, where alimony and/or child support payments are likely experiences. In many instances, new couples have never discussed such expenditures, and in such cases misunderstanding regarding old and new responsibilities may occur. And finally, as previously indicated, it must be recognized by everyone involved in dealing with reconstituted family processes that good family relationships are not an instant accomplishment and must be given an opportunity to develop over time.

Successful Reconstituted Family Functioning   In spite of the difficulty under which these families begin, not all of them struggle for identity and adjustment in relationships throughout the family life cycle. Some families are able to develop sound relationships between family members early in the new family's existence. A number of conditions contribute to successful development of reconstituted family structure and functioning. For example, the ages of children who are brought into the family may have impact on the stepparent-stepchild relationship as well as on the functioning of the sibling subsystem. Younger children usually have less difficulty in forming intrafamilial relationships in the new family than adolescents, who are more likely to have a stronger attachment to the biological family by reason of a longer association and a deeper appreciation of the fabric of this family and their role in it. Another factor is the individual life cycle of the adolescent. This stage of development is characterized by the adolescent's struggle with issues to identify and the desire for independence, which are demonstrated by rebellion against authority and disagreement with measures of control. The preferred posture of adolescents is freedom and autonomy rather than forming a new attachment to a stepparent with whom, in most cases, they are totally unfamiliar. This would involve not only giving up freedom but also being placed in the position of being controlled by an unfamiliar adult who is taking the place of the natural parent. This usually contributes to the difficulty in establishing relationships that is experienced in many reconstituted families. When the stepchildren are adults who do not occupy the reconstituted family household, the possibility of establishing acceptable working relationships is usually good. Additionally, adolescents have more adjustment difficulties to stepfamily living than do younger children; and adolescents girls have more difficulty adjusting to the stepparent than do adolescent boys (Hetherington et al., in DeGenova & Rice, 2005).

Parenting experience by the new couple is useful in developing the family in cases where children from previous families are involved. Parents with experience in dealing with children bring to the new family some knowledge of what to expect from children and how to relate to them in a number of circumstances. While this does not guarantee instant adjustment, it adds a positive dimension to the process.

Good Relationship between Partners   As architects of the family, the couple must maintain a good relationship if they are to guide the development of the family successfully. This takes on added importance in the reconstituted family, where bonding between the couple is more difficult to achieve than in the case of the natural family. In order to achieve and maintain a good relationship, the new couple must be able to communicate with clear messages that spell out their wishes, expectations, joys, and fears as related to their lives together and the establishment of the new family. There must be agreement on matters pertaining to family functioning and their roles in this process. They will also need to support each other in the performance of their respective parental roles. A good relationship between the parents, together with mutual support and cooperation, is among the necessary ingredients for successful family functioning.

Relaxed Atmosphere for Children   Children from previous marriages who enter the reconstituted family often resist establishing relationships, especially with stepparents. A major factor in this resistance is their attachment to biological family networks and the difficulty they experience in relating to a reconstituted family network at the same time. The greatest conflict is experienced in relating simultaneously to biological and stepparents. This problem can usually be overcome if the stepparent does not insist on instant positive relations with the child and allows the relationship to develop gradually. It is also important that children be given the opportunity to continue relating to both natural parents. In this kind of relaxed atmosphere, children usually learn to respond positively in reconstituted relationships, which enhances the functioning of the family.

Mature Relationship between All Parental Figures   Much of the difficulty experienced in reconstituted family functioning can be ameliorated if a mature relationship exists between the parental adults. Such a relationship requires abandoning attempts to both avenge previous wrongs and to compete for the affection of children. For example, no adult should demand total loyalty from children who must divide their time and attention between two sets of parents. Instead, they should be encouraged to relate to both natural parents and stepparents. Children's visits with the natural parent outside of the reconstituted family should be made as easy and convenient as possible. If negative feelings still exist between the natural parents, this should not be a topic for discussion with children nor should family boundaries be interfered with by criticism of rules and expectations of stepparents or natural parents. If these adults can relate in a civil manner, children will enjoy their time with them and the families will more likely function in a satisfactory manner.

BOX 12.1	Cultural Differences

One study of cultural differences among stepfamilies was reported in DeGenova and Rice (2005). Berger found cultural differences between American stepfamilies and Israeli stepfamilies, with the Americans thinking of their newly formed family as "different," versus Israeli families thinking of their families as similar to first-time married, nuclear families. Berger suggests that the American culture values individuality and personal happiness, leading stepfamilies to try and achieve this "happiness" goal for their new family. Since stepfamilies have a rather long period of adjustment (two to five years or longer), this happiness goal may be unrealistic and contribute to stepfamilies reporting low levels of satisfaction.

EVIDENCE-BASED TREATMENTS/ BEST PRACTICES

The practitioner who has worked primarily with the traditional intact nuclear family will need to understand what is different about the reconstituted family. A family systems approach with an educational component is recommended for work with all families, regardless of the stage of development or the nature of composition. And while the same therapeutic skills used in treating the nuclear family are also used in work with reconstituted families, the dynamics underlying reconstituted family problems are often quite different from the dynamics of nuclear family problems. An understanding of the differences and a few specific guidelines for intervention will add to the likelihood of success when family maladjustment is the object of change. In this section, we will address specific assessment tools that may be helpful with blended families, as well as intervention guidelines.

Assessment Tools

Social workers and other professionals who work with these families should be careful not to approach them as if they fit neatly into the traditional pattern of the nuclear family. This is a family whose members do not share a common history, and one needs to be aware of what is unique about the structure of this type of family and the common feelings and situations its members experience. Assessment tools can help with this process. Maps and genograms may be used to begin to identify family members and organize family members into their respective families of origin. Sculpting techniques or other role-playing techniques are helpful in identifying family members' patterns of interrelating, as well as helpful with children, especially teens. They like this type of dramatic approach. Standardized measures to be considered for assessment and monitoring include the Adult-Adolescent Parenting Inventory, Child's Attitude toward Mother or Father, Conflict Tactics Scale, Parental Bonding Instrument, and so forth (Corcoran & Fischer, 2000).

Table 12.1 | Assessment Instruments

Measure	Description	Reliability	Validity	Source
Adult-Adolescent Parenting Inventory	The AAPI is a 32-item measure designed to assess parenting and child-rearing strengths and weaknesses in four areas: inappropriate developmental expectations of children, lack of empathy toward children's needs, belief in the use of corporal punishment, and reversing parent-child roles.	Internal consistency reliability is from .65–.89	Extensive validity information is available. The measure clearly differentiates among different groups.	Bavolek, 1984
Child's Attitude toward Mother or Father	The CAF and CAM are 25-item instruments designed to measure the extent, degree, or severity of a child's problem with the parents.	Excellent reliability, with alphas of .95 and .94 respectively	Excellent known-groups validity	Hudson, 1997
Conflict Tactics Scale	The CT scale is a 15-item instrument designed to measure three family conflict resolution tactics: reasoning, verbal aggression, and violence.	Reliability coefficients range from .42–.96	Extensive support for its validity.	Straus & Gelles, 1990
Parental Bonding Instrument	The PBI is a 25-item instrument designed to measure parent-child bonding from the perspective of the child. Two variables are measured: caring (vs. indifference or rejection), and overprotection (vs. encouragement of independence).	Excellent internal consistency, with coefficients of .88 and .74 respectively	Good concurrent validity	Parker, Tupling, & Brown, 1979

SOURCE: Corcoran & Fischer, 2000.

Interventions

When the reconstituted family seeks professional help with problems related to family functioning, Collins, Jordan, and Coleman (1999) and Goldenburg and Goldenburg (2004) suggest that the starting point for assessment and intervention planning should be a psychoeducational approach. Knowledge of the tasks involved in completing a stepfamily identity will help give a direction to the young, developing family. These tasks are dealing with losses and changes, negotiating different developmental needs, establishing new traditions, developing a solid couple bond, forming new relationships, and creating a parenting coalition (Goldenburg & Goldenburg, 2004, p. 373). From there, interventions as needed to help the family achieve these tasks serve as a direction for continuing work with interventions such as grief work, communication training, problem-solving and negotiation training, marital counseling, family therapy to strengthen family members' bonds, and parent training.

Grief Work   "Embarking on a new relationship requires an 'emotional' divorce from the first marriage. Divorced adults must deal with their own fears about entering a new relationship" (Holman, in Collins et al., 1999, p. 78). The use of metaphors as in structural family therapy can be helpful in facilitating family communication about their feelings and emotions (Jongsma & Dattilio, 2000).

Communication Training   It is useful to learn what family members expect from each other, as this is likely to be a well-kept secret. It is not unusual to find that no one in the family has ever made his or her expectations known, in which case there are no guidelines for family members behaving in a manner that is totally satisfactory to other members. Helping family members express what they desire from each other introduces a new way of relating. This is especially true with stepparents, who usually enter into a new union without having addressed many important issues, such as role expectations and disciplining of the children. Stepparents do have ideas about these things, and practitioners should assist them in clarifying and formulating these ideas and expectations, supporting what is realistic, and helping them to understand and eliminate that which is related to fallacious beliefs often held by these couples. This includes such preconceived notions as believing that all family members will love each other and immediately adjust to each other, which will allow the family to go forward with its various tasks without difficulty. "Teaching assertiveness and communication skills (use of I messages, empathetic listening and reflective responding, undivided attention and good eye contact, respectful and controlled expression of emotions, etc.)" is recommended (Jongsma & Dattilio, 2000, p. 73).

Problem Solving and Negotiation Training   It should be kept in mind that members of the reconstituted family often bring different lifestyles to the task of developing a new family. These differences may center around such things as dress codes, entertainment preferences, disciplining children, attitudes toward sex or the use of alcohol, rules governing the conduct of family members at home and in interaction with others outside of the family, and so on. These differences may result in conflict between family members and should be evaluated as possible sources of difficulty in family functioning when the family comes for help. Jongsma and Dattilio (2000) recommend problem-solving therapy or sculpting to help families resolve these types of issues.

Marital Counseling   Sager and his associates (1983) suggest caution in setting goals for reconstituted families. Many couples come together with specific individual goals in mind, including the hope that this union will be a positive answer to all of the disappointments experienced in their previous unsatisfactory relationship. When failure to realize unrealistic goals brings the couple into treatment, they frequently try to achieve the same goals through the treatment process. In such cases, it is necessary to clarify the situation and establish realistic goals on which the work might be focused. Marital techniques as specified by Gottman (in Franklin & Jordan, 1999) can be helpful to guiding the couple in the development of a positive relationship.

Strengthening Family Members' Bonds   Collins and colleagues (1999) suggest that "boundaries in newly blended families need to be negotiated, and this can be a difficult task. Not only must members establish boundaries concerning physical space (sharing, property), but they must also decide how much emotional distance to maintain with new family members and agree upon roles that will work within this new family unit" (p. 79).

Contrary to the myth that instant love should exist between stepparent and stepchild, in some cases the relationship is characterized by competition or even a strong dislike for each other. When no basis for improving this situation can be found, we concur with Johnson (1980), who suggests accepting the fact that, in reality, a family does not exist and movement in this direction is not likely to occur in the near future. As a result, the ensuing process is usually one of waiting for the child to grow up and leave the family. In working with this situation, we also agree with her strategy and support intervention in the direction of the stepparent and stepchild spending as little time as possible together, with the natural parent assuming the major parenting responsibilities.

Parent Training   Jongsma and Dattilio (2000) suggest use of a parenting program such as Systematic Training for Effective Parenting (STEP) to help couples learn positive child management procedures. It may be useful at times to work separately with different subsystems of the reconstituted family in the same manner, as do many practitioners when working with the nuclear family. For example, when helping the new couple resolve issues around discipline and consolidating parental authority, work with subsystems at some point in this process might offer some advantages. The use of support groups for parents and children has also been found to be a profitable undertaking.

Table 12.2 | Research Studies

Family Psychoeducation	Other Family Treatments
Michaels (2000) designed a pilot stepfamily enrichment psychoeducational program to help family members understand common stepfamily relationship patterns, differentiated from intact families. Results are unreported.	Videka-Sharman (1989) performed a meta-analysis of 25 controlled studies of interventions for parental anger and abuse toward their children. The analysis revealed that social-learning, educational programs had greater effects than did psychodynamically oriented treatments.
	Forgatch and DeGarmo (1999) found that recently divorced mothers (versus controls) experienced positive changes in parenting behaviors, linked with changes in child behaviors. The intervention was parent management training.

TREATMENT MANUAL

The following is a summary of some of the steps of a treatment plan for blended families from Jongsma and colleagues (2000, pp. 71–77). The intervention is a blend of the techniques mentioned in the previous section, including education, parent and marital skills training, and so forth.

Behavioral Definitions

1. Parenting practices of biological parent versus stepparent are different.
2. Children align with the absent parent.
3. Adjustment to the new stepparent creates child behavior problems.
4. The new parental unit has difficulty resolving child issues such as parenting and so forth.

Long-Term Goals

1. Family members acknowledge the difficulties of blending and family, and agree to compromise.
2. Children accept the stepparent and show respect.
3. Stepparents learn a more flexible parenting style to better relate to the stepchildren.
4. The new parents negotiate a relationship, taking into account power and control issues.
5. Stepparents treat stepchildren fairly and with respect.

Short-Term Objectives

1. Family members each define their own family problems.
2. The couple identifies issues with their parenting style.
3. The couple learns better communication to improve their relationship.
4. The couple learns better parenting techniques to address their issues.
5. The couple strengthens their parental bond to avoid child triangulation and manipulation.
6. The couple each identify jealousies they may harbor about the spouse's relationship with the stepchildren.

Therapeutic Interventions

1. Create a safe place for each family member to share feelings and concerns.
2. Use metaphors or family sculpting to facilitate family discussions about problems.
3. Facilitate discussion about problems between stepchildren and stepparent. Help children talk about their feelings regarding the absent parent.
4. Use role-plays or modeling techniques to help stepparents discard strict or rigid interactions with stepchildren and learn new parenting strategies.
5. Teach parents assertiveness and communication skills to improve their relationship and to deal with difficult ex-spouses.
6. Use problem-solving and negotiation techniques to teach parents how to treat all children equally.

CASE EXAMPLE

This blended family consists of the mother, Ana, and her two daughters: Lisa, age 9; and Tina, age 2. The husband/stepdad is Ken, who has two children: Stacey, age 9; and Mark, age 12. The two older girls are experiencing jealousy at sharing their respective parent and sibling rivalry issues. Mark is exhibiting externalizing behaviors at home and school. He was caught raiding the liquor cabinet and selling small bottles of whiskey to the junior high football team. At school, Mark is rebellious toward his teachers and at home, toward his stepmother. Ken and Ana have disagreed about parenting the children. Ana believes Ken to be too strict, especially with her two girls. The younger girl, Tina, is not toilet trained, and Ken feels that it is because Ana babies her and that she should be spanked when she soils her clothing. The family was referred to the clinic by the girls' elementary school counselor, who got involved when Lisa and Stacey got into a fight in the lunchroom.

> **THERAPIST:** How are you all today? I'm Nancy Moore and I would like to get to know your family today. May we go around and have introductions from everyone to begin? (The family members introduce themselves, with the exception of Tina, who is introduced by her mom, Ana.)

> **THERAPIST:** In order for me to begin to get to know you and understand what's going on in your new family, I'd like to set some ground rules for our discussion today. Is that all right with everyone? (Nods all around.) I'd like to suggest that

we consider this office a neutral zone where anyone can say what they like and talk about their feelings without fear that others will get mad at them and try to get even with them later. Is that okay with everyone? (Again, nods from all.) (Step 1: Establish a neutral zone for family members to express themselves without fear of retaliation by other family members.)

THERAPIST: In the introductions, I heard you say that all of you children, except Tina, play soccer. I would like for us to try and talk about your family as a soccer team, if you would be willing to try that. For example, Ana, if you were on the family soccer team, what position would you play?

ANA: I would not be a member of the team but the referee. I feel like I am always trying to solve somebody's problem and that I am in the middle of everything that happens, even between the kids and Ken!

THERAPIST: Thank you, Ana, I can see that the referee position might be a stressful one that we will want to talk about more later on. Ken, what position do you play on the team?

KEN: I am definitely the coach. It is my job to keep everybody in line and to decide on the plans.

THERAPIST: Thank you Ken. That's a job with a lot of responsibility! (The therapist continues with the three older children. Mark describes himself as the one with the ball, the forward; while Lisa and Stacey fight over which one of them should be the goalie. The family is unanimous that Tina is the cute team mascot in the cheerleader uniform.) (Step 2: Utilize such techniques as metaphors or family sculpting to facilitate family members in talking openly about their feelings and emotions over present conflicts with one another.)

THERAPIST: Lisa and Stacey, tell me if you often have the kind of disagreement that I saw here, about who would be goalie, at home about other things.

LISA: Yes, all the time! When Ken married mom, Stacey moved into my room and she makes a mess of my stuff! And Ken backs her up! He never takes my side, but he tells me I have to do what he says. I don't think so! He's not my REAL father! (Step 3: Facilitate open dialogue between the disgruntled children and the stepparent or adoptive parent. Explore the child's feelings of disloyalty to his/her biological parents.)

THERAPIST: Lisa, tell me about your dad. Does he live close? Do you see him often? (Step 4: Facilitate release of the child's feelings that may be inhibiting acceptance of the stepparent's directives.)

THERAPIST: No, he moved up north to take another job. And I only get to see him on holidays and in the summer. I don't know why he had to move so far away! (angrily) He could have kept his old job. And then Ken thinks he can just come in and take my dad's place and boss us around and tell us what to do all the time.

Subsequent sessions would continue with the following:

Step 5: An assessment of the strictness or rigidity of the stepparent's style and whether it may be interfering with acceptance by the children.

Step 6: Use of role-playing and modeling to help the parent consider more flexible alternative methods.

Step 7: Education about assertiveness and communication skills, and so forth.

Table 12.3 | Treatment Manuals

Manual Reference	Author's Contact Information
McFarlane, W. R., Deakins, S. M., Gingerich, S. L., Dunne, E., Hornen, B., & Newmark, M. 1991. *Multiple-Family Psychoeducational Group Treatment Manual.* New York: Biosocial Treatment Division, New York State Psychiatric Institute.	http://w3.ouhsc.edu/bpfamily/ Detail/McFarlane. html
Adler-Baeder, F. *Smart Steps for Adults and Children in Stepfamilies.* http://www.smart-marriages.com/step.institute.html	Stepfamily Association of America http://ecommerce.4w.com/step fam/booksandtapes.htm
This 12-hour research-based, educational program curriculum is for remarried or partnering couples and their children, and focuses on building couple and family strength.	
The program uses informational presentations, hands-on exercises, group discussions, and media. The 250+ page curriculum includes leader lesson guides for adult and child programs, background readings, hand-out masters, resource list pre/post-evaluation questionnaires, two videos (*Stepmom* and *Smart Steps Video Vignettes*), and CD with Microsoft ®PowerPoint® slides, hand-out files, and evaluation questionnaires.	
Taylor, C., and Taylor, G. *Designing Dynamic Stepfamilies: Bringing the Pieces to Peace.* http://www.designingdynamicstepfamilies.com/	

SUMMARY

The breakup of a couple relationship, which often results in creation of a new family, is by no means a novelty in contemporary society. However, it is still viewed by some as a departure from the accepted norm. As a result, society has failed to define norms for the reconstituted family to establish guidelines for the appropriate behavior of its members. This has contributed to the confusion surrounding this new family, which responds to several different titles.

This family has a number of unique features, most of which do not make for a quick and easy adjustment among family members. The family is frequently seen in treatment as it struggles to stabilize its processes and become an organized unit. It is generally accepted that a family systems approach is

The one-of-a-kind, eight-part, VHS/DVD series shows the process for designing a successful stepfamily with intriguing illustrations and real life stories from the Taylors and others. This series serves to enhance the Smart Steps educational curriculum by using living examples to illustrate the principles taught. Ready to use for workshops, small groups, and home study. It comes with a comprehensive secular or Christian study guide. Total running time: 4 hrs 24 min.

Unavailable

Burt, M. (1989). *Stepfamilies Stepping Ahead: An 8 Step Program for Successful Family Living*. Stepfamilies Press.

This resource includes the following:

- *Guidelines for Stepfamilies*. Emily and John Visher
- *Stages in Becoming a Stepfamily*. Patricia Papernow
- *Myths about Stepfamilies*. Mala Burt

A stepfamily can feel like a comfortable and nurturing place to live when you have knowledge about how stepfamilies work and the stages of stepfamily development. Some things can change. Some things can't. Learn how to tell the difference and put your energy where it will count. Included is an eight-step, action-based program that can lead to success. Suitable for one person, a family, and groups. Themes: how stepfamilies are different; stages of stepfamily development.

---

most applicable to assessing and treating reconstituted family problems. The use of support groups is also effective. It is helpful for practitioners who engage these families in treatment to be aware that the dynamics underlying reconstituted family problems are not always the same as those associated with the nuclear family. Therefore, this family cannot be viewed in exactly the same manner as the nuclear family. And practitioners must be aware of their own attitudes as well as their personal experiences as they relate to the family as a functioning unit.

It is difficult to visualize the future relative to the place of the reconstituted family and how it will be viewed as an entity among other groupings in society. Nevertheless, it is a family form that will continue to exist, and we must strive for the most effective ways of understanding and dealing with these adults and their children.

BOX 12.2	Internet Resources

Due to the living nature of the Internet, website addresses often change and thus we have not printed the addresses in this text. Links to the following websites are posted at the Book Companion Site at www.wadsworth.com.

The Stepfamily Association of America—provides resources, information, and supports for stepfamilies

Santa Cruz Guide: Stepfamily Association of America—guide to marriage and family counselors, mental health clinics

Research-Connect.com—a section of the Stepfamily Association of America that includes research information on a variety of subjects for stepfamilies

BabyCenter.com—a section of the Stepfamily Association of America that includes information about home and family life

YourStepfamily.com—a magazine on stepfamily issues from the Stepfamily Association of America

Stepducks.net—provides stepfamily resources and support, with information on babies and children, including support from experts

DMOZ.org—open directory project with information and fellowship opportunities for stepfamilies, including a stepmom group, articles, advice, books, message board, and other blended family resources

Ohioline.osu.edu—Ten Steps Toward Successful Stepparenting, active parenting, helping children understand other cultures, and other family resources

All-the-Internet.com—a directory for family and parenting, including stepmom group articles, advice, books, message board, and other blended family resources

Stepmomgroup.com—Marriage Builders Alliance with resources including divorce recovery, Christian resources for pre-remarital couples, stepfamilies, and the churches that serve them

DISCUSSION QUESTIONS

1. Think of a blended family that you know, either in your field or work setting, or personally. Evaluate this family's adjustment using some of the assessment techniques listed here.
2. Design a treatment plan for the family you evaluated.
3. Discuss with classmates some of the societal or cultural contributions to stepfamily problems.

References

Collins, D., Jordan, C., and Coleman, C. 1999. *An Introduction to Family Social Work*. Chicago: Peacock.

Corcoran, K., and Fischer, J. 2000. *Measures for Clinical Practice,* 3rd edition. New York: Free Press.

Dattilio, F. M., and Jongsma, A. E. 1970. *The Family Therapy Treatment Planner.* New York: John Wiley & Sons.

DeGenova, M. K., and Rice, F. P. 2005. *Intimate Relationships, Marriages, and Families,* 6th edition. Boston: McGraw-Hill.

Duncan, S., and Brown, G. 1992. "RENEW: A Program for Building Remarried Family Strengths." *Families in Society* 73:144–58.

Franklin, C., and Jordan, C. 1999. *Family Practice: Brief Systems Methods for Social Work.* Belmont, CA: Brooks/Cole.

Goldenburg, I., and Goldenburg, H. 2004. *Family Therapy: An Overview,* 6th edition. Belmont, CA: Brooks/Cole.

Hobart, C. 1989. "Experiences of Remarried Families." *Journal of Divorce* 13: 121–44.

Hobart, C. 1990. "Relationships between the Formerly Married." *Journal of Comparative Family Studies* 21:81–97.

Johnson, H. C. 1980. "Working with Stepfamilies: Principles and Practice." *Social Work* 25(4):304–08.

Jongsma, A. E., and Dattilio, F. M. 2000. *The Family Therapy Treatment Planner.* New York: John Wiley & Sons.

Jongsma, A. E., Peterson, L. M., and McInnis, W. P. 2000. *The Adolescent Psychotherapy Treatment Planner.* New York: John Wiley & Sons.

Kent, M. O. 1980. "Remarriage: A Family Systems Perspective." *Social Casework* 61(3):146–53.

Minuchin, S. 1974. *Families and Family Therapy.* Cambridge, MA: Harvard University Press.

Sager, C. J., Brown, H. S., Crohn, H., Engel, T., Rodstein, E., and Walker, L. 1983. *Treating the Remarried Family.* New York: Brunner/Mazel Publishers.

Schulman, G. L. 1972. "Myths That Intrude on the Adaptation of the Step Family." *Social Casework* 53(3):131–39.

Smith, T. 1991. "Family Cohesion in Remarried Families." *Journal of Divorce and Remarriage* 17:49–66.

Stuart, R. B., and Jacobson, B. 1985. *Second Marriage.* New York: W. W. Norton & Co.

Thompson, C., and Rudolph, L. 1992. *Counseling Children,* 3rd edition. Pacific Grove, CA: Brooks/Cole.

Visher, E. B., and Visher, J. S. 1979. *Step Families: A Guide to Work with Stepparents and Stepchildren.* New York: Brunner/Mazel Publishers.

———. 1982. "Step Families and Stepparenting." In *Normal Family Processes,* ed. F. Walsh. New York: Guilford.

———. 1990. "Dynamics of Successful Stepfamilies." *Journal of Divorce and Remarriage* 14:3–11.

Wald, E. 1981. *The Remarried Family.* New York: Family Service Association of America.

Index